THE GODS
HAVE LANDED

New Religions
from Other Worlds

Edited by
James R. Lewis

State University of New York Press

Published by
State University of New York Press, Albany

For information, address State University of New York Press,
State University Plaza, Albany, N.Y., 12246

Production by Marilyn P. Semerad
Marketing by Bernadette LaManna

Library of Congress Cataloging-in-Publication Data

The Gods have landed : new religions from other worlds / edited by
  James R. Lewis.
      p.   cm.
   Includes bibliographical references and index.
   ISBN 0-7914-2329-8 (hc : alk. paper). — ISBN 0-7914-2330-1 (pb :
alk. paper)
   1. Unidentified flying object cults. 2. Unidentified flying
object cults—United States. 3. Unidentified flying objects-
-Religious aspects. 4. United States—Religion—20th century.
I. Lewis, James R.
BP605.U526 1995
299—dc20   94-10333
                                                                    CIP

10 9 8 7 6 5 4 3 2

CONTENTS

LIST OF ILLUSTRATIONS

ACKNOWLEDGMENTS

First of all, I would like to thank my wife Eve for her loving support, both for myself and for this project. Second, I would like to thank Charles H. Long for his continuing interest in this wayward student. Third, I would like to thank J. Gordon Melton, colleague and friend, who originally sparked my interest in UFO religion. Fourth, a special word of thanks to the contributors: Without their dedication to rigorous, creative scholarship this volume could never have come into being.

Thanks to the University of Hawaii Press for permission to use Robert S. Ellwood's "Spiritualism and UFO Religion in New Zealand," the substance of which was incorporated into UHP's *Islands of the Dawn: The Story of Alternative Spirituality in New Zealand*. Thanks also to J. Gordon Melton and George M. Eberhart for permission to use "The Contactees: A Survey" and "The Flying Saucer Contactee Movement." Finally, I would like to acknowledge that earlier versions of George Kirkpatrick and Diana Tumminia's "Unarius: Emergent Aspects of an American Flying Saucer Group," John A. Saliba's "UFO Contactee Phenomena from a Sociopsychological Perspective," and Susan Jean Palmer's "Women in the Raelian Movement" appeared in *Syzygy: Journal of Alternative Religion and Culture*.

INTRODUCTION

On the morning of the third day there were thunders and
lightnings, and a thick cloud upon the mountain. All of the
people in camp heard a sound like a loud trumpet blast, and
trembled. Then Moses brought the people out of camp to
meet God, and they took their stand at the foot of the mountain. Mount Sinai was wrapped in smoke, because the Lord
was descending upon it in fire. The smoke of it went up like
the smoke of a furnace, and the whole mountain quaked. As
the sound grew louder and louder, Moses spoke, and God
answered him in thunder. And the Lord landed upon Mount
Sinai.

—Exodus 19:16-20

While the tale of Moses' encounter with Yahweh is familiar to
everyone raised in the Judeo-Christian religious tradition, few would
connect that story with contemporary interest in UFOs. Yet it is not difficult to see how one might interpret the above passage as describing
the landing of some great spaceship on Mt. Sinai. Utilizing suggestive
narratives about sky gods from the Bible and from many other religious and cultural traditions, a popular writer by the name of Erich
von Däniken theorized that the "chariots of the gods" described in
ancient mythology were really the space vessels of an extraterrestrial
race concerned with the fate of humanity. While von Däniken's speculations have been severely criticized, it is nevertheless clear that his
ideas struck a respondent cord in the public imagination. The significance of the connections he perceived may, however, lie in precisely
the opposite direction from what he theorized. Let us, therefore, invert
von Däniken's hermeneutic and consider how a religious tradition
emphasizing sky gods might influence one to invest religious significance in the contemporary phenomenon of unidentified flying objects.

Historically, the human race has derived spiritual meaning from every dimension of the environment. For reasons that are too complex to develop in this short space, the Western religious tradition desacralized the Earth, and came to imagine God as residing in the sky. The celestial abode of the Deity is clear from certain events in Jesus' ministry as recorded in the Gospels. The many relevant incidents include:

1. His reference to God as "Our Father who art in Heaven."
2. The Holy Spirit's descent from the sky following Jesus' baptism.
3. His return to the heavens after leaving his disciples in the book of Acts.

These are only a few examples of a marked tendency in the Old and New Testaments to portray divinity as being somehow "located" in the sky. To recast this observation in more contemporary terms, we might say that the deity of Western religions is—in some sense—an "extraterrestrial" being. There are, however, many other characteristics of UFOs that link them to the religious consciousness.

One of the classics of religious phenomenology is Rudolf Otto's *The Idea of the Holy*. In this work, Otto carefully distinguishes fundamental religious experience—humanity's naked confrontation with the Sacred—from the other components of religion, and then proceeds to analyze this primordial experience into component parts. According to Otto, one encounters the Sacred as a powerful, alien reality that does not belong to the world of ordinary human existence. This experience encompasses components of both fear and attraction: The Sacred simultaneously repels and fascinates; it is "uncanny" and "awesome." The Sacred is also mysterious—something we cannot grasp with our rational minds, yet which we endlessly attempt to understand.

The parallels between religious experience and UFO experiences are clear enough. UFOs are uncanny and mysterious. If the reader has seen the movie *Close Encounters of the Third Kind*, she or he will recall the climactic final scene in which the mother ship appears: This enormous piece of alien machinery is experienced by the gathered officials and technicians as both beautiful and frightful—an incomprehensibly awesome power before which they feel like helpless children. This is precisely the kind of encounter that Otto characterizes as religious.

That flying saucers and their inhabitants have come to be invested with religious meaning should not, therefore, be surprising. This religious meaning can be manifested overtly in such explicitly religious organizations as the Unarians and the Raelians (described elsewhere in the present volume). It can also be manifested less obviously, in the form of certain themes and patterns that—when cloaked in the guise of flying machines—are not immediately recognized as religious, but which fulfill religious functions.

The great psychoanalyst Carl Jung, for example, pointed out that the theme of humanity's rescue by extraterrestrial beings is a religious myth recast in technological guise: Modern people who are no longer able to believe that humankind will be saved by God *can* believe that we will be saved by powerful, godlike beings from other worlds. In an expression that succinctly captures this general interpretative approach to UFOs, Jung referred to flying saucers as "technological angels."

The present anthology is a comprehensive account of the religious dimension of the UFO/flying saucer experience. Chapters range from analyses of the religious meanings attached to this phenomenon by the larger society to surveys of specific movements that claim inspiration from "Space Brothers" and other extraterrestrial sources. Although the wealth of existing sociological, psychological, and anthropological articles suggests that this is an important phenomenon, few book-length studies exist. *The Gods Have Landed* fills this gap, providing readers with a richly textured, interdisciplinary approach to UFO religions.

Ufologists—as those with a serious interest in this phenomenon refer to themselves—usually date the emergence of UFOs into the public consciousness from Kenneth Arnold's sighting on June 24, 1947, and the emergence of interpretations of the phenomenon to George Adamski's reported encounter with flying saucers on November 20, 1952. In the first chapter, "The Contactees: A Survey," J. Gordon Melton discusses religious movements and thinkers that relied upon extraterrestrial wisdom long before 1947. He also calls attention to the continuities between these earlier contactees and current UFO religions.

John A. Saliba's "Religious Dimensions of UFO Phenomena" is a comprehensive introduction to the various ways in which UFOs can be regarded as religious. The different types of interests people have in UFOs are first distinguished, showing how they are related to the kind of UFO organizations and associations and to the type of alien creatures believed in. Second, three categories of UFO groups, movements, or cults are outlined and a few examples of each given. Third, the various forms of Christian interpretations of UFO phenomena are briefly described. Fourth, the major religious themes which have already become part of the UFO subculture are analyzed. Finally, an attempt is made to assess the importance and significance of UFO religions.

The phenomenon of supposed abductions by inhabitants of flying saucers did not attract much attention until the early 1970s. Accounts of abductee experiences have, however, come to dominate the UFO field, so that books published on abductions now outnumber books on all other UFO subjects combined by a substantial margin. John Whitmore's "Religious Dimensions of the UFO Abductee Experience" presents a detailed analysis of this phenomenon, and demonstrates the various ways in which abduction experiences reflect more traditional religious patterns.

George Kirkpatrick and Diana Tumminia's "Unarius: Emergent Aspects of an American Flying Saucer Group" provides an overview of one of the more interesting UFO organizations. Famous for its prophecy, the Unarius Academy of Science awaits the landing of starships in the year 2001. In the interim, Uriel (Ruth Norman), Archangel and Cosmic Visionary, channels messages from the Space Brothers and leads Unarians through group past-life therapy sessions. This chapter presents an overview of the emergent processes involved in the growth of Unarius along with data on characteristics of the membership.

Susan Jean Palmer's "Women in the Raelian Movement" focuses on another highly interesting UFO group. The Raelians are one of the few new religious movements (NRMs) that tolerates sexual ambiguity and encourages homosexual expression. While the Raelians are characterized by traits that usually promote sexual equality and female leadership in NRMs, there are surprisingly few women in leadership positions in the Raelian hierarchy. Palmer's chapter gives an overview of this movement while exploring the factors that tend to keep women out of the hierarchy.

Robert W. Balch is well-known among sociologists of religion for the papers he has published over the years on the "Bo and Peep" UFO group. In "Waiting for the Ships" he retells the story of the mysterious couple known as "the Two," and the history of their group from its origins in Texas through 1980 when Balch stopped collecting systematic data. He also discusses why voluntary affiliation was not sufficient to create a committed, deployable membership. Genuine commitment did not develop until Bo and Peep introduced social influence processes such as regimentation and certain mental exercises.

Spiritualism and flying saucer groups, like many other nontraditional religious movements, have been highly successful in such areas of the world as New Zealand. The transmission of UFOism to New Zealand in the present century exhibits certain remarkable parallels to the transmission of spiritualism in the preceding century. Robert S. Ellwood's "Spiritualism and UFO Religion in New Zealand" analyzes this parallel in some detail. In both cases, visiting speakers from the U.S. or the U.K. generated considerable media publicity, and left behind much controversy as well as small groups of enthusiastic believers.

Certain skeptical scientists and tabloid journalists have naively asserted that, if the existence of extraterrestrial intelligence was to be decisively proven, traditional Christianity would collapse. Ted Peters's "Exo-Theology: Speculations on Extraterrestrial Life" demonstrates why this view is mistaken. The first part of his chapter surveys historical and contemporary Jewish and Christian thinkers who have integrated such a possibility into their theology. The second part of the chapter examines the fundamentalist literature of the 1970s that tended to demonize UFOs, and which may have given outsiders the false impression that the Christian tradition was unduly Earth centered.

The present volume concludes with two comprehensive bibliographic surveys. John A. Saliba's "UFO Contactee Phenomena from a Sociopsychological Perspective," the first of these review chapters, provides a systematic overview of social-scientific articles on UFOs. This chapter is especially useful for its summaries of most existing interpretations of this phenomenon. The concluding chapter, J. Gordon Melton and George M. Eberhart's "The Flying Saucer Contactee Movement, 1950-1994: A Bibliography" provides a comprehensive listing of both primary and secondary sources.

1

THE CONTACTEES: A SURVEY

J. Gordon Melton

In the 1950s, in response to the flying saucer phenomenon, there arose a group of people who claimed that they had personally contacted the occupants of these odd craft. They asserted that the saucers were in fact space craft and the occupants our brothers and sisters from space. A few even claimed to have traveled to distant planets or taken a ride in space.

That such people began to populate the gatherings of flying saucer buffs became a concern of many who proceeded to condemn them as kooks or dismiss them as the lunatic fringe. There were few who saw any value in what the contactees, as they came to be known, had to say. They were an embarrassment to sober research into the unusual aerial phenomena called unidentified flying objects.

During the 1970s, however, ufologists began to take a new look at people who claimed direct contact with flying saucer entities. Their experiences have been designated "close encounters of the third kind" and special interest has arisen around a particular CEIII, the abduction. Leo Sprinkle began annual gatherings of contactees in 1980, (cf. see *Proceedings of the Rocky Mountain Conference 1980*). Rarely, however, have contemporary researchers checked their cases in the light of the prior claims of such contact. This chapter is an initial attempt to offer some direction as to how that task might be pursued.

Typical of the stories of these contactees are those of Willard M. Magoon (Magoon 1930) and Guy Ballard (King 1935, 243-60). Magoon reported his experience many years after it had occurred to him as a young man in the early part of this century. He went to Mars, which he described as a beautiful, lush planet of forests, parks, and gardens. He had not planned the journey but had been taken there by some "unseen force." In his account, he says that the Martians were far ahead of earthlings in development, especially technologically. They already had automobiles and radios. They were also invisible and he could only sense their presence.

From his experience he gained a deep sense of responsibility for himself. "I could not depend upon someone else to do the work, it could not be done that way." He also admonished the religious leaders of his day not to fear scientific progress. It could not touch true religion.

Guy Ballard's adventures begin on the side of Mt. Shasta in northern California. Here he encountered a mysterious being who began to teach him the mysteries of the ages. On New Year's Eve, the teacher told Ballard to prepare himself for a gathering at the Royal Teton Mountain. At seven in the evening, they left Ballard's house and journeyed inside the mountain to a vast cavern. Once assembled, Ballard and 105 others became host to 12 Venusians who appeared in their midst in a blaze of light. During the course of the visit, the Venusians played the harp and violin much to the delight of all. On a large mirror they showed scenes from their home planet of advanced scientific and technological achievements. They also revealed a future dissipation of the dark forces threatening the earth and the gradual coming of a time of peace and goodwill.

These accounts are typical, as noted above, but more interesting than most in that Magoon's was published in the 1930s and Ballard's appeared in 1935. More than a decade before Kenneth Arnold gave us flying saucers and almost two decades before Adamski introduced us to Orthon, Magoon and Ballard were in contact with Martians and Venusians. And even more fascinating, these two are not just isolated anomalies, but fit into a tradition of claims of extraterrestrial contact that covers the two centuries before Arnold and Adamski. These two hundred years of reports of contacts with outer space provide needed additional material to compare and contrast with modern contactee claims, CEIIIs, and abductions.

This chapter surveys over one hundred contactees from the 1750s to the present. Included are all known cases of claims of extraterrestrial contact prior to 1952, all contacts reported from 1952 to 1964, and all post-1964 contacts published in book form through 1980. The central characteristics of the contactee phenomenon will be highlighted and the contactees placed in their more appropriate context, that of the occult religious tradition, to which these accounts show many similarities. In the concluding section, some reflection on contactees and current research on CEIIIs and abduction cases will be offered.

THE BEGINNING

In 1758 Emanuel Swedenborg, the famous Swedish scientist and seer, published his cosmological treatise *Concerning Earths in the Solar*

World, Which Are Called Planets; and Concerning Earths in the Starry Heaven; and Concerning Their Inhabitants; and Likewise Concerning the Spirits and Angels There from Things Seen and Heard (Swedenborg 1758). In this volume the renowned scientist informed the world that he had personally traveled to the various planets of the solar system and even beyond to the planets of the starry heavens. He described each in turn. For example, he recorded details of Martian anatomy and physiology. He reported on their unique social system where each individual found his way into a society of people of like mind and temperament: "Everyone there lives content with his goods, and everyone with his honor, in being esteemed just, and one that loves his neighbor" (p. 52).

Swedenborg represents a transition in the literature of the West. His book appeared in the midst of a century known for the popularity of the "fantastic voyage" novel.[1] In these novels, which were turned out by dreamers all over Europe, the hero travels to some spot remote to his/her home setting. The spot may be outer space, the inner earth, a far land (like Gulliver), or a future time. Once in the new locale, the hero discovers an ideal society. The author writes his/her account as a parable or call to action for the readers. The books dealt primarily with issues of social justice, technological progress, public education, and moral welfare.

Swedenborg's *Earths in Our Solar System* became a first. It reads much like any other fantastic voyage novel, with the exception that it claims to be an account of an actual trip to outer space. The trips to the planets were not seen by Swedenborg as merely figments of his imagination or projections of his hopes for the world. Swedenborg would soon be followed by others who claimed that they had actually traveled to outer space or to the inner earth or had met inhabitants of these places.

Possibly the most famous claim, nearly a century and a half after Swedenborg, was by a French medium, Helene Smith. In her account, she traveled to Mars in the 1890s; she returned to describe the Martians and drew pictures of the animal and plant life. She learned Martian, which she spoke and wrote. Fortunately for us, she turned over all of the data concerning her intercourse with Mars to psychologist Theodore Flournoy, who analyzed it and published his results (Flournoy 1900).

Among his other reflections, Flournoy discussed fully the Martian language. He discovered that Martian was, as he termed it, merely "an infantile travesty of French"; each Martian letter had French cognates. Smith had created a new language wholecloth, and one is immediately reminded of recent research on glossolalia (Samarin 1972): people who speak in tongues create a new language which is an infantile, cut-down version of the language they speak normally.

The cases of Swedenborg and Smith raise the central issues of contactee claims, all of which revolve around the rather parasitical relation that occult religion has to both popular science and research into the paranormal. Naively, the contactees claim to report on reality in an objective and even scientific manner. They draw upon popular scientific assumptions and reflect upon the current state of knowledge. Smith, like her American contemporary Sara Weiss (1906), reports in great detail on the Martian canals. Astronomer Percival Lowell had just published his first book detailing the "discovery" by the Italian G. V. Schiaparelli of the canals and the confirmation by the French astronomers in the 1880s. Interestingly, Swedenborg visits each planet known to exist in the 1750s on his way beyond the solar system to the starry heavens, but fails to note the existence of Uranus, Neptune, or Pluto.

Thus the contactee material (like occult material in general), when looked at in historical perspective contains mistake after mistake as it attached itself to popular scientific theories and conclusions that would later prove to be incorrect. This ongoing relationship to scientific error serves to focus more clearly the true intent of the material—to offer moral, metaphysical, and theological reflections on those areas of science and society considered crucial to the contactee. Therefore, while Swedenborg could comment upon human anatomy and the social order, and Smith on the possible life-on-other-planets implications of the sighting of canals on Mars, more recent contactees have commented upon the atom bomb and social disintegration in the urban setting.

Also, being tied to science as they are, contactees have continually shifted their model of scientific thought, again like the occult community in general. In the early nineteenth century, mesmerism gave a scientific cast to occult speculation, but was replaced before the century was over by the wedding of spiritualism with Darwinism and Newtonian worldviews. Both are reflected quite strongly in the various spiritualist creeds written in the late 1800s.

Most nineteenth- and early-twentieth-century contact with extraterrestrials occurred in a spiritualist context, more likely than not in a séance. The prime mode of contact was a phenomenon quite familiar to psychic researchers, namely "astral travel." A person experiencing astral travel senses his/her body and consciousness separately, and while the body remains in one place, the consciousness travels around. Thus Swedenborg and mediums like Smith and Weiss could go into trances and travel to the various planets. A series of out-of-body experiences, as astral travel is also known, was described by Albert Bender who started the whole man-in-black myth (Bender 1962).

By means of their space contact, contactees could replace the authority of the religious tradition they had cast away. They invoked the momentary authority of science (considered as a body of knowledge) which they bolstered with the additional information of direct contact with a new and equally authoritative source of information. Each provided a launching pad for the "religious" speculation they really desired.

Summarizing the large number of pre-Adamski contacts yields some interesting patterns. First, outer space contact, with the exception of Swedenborg's romp through the galaxy, is confined to the known solar system and almost totally to Mars, Venus, and the Moon.[2] Venus gradually replaces Mars during the twentieth century as the favorite contact planet.

Second, contact is established by some psychic/occult means. The most helpful tool is astral travel. Through astral travel, they could do what flying saucers would later also allow them to do. They could traverse long distances in relatively quick time without worry about such mundane items as g-forces, the vacuum of space, and escape velocities. In no case did a contactee claim to use any kind of spaceship. Rather, following the lead of the fantastic voyage novels, contactees either traveled astrally, woke up from a sleep to find themselves mysteriously transported to their destination, or experienced some form of what might be termed dematerialization. (John Carter, Edgar Rice Burroughs's earthling on Mars, traveled by a mysterious dematerialization process.)

Third, once contact is made, communication is by telepathy. Contactees seem astute enough to know about language barriers and some know language syntax barriers to direct translation. Telepathy solves both problems in that concepts, not words, are communicated. Smith was exposed in her Martian communication because she did not fully understand the relationship between languages.

Fourth, contactee accounts emphasize the message which is usually metaphysical. The information concerning the planet serves merely to authenticate the lesson to be learned. Weiss's contacts with Mars were meant to validate spiritualism while more clearly defining points upon which spiritualists had failed to reach consensus. Immo, her Martian contact, talks through Weiss to the larger spiritualist community:

In planetary language, which all advance spirits understand, Evon Thia (Martian words roughly translated as "for love's sake") is the watchword of all engaged in the endeavor to uplift humanity on both the physical and spirit planes of being; and such spirits strive ever to unfold such mentalities as are sensitive to their approach; for only through sensitives can the truth of the continuity of existence be demonstrated. (Weiss 1906, 11)

In so many words, the Martian is verifying a major spiritualist doctrine of belief in the necessity of mediums. Such conclusions far outweigh any information about life on Mars that were also included in the contact.

Finally, a religious context was almost always assumed. Swedenborg went on to found the Church of the New Jerusalem, the first of the modern occult religions. Spiritualism, which was strongly based upon Swedenborg's teachings, at least in its earlier stages, was the home for most of the others—Smith, the Dentons, Weiss, and Magoon. Austrian Franz Loeber began his own occult religion, as did John Newborough.[3]

We are now in a position to examine Madame Helena Petrovna Blavatsky's role in shaping the contactee picture. Students of religion will immediately recognize the name as one of the founders of the Theosophical Society, the single most influential occult body of the modern era. An ex-spiritualist, Blavatsky created a new occult system which included a hierarchy of "ascended masters." These masters, functioning like a gnostic pantheon, formed a structure of "supernatural" beings between humanity and the Divine. In Blavatsky's system, humans dealt more with the masters who were close and relatively accessible, than directly with the remote and very abstract, impersonal deity.

Little recognized, and certainly not emphasized by either Blavatsky or modern theosophists, Blavatsky included among the hierarchy masters who dwelt on Venus and with whom she was in contact. These masters she termed the Lords of the Flame and the Lord of This World, the head of the hierarchy for humanity. Under these Venusian lords are the Lords of the Seven Rays (or colors) who have direct contact with human adepts such as Blavatsky (Ransom 1938). Theosophists have, as a whole, focused their attention upon the material that the masters delivered through their main teachers, Blavatsky, Annie Besant, Charles Leadbeater, and Alice Bailey.

However, Guy Ballard, upon making contact with these masters, including the Venusian Lords of the Flame, built his own version of occult religion by emphasizing the direct and frequent ongoing contact with the masters. Members of his Great I AM religion gathered to hear the latest word from the masters, instead of gathering to study what Madame Blavatsky had written years ago in a book claimed to be inspired by the masters. Not only did Ballard become the first to actually build a religion on contact with extraterrestrials (as opposed to merely incorporating the extraterrestrial data into another already existing religion), but his emphasis was placed upon frequent contact with the masters from whom he received regular messages to the followers of the world contactee movement. The movement took over the I AM hierarchy and changed it into a space command hierarchy.

PRE-ADAMSKI AND THE 1950S CONTACTEES

Having surveyed the contactees of the pre-Adamski era, one naturally wonders how these contactees compare with the Adamski era contactees. The characteristics of the 1950s contactees have been summarized in a previous paper by this author (Melton 1980, 278-395), and the comparison is remarkable.

First, in the 1950s, contact remains with the three primary planets—Mars, Venus, and the Moon—but expands to include regular contact with Saturn, Jupiter, and Clarion, the mysterious twin of Earth on the other side of the sun.

Second, the flying saucer remains the only new element in the contactee story. It tends to replace astral travel as the means of getting around, both by extraterrestrials and by earthlings tripping into outer space for the first time. The saucer is not essential, however, and in many accounts in which it appears, it is obviously an additional frill. In many contactee accounts during the fifties, no flying saucer is included at all. Venusians walk the streets of urban America ready to talk to anyone aware enough to recognize them. Others are never seen but communicate directly with the Earth contact via telepathy. A few simply materialize in the person's presence when they wish to make themselves known. Astral travel is by no means forgotten and remains central to the accounts of such famous contactees as Angelucci and Michaels.

In Thomas Blot's 1891 account of his contact with a Martian (Blot 1891), the Martian suddenly appears at his rural home and begins to talk in clear English about Mars. Blot's account is unique in that most pre-Adamski contactees communicated via telepathy. Most post-Adamski contactees also communicate by telepathy, but a high percentage of the extraterrestrials, like Blot's Martian, speak English. Where such direct communication occurs, however, other paranormal events occurred to set the encounter apart from the mundane. Levitation, automatic writing, the ability to see through solid objects, and dematerialization were typical.

Thus, while the fifties contactees solved the language problem both by telepathy and the superintelligence of the extraterrestrials, they kept a "mysterious," a paranormal, aspect to the contact prominent. Those reading the accounts could thus be alerted that they are receiving much more than the straight account of a witness to a more or less unusual event.

Third, the contactees of the fifties continued to place much more emphasis upon the moral, metaphysical, and spiritual messages they received than on straight information of a "scientific" nature about outer space, space travel, or other mundane matters. Given the history of the pre-Adamski contactee accounts, we are no longer surprised, for we now understand that the contactee sees his/her task as delivering a message that has come out of either reflection upon, or an intuitive grasp of, the implications of modern science and culture. Thus, the contactees are naturally concerned with the effects of atomic power, war, pollution, and the need for the human family to come together.

Fourth, having noted the other likenesses between the pre-Adamski contactees and their fifties counterparts, we are not surprised to also find them operating in a religious context. More than half founded their own occult religion or became prominent in one founded by another. Almost all became involved in the two contactee ecumenical structures founded by George Van Tassel and Gabriel Green. Many had come out of spiritualist church or occult groups, such as Norman, Brady, and Lee. No less than five different groups were led by Adamski devotees.

FROM 1960 TO THE PRESENT

By 1960 occultists drawing on the massive body of occult teachings had created a new religious movement. With material from spiritualism, Theosophy, and the Great I AM, they found in the flying saucer a new image and a new concept around which to build their peculiar variations of occult belief. They followed a pattern set in the two hundred years between Swedenborg and Kenneth Arnold. They found in Adamski and other early contactees their prophets (and it matters little whether the prophets really believed their messages), and in Van Tassel and Green their organizers, their bishops, and overseers.

The crucial organizational development of the flying saucer movement in the 1950s made the future development over the next decades somewhat predictable. The movement followed the pattern of many new religions. They became institutionalized, with strong organizations developing around some contactees and many weak ones dying when the leader died or lost interest. Two organizations, Unarius, headed by Ruth Norman (Norman n.d.), and Mark-Age (*History* 1975), led by a group of four in Miami, Florida, became the largest contactee bodies, with groups across the United States. They were followed by Understanding, Inc. (Dan Fry) and the various Adamski groups, now thoroughly splintered.

As with other psycho-occult groups, new people with experiences of a kind promoted by the groups continued to appear. Some, such as Uri Geller (1975), became quite famous and had groups form around their revelations. Beti King (1976) moved from classic spiritualism, where she had been a medium. Warren Goetz (1974) and Elna E. Kenney (1974) (both Adamski followers), and Greta Woodrew (1981) represent a second set of leaders who emerged as contactees from within existing contactee organizations.

The contactees of the 1960s and 1970s follow the pattern set in the 1960s with one major exception. They have had to respond to increasing knowledge brought to the public consciousness that very little chance for intelligent life in this solar system exists. Therefore, they have had to abandon talk of contact with not just Mars and Venus, but Jupiter, Saturn, and the outer planets as well. All of the new contactees to emerge in the last decade either fail to reveal the planet from which their extraterrestrials come, or place it on the remote edge of the universe, far from the prying eyes of the space programs. Thus Woodrow Derenberger(Derenberger and Hubbard 1971) entertains visitors from Lanulos, and Oscar Magosci (1980) visits Argona of the Omm-Onn Solar System, a member of the Psycheon Federation Worlds. But most extraterrestrials keep their origins vague, as an exchange initiated by French contactee Claude Vorilhon shows:

> "Where do you come from?" he asked.
> "From far away . . ."
> "Do you speak French?"
> "We speak all of the languages of your world."
> "We come from a distant planet about which I will tell you nothing for fear that if the men of the earth weren't wise enough they could come to trouble our peace." (Vorilhon 1975)

The flying saucer movement has taken its place as a significant segment of the occult/psychic community in the United States.

Interestingly enough, it suffered little in the wake of the Condon report, which killed and weakened so many UFO groups—a further indication of its essentially religious nature. It appears at present to be stable and growing slowly. It seems impervious to the dangers of information produced by the space program, but the continuing spread of information on conditions in space may still have a strong effect on the movement in ways not yet apparent.

CONCLUSIONS AND SUMMARY

This survey of the contactee movement has verified a conclusion reached earlier that the flying saucer movement is in effect a new branch of occult religion. It follows the patterns of occult religious bodies and draws most of its content from general occult teachings.

As such, the contactees, both the more famous ones of the 1960s and the more recent ones, should be approached as participants in an occult religious movement. They are not kooks, but they are people who have been swept into a movement because of a direct experience with some extraordinary occurrences. These occurrences resemble most closely common visionary and psychic experiences cast in a framework of space age technology.

The contactees, also, hold little promise of supplying any useful information on the nature of the physical universe or outer space. They seek as a group religious, not scientific, goals, though they live in an age that demands some lip service to science and some technological sophistication, even in religious matters. In their naiveté, they do not see the lines between their religious quest and the search for information about unidentified flying objects. When they mix with UFO investigators, all of the tensions of putting religious people and secular scientists together are compounded by the anxiety of ufologists over the legitimacy of their pursuit and the desire of the contactees to share their experiences.

In one sense, the contactee phenomenon is quite separate from the attempt to understand unidentified flying objects. It has, nevertheless, particular interest in the recent focus of attention upon close encounters of the third kind and abductions. Prior to the mid-1960s, all of the CEIIIs which received any attention from the public were the contactee cases. They form the *only base* of case material with which to compare more recent cases.

The need to use contactee cases as a base of investigation became obvious in at least one prominent ufologist's treatment of contactees as "messengers of deception." In Vallee's case (Vallee 1979), the naiveté concerning occult and religious phenomenon in general destroyed the work of one ufologist willing to take the reports of close encounters seriously. But Vallee's theme repeats itself in less extreme ways in other literature, such as that treating the Anreasson affair (Fowler 1979).

As ufologists, we are weak methodologically when we rely too heavily upon case studies, as opposed to comparative studies of many similar cases. We also approach CEIII cases with a basic ignorance of common psychological and parapsychological material. We do not recognize astral travel. We do not understand psychokinesis. We grossly underestimate the power of the human mind, especially when in a disassociated state of consciousness such as hypnosis, to produce the most remarkable material, material completely impossible for the normal waking consciousness to acquire.

If there is any factual content to the stories of abductions and close encounters, especially those cases investigated through hypnosis, that content must first be tested in the light of equally strong content from competing accounts of close encounters with unusual beings by mediums, shamans, and visionaries. These people have for years been abducted by both fairies and flying creatures, and encountered demons, ghosts, and angels.

Finally, in gathering case studies of close encounters, the case material is incomplete without vital data on the total life of the contactee and follow-up studies on the result of that contact upon the life of the individual(s) involved. Only by becoming more sophisticated in our approach to contactee-like cases will we be able to lift the study beyond the esoteric interests of a few UFO buffs and make a genuine contribution to the body of scientific knowledge.

NOTES

1. On the fantastic voyage, see Philip B. Gove, *The Imaginary Voyage in Prose Fiction* (New York: Columbia Univ. Press, 1941). See also Noel Deisch, "The Navigation of Space in Early Speculation and in Modern Research" (*Popular Astronomy* 38, [1930]: 73-88.

2. William Denton, *Soul of Things* (Wellesley, Mass.: Mrs. E. M. F. Denton, 1873). Vol. 3. This volume contains accounts of a group of people who claimed contact with extraterrestrials from several planets they had visited.

See the *Encyclopedia of American Religions* by J. Gordon Melton (Detroit: Gale Research, 1992), Vol. 11 for an account of the various occult religions as founded by Loeber and Newborough and Madame Blavatsky.

REFERENCES

Bender, Albert K. 1962. *Flying Saucers and the Three Men*. Clarksburg, WVa: Saucerian Books.

Blot, Thomas. 1891. *The Man From Mars*. San Francisco: Bacon & Company.

Derenberger, Woodrow W., and Harold W. Hubbard. 1971. *Visitors From Lanulos*. New York: Vantage Press.

Flournoy, Theodore. 1900. *From India to the Planet Mars*. New York: Harper & Brothers.

Fowler, Raymond E. 1979. *The Andreasson Affair*. England Cliffs, NJ: Prentice-Hall.

Geller, Uri. 1975. *My Story*. New York: Praeger Publishers.

Goetz, Warren. 1974. *The Intelligence of the Universe Speaks*. The Author.

"History of Mark-Age" in special issue *Main*, #22, June-July, 1975.

Kenney, Elna E. 1974. *Under the Saucer's Shadow*. New York: Vantage Press.

King, Beti. 1976. *Diary From Outer Space*. The Author.

King, Godfre Ray (pseudo. of Guy Ballard). 1935. *Unveiled Mysteries*. Chicago: St. Germain Press.

Magocsi, Oscar. 1980. *My Space Odyssey in UFOs*. Toronto: Quest Group Publications.

Magoon, Vidsa Greenwood. 1930. *Willard M. Magoon/Psychic and Healer*. Newport, Vt: Wm. S. Bullock.

Melton, J. Gordon. 1980. "UFO Contactees—A Report on Work in Progress." In *Proceedings of the First International UFO Conference*, edited by Curtis G. Fuller. New York: Warner Books.

Norman, Ruth. N.d. *A Space Woman Speaks from Planet Earth*. El Cajon, Calif.: Unarius.

Proceedings of the Rocky Mountain Conference on UFO Investigation (Contactee Conference). 1980. Laramie, Wyo.: School of Extended Studies/Univ. of Wyoming.

Ransom, Josephine. 1938. *A Short History of the Theosophical Society*. Adyar, India: Theosophical Publishing House.

Samarin, William J. 1972. *Tongues of Men and Angels*. New York: Macmillan.

Swedenborg, Emanuel. N.d. *Earths in Our Solar System*. Boston: B. A. Whittemore.

Vallee, Jacques. 1979. *Messengers of Deception*. Berkeley, Calif.: And/Or Press.

Vorilhon, Claude. 1975. *"Real" Space Aliens Took Me to Their Planet*. Waduz, Lichtenstein: Face.

Weiss, Sara. 1906. *Decimon Huydas*. Rochester, N.Y.: Austin Publishing Co.

Woodrew, Greta. 1981. *On a Slide of Light*. New York: Macmillan.

2

RELIGIOUS DIMENSIONS
OF UFO PHENOMENA

John A. Saliba

In 1987, the Gallup Poll conducted a telephone survey to assess the national opinion on unidentified flying objects. Four basic questions were asked of those interviewed: (1) "Have you heard or read about UFOs?"; (2) "Have you, yourself, ever seen anything you thought was a UFO?"; (3) If you are aware of the UFO phenomenon, "in your opinion, are UFOs something real, or just people's imagination?"; and (4) "Do you think there are people somewhat like ourselves living on other planets in the universe?" (Gallup 1988, 52-54).

The results showed that over 88 percent of the population had some awareness of UFOs and 9 percent claimed to have seen something that could have been one. About 50 percent of the sample thought that UFOs were real objects and not constructs of the imagination and that intelligent beings existed somewhere else in the universe. Over 50 percent of the those who believed in UFOs had attended college. Men were found to be more likely than women to believe in the existence of intelligent life on other planets, though men and women shared the same opinions about UFOs. People over fifty years old were less convinced both about extraterrestrial life and UFOs.

Comparison between the Gallup surveys demonstrates that beliefs about flying saucers have not changed much since the late 1970s. It also shows that interest in UFOs runs high, an interest which is easily confirmed by introducing the topic of UFOs in a variety of social situations.

The 1987 Gallup Poll, however, left a lot of questions unanswered. It failed to distinguish, for instance, between (1) the various types of interests, religious and otherwise, people have in UFOs; (2) the different opinions regarding the probability and types of extraterrestrial life; and

(3) the conflicting reasons that have been advanced to explain why alien spacecraft have been visiting the planet Earth. Moreover, (4) it made no effort to gauge scientific opinion on the matter. And finally, (5) it omitted to examine the relationship between belief in UFOs and religion and to explore how, and to what extent, people get involved in flying-saucer religious groups, societies, movements, or cults. No statistics are provided to indicate what percentage of those who believe in UFOs assign a spiritual or religious interpretation to their presence. Defending the position that there are other forms of intelligent life in some distant solar system is very different from maintaining that advanced aliens have come from the planets within our solar system or from outer space to save the human race from spiritual and/or nuclear catastrophe, or to lead the human race to its next step in evolutionary development. Similarly, suggesting that flying saucers are the advance party of an alien invasion that aims to conquer and colonize planet Earth is not the same as affirming that UFOs are diabolical manifestations aimed at leading humans away from God or angelic visitations warning them of some impending doom.

This chapter draws attention to the religious aspects of the UFO phenomenon. First, the different types of people interested in UFOs are distinguished, showing how they are related to various kinds of UFO organizations and associations and to the type of alien creatures believed in. Second, three categories of UFO groups, movements, or cults are outlined and a few examples of each given. Third, the various forms of Christian interpretations of UFO phenomena are briefly described. Fourth, the major religious themes, which have already become part of UFO subculture, will be analyzed. Finally, an attempt will be made to assess the importance and significance of UFO religions.

TYPES OF PEOPLE INTERESTED IN UFOS

The subject of flying saucers is a topic that arouses the curiosity and interest of many different individuals. It is a topic that can be both exciting and foreboding. The literature reveals several types of people who think that searching for signs of extraterrestrial life and/or investigating UFO reports and contactee stories are worthwhile projects, and who exhibit various levels of enthusiasm about the flying saucer phenomenon. It may be of some help to distinguish, from the very start, the various types of "ufologists," even though the categories should not be rigidly compartmentalized. The possibility that intelligent extraterrestrial life forms exist and might be visiting and exploring the Earth attracts the attention and concern of (1) natural scientists, (2) social scientists, (3) government officials and military experts, (4) adventurers, and (5) religious individuals.[1] While it is relatively easy to identify these categories of people, it should be stressed that their interests overlap. Those contactees, for example, who believe that they have a religious mission may also rely on astronomical data to buttress their basic claim, namely that UFOs really exist.

The aforementioned types of people can also be distinguished by the kind of activities they participate in, the organizations they join, their descriptions of what UFO entities look like, the nature of their commitment to UFO ideology, and the level of involvement in activities relating to alien visitors.

Natural Scientists

The first major group of people who have examined UFO reports are the natural scientists, particularly physicists, chemists, and astronomers (Billingham 1981; Bova and Preiss 1990). Exobiology, the study of extraterrestrial life, has become a reputable subdiscipline in the biological sciences (Angelo 1985). Well-known scientists (Asimov 1979; Hoyle and Wickramasinghe 1978) have considered whether the presence of life elsewhere in the universe is at all feasible and have speculated on the type of extraterrestrial environment that would support it. They have further directed their efforts to finding concrete evidence that human beings are not alone in the cosmos.

Physicists are intrigued by the advanced technology that the purported builders of flying saucers must have developed. The speed and maneuverability of space vehicles, particularly if they have their origin in other galaxies, would point to a highly advanced civilization that would make our own appear technologically primitive. The research of physicists is hampered by lack of empirical evidence. No spacecraft or remnants from crashed vehicles have been examined at close range and reports of flying saucers are far too imprecise to warrant any definite conclusions.

Chemists are concerned with the minimal biochemical conditions that are necessary to sustain life as we know it in our solar system. Writing on the possibility of extraterrestrial life in the solar system, Norman Horowitz (1986, 144) writes:

Carbon is the characteristic element of terrestrial biochemistry. . . . The abundance of carbon in the cosmos is also very great, and a

variety of evidences—laboratory experiments, analysis of meteorites, interstellar spectroscopy—show that the formation of
organic compounds like those found in living matter occurs readily and on a large scale in the universe. It is therefore probable
that if life exists in the universe, it is also based on carbon chem-
istry.

Horowitz concludes, however, that there is no evidence of life in our
solar system. Since sufficient information to express any explicit conclusions or even solid opinions about the likelihood of life elsewhere in
the cosmos is as yet unavailable, he leaves open the question of whether
extraterrestrial life forms are present in other parts of the universe.

Astronomers (e.g. Ashpole 1989; cf. Mitton 1977), too, have entertained the idea that, given the vastness of the universe, conditions suitable for the origin and maintenance of life might be present also on
other planets in remote solar systems. Locating such life, whether it be
through radio contact or by some closer encounter here on Earth or in
space, would open up new horizons for research. Some physicists,
chemists, and astronomers are fascinated by the implications that the
existence of, and contact with, flying saucers might have on space travel,
as well as on understanding the genesis and evolution of life and on
expanding our knowledge of the laws of nature as a whole.

Not all these scientists are involved in UFO organizations. In
many instances, they limit themselves to writing books on the topic
and to presenting occasional talks at scientific conferences and UFO
panels. Some have formed or joined organizations whose main purpose is to investigate UFO reports, examine the evidence that is
adduced to verify their existence, and interpret their significance. In
general, scientists admit that "the majority of all recorded UFO sightings
are eventually identified" as "the result of observers innocently misinterpreting the appearance of unusual but perfectly natural phenomena" (Richards et al. 1991, 136). Some maintain, however, that since a
small percentage of sightings and contacts cannot be explained, it is
legitimate to seriously consider whether UFOs might be extraterrestrial visitations from other galaxies.

Scientific reflections on the possible types of intelligent extraterrestrial life differ substantially from those we find in most UFO cults
and movements. Scientists who speculate on the likely forms of extraterrestrial life disagree about whether the course of evolution in other
galaxies should proceed along paths similar to that of Earth. Fred Hoyle
(1957) and Lewis Beck (1985), for instance, have argued that life and
civilization in space need not be depicted anthropomorphically. Holye

has proposed the original idea that life elsewhere could be conceived as a vast intelligent cloud that lives in space, relies on stellar energy for food, and depends on a radio-based nervous system. Bieri (1964), on the other hand, has rejected such conjectures and maintains that life on other planets would have evolved along the same lines as that on Earth.

There are many organizations throughout the world studying UFO phenomena (cf. Clark 1990). Among the most well-known investigative associations in the field are the Center for UFO Studies (CUFOS) founded by astrophysicist J. Allen Hynek (cf. 1977), the Mutual UFO Network (MUFON), the National Investigations Committee on Aerial Phenomena (NICAP), the Aerial Phenomena Research Organization (APRO), the British UFO Research Association (BUFORA), the Canadian UFO Research Network (CUFORN), and the French Groupes D'Études des Phénomènes Aérospatiaux Non Identifies (GEPAN). Though some members of these groups believe in flying saucers, the research conducted by these organizations is professional and involves technical advisors, scientists, and aviation experts. These organizations do not hesitate to give conventional explanations of UFO phenomena, which they do not normally imbue with metaphysical or religious significance.

Social Scientists

The second group of scholars interested in UFO phenomena are social scientists, mainly, psychologists, psychiatrists, and sociologists, who have studied UFO reports, particularly those that describe encounters with, and abductions by, alien beings (cf. Saliba 1992). Their research has been directed not at envisioning the type of technology that is needed to produce such an advanced craft capable of traveling over large distances through space, but rather at the type of people who actually report UFO sightings and contacts and who are convinced of the existence of UFOs. Briefly stated, sociologists look for the correlations between UFO contacts and social and cultural factors. Psychologists and psychiatrists, on the other hand, examine what kind of personality is likely to have a UFO experience. They explore the relationship, if any, between UFO contactees and any mental, emotional, or psychological state or illness that might have been responsible for their alleged encounters. The majority of behavioral scientists start from the assumption that UFOs are not, or have not yet been proved to be, physical, empirical objects. Consequently, they can study only the reports themselves and the people who claim to have had encounters with alien craft and/or intelligent beings.

Social scientists interested in the UFO phenomenon usually participate in discussion groups or panels in various professional educational societies and conferences. Some may be involved in counseling people who claim to have been contacted by flying saucers. Because social scientists do not, as a rule, believe in UFOs, they do not join UFO religious groups except, sometimes, for the purpose of studying them by the method of participant observation. Social scientists make no speculations about the kind of alien beings that might be visiting Earth in their spacecraft. Their interest lies rather in the ways in which alien creatures are perceived and in the social, cultural, and psychological processes that are held to contribute to the forms they take.

Government Officials and Military Experts

A third group of people who have been concerned about flying saucers are government and military leaders. Particularly in the late 1940s and early 1950s, when the view that flying saucers might be secret Russian planes was popular, the presence of UFOs could easily be given both a military and political significance. A more daring explanation is that UFOs are spaceships of alien intelligences and are part of an advance guard of an armada that is planning to take over the Earth. The public appears to be amenable to such interpretations as the panic during the radio broadcast of Wells's *War of the Worlds* (1938) clearly shows (cf. Wells 1960 and Cantril 1966).

Some aspects of Western culture encourage the idea that space people and/or invaders exist. Science fiction literature, the movies, and the news media attract the attention of many readers and viewers with their portrayal of creatures from outer space. Classic science fiction movies, such as *The Day the Earth Stood Still* (1951) and *Earth vs. the Flying Saucers* (1956) are good examples of such interest and concern. More recent movies, like *Star Wars* (1977), *Close Encounters of the Third Kind* (1977), and *E.T.: The Extra Terrestrial* (1982), and the popular TV serials and movies (1979, 1982, 1984, 1986, 1989) on *Star Trek*, are even more explicit in their characterization of space people as carrying on campaigns of exploration, war, and conquest similar to those that have been often conducted by people on Earth.

Though the U.S. military has shown interest in the UFO phenomenon and, though the U.S. government did conduct a thorough investigation in the 1960s, there is little evidence that UFOs are part of contemporary political agenda and/or that the United Nations or any of major world powers are concerned about an impending attack from space. The Condon report (Condon 1969) seems to have put to rest any fear of an alien invasion.

Today, there are no politically active groups that take the UFO phenomenon seriously, much less as a threat. In spite of allegations to the contrary (cf., e.g., Blum 1990a), there is little substantial evidence that the U.S. government has a top-secret group studying UFOs. Some funds that maintain university-sponsored programs (such as the Planetary Society's Project META at Harvard University and the Search for Extraterrestrial Radio Emissions from Nearby Developed Intelligent Populations at the University of California at Berkeley, both designed to continue to look for life in space), may be indirectly sponsored by the government (cf. McDonough 1992). NASA's Search for Extraterrestrial Intelligence program (SETI) is also partly funded by the government (Blum 1990b; Papagiannis 1990). But the only political aspect of these programs is the process of getting the money allocated for specific research purposes. There is little hard evidence, moreover, for the so-called "conspiracy of silence" of which official agencies are sometimes accused (Evans 1987a). Several recent efforts (Fawcett and Greenwood 1984; Good 1988) to revive this theory have not been able to convince the scientific world, because they have not been documented by reliable physical documentation. Further, government agencies never seem to have speculated on what aliens might look like and have adopted the scientific attitude that, while allowing for the possibility that life forms on other planets may be quite different from those on Earth, it is futile to suggest the specific forms they might take.

Adventurers and Hobbyists

The fourth type of UFO enthusiasts are those who are in search of adventure or who approach flying saucers with the mentality of a hobbyist. Modern developments in technology, communication, and means of travel have brought people on Earth closer. There are few, if any, new lands or civilizations to discover or conquer. The achievements in space since the mid 1960s have opened up a new frontier, raising high hopes that human beings can eventually travel to distant planets and make contact with different worlds inhabited by all kinds of intelligent creatures. Screen depictions of space travel portray a human yearning to embark on new and challenging voyages, to discover unknown planets, to meet strange-looking, intelligent beings, and to learn about different cultures. This kind of adventurous mood, manifested so obviously in popular movies such as *2001: A Space Odyssey* (1968) and its sequel *2010* (1984), has also been adopted by popular magazines like *Omni*, which sometimes carries a feature entitled "UFO Update."

These UFO dilettantes often participate in loose organizations or platform societies that provide a forum for speakers who discuss various aspects of the UFO phenomenon. These societies function, not as closely knit cults that require membership and commitment, but rather as open places where views on UFOs are exchanged and UFO contactees relate their experiences. They include among their speakers experts in various fields of the occult sciences, like astrology, reincarnation, and the human aura. They tend to attract people who are interested in mystical experiences and who do not hesitate to bestow a religious or spiritual meaning to sightings of, and contacts with, UFOs. These groups operate, in the words of Rodney Stark and William Bainbridge (1983), as "audience cults." The Saucer and Unexplained Celestial Events Research Society and the Amalgamated Flying Saucers Clubs of America may be examples of this kind of group, whether or not they officially stress the need to conduct scientific research on UFOs.

These UFO enthusiasts are likely to characterize alien creatures as somewhat different from human beings. The aliens, however, are recognizable as some form of advanced animal life and often exhibit the same interests, problems, and desires that are part and parcel of human life. The depiction of aliens in the movie industry would come close to how these adventuresome ufologists conceive of alien life forms. Non-psychic contactees, that is, those who have had UFO encounters but have not become mediums for the religious messages of UFO creatures, might also have influenced the manner in which UFO beings are portrayed both in art and in the news media.

Religious Individuals

The final group of ufologists is made up of people who believe that UFOs exist and bring with them an important religious or spiritual message. These ufologists, however, disagree both about the nature of flying saucers and their occupants and about the message they bring. They may be classified in two broad types of believers: those who see alien encounters as psychic contacts with superior beings and those who interpret their appearances within the framework of traditional Christian apocalyptic theology.[2]

The first is made up of individuals who maintain that the space creatures piloting the UFOs have actually contacted select human beings and conveyed information that relates to the well-being of the human race and/or the planet Earth. These messages are supernatural, psychic, or paranormal manifestations or revelations that deal with some of the ultimate questions about life and the urgent needs of planet Earth. UFO encounters are thus comparable to traditional religious or mystical experiences. Moreover, these contactees frequently feel they have become entrusted with a mission. Through mediumship, or some other psychic means like telepathy, they become prophetic bearers of instructions and information from alien creatures, spiritual beings, or the Ascended Masters, all of whom are linked with intelligent and superior life in other planets within or outside our solar system.

Those who have accepted these contactees as genuine channels of extraterrestrial beings sometimes form associations or organizations whose tasks are to propagate the revelatory messages of the aliens and to prepare themselves and the human race for an apocalyptic future. The ideology of these groups is religious in orientation and the spiritual messages they accept from the flying saucer occupants or from outer space beings contain the traditional themes of salvation, prosperity, spiritual growth, and healing. It is these groups which often form cults or new religions centered around individuals who, by channeling extraterrestrial messages, assume prophetic and/or mystic roles.

Many of the best descriptions of extraterrestrial beings come from psychic contactees. The character and appearance of alien creatures vary enormously. Some, such as those portrayed by the Aetherius Society, are saintly, benevolent, and attractive human figures, like the Master Jesus, who is believed to be a being from the planet Venus. Others, like those depicted by Whitley Strieber (1987), are terrifying and malevolent entities who seem to appear from nowhere and to be intent on using the human race for their own nefarious plans.

Several attempts have be made to outline the forms in which aliens have appeared to their chosen contacts. Richard Hall (1988, 66) offers a simplified classification of what the "humanoids" look like. He writes that there are three basic types within which considerable variation exists:

Diminutive: typically 3-4 feet tall, disproportionate large heads, slender bodies, often clothed in "coveralls," and sometimes with transparent bodies. (Humanoid form.)

Average: about 5-6 feet tall, human-like in appearance and behavior, in fact sometimes indistinguishable from humans except for the association with UFOs. (Human form.)

Giant: perhaps 8-12 feet tall with oversize, often grotesque features. (Monster form.)

The inadequacy of this typology is indirectly admitted by Hall himself since he finds it necessary to add a fourth type of humanoids. He states (1988, 67) that "a fourth category of entity sightings indicates that some of the beings associated with UFOs probably are not purely biological beings. A number of reports suggest that some of the 'humanoids' are robots or androids." Moreover, in his representative sample of humanoid reports (Hall 1988, 61-63), he schematically describes twenty-five UFO beings, none of which correspond to his monster form.

A more comprehensive typology has been devised by Alvin Lawson (1980, 32), who distinguishes six types of UFO entities seen by those who have claimed close encounters of the third or fourth kind:

Human—clearly human in general appearance, size, and body movement.

Humanoid (humanlike)—often short, with a large head, large eyes (but remaining facial features are often underdeveloped), and a hairless body.

Animal—distinctly mammalian, reptilian or fishlike features, such as fur, claws, tail, scales, pointed ears, vertical pupils.

Robot—often wears "padded space suit" and bubble-dome head-gear, but sometimes has metallic body; mechanical movement common.

Exotic—beings with bizarre characteristics such as grotesque anatomical development, qualities of two or more entity types (human-robotic, humanoid-animal), or so unique as to be difficult to classify.

Apparition—ghostly creatures which may dematerialize, change shape, pass through walls, but may assume solid form.

It should be noted that the UFO literature of psychic contactees is not always clear about both the place of origin of flying saucers and the nature of their occupants. The opinion that space creatures come from faraway galaxies is common. However, many psychic contactees hold that UFOs actually come from planets in our solar system and that their occupants are more advanced entities from Venus, Mars, etc., who occasionally visit and live on Earth. Although modern space exploration has discounted the possibility that life exists elsewhere in our solar system, the view persists among members of several contemporary UFO movements (such as the Aetherius Society and the Summit Lighthouse) that the Ascended Masters stem from nearby planets. The majority of UFO cults or new religions, particularly those within the neo-I AM tradition (described below), are based on the assumption that UFOs come from our neighboring planets. Those who believe that aliens come from nearby planets argue that the scientific view that considers these planets lifeless and/or unable to support life does not necessarily contradict their own position. They insist that the Masters who live on other planets are obviously adapted to the conditions that prevail there. Surely, human life, as we know it on Earth, cannot survive on the planets in our solar system. However, radically different forms of intelligent life might exist elsewhere, even though scientific investigations have not yet discovered them.

There is, further, some confusion as to whether the aliens have physical bodies. Some psychic contactees insist that UFOs are physical in nature and that their occupants are similar to human beings, in the sense that they have a material body with the same basic outline and features as those of human beings here on Earth. Many contactees, however, write about UFOs and space beings as if these were psychic phenomena (cf. Andrews 1980), belonging to a different time/space dimension that lies beyond the scope and province of modern science. Or again, UFO occupants are spoken of as superior and/or spiritual beings or saints who once lived on Earth before they ascended to a higher level of existence. The portrayal of UFO beings as psychic or spiritual entities makes them impervious to objective and empirical detection and investigation that are the hallmark of modern science.

The second type of believers in UFOs are those who bestow on their presence a Christian interpretation, often linking them to apocalyptic times (cf. Inglesby 1973; Ogden 1963). Unidentified flying saucers need not be physical entities containing aliens from some other planet. They could be the product of supernatural forces and their occupants supernatural beings. They are, basically, signs or symbols whose meaning and/or message needs to be interpreted rather than channeled. Those who decipher the signs are exegetes or theologians, not mediums; they are preachers rather than seers or shamans. Consequently, the tendency to form cults or new religious movements that center around the teachings of a particular leader, though not completely absent, is less strong. While the members of organizations that revolve around psychic contactees are actually making a new commitment to a religious group that doesn't fit into the Judeo-Christian tradition, those Christians who accept the presence of UFOs as a religious event are not necessarily changing their religious affiliation, even though their understanding of flying saucers may place them on the fringes of Christianity.

Unlike psychic contactees, Christian believers in UFOs do not usually suggest that flying saucers come from any particular region of the universe. Rather, they maintain that UFOs are being sent by God or the devil, depending on whether their mission is beneficent or nefarious. In like manner, these Christians do not claim that they have contacted the occupants of alien spaceships. Nor do they usually provide us with novel and vivid descriptions of the aliens. Because their interpretation of UFOs is colored by their Christian worldview, they are more likely to view the aliens in those traditional forms in which angels and/or devils have been illustrated in Christian art.

TYPES OF UFO CULTS AND MOVEMENTS

There is ample evidence to show that speculations about whether other planets are inhabited are not new in the history of Western culture and can be traced back at least to the seventeenth century, particularly to the work of Emanuel Swedenborg (1915). That this belief has at times led to the establishment of religious movements is also well documented (Ellwood 1980). But scholars disagree about the historical roots and the ideological mold of UFO groups. David Stupple (1984) thinks that the Theosophical movement of the nineteenth century was instrumental in the development of a cosmology that included the notion that benevolent beings from other planets were highly evolved adepts who periodically visit the Earth and who continue to be interested in human welfare. Contact with these spiritual beings, known as the Great White Brotherhood, can be achieved through paranormal means. Splinter groups from the Theosophical Society, like the I AM movement, further developed the ideas about Space Masters and their relationship with planet Earth. Individual contactees, who were responsible for passing on the advanced spiritual knowledge of these Masters and announcing their timely interventions, attracted clienteles that developed into religious movements or cults.

Stupple (1984, 136), however, indirectly admits that his position is not without problems. In classifying the various UFO cults he states that one type is made up of "the neo-I AM sects which acknowledge the existence of flying saucers but *do not claim contact* with them." In which case, of course, these neo-I AM sects would not be UFO cults at all, since contact with extraterrestrials is central to any UFO movement.

Other scholars prefer to trace the roots of UFO groups to spiritualism. Gordon Melton (1989) includes them in the "Spiritualist, Psychic, and New Age Family," while he places the Theosophical Society and the I AM movements into a distinct category, the "Ancient Wisdom Family." Robert Ellwood and Harry Partin (1988, 116) agree with Melton, though they recognize that the Aetherius Society is an exception since it has been definitely influenced by Theosophy. Contactees are similar to spiritualist mediums, the former receiving messages from superior, nonearthly beings, the latter from the spirits of the dead who are also not on this earthly plane.

Many UFO groups have borrowed heavily from both spiritualism and Theosophy. They have incorporated in their ideology the concepts of cosmic wisdom and cosmic masters who exist on other planets. Their leaders often channel, or communicate with, these masters through some psychic means (such as telepathy) or by entering into a trance like state. Probably the main difference between UFO cults and the neo-I AM movement is that the former hold that the Masters not only live on other planets, but also visit the Earth periodically in spaceships. For neo-I AM groups channeling the messages of the Masters from other planets is an important activity. But these Masters, unlike those of UFO groups, do not visit the Earth in flying saucers. The Church Universal and Triumphant (the Summit Lighthouse) is a good example of this type of neo-I AM movement, since it teaches that there are cosmic masters whose messages are channeled through Elizabeth Claire Prophet.[3] Jesus, according to the Summit Lighthouse, is a highly evolved Venusian who came on Earth to assist humankind. But there is little interest in flying saucers as such and members are not encouraged to pursue the topic. Essential to any UFO cult or religion is the belief that one or several individuals are in touch with beings in flying saucers and regularly fulfill the role of mediums who transmit prophetic messages, religious teaching, and moral instructions.

It is not easy to pinpoint the distinguishing features of the various types of psychic (religious) UFO groups, because the several names of the space masters or UFO people appear with astounding regularity and the religious messages and spiritual instructions are very similar in content. Without attempting, and much less claiming, to have found a solution to the debate briefly outlined above, it is here suggested that UFO movements be conveniently divided into three major types: (a) those that rely heavily on the Theosophical tradition, particularly the I AM branch; (b) those whose roots stem more directly from the spiritualist tradition and have accepted the belief that superior beings in flying saucers are in touch with the human race through selected mediums; and (c) those that are essentially Christian movements, since they endeavor to interpret their UFO sightings and experiences within the context of Christian teachings. The last-mentioned groups need not be cults in the strict sense, since their members do not abandon their previous religious affiliations and are not required to commit themselves to and accept a relatively new ideology, religious practice, and lifestyle.

UFO Groups in the Neo-I AM Tradition (cf. Ellwood 1988)

There are several neo-I AM groups that believe that their leaders are in touch with space brothers and sisters who are, by and large, the Masters of the Theosophical Society. These superior beings visit the Earth in flying saucers or at least oversee its inhabitants from their vantage point in space. They deliver their messages to the human race through mediums, usually on a regular basis. In general the mediums of each movement hold a monopoly over access to the space relatives. They play the role of "mystagogues" in Weber's use of the word; in other words their function is to perform sacraments, that is, "magical actions that contain the boons of salvation" (Weber 1956, 54). Weber's theory has been applied to the Aetherius Society by Roy Wallis (1974), who sees its founder George King as a typical mystagogue, and to Unarius by Kirkpatrick and Tumminia (n.d.). Probably the best example of a UFO religion in the neo-I AM tradition is the Aetherius Society, one of the oldest and most organized flying saucer movements (Ellwood and Partin 1988, 126-32). Though sometimes included under spiritualist groups (see, for example, Melton 1989, 677), the Aetherius Society is a model of a UFO religion because belief in flying saucers is central to its religious ideology. George King, its founder and leader, is held to be the "Voice of International Parliament" and the "Primary Terrestrial Mental Channel" of several cosmic masters who, through him, communicate on a regular basis with the human race. Like the Summit Lighthouse, the Aetherius Society believes that Jesus is an advanced being from the planet Venus who speaks through a human channel. But the members of the Aetherius Society also hold that Jesus and other space entities (like Mars Sector 6 and Jupiter 92) travel in flying saucers, that constantly hover over the Earth protecting it from evil forces and warning humans of impending calamities. Through George King, these masters from the planets in our solar system carry out their plans to protect human beings from ecological disasters, to encourage them in their good work on Earth, and to provide guidance for the spiritual development of the human race.

UFO Groups More Directly Related to the Spiritualist Tradition

The second (and probably more common) class of UFO groups is made up of those that are not linked with the neo-I AM movement or whose connections with this tradition are rather tenuous. They belong more appropriately to the spiritualist tradition of mediumship. Members in these groups believe that certain individuals are in direct contact with UFO beings, but spacecraft from other planets play little or no role in their worldview.

The organization known as Mark-Age (cf. Melton 1989, 680) provides an illustration of how the belief in beings from outer space can be incorporated in what is essentially a contemporary form of spiritualism. Yolanda, the main channeler in Mark-Age, is a telepathic medium through which the Theosophical Masters speak to human beings. While the Masters are held to live on other planets, they do not visit the Earth in flying saucers. In fact, Mark-Age teaches explicitly that spacecraft are not physical objects constructed by a technologically superior race on another planet. Their existence is in the ethereal realm.

One can include the Universarium Foundation (Melton 1989, 1024) within this category. Borrowing heavily from the I AM tradition, this organization maintains that the Ascended Masters are from outer space. But the stress is on the messages which are transmitted through mediumship. All these groups differ from traditional mediumship in that their leaders are in touch, not with the spirits of the dead, but rather with exceptional entities who are not human beings at all. They differ from UFO groups because their beliefs and practices do not hinge on the existence of flying saucers. Unlike the Aetherius Society, they do not keep track of UFO sightings, interpret their significance, or use them to corroborate their religious beliefs.

In some cases many aliens are said to have taken over human beings here on Earth in order to help the human race advance to a higher level of consciousness. Meditation, retreats, and instructions on occult topics are common practices in these movements.

One of the most outstanding examples of this type of UFO movement is the Extraterrestrial Earth Mission of Sedona, Arizona.[4] The mission's founders and leaders, Savizar and Silarra, claim to be "extraterrestrial walk-ins" who channel various extraterrestrial masters with the intention of furthering the planet Earth's divine awakening. One of the mission's promotional leaflets makes the following statement on its founders:

> Savizar and Silarra describe themselves as multi-dimensional entities that have emerged from extra-terrestrial sources. Inhabiting human bodies subjects them to the impact of Earth's existence and they must use the same Universal Principles as everyone else on this planet in order to deal with that. What is extraordinary

about them is their intense purposefulness and willingness to experiment with possibilities for the co-creation of Heaven and Earth. They are quite human and ordinary in many ways and yet they demonstrate a level of wholeness and oneness with the Universe that allows the courage and strength to stand naked in their truth.

Savizar and Silarra state that they are the third team of aliens, who have inhabited the same human bodies, and that there are millions of aliens who have likewise taken over the physical bodies of men and women all over the Earth. It is obvious that Savizar and Silarra are not just channelers or mediums of cosmic masters or space brothers and sisters. They have been literally taken over or possessed and, thus, transformed into vehicles of cosmic wisdom and power. They articulate their mission, which is one of service to planet Earth, as follows:

We are the third team of extraterrestrial walk-ins who have inhabited these bodies. Being extraterrestrials, we have many different ways of perceiving, relating to, and articulating the evolutionary phenomenon that faces the inhabitants of Planet Earth at this time. It is time to awaken and co-create a world that has never been here before. A World that is most easily described as Heaven on Earth.[5]

Christian UFO Groups

The possibility that other intelligent beings exist in some parts of the universe raises several questions from a Christian theological viewpoint (Zubeck 1961; Jennings 1978). Their origin, their spiritual condition, and their relationship to God would all have to be specified. One can argue, however, that prolonged theological speculation and debate about the physical nature and spiritual state of extraterrestrials are not worth the trouble until one knows more about them.

On the other hand, the belief that these intelligent beings are actually visiting us in flying saucers brings with it an element of urgency. How does the presence of UFOs fit into the Christian worldview? Does the Bible provide any clue to the meaning of UFO phenomena? One particular Christian organization, the Christian Research of Aerial Phenomena, is dedicated to investigating flying saucers from a biblical perspective.[6] Though not a religious movement or cult, this organization is made up of Christians who not only believe in UFOs, but who also think that their presence should be of concern to the governments of the world, to the public in general, and to Christian churches.

Christian UFO cults come into being when the presence and activity of flying saucers are accepted as central to the Christian message, which is interpreted anew by prophetic leaders who claim some connection with and/or knowledge of space creatures. One such cult, which flourished in the mid 1970s, called itself the Human Individual Metamorphosis. Also known as the UFO People, this group has received considerable attention from scholars.[7] Its leaders, Herff Applewhite and Bonnie Nettles, who referred to themselves by various exotic names such as "Bo and Peep" and "Pig and Sow," began preaching their flying-saucers gospel on the West Coast of the United States. Their claim is that they had come to Earth in a spacecraft with the specific mission of preparing prospective members to graduate to their next level of being. Their theology is based on the biblical theme of the imminent coming of God's Kingdom, which they see heralded in the advent of flying saucers. They are so convinced that UFOs will come to rescue the human race in the near future that they travel with their followers from hilltop to hilltop in expectation of their advent. People who join this movement literally abandon all to make themselves ready for the coming of the Kingdom.[8]

Applewhite and Nettles argue that the human condition has been so chained by cycles of reincarnation that only escape from our planet, doomed to destruction by pollution and decay, could save the human race. Salvation means the attainment of the Kingdom of God which is a physical place located outside the Earth's atmosphere, somewhere in the vast cosmos. Those who will be saved will be "beamed up" by a flying saucer and transformed into a higher level, that of resurrected people. By renouncing their possessions and desires, members would purify their bodies and make themselves ready to be saved, that is, picked up by flying saucers. This message is buttressed by copious references to the Bible. Applewhite and Nettles do not claim to be in touch with the Ascended Masters through channeling, nor do they advocate any new teachings or convey cosmic wisdom. They do not reflect the theology of the I AM movement, nor display the mediumship ability of classical spiritualists. Even though they declare that their origin is extraterrestrial, they behave as prophetic figures who have been assigned the task of announcing the coming of salvation. Although many Christians would disagree with their theological stance, their message can be interpreted as an attempt to relate some basic Christian beliefs with current human conditions and problems and to present the Christian message in the language of the contemporary myth of flying saucers.

TYPES OF CHRISTIAN INTERPRETATIONS

The belief in the presence and activity of UFOs is not limited to those individuals who have had close encounters with flying saucers or joined a UFO cult. Convinced of the reality of UFOs, many Christians have reread the Bible, found hidden references to UFOs, and bestowed a religious meaning upon their existence and their current activities.

UFOs and the Bible

The reader who, for the first time, ventures into the abundant literature on the UFO phenomenon will be surprised by the many books and articles dedicated to the study of UFOs and the Bible (Catoe 1978; Rasmussen 1985; and Eberhart 1986). The main hypothesis advanced is that the presence of UFOs is corroborated by the Bible, many stories of which can only be properly understood in the framework of UFO theory. Two distinct types of biblical interpretations have emerged. The first attempts to cling to the traditional Christian view which stresses God's creative and salvific activities, but adds the theory that beings from outer space represent messengers from God. In other words, God's action in the world is carried out through the work of space creatures who act, like angels, as agents of God. The second replaces God and the supernatural with superbeings who inhabit other regions in the galaxy and who are responsible for the creation of the human race and its development.

Scripture is the starting point for both types of proponents who see references to UFOs in most of the extraordinary accounts and miraculous stories of the Old and New Testaments. Barry H. Downing (1968), one of those who strongly maintain that the Bible contains plenty of evidence that flying saucers have been visiting the Earth from ancient times, divides biblical UFOs into two categories: "(1) those that seem to be connected with what we might call psychic phenomena and (2) those that we would now call 'multiple witness' sightings" (Downing 1980a, 53-54). As examples of the first type he cites prophetic experiences recorded in the Bible, such as the deep sleeps of Abraham (Gen. 15:17) and Jacob (Gen. 28:12). These sleeps he interprets as a form of trance that can be compared to the hypnotic state during which modern UFO contacts remember their encounters with extraterrestrial beings. Similarly, Ezekiel's two famous visions (Ezek. 1 and 10) may also be counted as UFO experiences under trance conditions.

Many incidences recorded during the Exodus of the Israelites from Egypt provide excellent cases of multiple witness sightings. The parting of the Red Sea is said to have been caused by unidentified flying objects and the cloud that guided them across the wilderness (see, for instance, Exod. 13:21) is compared to contemporary cigar-shaped UFOs (cf. Downing 1990). In the same way Ezekiel's ascension (2 Kings 2) in a "chariot of fire" is one of the biblical narratives most often quoted to document the existence of flying saucers in biblical times. In the New Testament, the appearance of angels to the shepherds at the birth of Jesus (Luke 2:9), the bright cloud seen by the three apostles at the transfiguration of Jesus (Matt. 17:1-8), the scene described at the baptism of Jesus (e.g., Matt. 3:13-17), and his ascension in a cloud (Acts 2:9) are all similarly explained as UFO experiences.

The first view tries to fit modern UFO sightings and contacts into the fabric of Christian thought, which conceives of God as active in human history. The New and Old Testaments represent two revelations through major UFO contacts. In other words, while maintaining the traditional Christian view that God has revealed himself to human beings and that divine manifestations are contained in the Bible, biblical revelations are said to have come to humankind through the medium of UFOs. The supernatural takes on a technological form in order to make known to human beings God's plans and intentions. God's activity on Earth continues today through UFO encounters, which constitute a modern form of divine revelation.

The use of the UFO theory as a hermeneutical principle of biblical interpretation faces two serious objections, one stemming from biblical scholarship, the other from systematic theology (cf. Soulen 1981; Hagan et al. 1985; Grant 1965). Those who claim that certain narratives in the Bible refer to UFOs are using flying saucers as a method for understanding the meaning of the text. In other words, the presence of UFOs is taken for granted and then the Bible stories are interpreted in the light of this assumption. This approach to the Judeo-Christian study of the Bible is relatively new and one wonders whether it has any chance of leaving much impact on the kind of biblical studies that take place in seminaries, colleges, and universities. Biblical scholars are likely to object strongly to the use of belief in UFOs as a principle of hermeneutics. The main reason for this is obvious: the existence of UFOs is a statement of faith and their alleged presence in biblical times is a hypothesis. UFOs, therefore, cannot be the method of eliciting the meaning of the scriptural text, since they themselves are an interpretation of the same text.

Systematic theologians are also likely to raise difficulties against UFO exegesis. Those who opt for a literal interpretation of the Bible will find it practically impossible to harmonize their worldview both with the idea of extraterrestrial life and with the interference of space intelligences in the history of the human race as depicted by the Bible. Others can complain that this approach to the Bible indirectly challenges the manner in which the Bible has been traditionally understood. Besides, the claim that revelations through UFOs have continued up to the present age contradicts the common Christian belief that revelation came to an end with the New Testament and, moreover, requires radical rethinking of the common Christian doctrines of creation and redemption (cf. Butterworth 1969; McDonagh 1986; Wiederkehr 1979).

The second view not only reinterprets the Bible; it also changes its focus. God becomes an astronaut, a superior being who lives in a more advanced civilization in some other faraway galaxy. Divine revelations are nothing but teachings from space creatures and miracles are awesome interventions by intelligences who are technologically superior to the human race. The supernatural, in this view, is reduced to the super-technological. God is a superior humanoid creature living on another planet. He has made himself immortal through technology and has created the human race on Earth for his amusement.

Erich von Däniken's theory (1969, 1973) about flying saucers and their influence on Earth is probably the most well-known and popular attempt to create a worldview in which extraterrestrials play the leading role in the evolution and development of the human race. His untiring efforts to corroborate it by scientific evidence, archaeological discoveries, and technological inventions seem convincing to many people, even though they have been largely spurned in the scientific world (Peters 1977b; Omohundro 1976). Däniken's view of the fantastic origins of the human race is summarized by John Allan (1976, 22; cf. Däniken 1973, 46):

> In the unknown past . . . there was a battle in the depths of the galaxy between two space people like us. The losers escaped in a spaceship to earth, and built tunnel systems underground to avoid detection by the pursuers. Eventually they emerged from their tunnels and began to create human life "*in their own image* from already existing monkeys." After that they had decided that the evolutionary process was too slow, and in impatience wiped out "those who did not follow the biological laws laid down." Subsequently, men began to dig underground hideouts themselves, for fear of "divine judgment." Eventually the astronauts took off from fresh fields and pastures new, but still they're watching us, curious about the results of their experiment.

R. L. Dione's works (1969, 1976) provide many illustrations of how the UFO theory can be used to reinterpret traditional religious tenets in a more scientific manner. Two examples from the New Testament should suffice to show how some ufologists are rereading the Bible. The Gospels relate many stories about how Jesus cured the crippled and the lame. Dione maintains that these were not genuine miraculous cures. In his opinion, what actually took place was that extraterrestrials had previously hypnotized certain people so that their infirmities were psychosomatic. These apparently sick people were programmed to respond to the suggestions of Jesus that led to their being instantaneously healed.

Another example is the New Testament account of the story of the Virgin Birth, a Christian belief that found its place in the early creeds. The Virgin Birth has been subjected to various interpretations by Christian theologians (cf. Brown 1977) and social scientists alike (Saliba 1975). In traditional Christian theology it has often stood as a sign of God's intervention in human history and as a proof of the divinity of Christ. Some ufologists (cf. Dione 1969; 1976) have seen it as an example of space technology brought about by the intervention of beings from outer space. Accordingly, the story of the Virgin Birth refers to the advent of a flying saucer whose occupants injected the mother of Jesus with the sperm of the space creature from another world or planet. Mary can still be said to have been literally a virgin, though no miracle or supernatural intervention occurred.

The theories of von Däniken and Dione are examples of both secularization and remythologization. They secularize religion because they remove the supernatural: the miraculous (supernaturally produced) events in the Bible become activities of superhuman beings from other planets, who possess superior technological and psychic powers. God, the transcendent creator and miracle worker of Judeo-Christian thought, becomes a technician and scientist whose knowledge and skill by far surpass those of human beings. God's activities do not require supernatural explanations, for they are nothing but practical and medical procedures that are so advanced that they appear miraculous or magical in the context of our inferior and underdeveloped culture. They remythologize it because they introduce an element of mystery and a preternatural force that is beyond our scientific knowledge. They create another realm of beings which is not quite spiritual nor material. By postulating that UFOs are objective spaceships that somehow elude our established methods of empirical verification, they reintroduce that element of paradox that is at the heart of all religions.

Both approaches are likely to be rejected by the majority of Christians. However, those Christians who believe in UFOs and still prefer to maintain their allegiance to traditional Christianity have proposed more orthodox interpretations of the presence and activities of flying saucers. The presence of mysterious objects in the sky can readily be deciphered as angelic or demonic visions and linked with apocalyptic times.

UFOs as Angelic or Demonic Manifestations

Although many believers in flying saucers maintain that their inhabitants are friendly, not all accounts of UFO contacts are serene and congenial. Space intelligences can be either beneficent or nefarious beings. They belong to a universe where the moral order is flawed. Like their intelligent counterparts on planet Earth, they have the ability and responsibility to choose between good and evil. As in religious worldviews, good and evil in UFO mythology are given cosmic proportions. They are perceived as two diametrically opposed forces at work in the universe. They are constantly at war with each other. They not only represent symbolically the relentless wars that have been waged throughout the history of humankind, but they also are participating in the struggles that are part and parcel of human life on Earth.

Although UFO cults and movements usually stress the good aspects of alien beings, some groups unite both the negative and positive features of extraterrestrials in a coherent cosmology. The Aetherius Society, for instance, believes that its founder is in touch with various Ascended Masters, who circle the Earth in flying saucers to assist its inhabitants in their spiritual development and to defend them in times of crises. These godly beings have the mission of saving us not only from our own ignorance and misdeeds, but also from outside powers that are beyond human control. Members of this society believe that these Masters have, on several occasions, saved the Earth from an invasion and destruction engineered by the advanced and compassionless scientists of a dying world, referred to by its pseudonym "Garouche," which is ruled by four evil intelligences. On one occasion, Master Aetherius, with the help of nine thousand spacecraft from his planet Venus, came to the rescue and averted the danger by encircling the Earth with an impenetrable shield.[9]

The descriptions of UFO activities by contactees can, therefore, be generally classified into two main categories. One depicts the aliens as angelic and attractive youth who appear suddenly in a bright light and who are genuinely interested in the well-being of the human race.

These travelers from other regions of the cosmos care for the human race and its welfare, particularly in the current, unparalleled troubled times in human history. Many of the UFO messages, channeled through people who believe they have been designated for the task, show concern for the present human plight, which has been brought to a head by the development of nuclear power and the misuse of Earth's natural resources that has led to a serious ecological crisis. The aliens are calling us back to our senses, warning us that the destruction of the Earth lies ahead, if we do not reform, and guiding us in our efforts to preserve the Earth. Religious goals, such as spiritual transformation, redemption from earthly woes, creation of a paradisal condition in this life, and preparation for a higher life form after death are among the benefits that UFO occupants impart through human contactees.

The second trend is to look on aliens as dangerous and terrifying creatures or negative astral entities, whose activities are violent and hostile (Tyson 1977). They are unwanted intruders in human life because their intentions are inimical to the well-being of the human race. They are superior invaders who are secretly watching us and experimenting on human life (just as humans experiment on animal life here on Earth). They make continuous attempts to interrupt human contacts with our space relatives. Their final goal is to conquer, subdue, and control the Earth and its inhabitants (Steiger 1988, 142ff.). Such a theory about the purposes of flying saucers is corroborated not only by abductees (such as Strieber 1987) who have had frightening UFO experiences, but also by some influential writers on the UFO phenomenon (cf. Hopkins 1987). Even though less alarming views of the abduction experiences have been offered (Ring 1989), some still persist in presenting a rather disturbing view of UFOs and the intentions of their occupants. Jacques Vallée (1990), for instance, maintains that UFOs are not necessarily invaders from another planetary system. They represent a far more subtle and serious threat to humankind. Vallée (1979, 21) summarizes his position as follows:

> UFOs are real. They are an application of psychotronic technology; that is, they are physical devices used to affect human consciousness. They may not be from outer space; they may, in fact, be terrestrial-based manipulating devices. Their purpose may be to achieve social changes in this planet. Their methods are those of deception: systematic manipulation of witnesses and contactees; covert use of various sects and cults; control of the channels through which alleged "space messages" can make an impact on the public.

Vallée (1979, 70ff.) corroborates his thesis by giving several examples, such as the group known as Human Individual Metamorphosis (mentioned earlier), which, he thinks, is a dangerous organization that uses traditional religious themes and adverse social conditions to establish its doctrine of salvation and manipulate its believers.

The view that there are both benign and malicious superbeings at large in the cosmos who are engaged in the eternal fight between good and evil is amenable to philosophical and religious overtones. It can also be harmonized with Christian theology, where the battle between the good and bad angels represents the universal struggle between the divine and the demonic, a struggle that has both cosmic and earthly proportions. The good aliens can be said to be angels sent by God to help humankind, while the evil ones are demonic beings and forces that are determined to draw human beings away from God.

If UFOs are friendly creatures from a space civilization that is more advanced than the Earth's, then one can picture them as benign quasi-supernatural or superhuman beings who have no evil intentions toward humankind. George Adamski (Leslie and Adamski 1953) claims that space people have told him of their many visitations in biblical times. He maintains that the Bible has many references to other worlds (Gen. 6:2-4; Heb. 1:2, 11:3; John 14:2) and that Jesus himself told his disciples that he was not of this world (John 8:23). The flying saucers' occupants originate from the many different worlds created by God. When they visited the Earth in ancient times they were called "angels" by human beings who interpreted their divine mission as a benevolent intervention by God or the gods. There is consequently nothing to fear from the strange objects flying in the sky. Reacting to reports that the U.S. Air Force has shot at UFOs, Adamski remarks that the human pilots have attacked angels or messengers of God. He writes (cf. David 1970, 334):

> The saucers are not here to harm or frighten any one. They have injured no one, although they have been accused by those who do not understand their purpose. They have not committed hostile acts against our planes or kidnaped their crews. Some may have been taken—just as Elijah was—and later returned to teach what they know.

To Adamski, the function of flying saucers' occupants is similar to that of guardian angels in Christian thought. They are sent to help us, offer us guidance, and instruct us in times of trouble. They are divinely commissioned missionaries or saviors. Adamski makes an effort to give a Christian interpretation of UFOs and their occupants. In fact he veers from traditional Christian doctrine when he holds that Jesus was, like many other extraterrestrials, a visitor from another planet who came on Earth as a missionary. This theme, that space people are benevolent beings (angels), has been adopted by some Christian writers who look on them as messengers of God sent with a mission to protect and deliver us from evil. Billy Graham (1986, 20), though not quite endorsing this view, leans towards it.

But flying saucer occupants can be identified not only with the angels of the Judeo-Christian tradition, but also with the demons of the same tradition. Once they are imagined as powerful, adverse beings intent on inflicting harm on human beings, they can easily become classified with the evil angels that go about doing the work of Satan.

Several Christian writers have done precisely that. John Weldon and Zola Levitt (1975), in a major Christian fundamentalist work on flying saucers, have strongly maintained that UFOs are manifest signs of satanic presence in the contemporary world. They argue that there is a very clear relationship between belief in, and contact with, UFOs and occult phenomena, which themselves are evil and diabolic. Whether UFOs are real, physical machines that come from other planets is not that important. What counts is that people see them and their presence as demonic manifestations. Put in another way, demons make people see UFOs by "temporary manipulations of matter and energy" (Weldon and Levitt 1975, 135). Sightings of and contacts with extraterrestrials are direct or indirect associations with the devil himself. In Weldon and Levitt's own words (1975, 121):

> [UFOs] are a manifestation of demon activity. They are here to misguide the multitudes and they are doing pretty well. They have judiciously utilized their powers through selected people to fascinate the masses, and they have widely promulgated their doctrines.

Moreover, this view of UFOs as demonic manifestations or apparitions fits comfortably with the theory that connects UFO phenomenon and encounters with the perceived current resurgence of evil in our times, a revival that can be read as an apocalyptic sign that the end of the world is not far off. Weldon and Levitt (1975, 106) have, once again, summarized this position in passionate language:

> All of what we are witnessing in the fields of the occult, the UFO's, the false messiahs—even inflation and famine—lines up

well with what the prophets expected of the period known as the end time. True Christians, with their faith in things unseen, are never staggered by the idea of invisible forces of evil, and they are the last either to doubt or fear the strange phenomenon of this age.

Bob Larson, writing on the New Age movement, points out that UFO beings give messages that are consistent with New Age ideology that ascribes a divine inner nature to human beings. Because this teaching is in direct conflict with the Bible, he concludes that "extraterrestrials are demonic beings, part of the delusions prophesied for the end of this age" (Larson 1989:254).

Many Christian writers hold that the occupants of UFOs are demons, disguised as angels, sent by Satan to seduce and lead people away from the truth and to establish his own evil kingdom.[10] They cunningly draw our attention away from the Bible. In the words of one author (Hymers 1976, 141):

> They [i.e. the UFOs] set the stage for a supernatural, or at least an extraterrestrial, solution for world problems; and then they attack the credence of the Scriptures, the true solution.

Since their mission is to lead people to abandon their orthodox Christian beliefs, they represent the anti-Christ. In the New Testament the anti-Christ (cf., e.g., 1 John 2:18-22 and 4:2-4) represents the enemy of Christ who desires to counteract the salvific action of God. He is equated both with the "man of sin" in one of the Pauline letters (2 Thess. 2:3-10) and with the "beast" of the Book of Revelation. He is expected to make his appearance during the great apostasy that must precede the return of Christ. He is depicted as one person or several individuals, or as a personification of all forces hostile to Christ. Flying saucers and their occupants could be fitted into this theological mold without much difficulty.

UFO encounters and abductions are, therefore, a form of diabolical intervention. Those who act as mediums and pass on the messages and teachings of the aliens are experiencing a form of demonic possession. From a religious point of view, UFO occupants are transformed from warlike colonizers from space into demonic forces that intend to undermine the teachings of the Bible and to overthrow Christianity. Their influence is so pervasive and their resources so powerful that they can only be interpreted as a sign that the final cosmic struggle between good and evil is close at hand.

UFOs as Apocalyptic Signs

Once UFOs are linked to angelic or diabolical activity, the many reports of sightings and encounters can easily be explained as a sign that we are living in apocalyptic times. Ruth Montgomery (1985, 21) subscribes to such a view. She states that the aliens in vehicles from outer space have the mission of awakening human beings to the realization that their final destruction is imminent unless, of course, better ways of settling disputes between nations are found. The Earth, in her view (1985, 51; cf. Barton 1969), will shift on its axis in the year 2000, with catastrophic results, including the death of most of its inhabitants. The space people will save many of the enlightened souls by evacuating them in galactic fleets and later returning them to Earth for its rehabilitation or recolonization.

UFOs, thus, can be the heavenly sign that heralds the Second Coming of Christ with its consequent judgment. They are an indication that the decisive great battle of Armageddon is not far away. And they serve as a warning that human beings should prepare themselves for this event (cf. Inglesby 1973; Ogden 1963). This understanding of UFOs can be seen as a modern expression of apocalyptic and millenarian thought that has been a constant factor in Christian theology.

RELIGIOUS THEMES IN UFO PHENOMENA

One of the most appealing aspects of UFOs is their religious content and structure. UFOs can readily function as a religion for several reasons. They deal with important and often ultimate issues in human life; they contain references to entities that bear some resemblance to traditional religious beings, such as gods, supernatural heroes, angels, and devils; and they appear to have a spiritual or transhuman nature, since their presence is not susceptible to modern empirical investigation. At least seven major religious themes or elements dominate accounts of UFO sightings and contacts: (1) mystery; (2) transcendence; (3) belief in spiritual entities; (4) perfection; (5) salvation; (6) worldview (the ascription of meaning and purpose to the universe); and (7) spirituality.

Mystery

Those individuals who have had a close encounter with UFOs and their alien inhabitants are understandably convinced of the mysterious element in their experience. What is even more noteworthy is that those who have not had this experience often write about it in a similar vein. The aura of mystery in which these encounters are expressed and relayed to the general public is astounding (cf., e.g., Evans 1979; Cazeau and Scott 1979; Blundell and Boar 1990). This sense of mystery is enhanced by the nature of the flying saucers themselves, which travel at enormous speeds and are extremely elusive. Reports of UFO encounters, especially stories of abductions, leave a lot of questions about the aliens' methods and intentions unanswered. The veil of secrecy that so frequently surrounds the subject brings "an aura of mystery and glamour to the whole question" (Moore 1970, 1002).

The UFO phenomenon is a mystery in the sense that the nature and intentions of the aliens are hidden and apparently unknowable. At the same time, UFOs open up new vistas for human understanding and for solving such classical puzzles as the Bermuda Triangle, the case of the knowledge of the star Sirius by the Dogon of Mali in West Africa, and the amazing sculptures of the Incas of Peru (Temple 1977; Story 1980, 113ff.; Oberg 1982, 121ff.). Religion has always provided answers to questions which science has not yet solved or which lie beyond the province of scientific inquiry. Even though many scholars have pointed out that these alleged riddles can be easily solved without recourse to the intervention of aliens who visited the Earth in flying saucers (Story 1980, 219ff.), they still are presented as unfathomable phenomena which no human ingenuity can account for.

Scholars who have given different interpretations of UFOs seem to agree on the mystery element. Ronald Story (1980, 140), for example, who has studied the religious aspects of the UFO movement, remarks:

> What gives rise to the "mystery," is that even after such reasonable explanations are taken into account, there still remains a residue of seemingly inexplicable phenomena; things and events which do not seem to fit reasonably into the acceptable framework of existing human knowledge.

Writing from a psychological viewpoint, Thomas Bullard (cf. Bartholomew 1989, iii-iv) reflects on why the quest of mystery often dominates UFO accounts:

> News from heaven always carries a fascination of its own, unrivaled among any discoveries we can make on our own. The urge to imagine someone or something greater than oneself never dies. In an intensely hard-headed, mechanistic age the story may assume a muted form and offer only a mild sort of amazement, but in more accepting times the myth enlarges, the other world distances itself from the everyday and grows in numinous power.

In a more skeptical frame of mind, Philip Klass (1968, 1974) lists several unusual behaviors of UFOs and argues that they appear mysterious only when they are assumed to be spaceships made by intelligent beings on some other planet. In other words, it is the reports, not the phenomena themselves, that are mysterious. Klass argues that UFO sightings can be explained as natural events, such as freak atmospheric electrical phenomena, weather balloons, and meteorites.   He points out (1968, 275) that the tendency to interpret unusual phenomena by invoking mysterious forces is common in human history:

> In centuries past, primitive man was forced to devise supernatural explanations for such startling events as a solar eclipse and lightning. Today these are recognized as natural phenomena, although our understanding of lightning is still far from complete, for the ways of nature are complex and some of her secrets are not easily penetrated. It is ironic, and yet in some ways understandable, that today there are those who invoke the Space-Age version of the supernatural—extraterrestrial visitors—to explain a mysterious natural phenomenon.

The questions raised by the very presence of UFOs add to the mystery that surrounds them. There is no agreement as to the intentions, hostile or friendly, of these vastly superior aliens. The claims by different people that they are receiving unique messages from alien beings or masters add to the enigmatic quality which so many of the transmissions have. Several intriguing and puzzling questions are left unanswered. For instance, why is it that these technologically advanced beings, some of whom must have spent several decades traveling at the speed of light to reach planet Earth, have appeared to only few, relatively unknown people, mostly in remote areas and at night? The answer often given to this question, that most people are not yet prepared to meet these beings face to face, does nothing but increase the sense of mystery.

Or again, one can ask why is it that these highly advanced aliens have not taken the logical step of making their presence openly known to, and establishing contact with, official agencies like the United Nations? A common reply, that such contact with the world powers have been made and either ignored or purposely keep secret, is both inscrutable and melodramatic. Much discussion has taken place over the possibility that there has been a conspiracy to cover up the whole flying saucer issue. The question whether, for example, the U.S. government has been attempting to conceal its own clandestine activities, its secret research in UFO phenomena, its classified knowledge of alien spacecraft and creatures, or its own ignorance is one of those classic conundrums that cannot be unraveled. What is clear is that the enduring accusations, namely that the government has been withholding from the public vital information on UFOs and/or has been involved in some covert operation related to flying saucers, have become part and parcel of the UFO subculture and have magnified the aura of mystery that clouds the UFO phenomenon (Evans 1987a; Fawcett and Greenwood 1984).

This sense of mystery is often highlighted by the connection made between UFOs and psychic and occult phenomena. Aliens have the ability to use clairvoyance and telepathy to deliver their instructions and messages. Or they may use trance conditions, similar to those of spiritualist mediums and New Age channelers. No wonder UFO encounters become eerie occurrences that are quite beyond human reach, making them amenable to all kinds of bizarre, foreboding, and far-fetched interpretations.

Transcendence

Unidentified flying objects are essentially sky phenomena that readily become symbols of transcendence. They are believed to come from planetary systems that are outside the perceivable limits of human endeavor. They soar above us, effortlessly, almost within our grasp. Yet, they are intangible and evasive. They inspire our imagination, arouse within us a sense of wonder, nourish our fear of the unknown, and instill in our hearts a spark of hope. Although UFO occupants are often described as if they had physical bodies, they seem to be spiritual or psychic, rather than material, beings. Their nature appears to be radically different from that of human beings, surpassing it not only in degree, but also in kind. It resembles that of the angels or saints in heaven, because it frees them from the limitations of matter and from the restrictions of the time-space dimension in which humans are trapped. When UFO beings are equated with the Ascended Masters, they become, even more clearly, religious entities that are beyond our universe and thus not subject to our scrutiny. This explains why some scholars (e.g., Evans 1984) have compared their appearances to selected contactees to the apparitions of the Virgin Mary.

Sky gods have figured prominently in the religious history of the human race. From ancient religions to more recent ones, the link between the supreme being or the gods and the sky has been a constant dominant feature. Examples of this connection are numerous

(Eliot 1976). The ancient Egyptians believed that their pharaohs had to be buried with special rites in order that they could join the sun god in the heavens. The ancient Romans held that Romulus, the founder of their city, was taken up into the sky by Jupiter. The Judeo-Christian tradition places God in the sky or in heaven, from where he rules. There are plenty of biblical examples, such as the descent of God on Mount Sinai and the Ascension of Jesus into heaven, that give incontestable evidence of the central role that the sky has played as a suitable symbol to express the transcendental nature of the almighty.

This theme of transcendence, which is also found in science fiction literature (Hopkins 1960), is at the core of UFO movements and cults. The transcendent nature of UFOs is, at times, defended with the same zeal that the existence of God is in the Judeo-Christian tradition.

Belief in Supernatural Entities

Related to the theme of transcendence is the belief that both the aliens from outer space and their mediums on Earth are superhuman entities that transcend human nature. The Ascended Masters are reminiscent of the angels and/or Christian saints to whom people pray for all kinds of needs.

In a leaflet describing its "permanent celestial message," the Cosmic Circle of Fellowship, a UFO group founded by William Ferguson, expresses its beliefs in UFOs as follows:

> The Cosmic Circle of Fellowship is a religious organization of the sovereign State of Illinois, under the complete guidance of Celestial and Immortal Beings from Outer Space. The messenger of these space beings is William Ferguson of the Planet Earth, and other Priests and Priestesses, who have been and will be, elevated to the Priesthood of the Cosmic Circle of Fellowship.
>
> We teach the New Age Truth, given to us by the Spirit of Truth from the Holy Triune.
>
> We worship only the Alpha and the Omega, who are the First Cause, (Everliving). We adore many Celestials and Immortals, who are working with us and guiding us. We invite all people of the Planet Earth to join us in fellowship and the worship of Alpha and Omega.

In a similar way the individuals who transmit the messages of the intelligent beings from other planets are themselves ascribed superhuman qualities which raise them far above human beings, sometimes almost deifying them. Supporters of George Adamski, for instance, claimed that he "had a series of experiences that indicated he was something more than an ordinary earth person" (Stupple 1980, 267).

The members of the Aetherius Society lavish Dr. George King with all kinds of achievements and qualities. Besides having been awarded many university degrees and civil recognitions, he is also a metropolitan archbishop, a prince, and a Knight of Malta. He is the primary extraterrestrial channel. He has been assigned the task by the Cosmic Masters to perform several missions for the benefit of planet Earth and the welfare of its inhabitants. He possesses great spiritual and occult skills, having mastered Yoga at an early age. As a spiritual teacher he reveals cosmic truths to the world. All this raises him far beyond the average human being and leads those who believe in him and his mission to speak of him with great reverence and awe.

Ruth Norman, the leader of Unarius Academy of Science, another UFO movement, is venerated by her followers. Known as Uriel, she plays the role of a divine being and participates in the work of spiritual hierarchy that presides over a confederation of planets. Kirkpatrick and Tumminia (1992, 160-61) call her the "Magical Madonna" and a "Mother Goddess." They describe her role as mother goddess or space goddess as follows (Kirkpatrick and Tumminia n.d., 8-9):

> Uriel stands for Universal Radiant Infinite Eternal Light. When Ruth Norman arrives in the persona of Uriel all members of Unarius assemble and focus their attention on her. Uriel claims over two hundred previous reincarnations. . . . Two reincarnations are recognized mother goddess figures, Kuan Yin, the Chinese Goddess of Peace, and Isis, the Great Mother Goddess of Egypt. . . . She is portrayed in their iconography as a kind of mother goddess. The glorification of Uriel is ever present in Unarius.
>
> In 1973, Uriel announced she had progressed in her evolution to become a healing archangel. . . . In 1974, Uriel received knowledge from the inner worlds that she is "The Spirit of beauty, Goddess of Love." In this form she wields the sword of truth, holds the Book of Life, and projects healing beams of light from her eyes. . . . Mrs. Norman declared that her powers and duties had increased in 1981. At a ceremony at the Unarius Center, Uriel appeared as the Cosmic Generator, or the direct supplier (in conjunction with the spiritual hierarchy) of the "Light-Force Energies into the earth worlds."

The portrayal of both aliens and their mediums on Earth as divine or semi-divine beings places UFO movements within the framework of traditional religions. The belief systems and ritual practices found in these movements parallel those found in many religions, past and present.

Perfection

The attributes of UFO occupants are generally those ascribed to supernatural beings, spiritual entities, or gods, who differ from mere humans in their intellectual, spiritual, and moral state. Accounts and descriptions of UFO occupants by contactees and abductees emphasize the superior state of these outer-space beings. Perfection, immense power (often used for healing purposes), and omniscience are among the common qualities of UFO occupants.

Carl Jung (1958) remarked that the circle, the most common shape given to flying objects,[11] is an archetypal symbol of perfection and can be traced to many religions. The circle (which, in paintings, appears as a halo over the heads of Christian saints) has been used from ancient times to mark the boundary of the area considered sacred or full of magical power and, thus, set apart from daily activities and protected from evil influences. Both the occupants of flying saucers and their machines are entities that cannot been seen by the human eye of the average human being.

The power ascribed to the extraterrestrial visitors by far outstrips that of humankind. Given the assumption that UFOs have come from distant planets or stars, one can only conclude that their occupants' civilizations have developed technologies that makes ours look like those of the Stone Age. Some claim that great human achievements of past civilizations, like the pyramids of ancient Egypt, could only have been constructed by people from an alien culture.

Not only do the aliens have unsurpassed mastery over the forces of physical nature by which they could easily overpower our greatest technological achievements; they are also imbued with paranormal power, like telepathy, which gives them a new avenue through which they can influence human thought and behavior. These psychic powers give the aliens an almost unlimited knowledge of, and control over, human beings.

Jacques Vallée (1987, 318), for instance, maintains that flying saucers represent a superior kind of psychophysical technology:

UFO Phenomenon is the product of a technology that integrates physical and psychic phenomena and primarily affects cultural variables in our society through manipulation of physiological and psychological parameters in the witnesses.

Though the power which flows from such a technology does not make UFO occupants omnipotent, it would certainly provide them with a strength that is beyond human comprehension and with the ability to influence and control all human activities.

Salvation

The mission of UFOs is frequently described as one of redemption. Among the more common themes contained in messages from aliens are the cure of all diseases, the deliverance from the destructive forces of atomic power, and the transportation to a new planet where there will be complete security, wealth, and cooperation. UFO literature of the 1950s and 1960s is full of warnings about the potential outcome of atomic fallout and wars (Mitchell and Mitchell 1959; Stranges 1960), thus stressing that humanity needs redemption.

In UFO religions, just as in traditional Judeo-Christian theology, salvation or redemption is conceived as coming from outside. In other words, while the cooperation of human beings is necessary if the planet is to be saved, the intervention of superior intelligences from other planets is considered essential. The Aetherius Society advocates such a view of salvation. In *The Twelve Blessings of Jesus* (King 1958), the fourth blessing is directed towards "the Planetary Ones." These cosmic masters, we learn, have answered the call of even higher beings to save the planet Earth. They are said to have sacrificed their spiritual homes, peace, friendship, and their own salvation to fulfill their mission. They suffer in silence in order that human beings might be saved. They vicariously take over the bad karma of the human race.

More simply, salvation can be seen as an intervention from space beings that will lead the human race to its next stage of development or evolution. William Ferguson (n.d., 7), describing his experience on a spacecraft and conversation with the oligarchs of the planet Venus, states:

> They [the oligarchs] told me to tell the people of the planet Earth, that all unidentified flying objects are here to help the planet Earth. They are here to help the planet at the time when it is approaching its next evolutionary step. The next evolutionary step is a Four Dimensional consciousness, and after that, a complete change so that the Three Dimensional body will be able to change its frequency and go into Four Dimensions, at will.

Religious Worldview

Flying saucers also provide contemporary society with alternative cosmologies or worldviews to those offered by traditional religions and modern science. Because of the current interest in anomalous phenomena, about which religion and science have little to say, people are turning to other sources for information. Many of the answers that religion and science give to some of the perennial questions of life, such as those regarding the origins of the human race, remain somewhat ambiguous, if not contradictory. Von Däniken's theory of human origins is an excellent example of a myth that unites contemporary space technology with UFO phenomenon. It combines the religious quest for absolute answers with the objectivity of scientific certainty. In a society where religion and science are in conflict, a conflict that creates many tensions and contradictions, von Däniken presents a worldview that brings together religion and science in an apparently harmonious union (Ashworth 1980). This approach is similar to the Christian fundamentalist insistence that science cannot contradict belief and that beliefs can, in fact, be substantiated by direct empirical evidence that no honest inquirer can reject.

The originality of the worldview that comes with belief in UFOs is evident when one compares it to the views of the universe that are available in religious creeds and scientific literature. Religion, particularly in the Judeo-Christian tradition, has offered little scope for speculation on the nature of the universe as seen through the eyes of modern astronomical discoveries and scientific achievements. In other words, religious views of the universe are utterly earth-bound. Religious cosmologies give human beings a central and significant role in creation. They fail, however, to include any theoretical formulations about the possible existence and theological implications of other intelligent life on other planets. From a literal interpretation of the Bible one could reach the conclusion that the Earth is located at the very center of the universe and that it is the only place inhabited by intelligent beings, who represent the peak of creation. It is, therefore, not surprising that Christian fundamentalists find it hard to believe that superior forms of life are not only present in other regions of space but have also been visiting the Earth for centuries.

One major difficulty with the traditional religious worldview is that it cannot be easily harmonized with modern astronomical knowledge. Original theories about the origin and evolution of human life and its relationship to extraterrestrial intelligences provide a broader base for theological reflection. They seek to establish a religious worldview or cosmology that places the Earth and its inhabitants in a more realistic perspective. By so doing, they establish different theological assumptions about the creation of the world and of the human race and the involvement of God in the complex process of development or evolution.

Science, on the other hand, has all but reduced the human race to a slightly more advanced, evolved sample of the animal species. It does not bestow any cosmic significance to being human, nor does it assign any special destiny for human beings, whose chances of survival for a long period of time may not be too promising. The human race remains completely earth-bound in its origin and development, which can be easily accounted for without recourse to supernatural explanations or extraterrestrials invasions. Because hard empirical evidence on flying saucers is unavailable, scientific theories about the origin and evolution of the human species do not include alien involvement (Cohen 1987; Allen and Briggs 1989). Speculations or hypotheses about the extraterrestrial origins and/or development of the human race are ruled out as unrealistic and far-fetched.

The UFO worldview unites, to some degree, religious and scientific views of the origin of the human race. Like the common Judeo-Christian religious point of view, it maintains that human beings are not just evolved animals. They are, rather, descended from above, making them superior to the animal world and "a little less than the angels." And like the modern scientific worldview, the origin of humankind is traced, not to the direct, supernatural act of creation by a supreme God, but through physical, natural descent from mighty creatures from other parts of the universe.

Spirituality

Encounters with UFOs, particularly those of the third and fourth kinds, are intense experiences that are easily comparable to those of Christian mystics and visionary saints. Bertrand Meheust (1987) detects a timeless structure behind abduction stories, which have frequently transformed the lives of contactees. Personal experiences like those of Whitley Strieber may sound unbelievable, but it is difficult to miss the process of change that he underwent as he recalled his alleged encounters with strange nonhuman beings.

The encounter experience has been likened to a rite of passage and a rebirth (Evans 1987b, 237ff.; Meheust 1987, 355). Rites of passage, common in many nonliterate societies, are ceremonies that mark a crucial stage in an individual's life, particularly in the important and critical conditions at birth, puberty, marriage, and death.[12] In these societies, rites of passage radically alter one's social identity and imbue the participant with a new role and sense of duty and a different kind of self-consciousness. Whether or not the decline of such rituals in the West creates the need for new ones to emerge is debatable. So also is the assumption that the experience of encounter and/or abduction is a rite of passage which resolves an individual's identity crisis.

What is clear is that the contactee goes through a change in self-awareness that has religious connotations. For, through the experience of encounter with these superior beings, one feels that one has come in contact with something divine or transcendent and that, consequently, one has undergone a developmental change in one's spiritual condition. In other words, the contactee experiences a religious growth and acquires a status or prestige that surpasses that of other humans, who have not been fortunate enough to have been approached by aliens in their flying saucers. The contactee becomes a person set apart, which may explain, to some degree, why he or she enjoys popularity and/or succeeds, on occasion, in attracting a following. Moreover, contactees can acquire a sense of duty, destiny, and mission, which further sets them apart and, in typical prophetic expression, usually evokes ridicule and/or persecution.

The change that occurs in contactees, however, is not only in self-consciousness, but also in lifestyle. They experience a rebirth, a transformation, or a new beginning, at times leading to a career change and to the adoption of a different worldview that is more concerned with modern issues, like war, ecology, and nuclear energy. Another factor in this rebirth can be seen in the similarities between accounts of abductees' encounters and the birth process and near-death experiences (Lawson 1980, 34-35).

Evans (1987b, 239-40) thinks that the encounter and/or abduction experience is an archetypal initiation process because it contains the following elements: (1) it is usually a solitary experience; (2) it occurs, as a rule, in isolated places, away from crowds; (3) wise superior beings take the initiative and guide the contactee; (4) light seems to be the dominant symbol in encounters of the third and fourth kinds; (5) there is a sexual element (the preoccupation with genitals) in the medical examinations that aliens reportedly perform on those humans they abduct; and (6) the absence of bird song and other animal noises in many encounter stories. What is interesting in Evans's analysis is the similarity between the experiences of abductees and those of mystics.

Becoming a member of a UFO movement often involves an initiation which connotes the beginning of a spiritual development through a series of stages or grades. The restriction of some written materials, course instructions, and meetings to some initiates endorses the view that they are actually making progress to higher spiritual levels of knowledge and consciousness. Grades and levels of initiation within the same organization support the same position.

THE IMPORTANCE AND SIGNIFICANCE OF UFO RELIGIONS

This chapter has drawn attention to the current interest in flying saucers, to the spiritual overtones with which they are often clothed, and to the variety of religious interpretations of their origin, meaning, and purpose. The scholar who investigates the UFO phenomenon of the late twentieth century will wonder what kind of significance it has for contemporary religions and culture. Four major hypotheses of UFO religions can be constructed, and are outlined below.

UFO Religions as Fads

Although many people seem to believe in UFOs, not many have been willing to dedicate themselves to the ideology and practices of UFO cults. Membership in such groups has always been relatively small and there is no reason to suggest that any group is likely to experience significant growth in the near future. Whether, and to what extent, the rise of these new religious bodies has any great significance is a moot question. The religious views expressed by many believers in UFOs often appear so unrealistic and hilarious that one has every reason to wonder whether they are nothing but minor aberrant idiosyncrasies that will have little or no impact on the major religious traditions and mainstream culture. Are UFO cults, then, simply a modern, trivial, quasi-religious fad, that has little significance either for society as a whole or for current religious developments taking place in the West?

Kevin McClure (1987, 351) has expressed the view that modern UFO cults are rather inconsequential. He thinks that, although the members of these movements are sincere in their commitments, some of their views and practices are just too ridiculous to be given much attention:

> Personally, I regard the collected evidence of the UFO phenomenon as tenuous and frail, but also as important and interesting. The cults and belief groups that have developed from it (i.e., the UFO phenomenon) are themselves fascinating, but if I were to summarize their significance in the subject as a whole, and their bearing on its interpretation and understanding, I would have to conclude that they warrant our interest, and maybe our sympathy. But not a great deal of our time.

McClure's position might be justifiable, if one limits one's view to UFO cults or movements. But the religious aspects of the UFO phenomenon are much broader than cultic involvement. Truly enough, only a small minority of a given population assigns religious meaning to flying saucers. The importance of such a phenomenon, however, may not lie in the number of people who believe that UFOs exist and are linked with the spiritual and/or psychic state and development of the human race, nor in the actual tenets and ritual practices that emerge from such beliefs. Rather, the religious meanings that have been so freely attached to UFO encounters are of value because they might indirectly (1) reflect certain cultural trends and religious developments, and (2) point to some of the problems which traditional religions are facing at the end of the twentieth century.

UFO Movements as Pseudo-Religion

A second position would argue that, in spite of the indications to the contrary, the UFO phenomenon does not constitute a genuine religion. If one maintains that belief in the supernatural (in the Christian theological sense) is essential to any religious system, then it is easy to minimize the religious elements found in the UFO phenomenon.[13] Believers in UFOs appear to stress the paranormal or preternatural powers of the space beings. UFOs tend to be psychic or paranormal, rather than supernatural, manifestations. Their occupants are only superior quasi-human beings, even though they often assume the roles and activities ascribed to God in the Judeo-Christian tradition or to the gods and goddesses in many religions.

As was pointed out above, some biblical interpretations influenced by the UFO phenomenon tend to replace divine intervention with reference to superior extraterrestrial beings. In this case, while maintaining the option of postulating a creator, the UFO hypothesis attempts to explain biblical history without assuming the existence of a personal God who directs and intervenes in human life. UFO movements can be considered pseudo-religions in the sense that they present a somewhat secularized version of biblical religion, replacing God or the gods with superbeings from outer space (cf. Blumrich 1974).

Ted Peters maintains that the UFO phenomenon is a "scientized myth." UFO believers have accepted the modern scientific view of the universe. However, "they do want a celestial savior, but that savior will not be mysterious; instead, he will be fully comprehendible and scientifically explainable according to the laws of nature" (Peters 1977a, 267). This would tend to eliminate the sacred dimension from all encounters with flying saucers and from speculations about the universe and human destiny.

UFOs as Symptoms of Religious, Cultural, and Psychological Issues in Western Culture

A third interpretation of the UFO phenomenon is common particularly within the social sciences (cf. Saliba 1992). Underlying sociopsychological explanations of UFOs is the assumption that encounters with UFOs are a product of several distinct human factors, namely the cultural condition prevalent in society and the psychological state of human beings. Like all other religious movements, the UFO phenomenon is related to cultural change and social and intellectual dislocation. One therefore has to examine it not as a religious event by itself, but in relation to other developments in the current world. UFOs can thus be seen, for example, as an attempt to come to terms with the conflict between science and religion or as one aspect of the resurgence of religious fundamentalism in different parts of the world. From a psychological point of view UFO cults and movements cater to the individual need for security in a world of religious changes and social upheaval, or they may be unusual or pathological expressions of human emotional and intellectual crises.

UFOs as a Harbinger of a New Religion

A final opinion would insist on the religious dimensions and functions of UFO phenomena. Beliefs about, and practices surrounding, flying saucers constitute an original religious worldview that takes into account modern knowledge of the universe and technological advances that include space travel.

Barry Downing (1980b) lists six major theories that compare traditional religious beliefs to those about UFOs. Belief in UFOs (1) is similar to traditional religious beliefs in that both are systems of make-believe; (2) substitutes traditional religion with a "true science," since UFOs, unlike the tenets of most religions, can be subjected to empirical proof; (3) replaces the transcendental God of the Bible with an astronaut who has superhuman power and knowledge; (4) suggests that both UFOs and religion have a common ground in the unconscious and consequently that both faiths stem from within the human person; (5) unites UFOs with demons; and (6) represents some kind of divine power. He omits, however, one area of comparison that might account for the uniqueness of UFO religions, namely that they offer an innovative worldview that demands one's involvement and commitment.

One can postulate that UFO phenomena are a new type of religion that attempts to formulate a worldview that is more consistent with the culture and technology of the twenty-first century. UFOs are some kind of unspecified power or force that permeates the whole universe and directs, at a deep unconscious level, human destiny (cf. Vallée 1975). They are "the Force" of *Star Wars*. This new religion would represent a radical change from the Judeo-Christian view of a personal God who intervenes in history. It may take two separate forms. On the one hand, it could adopt a pantheistic view of nature (consistent with the New Age movement), which sees God not as a person, distinct and separate from the material world, but rather as a spiritual reality in which all life participates. On the other, it could develop a rather secular worldview, which maintains that the existence and visitations of superior aliens from space are devoid of any supernatural content and can be subjected to the same objective and empirically verifiable principles of modern science.

CONCLUSION

The UFO phenomenon is a complex one and is amenable to various interpretations. While none of the aforementioned hypotheses are likely to receive universal acceptance, there is little doubt that the claims made by those who have made contact with aliens from other worlds raise some puzzling questions for religionists and scientists alike.

The widespread interest and belief in the presence of flying saucers is, in the opinion of this writer, an extreme example of the human quest to make religion relevant to life, to instill a cosmic dimension into an earth-bound religious worldview, and to inject into spiritual experiences the element of scientific verifiability. UFO cults will probably remain a minor section of the tapestry of religious movements and spiritual renewals that have swept through the West since World War II. Whether or not they will all pass away into oblivion in the near future will not affect their status as excellent examples of the ingenuity and creativity of the human spirit. As such, they are a component of the social and religious history of the human race. They have become, in the words of one sociologist (Miller 1985, 120), "part of our basic culture and social structure." They deserve some attention, not necessarily because of their lasting impact on culture and religion, but because of the implicit lessons that their emergence has. The significance of UFO cults and movements might lie in the contribution they make to our understanding of what religion is, what human crises and conflicts it ventures to resolve, and what future trends it might follow or avoid.

NOTES

1. This is an adaptation and expansion of Michael Schultz's (1980) three-fold distinction between *(a)* investigations groups, *(b)* platform societies, and *(c)* religious cults.

2. In a posthumously published article, David Stupple (1984; 135ff.) distinguished between psychic and non-psychic contactees. The latter are those who report bizarre adventure stories involving apparent extraterrestrial craft and/or alien beings and who believe in UFOs but have a hobbyist,orientation and may become active in flying saucer clubs. In this chapter it is suggested that they belong more appropriately with those whose beliefs and interests in UFO are not religious in nature. Psychic contactees, however, not only believe that UFOs are real but ascribe religious significance to their presence and activities.

3. This church publishes a lot of materials through the Summit University Press. See, for instance, Prophet (n.d.) where the messages of the ascended master El Morya as channeled through Elizabeth Claire Prophet are transcribed. Prophet (1976) has also written a general book on the Great White Brotherhood.

4. Besides a number of tapes that record the talks of the leaders, this mission publishes a quarterly magazine called *Light Speed* which includes extraterrestrial transmissions and the listing of the mission's meetings and other events.

5. *Light Speed* (Oct./Nov./Dec. 1989): 1.

6. The materials published by this association include essays that propose the view that the appearance of UFOs are demonic interventions heralding the Second Coming.

7. The main researchers of this group are Robert W. Balch and David Taylor. Consult, for example, Balch and Taylor (1976, 1977) and Balch (1980, 1982, 1985). For ethnographic data on the UFO People see Hewes and Steiger (1976).

8. Though less prominent than it was in the 1970s, the UFO People are not yet a defunct group. Herff Applewhite has since died, but a small band of followers are apparently still waiting for the advent of the flying saucers.

9. See the Aetherius Society's publication *Cosmic Voice*, 14 (Feb./March 1958): 9ff., where the event is described in some detail. Cf. also *Cosmic Voice* 25: 22.

10. See, for example, Seagraves (1976, 1977); McConnell (1967); Lindsay (1972); Grant (1959); and Allnut (1978).

11. Hitching (1978: 188) gives thirty-one varieties of UFO shapes, of which seventeen are clearly circular.

12 . See Van Gennep (1960) and Turner (1969). Van Gennep's theory has been applied to the new religious movements by Melton and Moore (1982).

13. One should note that the word "supernatural" has had different shades of meaning in the history of Western culture and that it cannot be assumed to be universally applicable.

REFERENCES

Allan, John Robertson. 1976. *The Gospel According to Science Fiction: God Was an Ancient Astronaut, Wasn't He?* Libertyville, Ill.: Quill Publications.

Allen, Keith, and Derek Briggs. 1989. *Evolution and the Fossil Record.* London: Belhaven.

Allnut, Frank. 1978. *Infinite Encounters.* Old Tappan, N.J.: Spire Books.

Andrews, Arlan K. 1980. "Psychic Aspects of UFOs." In *Encyclopedia of UFOs,* edited by Ronald Story, 286-89. New York: New English Library.

Angelo, Joseph A. 1985. *The Extraterrestrial Encyclopedia: Our Search for Life in Outer Space.* New York: Facts on File Publications.

Ashpole, Edward. 1989. *The Search for Extraterrestrial Intelligence.* London: Blandford Press.

Ashworth, C. E. 1980. "Flying Saucers, Spoon-bending, and Atlantis." *Sociological Review* 28:253-76.

Asimov, Isaac. 1979. *Extraterrestrial Civilizations.* New York: Crown Publishers.

Balch, Robert. 1980. "Looking Behind the Scenes in a Religious Cult." *Sociological Analysis* 41:137-43.

————. 1982. "Bo and Peep: A Case Study of the Origins of Messianic Leadership." In *Millennialism and Charisma,* edited by Roy Wallis, 13-72. Belfast: Queen's University Press.

————. 1985. "When the Light Goes Out, Darkness Comes: A Study of Defection from a Totalistic Cult." In *Religious Movements: Genesis, Exodus, and Numbers,* edited by Rodney Stark, 11-55. New York: Paragon House.

Balch, Robert, and David Taylor. 1976. "Salvation in a UFO," *Psychology Today* 10, no. 5:58, 61-62, 66, 104.

————. 1977. "Seekers and Saucers: The Role of the Cultic Milieu in Joining a UFO Cult." *American Behavioral Scientist* 20:839-60.

Bartholomew, Robert E. 1989. *Ufolore: A Social Psychological Study of a Modern Myth in the Making.* Stone Mountain, Ga.: Arcturus Book Service.

Barton, Michael X. 1969. *Discs, Destiny, and You.* Clarksburg, W.Va: Saucerian Press.

Beck, Lewis White. 1985. "Extraterrestrial Intelligent Life." In *Extraterrestrials: Science and Alien Intelligence,* edited by Edward Regis. Cambridge: Cambridge University Press.

Bieri, R. 1964. "Humanoids on Other Planets." *American Scientist* 52:425-58.

Billingham, John, ed. 1981. *Life in the Universe.* Washington: NASA.

Blum, Howard. 1990a. *Out There: The Government's Secret Quest for Extraterrestrials.* New York: Simon and Schuster.

———. 1990b. "SETI: Phone Home." *New York Times,* magazine section, October 21, pp. 33-37, 76-78.

Blumrich, Josef. 1974. *The Spaceships of Ezekiel.* New York: Bantam.

Blundell, Nigel, and Roger Boar. 1990. *The World's Greatest UFO Mysteries.* New York: Berkley.

Bova, Ben, and Byran Preiss, eds. 1990. *First Contact: The Search for Extraterrestrial Intelligence.* New York: Penguin.

Brown, Raymond. 1977. *The Birth of the Messiah: A Commentary on the Infancy Narratives of Matthew and Luke.* Garden City, N.Y.: Doubleday.

Butterworth, Robert. 1969. *The Theology of Creation.* Cork, Ireland: Mercier Press.

Cantril, Hadley. 1966. *The Invasion from Mars: A Study in the Psychology of Panic.* New York: Harper.

Catoe, Lynn E. 1978. *UFO and Related Subjects: An Annotated Bibliography.* Detroit: Gale Research.

Cazeau, Charles J., and Stuart D. Scott. 1979. *Exploring the Unknown: Great Mysteries Reexamined.* New York: Plenum Press.

Clark, Jerome. 1990. *The UFO Encyclopedia, Vol. 1: UFOs in the 1980s.* Detroit: Apogee Books.

Cohen, Bernice. 1987. *The Cultural Science of Man.* London: Codek.

Condon, Edward V., ed. 1969. *Final Report of the Scientific Study of Unidentified Flying Objects.* New York: Dutton.

Däniken, Eric von. 1969. *Chariots of the Gods?: Unsolved Mysteries of the Past.* New York: Berkley Publishing.

———. 1973. *Gold of the Gods.* New York: Putnam.

David, Jay. 1970. *Flying Saucers Have Arrived.* New York: World Publishing Co.

Dione, R. L. 1969. *God Drives a Flying Saucer.* New York: Exposition Press.

———. 1976. *Is God Supernatural?: The 4,000 Year Misunderstanding.* New York: Bantam.

Downing, Barry H. 1968. *The Bible and Flying Saucers.* Philadelphia: J. B. Lippincott.

———. 1980a. "Biblical UFO Sightings." In *Encyclopedia of UFOs,* edited by Ronald Story, 53-54. New York: New English Library.

———. 1980b. "Religion and UFOs." *Encyclopedia of UFOs,* edited by Ronald Story, 305-6. New York: New English Library.

———. 1990. "Did a UFO Part the Red Sea?" *UFO: A Forum of Extraordinary Theories and Phenomena* 5, no. 2:16-21.

Eberhart, George M. 1986. *UFOs and the Extraterrestrial Contact Movement.* Metuchen, N.J.: Scarecrow Press.

Eliot, Alexander. 1976. *Myths.* New York: McGraw-Hill.

Ellwood, Robert. 1980. "Religious Movements and UFOs." In *Encyclopedia of UFOs,* edited by Ronald Story, 306-9. New York: New English Library.

———. 1988. "Making New Religion: The Mighty I AM Movement." *History Today* 38:18-32.

Ellwood, Robert, and Harry Partin. 1988. *Religious and Spiritual Groups in Contemporary America.* Englewood Cliffs, N.J.: PrenticeHall.

Evans, Hilary. 1979. *UFOs: The Greatest Mystery.* Secaucus, N.J.: Chartwell Books.

———. 1984. *Visions, Apparitions, and Alien Visitors.* Wellingborough, UK: Aquarian Press.

———. 1987a. "Conspiracy of Silence." In *UFOs, 1947-1987: The 40-Year Search for an Explanation,* edited by Hilary Evans and John Spencer, 359-63. London: Fortean Press.

———. 1987b. *Gods, Spirits, and Cosmic Masters: A Comparative Study of the Encounter Experience.* Wellingborough, UK: Aquarian Press.

Fawcett, Lawrence, and Barry J. Greenwood. 1984. *The UFO Cover-Up: What the Government Won't Say.* New York: Prentice-Hall.

Ferguson, William. 1955. *Five Hours with the Oligarchs of Venus*. Chicago: The Cosmic Circle of Fellowship, Inc.

Gallup, George, Jr. 1988. *The Gallup Poll: Public Opinion 1987*. Wilmington, Del.: Scholarly Research, Inc.

Good, Timothy. 1988. *Above Top Secret: The Worldwide UFO Coverup*. New York: William Morrow.

Graham, Billy. 1986. *Angels: God's Secret Agents*. Waco, Tex.: Word Books.

Grant, Robert M. 1965. *A Short History of the Interpretation of the Bible*. London: Adam and Charles Black.

Grant, Walter V. 1959. *Men from the Moon in America: Did They Come from a Russian Satellite?* Dallas: Faith Clinic.

Hagan, K., et al. 1985. *The Bible and the Churches: How Different Churches Interpret the Bible*. New York: Paulist Press.

Hall, Richard. 1988. *Uninvited Guests: A Documentary History of UFO Sightings, Alien Encounters, and Coverups*. Santa Fe: Aurora Press.

Hewes, Hayden, and Brad Steiger. 1976. *UFO Missionaries Extraordinary*. New York: Pocket Books.

Hitching, Francis. 1978. *The Mysterious World: An Atlas of the Unexplained*. New York: Holt, Rinehart, and Winston.

Hopkins, Budd. 1987. *Intruders: The Incredible Visitations at Copley Woods*. New York: Random House.

Hopkins, E. 1960. "New Maps of Heaven." *Theoria to Theory* (October):136-37.

Horowitz, Norman. 1986. *To Utopia and Back: The Search for Life in the Solar System*. New York: Freeman and Co.

Hoyle, Fred. 1957. *The Black Cloud*. New York: Harper.

Hoyle, Fred, and Chandra Wickramasinghe. 1978. *Life Cloud: The Origin of Life in the Cosmos*. New York: Harper and Row.

Hymers, R. L. 1976. *Encounters of the Fourth Kind*. Van Nuys, Calif.: Bible Voice.

Hynek, J Allen. 1977. *The Hynek UFO Report*. New York: Dell.

Inglesby, Eric. 1973. *UFOs and the Christian*. London: Regnery Press.

Jennings, Jack A. 1978. "UFOs: The Next Theological Challenge?" *Christian Century* (February 22):184-89.

Junq, C. G. 1958. *Flying Saucers: The Myth of Things Seen in the Skies*. London: Kegan Paul.

King, George. 1958. *The Twelve Blessings of Jesus*. Hollywood, Calif.: Aetherius Society.

Kirkpatrick, R. George, and Diana Tumminia. N.d. "California Space Goddess: The Mystagogue in a Flying Saucer Cult." Unpublished manuscript.

——. 1992. "Space Magic, Techno-animism and the Cult of the Goddess in a Southern California Contactee Group: A Case Study of Millenarianism." *Syzygy: Journal of Alternative Religion and Culture* 1:159-72.

Klass, Philip J. 1968. *UFOs—Identified*. New York: Random House.

——. 1974. *UFO Explained*. New York: Random House.

Larson, Bob. 1989. *Straight Answers on the New Age*. Nashville: Thomas Nelson.

Lawson, Alvin H. 1980. "Archetypes and Abductions." *Frontiers of Science* 2, 6:32-36.

Leslie, Desmond, and George Adamski. 1953. *Flying Saucers Have Landed*. London: Neville Spearman.

Lindsay, Gordon. 1972. *The Riddle of Flying Saucers in the Light of the Bible*. Dallas: Voice of Healing Publishing Co.

McClure, Kevin. 1987. "UFO Cults." In *UFOs, 1947-1987: The 40-Year Search for an Explanation*, edited by Hilary Evans and John Spencer, 346-51. London: Fortean Press.

McConnell, David E. 1967. *Flying Saucers of the Lord*. Miami: Economy Printing Co.

McDonagh, Sean. 1986. *To Care for the Earth: A Call for a New Theology*. London: Chapman.

McDonough, Thomas R. 1992. "Is Anyone Out There?" *Discovery* 13, no. 11 (November):84 85.

Meheust, Bertrand. 1987. "UFO Abductions as Religious Folklore." In *UFOs, 1947-1987: The 40-Year Search for an Explanation*, edited by Hilary Evans and John Spencer, 355-56. London: Fortean Press.

Melton, J. Gordon. 1989. *The Encyclopedia of American Religions*. 3rd ed. Detroit: Gale Research.

Melton, J. Gordon, and Robert L. Moore. 1982. *The Cult Experience: Responding to the New Religious Pluralism*. New York: Pilgrim Press.

Miller, David L. 1985. *Introduction to Collective Behavior*. Belmont, Calif.: Wadsworth.

Mitchell, Helen, and Betty Mitchell. 1959. *We Met the Space People*. Clarksburg, W.Va.: Saucerian Press.

Mitton, Simon, ed. 1977. *The Cambridge Encylopaedia of Astronomy*. New York: Crown Publishers, Inc.

Montgomery, Ruth. 1985. *Aliens Among Us*. New York: G. P. Putnam.

Moore, Patrick. 1970. "Flying Saucers." In *Man, Myth, and Magic*, edited by Richard Cavendish, vol. 8, pp. 1000-1003. New York: Marshall Cavendish Corporation.

Oberg, James E. 1982. *UFOs and Outer Space Mysteries: A Sympathetic Skeptic's Report*. Norfolk, Va. Donning.

Ogden, Richard. 1963. *Second Coming of Christ and Flying Saucers*. Seattle: Ufology Publications.

Omohundro, John T. 1976. "Von Däniken's Chariots: A Primer in the Art of Cooked Science," *Zetetic* 1, no. 1:58-68.

Papagiannis, Michael. 1990. "The Hunt Is On: SETI." *First Contact: The Search for Extraterrestrial Intelligence*, edited by Ben Bova and Bryan Preiss. New York: Penguin.

Peters, Ted. 1977a. "UFOs: The Religious Dimension." *Cross Currents* 27:261-78.

———. 1977b. *UFOs—God's Chariots?: Flying Saucers in Politics, Science, and Religion*. Atlanta: John Knox Press.

Prophet, Elizabeth Claire. N.d. *The Chela and the Path: Meeting the Challenge of the Twentieth Century*. Livingston, Mont.: Summit Lighthouse Press.

———. N.d. *The Sacred Adventure*. Livingston, Mont.: Summit Lighthouse Press.

———. 1976. *Great White Brotherhood in the Culture, History, and Religion of America*. Livingston, Mont.: Summit Lighthouse Press.

Rasmussen, Richard M. 1985. *The UFO Literature: A Comprehensive Annotated Bibliography of Works in English*. Jefferson, N.C.: McFarland and Co.

Richards, William, et al., eds. 1991. *UFO: The Continuing Enigma*. Pleasantville, N.Y.: Reader's Digest Association.

Ring, Kenneth. 1989. "Toward an Imaginal Interpretation of 'UFO Abductions'." *Revision* 11, no. 4:17-24.

Saliba, John A. 1975. "The Virgin Birth Debate in Anthropological Literature: A Critical Assessment." *Theological Studies* 36:428-54.

———. 1992. "UFO Contactee Phenomena from a Sociopsychological Perspective: A Review." *Syzygy: Journal of Alternative Religion and Culture* 1:63-93.

Schultz, Michael. 1980. "Sociological Aspects of UFOs." In *Encyclopedia of UFOs,* edited by Ronald Story, 340-41. New York: New English Library.

Seagraves, Kelly L. 1976. *Sons of God Return.* New York: Pyramid Books.

———. 1977. *The Great Flying Saucer Myth.* 2d ed. San Diego: Beta Books.

Soulen, P. N. 1981. *Handbook of Biblical Criticism.* 2d revised ed. Atlanta: John Knox Press.

Stark, Rodney, and William Sims Bainbridge. 1983. "Concepts for a Theory of Religious Movements." In *Alternatives to American Mainline Churches,* edited by Joseph Fichter, 3-25. New York: Rose of Sharon Press.

Steiger, Brad. 1988. *The Fellowship: Spiritual Contact Between Humans and Outer Space Beings.* New York: Doubleday.

Story, Ronald. 1980. *Guardians of the Universe.* New York: St. Martin's Press.

Stranges, Frank E. 1960. *Danger from the Stars.* Venice, Calif.: International Evangelism Crusade.

Strieber, Whitley. 1987. *Communion: A True Story.* New York: Beech Tree Books.

Stupple, David. 1980. "The Man Who Talked to Venusians." In *Proceedings of the First International UFO Congress,* compiled and edited by Curtis G. Fuller. New York: Warner.

———. 1984. "Mahatmas and Space Brothers: The Ideologies of Alleged Contact with Mahatmas and Space Brothers." *Journal of American Culture* 7:131-39.

Swedenborg, Emanuel. 1915. *Arcana Coelestia.* Vol. 9. New York: The American Swedenborg Printing and Publishing Society.

Temple, Robert. 1977. *The Sirius Mystery.* New York: St. Martin's Press.

Turner, Victor, W. 1969. *The Ritual Process: Structure and Anti-Structure.* Chicago: Aldine.

Tyson, Basil. 1977. *UFOs: Satanic Terror.* Beaverlodge, Alberta: Horizon House Publishers.

Vallée, Jacques. 1975. *The Invisible College: What a Group of Scientists Have Discovered About UFO Influences on the Human Race.* New York: Dutton.

———. 1979. *Messengers of Deception.* Berkeley, Calif.: And/Or Press.

———. 1987. "The Psycho-Physical Nature of the UFO Reality: A Speculative Framework." In *UFOs, 1947-1987: The 40-Year Search for an Explanation,* edited by Hilary Evans and John Spencer, 317-19. London: Fortean Press.

————. 1990. "Five Arguments Against the Extraterrestrial Origin of Unidentified Flying Objects." *Journal of Scientific Exploration* 4, No. 1:105-17.

Van Gennep, Arnold. 1909. *The Rites of Passage*. Reprint. Chicago: University of Chicago Press, 1960.

Wallis, Roy. 1974. "The Aetherius Society: A Case Study of the Formation of a Mystagogue Congregation." *Sociological Review* 22:27-44.

Weber, Max. 1956. *Sociology of Religion*. Boston: Beacon Press.

Weldon, John, with Zola Levitt. 1975. *UFOs: What on Earth Is Happening*. Irvine, Calif.: Harvest House Publishers.

Wells, H. G. 1960. *The War of the Worlds*. New York: Random House.

Wiederkehr, Dieter. 1979. *Belief in the Redemption: Explorations in Doctrine from the New Testament to Today*. Atlanta: John Knox.

Zubeck, T. J. 1961. "Theological Questions on Space Creatures." *American Ecclesiastical Review* 145:393-99.

3

RELIGIOUS DIMENSIONS OF THE UFO ABDUCTEE EXPERIENCE

John Whitmore

In recent times, the subject of UFO abductions has gained immense popularity, both with the public and with a small group of scholars and writers who have turned their attention to the UFO phenomenon. The number of people who claim to have been abducted by occupants of UFOs has been rising almost exponentially since the early 1970s when the subject was first granted acceptance by the media and the ufological community. With the publication in 1987 of Whitley Strieber's *Communion*, interest in abductions and abductees exploded. Strieber's account, written with skill by an accomplished author, presented the bizarre details of UFO abduction in an accessible way, spurring the book to the top of the *New York Times* bestseller list. In the wake of this success, talk shows on radio and television fed the public interest in the abduction phenomenon with a steady diet of reports of individuals who believed that they, too, had been abducted.

Contemporaneous with the rise in popularity of Strieber's book was the work of UFO researchers who were dedicated to examining abductions. Individuals like Bud Hopkins, whose own book *Intruders* (1987) made it to the bestseller list, came to dominate the field of ufology. Hopkins and those who share his methodology believe that UFO abductions are a widespread phenomenon that are not always remembered by the victims. Hypnosis is considered a powerful and reliable tool for retrieving these memories, which Hopkins and others argue reveal a specific pattern of action on the part of UFO occupants. In contradistinction to Strieber, who considers his own experiences to be mainly inexplicable, hypnosis-using researchers tend to have clearly defined theories about the nature and purpose of the abduction phenomenon. These theories have come to dominate the field of ufology. A quick examination of UFO books published in the last eight years reveals that books on abductions have outnumbered books on all other subjects related to UFOs combined, by a substantial margin. Popular magazines devoted to UFOs have become almost exclusively concerned with abductions in recent years.

The popularity of abductions has led to a proliferation of first-person accounts, both remembered consciously and retrieved through hypnosis, which are accessible to the researcher. These primary sources reveal a wealth of bizarre detail which is not wholly amenable to the neat theories of many ufologists. A careful examination of abduction narratives indicates that the patterns alleged to have been discovered by abduction investigators often have religious overtones or similarities with more traditional types of religious experience. In addition, the abduction experience is often given a religious meaning by the percipient, and these interpretations are habitually overlooked or ignored by the UFO investigator. The purpose of this chapter will be to examine the abduction phenomenon from the standpoint of religious studies, concentrating on the primary sources with careful attention to religious interpretations of the events that form the pattern of abduction experience.

Sketching the general characteristics of the phenomenon is the first step in such an analysis. In coming to grips with the claims of abductees and researchers, the practice of hypnosis must first be considered. The use of hypnosis to investigate UFO abductions dates back to one of the earliest instances of the phenomenon, the story of Betty and Barney Hill in 1963 (Fuller 1966). In the overwhelming majority of cases available for research, the memory of the abduction event was obtained or clarified through hypnosis. Typically, the abductee consciously recalls little or nothing about the experience. Certain telltale signs, such as unaccounted for spans of time, uneasy feelings associated with UFOs, or the sense of a presence in the bedroom before falling asleep, serve to clue the vigilant researcher into the possibility that an abduction has occurred (Hopkins 1987). Hypnosis is then generally used to explore the abduction experience.

While the reliance on hypnosis is heavy among abduction researchers, most seem to be aware of the difficulties inherent in the process. Hypnosis apparently allows access to a subconscious level of an individual's psyche, allowing him or her to recall repressed memories of actual events, but also making it possible to derive "memories" of things which have never happened (Klass 1988). Hypnotism greatly increases a subject's suggestibility, infusing him or her with a desire to please the questioner and making the subject very susceptible to leading

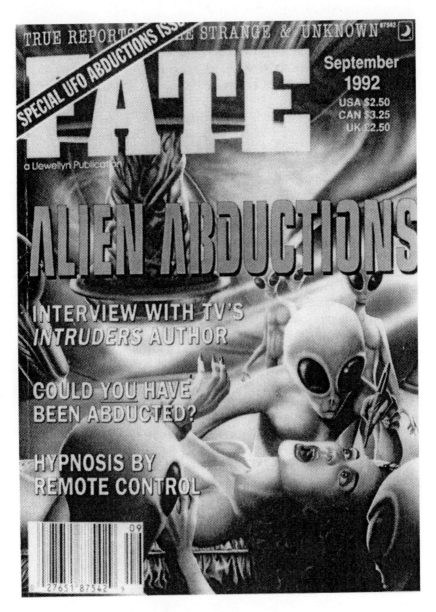

FIGURE 1. Alien Abductions

Abduction reports have superseded all other UFO-related topics as the most popular subgenre in the field. This relatively recent issue of *Fate* magazine (Sept. 1992) contains, among other relevant articles, a report on a survey that claims 3.7 million Americans have been abducted by aliens. (Photo courtesy *Fate* Magazine) questions (Jacobs 1992). Although they recognize these limitations, researchers, with few exceptions (Vallee 1988), contend that when used competently hypnosis is an accurate tool for uncovering factual details of the abduction event. It would be premature, however, to dismiss the possibility that many, if not all, abduction memories are confabulations of the subconscious, guided by the preconceptions of the hypnotist. Noted UFO debunker Philip Klass favors this view, and rather plausibly dismembers some better known cases by applying this theory. Scott Rogo (1990) also argues for a more psychological view of UFO abductions and his work applies psychoanalytical principles to abduction experiences, showing how such experiences could easily be products of the anxieties of participants.

The nature of accounts obtained through hypnosis is important for understanding the religious characteristics of the abduction phenomenon. As Jung (1958) has argued, specifically in relation to UFOs, the subconscious is a storehouse of religious ideas and symbols. Such symbols can become exteriorized through anxiety or stress. Thus, the religious imagery and interpretation brought out by hypnosis could be confabulations of the subject's subconscious and perhaps worked into a UFO narrative in an effort to please the hypnotist. In his research, Jung noted that certain complexes of religious symbols appeared time and time again in widely separated subjects. The prevalence of similar patterns in part gave rise to his theory of a collective unconscious, a fund of ideas and imagery shared by all people. This theory may also help to explain the similar patterns, filled with religious overtones, which abduction researchers claim to find among their subjects.

The applicability of a Jungian form of analysis to UFO abductions is further strengthened by the markedly dreamlike character of the experience. Dreams are the most common arena in which religious symbolism is encountered. One of the signs noted by abduction researchers as indicative of an abduction event is the prevalence of dreams containing UFOs or alien-related imagery. In many of the cases in which the abduction is at least partially recalled prior to the use of hypnosis, it is recalled as a dream rather than as an objective event. For example, Kathy Davis, the main subject of Bud Hopkins's bestseller *Intruders*, consistently believes that her experiences were a series of dreams about UFO abductions. In his investigation, Hopkins hypnotically examines the alleged abduction events by directing her towards these dreams and asking her to recount their details. Hopkins explains that Davis remembers these events as dreams in order to shield her psyche from the unsettling implications of their reality. Unless one is strongly committed to a theory of extraterrestrial genetic engineers, as is Hopkins, it is difficult to dismiss Kathy Davis's contention that the events were in fact dreams.

An examination of the available primary accounts of abductions also reinforces the dreamlike character of the phenomenon. Often the abductee reports being outside her body during certain stages of the event, or views herself in the third person throughout. Abductees report very common dream imagery during the course of their ordeals, such as floating or flying, falling endlessly, or appearing naked in a public place. Time and space appear disjointed in a nonsensical, dreamlike way. Day instantly becomes night, the inside of a room or craft appears far larger than its exterior dimensions would allow, and events which subjectively seem to have taken hours are found to have taken minutes, or vice versa. Massive structures or huge gatherings of people are reported in places familiar to the abductee, places where they could not possibly have been (Fiore 1989). The phantasmagoric texture of a reported abduction is arguably its prime characteristic, and, much like dreams of a more prosaic kind, the abduction contains patterns and images of religious significance.

The patterns alleged to exist in tales of UFO abductions are, upon first glance, quite convincing. The presence of so many intricate details concerning the appearance of the aliens, the procedures undergone, and the messages imparted to the victim seem to argue strongly against the hypothesis that abductees are simply lying. Researchers such as Hopkins and David Jacobs (1992) contend that these patterns only begin to make sense if the abductions themselves are objective events perpetrated by extraterrestrials with scientific motives. However, such researchers tend to ignore the religious connotations of these patterns and details.

Abductions often begin with the perception of light: extremely bright light that causes the percipient to become paralyzed, blinded, or generally disoriented. Sometimes the light renders the abductee unconscious. This intense light is usually identified as the light of a flying saucer or extraterrestrial vehicle. The religious symbolism inherent here is quite obvious. The appearance of a brilliant light is often said to herald an encounter with the divine Other. Paralysis, blindness, and disorientation are associated with this light. The experience of Saul on the road to Damascus, Muhammad on the Night of Power, or Arjuna in the *Mahabharata* are well-known examples of divine encounters which conform to the model. Bright lights and their attendant effects are stock harbingers of the numinous experience.

Alternately, the experience begins in the nighttime, at the abductee's home, right before falling asleep. The abductee sees one or more beings approaching her bedside, often after passing through walls or closed windows. The abductee usually feels paralyzed at this point, and often loses consciousness.[1] The bedside visitors then take the abductee into their craft, once again passing through walls and taking their victim with them. Visions of beings or faces over the bed before one falls asleep is among the most common of all hallucinations, occurring in the distinctive mental state that lies between waking and sleeping. The visions of abductees have analogies to the experiences of religious ecstatics and saints, who report seeing angels, demons, or revered religious figures coming to them in the night (Evans 1985). Often, these figures lead the mystic on a journey to view heaven or hell, or counsel him in religious matters. Strieber (1988) reports being transported by his visitors to strange, unearthly realms, as do Davis (Hopkins 1987) and Andreasson (Fowler 1990.).

After the light, the abductee encounters the aliens. The alien is, as the name suggests, the personification of the Other, utterly nonhuman. Although descriptions vary somewhat, the alien is described as having a large forehead, denoting superhuman intelligence; dressed in shining garments without seams or fasteners; with unblinking, penetrating eyes. The alien often floats or flies, and speaks to the abductee without moving its lips. This complex of attributes is standard for many types of supernatural beings, from angels as described in Christian medieval texts (Vallee 1988) to the devas encountered by Nala in the *Mahabharata*. The alien's appearance marks it as not of this world, and the technology which surrounds it, spacecraft and high tech machinery, shows it to be superior to humanity.

In their encounters with this superhuman Other, abductees report being floated upwards into a waiting craft. Oftentimes, they pass through walls or other obstacles and feel disembodied, as if their soul only were being taken to the UFO (Hopkins 1987; Fowler 1989). Aboard the ship, abductees report frightening details. They are poked, prodded, and molested, most often in a sexual manner. They are subjected to painful medical procedures by groups of aliens, and are even dismembered, body parts severed and organs removed, only to be reassembled (Hopkins 1987; Fiore 1991). After the physical ordeal, they are subjected to some sort of spiritual examination. An alien, generally taller or more authoritative than his fellows, probes their souls. Abductees often report feeling that their memories are being examined or their souls scrutinized, perhaps for some spiritual flaw. After this, abductees are given messages in their minds which they take back with them when they return to normal life. Often these messages concern the purpose of the alien's visit—to interbreed with humanity in order to produce a new hybrid race. Abductees are told that they themselves, or humanity as a whole, are somehow creations of the aliens. The messages can be eschatological in character, forecasting a coming catastrophe or the dawning of a new age.

This scenario has many exact parallels to traditional accounts of shamanistic initiations. Shamanism, an archaic religious complex centered around ecstatic visionary experiences, is widespread among primordial peoples across the globe. The psychological factors inherent in shamanism have been discussed (Silverman 1967) and the broad stages which characterize shamanistic initiation have been outlined (Halifax 1982), in ways that reveal striking similarities with the patterns of UFO abductions. Shamanistic initiations begin with the individual being pulled into the world of the Other, experiencing an isolation from society. They involve brutal physical and mental ordeals, often centering around dismemberment and torture. After being judged worthy by his tormentors, the shaman's nature and mystical ancestry are revealed to him, much as the abductee is given knowledge of her descent. The shaman is often given eschatological knowledge, and returns to society as a healer and religious authority chosen by the spiritual realm. Inexplicable healings and feelings of having been chose are also reported by UFO abductees. Both types of experience are extremely frightening, personality-altering encounters with the Other, perceived at least at first as the Jungian Shadow, mysterious and threatening to the conscious self. Both leave definite, permanent imprints on the psyche of the percipient.

The most important part of the procedures undergone by the abductee, at least in terms of the amount of time spent on it by abduction researchers, is the genital examination. Abductees, both male and female, report having their reproductive systems scrutinized by the aliens, either by hand or with sophisticated-looking instruments. Quantities of sperm and ova are obtained in a process often involving some type of sexual stimulation. In one very early abduction case, a Brazilian farmer actually had intercourse with an attractive female alien (Vallee 1989). Such direct means of obtaining genetic material are sometimes reported, but most often the abductee is aroused in some inexplicable mental way, and often brought by this shadowy means to orgasm (Hopkins 1987; Jacobs 1992). Abductees' minds are filled with erotic images, exciting them against their will. Female abductees are often vaginally penetrated at some point during their experience, and male abductees also tend to report anal penetration by some uncomfortable instrument (Strieber 1988).

The presence of this overt sexual imagery may at first glance offer no insight into the religious significance of the abduction phenomenon.

However, as Jung has noted (1958), sexual imagery is often found to be associated with the encounter with the Other. Sexuality is a powerful component of the individual psyche, and one of the primary arenas for the day-to-day confrontation with otherness is the individual's dialogue with the opposite sex. The sexual symbolism often associated with religious experience is in this view an underscoring of the otherness which typifies the encounter with the numinous.[2]

Some abductees report the healing of some ailment as a result of their abduction. The medical processes undergone are in these cases directed at correcting some chronic condition. Abductees claim that other humans aboard the UFO with them also undergo healings, and the aliens explain that these healings have a spiritual component as well as a physical effect. In one case, an abductee viewed a group of people who the aliens said was to be sent down to disadvantaged areas of Earth in order to engage in healing missions (Fiore 1989). The healing powers of God or superhuman beings have long been a subject of religious belief, and to find aliens involved in miraculous, if technological, healings is perhaps not surprising. The connection with shamanistic initiation, in which the shaman returns from his trip as a healer, has already been noted.

At some point in their experience, many abductees report meeting a leader of the aliens. This leader, who is usually physically distinguishable from his fellow aliens, spurs a strong reaction in the minds of the abductees. The alien often reassures the abductee, mysteriously removing any pain felt during the exam (Fiore 1989). Some abductees seem to feel that the alien leader is extremely "good," and bond to him in a warm, emotional way. The abductee implicitly trusts the leader, and feels as if she has known him all her life. Often, the abductee simply feels love for the alien (Jacobs 1992). The feelings may even be sexual, once again emphasizing the otherness of the encounter. Such feelings of goodness, trust, and deep love, linked in abduction cases to the alien leader, are in more traditional types of religious experience often predicated of the divine. The leader of the aliens is the ruler of the numinous realm of the Other into which the abductee is drawn, and is as such a personification of Otherness, in a manner analogous to God.

A more detailed examination of the messages received by abductees from UFO occupants reveals a wealth of religious details. The content of these communications is often extremely difficult for the abductee to recall, even under hypnosis, and requires great effort on the part of both the hypnotist and the abductee to uncover. Often, the abductee only remembers that she was given some sort of message, and is told by the aliens that she will be unable to remember the content until a later date, "when the world is ready to accept it" (Fiore 1992). These messages can be divided into four distinct classes, each with a specifically religious connotation.

The first type of message is the moral injunction. The aliens tell the abductee that humankind has been behaving very badly, and that if they don't mend their ways, the planet will suffer some sort of chastisement. Sometimes the moral message is quite practical; if the nations of the earth do not stop their constant bickering and experimentation with nuclear weapons, they will assuredly destroy themselves (Fiore 1989). Others are more metaphysical, proclaiming that humans must adopt a more loving attitude towards their fellows and their planet if they are to survive. Sometimes the aliens themselves claim that they will take an active role in the moral sphere, and are ready to destroy humanity if we do not spiritually mature or if we pose a threat to other worlds. These types of messages bear strong resemblances to the prophetic utterances of the UFO contactees of the '50s and '60s.[3] The theme that humankind's moral activity is the interest of some superhuman being is of course a stock theme of Christianity and most other religions, although in this case the judgment is meted out to man not by Jesus Christ but by a powerful alien race.

Other messages are more strictly apocalyptic in character, forecasting a horrible catastrophe on a worldwide scale that will bring about the end of history. Some form of drastic ecological collapse is currently the most popular scenario, ozone depletion or the corruption of the world's oceans being particularly favored (Strieber 1989). The human race however will survive, either by being transplanted to some safe planet to live in paradisiacal comfort, or through becoming one with the aliens through their process of hybridization. The union of man and alien, sharing in the technological power and moral strength of the latter, raised by this union to a superlative degree and redeemed from the perils of earthly existence, is the aliens' final goal according to these abduction narratives (Fowler 1990).

The theme of being chosen also forms an important part of the messages received by abductees. They are told that they are special or important to the aliens and that their experiences are part of some larger plan (Jacobs 1992). They are sometimes charged with conveying the aliens' message to the people of earth, or informed that the aliens have chosen to reveal themselves to humanity through them (Fiore 1989). They are often told that they will know when the time is right to reveal their election and the aliens' gospel.

Other messages claim to reveal the identity and purpose of the aliens. The aliens have come from a distant planet and are busy on earth performing some type of genetic experimentation (Hopkins 1987; Jacobs 1992). Abductees are basically breeding stock for these aliens, supplying them with the eggs and sperm needed for their hybridization mission. The aliens claim to be responsible for the genetic development of man from his primal ancestor (Fowler 1990). That is, they are the creators of humanity; they made us and have guided our evolutionary development and have even intervened in history. The aliens are returning in such great numbers now in preparation for the aforementioned catastrophe. In this scenario, the aliens perform many of the traditional functions of God. They create humanity, guide it through history, and eventually offer a form of salvation, all through a nearly omnipotent technology that replaces the miraculous will of God for modern humankind.

The content of these messages underscores a phenomenon that is encountered time and time again in an analysis of the UFO phenomenon—the projection of traditional religious themes onto a technological/science fiction framework. The parallels of these messages to doctrines of the Christian religion are particularly striking. In the moralizing messages, we get the sense that time is running out, that humans must reform or face judgment by the aliens who are superior not merely technologically but also, apparently, ethically. This is the message of the Old Testament prophet, warning of the calamities God will visit upon His people unless they mend their ways. Apocalyptic messages invoke images of Armageddon and mass catastrophe from which a faithful remnant will be preserved. Abductees are informed that they are chosen to play a special part in a suprahuman plan, and they must evangelize among the nonelect, spreading an alien gospel. The aliens' messages about themselves and the role they play in the development of human culture reveal history to be the unfolding of that plan, in order to produce a new, superior hybrid being—the next step in human evolution. The aliens take the place of a God of salvation history working for humanity's redemption. The goal of history, according to abduction narratives, is not the union of God and man in Christ; rather, it is the union of humanity and alien towards which the UFO godlings strive. The barely disguised grafting of these theological elements of America's most popular religion onto the bizarre phenomenon of UFO abductions argues strongly for that phenomenon's essentially religious nature.

The psychological profiles of UFO abductees reveal differences from those of nonabductees, differences which can be said to indicate the effect of some type of religious experience. Psychologist Kenneth Ring's recent study (1992) finds abductees reporting changes in their mentalities after their encounters. Abductees tend to become more spiritual in outlook, to see in the universe the workings of some supernatural force. Their religious views are more syncretic, finding in all religions some form of spiritual truth. Many abductees report paranormal talents gained as a result of their experience. The ability to cause electromagnetic disturbances, to travel out of body, or to read minds is often claimed. This pattern of personality change is quite similar to that found among people who report near-death experiences, another phenomenon with heavy religious overtones. These experiences, however subjective they may be, have powerful and long-lasting effects upon the psyche of the individual, prompting permanent changes in worldview and lifestyle. In this respect, UFO abductions are like the paranormal events connected with conversion experiences in Puritan New England or modern charismatic Pentacostals: intrusions of another world associated with adoption of a spiritual creed.

Considered in a broad and general sense, the very idea of UFO abductions is an intensely religious concept. Humans of all times and places have held some belief in beings of another order of intelligence— not gods, but sentient creatures different from humanity. This expression of the idea of the Other has traditionally fallen under the supervision of religion, which conceived of these beings spiritually and attributed their great powers to subtleness of nature or superior magical knowledge. The Other still takes this form in modern abduction tales, now a physical extraterrestrial possessing advanced technology rather than a djinn composed of fire. The aliens still retain magical powers— the ability to pass through walls, to fly, to speak with telepathy. As the demons and fairies of previous cultures, they kidnap humans and snatch babies for some inscrutable purpose (Vallee 1969).

To interpret the phenomenon of UFO abductions within a scholarly framework is a difficult task, considering the scope and detail that the phenomenon manifests. Even abductees have severe problems making sense out of their experiences, and tend to turn to researchers/hypnotists who hold highly imaginative views of what is happening for advice and guidance. On one level, abductions are simply uninterpretable. A dreamlike confusion seems to be the hallmark of these reports, and the statements of abductees, although somewhat consistent in terms of overall patterns, is at times widely contradictory. The experiences of many abductees after the abduction event (or between abductions in an ongoing case[4]) are so bizarre as to seem nonsensical. What is one to make of an abductee's report that sinister government agents, with fake identification and license plates, came to harass her about her experiences (Keel 1988)? Or of Kathy Davis's claim that unmarked black helicopters buzzed her house after UFO sightings (Hopkins 1987)? It is tempting to dismiss the entire subject of UFO abductions, and interpret them simply as the rantings of paranoids, yet to do this would be to ignore the significance they have for the study of religion.

The abductees themselves often tend to explain their experiences in terms of religion. Although some abductees strongly reject the idea that their terrifying encounters could have any spiritual significance, many interpret the aliens a priori as supernatural beings. The specific reasons for this will be postulated in the conclusion. At this point, it is interesting to note that the cases which are the most extensively documented and least manhandled by hypnotist-researchers show the most religious details and the greatest degree of personal consciousness on the part of the abductee that her experience was religious in character.

An excellent example is that of Betty Andreasson, whose ongoing abduction experiences have been the subject of three books (Fowler 1980, 1982, 1990). Andreasson herself, a devout Christian, believes that her abductors, as frightening as they are to her, are angels, servants of God. These aliens show an interest in the Bible and baptize her at the beginning of her encounters. They teach her spiritual lessons concerning the nature of the soul and resurrection, and take her out of her body to cavort with them as beings of light. She reports what can only be called a mystical experience, in which the aliens introduce her to a being called the One, with whom she experiences ecstatic union. Andreasson feels that the aliens, the Watchers as she calls them, guide mankind at the command of God, the One.

Whitley Strieber, the most famous of the abductees, also believes his experiences to have been primarily religious in character. Although raised a Catholic, Strieber no longer adheres to any organized religion, and his encounters lack the specifically Christian references of Betty Andreasson's. The "visitor experience," as he terms the abduction phenomenon, is concerned with the evolution of human consciousness, and the science used by the visitors is a "technology of the soul" aimed at heightening man's awareness of his spiritual dimension. He compares the aliens to demons, cosmic predators whose task it is to jolt humanity's spiritual capabilities by subjecting individuals to shock and pain. Upon attaining a sufficiently high state of consciousness, Strieber speculates, humanity may become a fit companion for God. Strieber believes that mystic experience is central to the solution of the UFO mystery, and adopts this attitude in his own investigations, encouraging people with similarly religious abduction experiences to speak out against the prevailing genetic experimentation theories of Hopkins and others (Conroy 1989).

The interpretation of abduction stories by UFO researchers also reveals undercurrents of religion. Many writers from outside the field of religious studies have noted the similarities between modern abduction accounts and the folklore of earlier years concerning fairies and "little people" (Bullard 1987). The belief in diminutive nonhuman beings has always been present in some form in Western culture, and as late as the last century Evans-Wentz (1966) was able to chronicle the details of a living belief in fairies in Scotland and Ireland. Fairies, like UFO occupants, enjoyed abducting humans and causing their victims to experience temporal distortions, periods of "missing time" resembling those that modern UFO experts say are reliable signs of an abduction. Fairies, it was believed, could not properly reproduce and needed the help of humans to sustain their species. Encounters with them were often erotic experiences for the humans involved, and sometimes led to a continuing series of contacts resembling the repeat abductions seen in modern stories. Fairies, however inexplicable their activities, had a firm place in the theology of their time: they were fallen angelic beings, condemned to spend history as exiles from heaven.

Throughout the Middle Ages, both scholars and lay people accepted a belief in incubi and succubi, sexually ravenous demons that invaded bedrooms to molest innocent Christians. These diabolical entities were only one of the folkloric cousins of modern alien abductors found in the medieval period. Medieval chronicles report sightings of flying ships captained by the strange denizens of Magonia (Vallee 1969), who often carried off humans to their land beyond the clouds. In even earlier times the legends of the Norsemen bear witness to belief in a race of dwarves who abducted human beings for the purpose of reproduction.

The existence of a diminutive species of creatures who fly through the air and steal humans for sexual purposes is a belief by no means confined to Western culture. Vallee (1989) notes similar folklore among Native Americans of Mexico and South America. Wherever the idea is found, the beings are always assigned a place in the religious framework of the culture and their existence and purpose is granted a religious significance. The persistent linkage of folklore and religion on this issue is suggestive in terms of the modern attempt to interpret UFO abductions. As will be argued in the conclusion, humanity appears to have no choice but to evaluate its confrontations with the Other in terms of some religious experience. To ignore this connection when interpreting abductions may well be impossible, and at any rate is not conducive to a complete understanding of the phenomenon.

Further strengthening the argument for the essentially religious nature of UFO abductions are the interpretive efforts of abduction researchers who, while not intending to raise issues of religion, still construct "theologies of abduction" when attempting to explain these phenomenon. Some, like Michael Persinger (1989), adopt what could be termed a reductionist position in regards to UFOs and abductions which can be equally well applied to religion. Persinger argues that abductions, as well as near-death experiences and mystical experiences, are the results of naturally occurring electrical charges affecting the temporal lobe of the brain. Such temporal lobe disturbances produce the hallucinations, disorientation, and heightened sense of meaning that are characteristic both of abductions and of religious experiences. Thus, in Persinger's view, religion and abductions are much the same thing: products of discombobulated brains.

Other researchers adopt interpretive schemes which border on the fantastic. Keel (1988) and Vallee (1988) argue that UFOs and abductions are encroachments upon our world by another reality, a distinct dimension of otherness harboring classes of beings of which humanity is not normally aware. Abductions and other paranormal events are the mechanism by which the intelligences of this alternate reality control humanity, manipulating our beliefs and opinions in a rather sinister fashion. The deities and demons which fill religions are based upon these intelligences, and abductions are simply the latest device being used by extradimensional beings to influence human development. The theory that our world is subject to control by alternate realities is used to explain everything from Bigfoot to appearances of the Blessed Virgin Mary.

By far the most popular scenario for interpreting the abduction experience is the theory that extraterrestrial biologists are using humans for genetic experiments. This is the stance adopted by the majority of UFO books and magazines towards the abduction phenomenon. Most of the well-known hypnotist-researchers, like Hopkins, are strongly committed to this view, and, due to the uncertainties of hypnosis discussed earlier, it is difficult to determine if the theory is derived from the subject matter, or if the extraterrestrial theory influences the hypnotic recall of the abductee. As noted, the idea that aliens were responsible for the creation and evolution of humanity in the manner described by abductees carries with it religious connotations.

An inseparable corollary to the notion that aliens are abroad kidnapping humans is the theory that the government is fully aware of this but conceals it from the public. Some argue that the United States and other world powers have cut a Faustian deal with the aliens, ignoring the extraterrestrial attacks on citizens in exchange for advanced technology (Hall 1988). Such a scenario pits a small group of the Elect who are knowledgeable about the aliens' existence and motives against

government conspirators who have sold out the human race to diabolical alien monsters. Other conspiracy theorists believe that our planet is
a pawn in a battle between two advanced alien species, one benevolent and concerned with human welfare, and the other evil and heart-
less with a desire to enslave humankind (Hamilton 1991). Abductions
are carried out by both sides, with the beneficent aliens spiritually edu-
cating people so that they may resist the sinister extraterrestrials who
abduct in order to torture and control. The government would appear to
be on the wrong side of this Manichean war of Light and Darkness,
and those who know must expose the conspiracy so that all people may
come to the aid of the good extraterrestrials.

Searching for some methodological underpinnings for a conclusive analysis of the abduction phenomenon has been a difficult task.
The scope and strangeness of abduction accounts strongly resist any
attempt to pigeonhole the phenomenon neatly, but the one consistent
thread that can be traced in the complex tapestry of abductions is the
theme of religion. Any theoretical exercise aimed at interpreting abductions must take religion into account. Throughout this discussion,
Jungian categories have been useful in coming to grips with the dynamics that seem to be at work in these stories. These categories allow the
inherent bizarreness and incomprehensibility that are characteristic of
abduction narratives to be preserved in the discussion, while also using
religion as a rallying point for understanding the patterns that emerge
from the confusing details. Since recollections of abductions are dreamlike and uncovered through a process of hypnosis in which the individual's subconscious can play a major part, Jung's psychological categories seem tailor-made for an analysis of the phenomenon. The concept
of the Other has been especially valuable for this investigation.

Whatever else UFO abductions may be, they are an encounter
with the Other. Every detail of an abduction story emphasizes the idea
of otherness. Abductees are subjected to an otherness of space, taken
aboard an extraterrestrial spacecraft and even at times pulled out of
their bodies, isolating them from any sense of the familiar. They experience an Otherness of time, which does not seem to flow at the same
rate or with the same laws as in day-to-day existence. They are surrounded by Other beings, aliens with visages and powers which are
simply not human. The aliens are physically Other, with their short
statures, enormous eyes, and oversized heads. They are sexually Other,
arousing the abductee and sparking feelings of love. They are spiritually
Other, superintelligent and either morally superior or clinically amoral.
The abduction experience is a very condensation of the strange and
unfamiliar.

As encounters with the Other, UFO abductions are essentially religious. Humanity seems to innately separate the prosaic from the unfamiliar, and the sacred from the profane. Things which do not fit into the definitions of the familiar humanity tends to sacralize. The sacred, the numinous, is that which is "wholly other," completely beyond the pale of human experience as normally considered. Abduction by aliens certainly falls into that category, and this is perhaps the reason for the tendency of abductees to interpret their experiences within some sort of religious framework. Researchers who devise interpretive scenarios tend to encounter religion whether they mean to or not, and even resort to theologizing about alternate realities and the final goal of human history. The otherness of the abduction phenomenon makes religion impossible to escape, and no understanding of the phenomenon can be complete without a consciousness of its religious nature.

Abduction narratives seem to emerge, at least in part, from the subconscious of the abductee. Thus, the stories often contain images drawn from popular culture as well as archetypal symbols drawn from the abductee's psyche. The myth of the flying saucer and its alien occupants has been an important part of Western culture in the years since World War II, and the image of the UFO has been used in literature and cinema to represent everything from the threat of communist invasion to the hope of a united world. The pervasiveness of UFOs in the popular consciousness has increased in recent years along with the number of abduction accounts. More interest in the phenomenon seemed to breed more accounts, which in turn increase the topic's popularity. Abduction accounts seem to absorb whatever details or issues are being discussed in the ufological community, leading to the interesting observation that abduction researchers tend to find whatever they are currently looking for within abduction accounts to support the theory of the day. The increased suggestibility characteristic of the hypnotic state makes it virtually impossible for researchers to hide their biases, and details of previous accounts are repeated by other abductees who pick them up from the hypnotist, from the media, or from UFO literature. The popular concerns of the day are invariably reflected in the abduction narrative, with worries about the environment replacing the fear of nuclear war as facets of the abduction account now that East-West tensions have eased. The ability of abductees to incorporate cultural symbols and concerns into their tales, coupled with the inherently religious nature of abductions as encounters with the Other, goes a long way towards explaining the religious themes discovered in the analysis of the patterns of abduction narratives.

An excellent example of this is the way in which abduction narratives incorporate characteristically American themes. UFO abductions seem to be primarily an American phenomenon; although several important cases have been reported outside the U.S., some argue that abductions are mainly confined to this country. Certainly, no other nation displays such an incredible interest in abduction stories. One reason for this could be the similarities of abductions stories to one of America's favorite literary themes, the captivity tale. Heavily influenced by theological motifs of early Protestant New England, emphasizing imprisonment and bondage, captivity narratives base themselves upon the capture of Americans by culturally distinct, physically different, alien Others: Native Americans, Barbary pirates, or the communist Vietnamese of a modern Rambo movie (Lewis 1989). The captives, usually women, are menaced by their alien captors, and such stories often concentrate on the details of their torture or rape. Anyone familiar with current tales of UFO abductions, especially as related in popular magazines, can recognize the connection. Here the Other is truly alien, non-human and extraterrestrial, whose actions are threatening but inexplicable. The abductees, 80 percent of whom are women, are tortured and sexually violated by bizarre medical experiments, the prurient details of which are discussed on afternoon talk shows. In standard captivity narratives victims are often rescued by a morally perfect hero who destroys the victim's tormentors; in abduction tales the hero is the researcher-hypnotist, who alone knows the chilling agenda behind the victim's capture. In captivity narratives American moral virtue is favorably distinguished from the savage excesses, sexual and otherwise, of the captors. The aliens of abduction narratives, coldly clinical and amorally utilitarian, treat their victims more like mere objects of scientific study, perhaps revealing a concern, often expressed in science fiction, that our modern society is becoming increasingly detached from human values.

The phenomenon of UFO abductions is a gold mine for scholars of religion. My brief examination of abductions in a search for patterns has revealed that these encounters can look quite similar to other more traditional forms of religious experience. Similar to dreams and called forth by the use of hypnosis, abductions manifest subconscious imagery which is often religious in nature. The general pattern of the abduction experience manifests congruencies with numinous encounters, and with archaic shamanistic symbolism. The consequences of the event for the abductee are the same as with other forms of subjective paranormal religious experiences. Even the interpretive scenarios developed by abduction researchers, which ignore the religious character of the abductee's experiences, are themselves rife with religious significance.

Finally, the abductee's own interpretations of the phenomenon show a propensity, or even a need, to understand the religious significance of the phenomenon. As an important theme in popular culture, abductions deserve to be investigated by trained scholars, employing a number of methodologies, in order to determine the significance they have for the study of religion. It would be a great shame to leave such a topic, so rich with potential for increasing the understanding of popular religious concepts, in the hands of amateur hypnotists and believers in spaceships and government conspiracies.

NOTES

1. The bright light associated with UFO phenomena may signal the transition to an altered state of consciousness. Michael Persinger (1989) argues that the perception of a bright light is a common hallucination associated with temporal lobe disturbances. Such disturbances could well take the form of images like those encountered in abduction narratives, especially when recalled through hypnosis. However, as Jacobs (1992) argues, abductees show no evidence of being prone to epileptic fits or other temporal lobe phenomenon.

2. Other characteristics of abductions, according to some researchers, include the implantation and later removal of fetuses, and the presentation to women of hybrid children. These particular events are rather recent developments found primarily in the works of researchers who are quite convinced of the extraterrestrial genetic theory, and who may be influencing their subjects' testimonies. At any rate, the religious significance of these episodes is by no means clear, and they have been largely ignored in this analysis.

3. For example, the writings of George Adamski, the famous contactee, contain interminable moralizing and sternly warn against the continuance of atomic experiments. See his (with Desmond Leslie) *The Flying Saucers Have Landed* (New York: Werner Laurie, 1953).

4. Many abductees report continuing abduction experiences that stretch back to early childhood. Once again, there is the possibility that these experiences are as much the product of the hypnotist's eagerness to uncover new "memories" as they are a result of the abductee's recollections.

REFERENCES

Bullard, Thomas E. 1987. *On Stolen Time*. Mount Ranier, Md.: The Fund for UFO Research.

Conroy, Ed. 1989. *Report on Communion*. New York: Avon Books.

Evans, Hilary. 1985. *Visions, Apparitions, and Alien Visitors*. Wellingborough: Aquarian Press.

Evans-Wentz, W. Y. 1966. *The Fairy-Faith in Celtic Countries*. New York: University Press.

Fiore, Edith. 1989. *Encounters*. New York: Doubleday.

Fowler, Raymond. 1980. *The Andreasson Affair*. Englewood Cliffs: Prentice-Hall.

———. 1982. *The Andreasson Affair, Phase Two*. Englewood Cliffs: Prentice-Hall.'

———. 1990. *The Watchers*. New York: Bantam.

Fuller, John G. 1966. *The Interrupted Journey*. New York: Dial Press.

Halifax, J. 1982. *Shaman: The Wounded Healer*. London: Thames and Hudson.

Hall, Richard. 1988. *Uninvited Guests*. Santa Fe: Aurora Press.

Hamilton, William. 1991. *Cosmic Top Secret*. New Brunswick: Inner Light Publications.

Hopkins, Budd. 1981. *Missing Time*. New York: Richard Marek Publishers.

———. 1987. *Intruders*. New York: Random House.

Jacobs, David. 1992. *Secret Life*. New York: Simon and Schuster.

Jung, C. G. 1958. *Flying Saucers*. Princeton: Princeton University Press.

Keel, John. 1975. *The Mothman Prophecies*. New York: Saturday Review Press.

———. 1988. *Disneyland of the Gods*. New York: Amok Press.

Klass, Philip. 1988. *UFO Abductions: A Dangerous Game*. Buffalo: Prometheus Books.

Lewis, James. 1989. "Assessing the Impact of Indian Captivity on the Euro-American Mind: Some Critical Issues." *Connecticut Review* (Summer).

Persinger, Michael. 1989. "The 'Visitor' Experience and the Personality: The Temporal Lobe Factor." In *Cyberbiological Studies of the Imaginal Component in the UFO Contact Experience*, edited by D. Stillings, 157-71. St. Paul: Archaeus Project.

Ring, Kenneth. 1992. *The Omega Project*. New York: William Morrow and Company.

Rogo, D. Scott. 1990. *Beyond Reality*. Wellingborough: Aquarian Press.

Silverman, J. 1967. "Shamanism and Schizophrenia." *American Anthropologist* 69, no. 2.

Strieber, Whitley. 1987. *Communion*. New York: Morrow/Beech Tree Books.

———. 1988. *Transformation*. New York: Morrow/Beech Tree Books.

Vallee, Jaques. 1969. *Passport to Magonia*. Chicago: Henry Regency Company.

———. 1988. *Dimensions*. Chicago: Contemporary Books.

4

UNARIUS: EMERGENT ASPECTS OF AN AMERICAN FLYING SAUCER GROUP

Diana Tumminia and R. George Kirkpatrick

The flying saucer group Unarius, with its forty-year history, has become one of the most enduring organizations within the American contactee movement. Unarius attracted the attention of the world at large because of the charismatic reputation of its recently deceased leader, Uriel, "Archangel and Cosmic Visionary." The group, known for its prophecy, awaits the landing of starships in the year 2001. Unarius has been the subject of countless newspaper and magazine articles as well as television and radio spots, but it has received little sociological attention. Begun in 1986, our research (Kirkpatrick and Tumminia 1992) has employed an extensive case-study methodology, which includes participant observation, questionnaires, and analysis of Unarius literature and films. Here we present an overview of the emergent processes involved in the growth of Unarius, along with data about the characteristics of membership.

As an ideal type, Unarius juggles a plethora of symbols and imagery. Contemporary theory might suggest that Unarius may be responding to a condition of postmodern fragmentation and the shattering of traditional modes of perception. Support for this analysis is found in its narrative pastiche of extra-institutional meanings with links to disparate traditions. However, its totalistic utopian vision of millenarian transformation runs counter to a strictly postmodern theoretical interpretation. Rather, it is our perspective that Unarian practices have evolved in a process of emergent norms (Turner and Killian 1987) driven by the narrative improvisations of its leaders and members. Gaining its first impetus from rumors about UFOs, the larger but diffuse magico-religious social movement that claims spiritual contact with extraterrestrials gave birth to numerous types of organizations. Turner and Killian (1987) caution against assumptions of unanimity in collective behavior. It follows that groups within contacteeism would fashion on the surface similar, yet ultimately different, interpretive careers. Unarius, for instance, carved its unique path slowly with many twists and turns, borrowing and inventing as it went along.

Over a period of forty years their philosophy has expanded in many directions. Sociologists Turner and Killian (1987) argue that influential individuals called "keynoters" play a critical role in defining a group's definition of reality. Keynoters set the emotional tone and frame the symbolic interpretations within budding collectives. In Unarius, Ernest and Ruth Norman led the way. With them, the group reached its present form through active elaboration upon themes which defined the situation of contact with beings from outer space as a benevolent one. In their view, contact was therapeutic and scientific. As the organization grew, interpretive innovation redefined the direction of the group to one of millenarian expectation with its prophecy. More innovation introduced a therapeutic expression in the form of past-life therapy. Further development of cohesive narrative tales added interpretive imagery to the normative practices. What follows is a brief descriptive history of the emergent-norm process in Unarius as an evolving socially constructed series of definitions of the situation. Later we offer a statistical portrait of the group.

FIRST CONTACTS WITH SPACE

Ruth, who would later be called Uriel, met Ernest Norman at a psychic convention in 1954. Their union brought forth their "mission." Previous to this Ernest Norman, adept at giving psychic readings, had worked with several spiritualist churches.[1] In a reading given at the time of their first meeting, Ernest Norman informed Ruth that she had once been the pharaoh's daughter who had found Moses in the bulrushes. Ruth became Ernest's helpmate, taking on the role of wife and typist. The mission began to blossom when Ernest started to receive transmissions from on high.

Ernest Norman clairvoyantly received transmissions from Mars and Venus. Beings on these planets described their cities to him. *The Voice of Venus*, originally published in 1956, describes the "healing wards" of the planet where psychically damaged souls are nurtured back to health. This and other channelings about spiritual planets comprise the set of books known as the Pulse of Creation Series. These

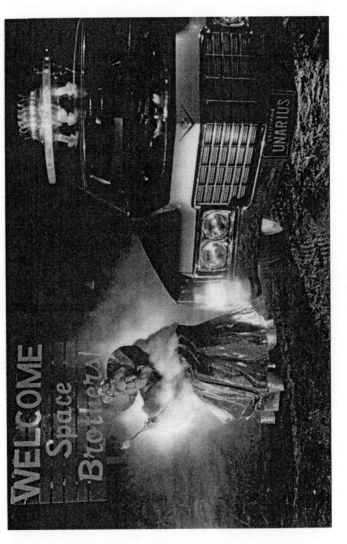

FIGURE 2. Uriel and the Space Cadillac

Out at the landing strip constructed for flying saucers, Uriel posed next to her "cosmic car." Also known as the Space Cadillac, it was specially painted with flying saucers to compliment the model mounted on top of the car. In her will, Uriel stated she would pick up the car when she returns to Earth with her spacefleet in 2001. (Photo courtesy Michael Grecco) spiritual planets (Venus, Eros, Orion, Muse, Elysium, Unarius, and Hermes) make up the "advanced teaching centers" and enlightened universities of the high astral realm. Homes of great teachers and ascended masters, the planets transmit knowledge and welcome astral travelers.

Contact with extraterrestrials is ambiguous at best; at worst, it has been portrayed as terrifying in science fiction film. The Normans defined the situation as educational, healing, and uplifting. During the fifties and early sixties, the Normans had a modest following. Besides personal contacts, interested people wrote to them and sent in pictures in order to obtain psychic readings through the mail. Ernest Norman kept channeling.

Over time, a series of basic teachings came forth from "Infinite Intelligence." In the early years of Unarius, these were given out in mimeographed form. Later they were typeset and published as *The Infinite Concept of Cosmic Creation*. This is the prime lesson book for a student of the science.[2] This twenty-lesson tome informs us that everything is energy: atoms, higher knowledge, our own bodies, and our experiences. This energy vibrates in frequencies and wave forms. Through scientific understanding of the vibrational energies we are in contact with all things: higher intelligence, the advanced teaching centers, and even our past lives. By being in tune with spiritual frequencies we can heal ourselves of mental and physical illness. Furthermore, a sleeping student may astral travel to the centers and universities of the spiritual planets where the great masters teach.

Throughout the sixties and early seventies, the Normans worked out of their home. They moved to several cities in California during this time, eventually settling in Escondido. In 1965 the Normans began to get more fully in touch with their past lives as Jesus and Mary Magdalene. During a Passover get-together, Ernest, Ruth, and a small band of students "relived" their experiences in the life and death of Christ. Their followers who were present admitted their complicity with the persecution. Those in contact by mail with the Normans sent in their testimonials with "realizations" of their guilt.

The sixties held another benchmark for Unarius. The Normans attracted two students who were given the spiritual names of Antares and Cosmon. They became "sub-channels" after the death of Ernest Norman in 1971. The mission did not die with Ernest, for Ruth followed in his footsteps and began to excel as a visionary. Channeling with the help of Antares and Cosmon, Ruth increased the number of messages from outer space and from the spiritual planets of the emerging cosmology.

TRANSITION AND GROWTH

At home during the early part of 1973, Ruth was overcome by higher energies which led to the appearance of ascended beings before her. Awash with the beauty of her vision, she related her story to Antares. Together they began to "view" the happenings in the city Parhelion on the planet Eros. Antares often describes this moment as "if a curtain was pulled away and we could see." Several days of channeling sessions were transcribed into a book called the *Conclave of Light Beings* (1973) which heralds the new transition in the Unarius mission.

Resplendent with evocative images, the pages tell of how Ruth was then engaged in an extravagant festival on the occasion of her marriage to the archangel, Michiel. Scenes described sacred temple flames, breathtaking gardens, and joyous greetings by flowergirls and trumpeters. In this vision Ruth was renamed "Queen Uriel, Queen of the Archangels" as she was crowned by the celestial form of her dead husband.

Ruth's transmission redirected the emotional tone of Unarius. Her followers enacted the marriage and crowning of Uriel at a local hotel ballroom. With Antares on her arm, the aged Ruth appeared in a wedding dress. The celebratory mood anticipated the expansion of Unarius and its mission to bring higher knowledge to earth. The momentum for contact increased.

More channelings propelled greater excitement. The *Tesla Speaks* series of books was born. The *Tesla Speaks* series consists of thirteen separate volumes of channeled revelations. Nicola Tesla, for whom the books are named, was a turn-of-the-century inventor. According to Unarius, Telsa was the reincarnation of the Archangel Michiel and a sympathetic Space Brother. In the first volume, Tesla facilitated the transmissions of messages from his fellow scientists, Albert Einstein, Louis Pasteur, William Crookes, and Robert Oppenheimer who now reside on the planet Eros.

In volume two, ascended philosophers and scientists, like Plato, Socrates, and Isaac Newton, lent their voices to praise Unarius. The third volume holds the channeled wisdom of John F. Kennedy and Dwight D. Eisenhower, among other statesmen. By the fourth and fifth volumes, the pace and the imagination of the channelings had accelerated, creating contacts with beings ("polarities") on thirty-two previously unknown planets. Volume Seven of the *Tesla Speaks* series is entitled *Countdown!!! To Spacefleet Landing*. Aside from messages from George Adamski and Orfeo Angelucci on the planet Venus, and good wishes from the dead astronauts Grissom, White, and Chaffee, a "revelation" dated March 17, 1974 states that Uriel was informed that a "spacefleet landing shall be instituted mainly for the purposes to inform the earth people of this great Intergalactic Confederation Project now being formulated. . ." (1974c, 177).

The Unarian prophecy had started to emerge. The thirty-two planets were sending their spaceships. The date of the predicted landing changed from 1975 to the year 2001. Unarians found the explanation for their misunderstanding of the proper date in their past-life karma. However, the substance of prophecy has remained the same and it is as follows.

PROPHECY 2001

Sixty-seven acres of land in the mountains of San Diego, California have been purchased for the landing of the starships in the year 2001. Expected to take place on Uriel's one-hundredth birthday, the landing will usher in a new golden age of "logic and reason." The current members of Unarius await the "vehicles of light" which will bring higher knowledge and gifts of technology to Earth. The starships, it is said, will land on top of each other. At the resulting saucer tower, the Space Brothers will set up a hospital and university. A gift of one additional ship will represent Earth in the tower.

The flying saucers are described as extremely large, sometimes five miles in diameter. Each of the ships will bring one thousand scientists to earth, a total of thirty-three thousand interplanetary scientists who will work for the betterment of all humankind. Only after they stabilize the consciousness of Earth will they become visible. The ships are expected to land first in the Bermuda Triangle. One of their first benevolent acts will be to recover the libraries of Atlantis and Lemuria. The contents of these libraries, said to be on thin metal plates somewhere in the debris of the sunken continents, will be given back to the Earth people. The Space Brothers have plans to train technicians with this knowledge in order to build crystal and gold computers and other wondrous technology.

Each level of the multilevel university formed by the spacecraft will be devoted to a particular science. The university will recreate the computers of Atlantis and Lemuria. Because technology will solve all economic and social problems, people can dedicate their lives to education and the service of humanity without having to work for a living. New methods of education will emerge, such as a cap which when placed on the head would enable a person to read "a book a night."

FIGURE 3. Prophecy 2001

As Uriel, Ruth Norman (1900-1993) is seated before a replica of the prophesied landing of spaceships in the year 2001. Elaborately costumed with her glittering cape, a scepter, and a tiara of stars, Uriel projected the loving energy of the Space Brothers. (Photo courtesy Michael Grecco)

They anticipate that the first ship will set a device which will telepathically explain the history of all the planets in the Unarian Confederation. Such electronic marvels will abound in the new educational era.

The university and medical center will be open to all, free of charge. Some of the gifts to Earth will be "advanced healing machines." The hospital will be able to heal mental as well as physical diseases with the help of the "psychic anatomy viewer." According to Unarian science, information about past lives leads to healing. As such, the "psychic anatomy viewer" will X-ray the "electronic body," a term used to describe the past-life karma as it is held in the electro-magnetic memory of the body. This machine will reveal any "malformations" and the exact time they occurred in a past life. With this information, a person is then thought to be able to release his or her problem. For example, if a person injured another during battle in a past life on Atlantis, the guilt would still be found in the "electronic body." According to Unarius, this might cause any number of illnesses which would heal upon receipt of this datum. This "psychic anatomy viewer" is expected to empty all hospitals, prisons, and asylums. Drug abuse and alcoholism will be unheard of in the age the new science will create.

The "most highly advanced" materials with which to build a new technology will be unloaded from the great ships. Celestial alloys, extraterrestrial construction tools, and interstellar electronics are awaited. The Space Brothers are to give earthlings the components of machines to clean up the environment. Space cargo of gold, crystals, lasers, and high-tech mirrors will be used to build a "Power Tower" of non-polluting energy. All transportation and communication systems will be fueled by this tower. The Power Tower will satisfy the energy needs for the entire planet, its cities, homes, and automobiles. It is said that the tower will link up with other Power Towers of the confederation. Thus, where energy signals cross, new planets of a higher frequency are to materialize. The Space Brothers are also expected to bring a weather-controlling apparatus that can renew the deserts and end all famine. The people of Earth are to build enclosed cities with perfectly modulated atmospheres.

The most important gift of the starships are the Space Brothers themselves. Powerful healers, they will eagerly train Earth people to change their own societies. The collective consciousness of the Space Brothers will "overshadow" the peace efforts of our planet. Portrayed as true humanitarians, the Space Brothers have genuine concern. It is said that the Space Brothers emanate "complete love and peace." Those who come in contact with them will have their consciousness raised to a "higher frequency." Humans will immediately experience their love.

This is how one spaceship is described as it travels closer to Earth to fulfill its mission:

> Throughout the entire craft, more than 500,000 square feet, was heard the sublime music. It was the electromagnetic harmony of the consciousness of 1,000 individuals who had been carefully selected to make this trip from their home planet; individuals who gained that development whereby their mentality was integrated with a higher spiritual nature of themselves.
>
> These persons were especially selected who had mastered the lower nature of their physical consciousness, an advanced race of Homo Sapiens with no blemishes on their bodies, reflecting their inner development. (Norman and Spaegel 1987, 3)

INTERPRETIVE INNOVATION

Uriel and her followers opened a storefront center on February 14, 1975. They attracted new students. Uriel's role expanded. As cosmic emissary to the starfleet, she prepared to greet the ships. The media picked up the story. Since then Unarius has rarely lacked publicity.

The introduction of the news about the Interplanetary Confederation and the prophecy of the spacefleet landing completely redefined the Unarian mission. In this new interpretive innovation, Uriel plays the role of cosmic emissary, uniting the confederation. The next years of the Unarius mission entailed continuous elaboration on this narrative theme. Subsequent channelings and psychic readings wove ever-expansive tales of a Unarian mission that was millions of years old. "True stories" of how Uriel and her followers had traveled throughout space and time together emerged. From planet to planet and from one historical period to the next, Unarians could trace their collective biographies. Their task now was to right the wrongs of the past, for they, themselves, had often thwarted the Unarian mission by actively engaging in evil deeds against Uriel and the Space Brothers. These never-ending tales gave form to the interpretive invention Unarians call past-life therapy.

Unarius had always provided psychic readings of past lives as a basis for healing. Readings were recorded and given to students. By the mid seventies past-life stories reached a critical mass, as forty students formed a stable community of believers. Unarius had started doing readings in groups. Thus, the tales from readings strongly intertwined. Originally called psychic group therapy, Unarian past-life therapy encouraged a student "to get in touch with his past" and "face his past." The "past" visits Unarians in "cycles," as it had in 1965 when Ernest and Ruth went through the "Jesus Cycle." During one cycle, Unarians may relive their lives together on Atlantis. In another, they experience a time when they banded together in spaceships to destroy other planets in the Orion constellation. Cycles are formally or informally announced by the leadership. Individuals may experience more than one cycle in any given time.

To fulfill class assignments in past-life therapy, students give oral and written testimonials about the content of their psychic readings and their personal revelations about "cycles." Students are also encouraged to come to experiential realizations on their own by recognizing memories of their past lives. The transcribed texts of therapy classes are turned into books.

When Unarius started making films and videos in the late seventies, students started to act out their past lives in costume for the camera. The films and books tell of an arduous journey which began, so to speak, long, long ago in a galaxy far away. For the sake of illustration one tale will be related here from the "Orion cycle." The tale resembles the story of a fallen angel. On the planet Aries, Antares, the formerly mentioned student of Unarius, was an advanced being. Uriel and Michiel, the archangels, were wayshowers who had planned to save the planet, Tyron, during an Ice Age. Antares devised his own plan without Uriel. In this manner, Antares fell through "ego." He appeared millions of years ago on Tyron in the Orion system. After many lifetimes Antares took on the body of Tyrantus, master of the galaxy and commander of doom. Tyrantus waged war on other planets. According to Unarian belief, present-day students of Unarius once resided in the Orion system. It was there they were enlisted to carry out evil deeds for Tyrantus. Students unwittingly took on the jobs of space commanders and starship crew members. As scientists, they conducted experiments on others. Breeding experiments, mutilations and transplants, and military research were performed at the bidding of Tyrantus.

In a new body, Uriel came to visit Tyrantus. Uriel arrived in a spaceship as Dalos, spiritual leader of the Pleiades star cluster. Because of their negative state, brought about largely through the influence of electronic devices, the Orion people conspired to torture Dalos (Uriel). Dalos was tortured for a thousand years by those who now call themselves Unarian students. Student accounts of the Orion cycle are found in the book, *The Decline and Destruction of the Orion Empire* (1979), and in the film by the same name.

FIGURE 4. Higher Teaching Center

Dressed in costumes which reflect the cultured life of the "higher teaching centers" on other planets, students listen to a reading of an "inspired" Unarian book. They sit beneath a beloved painting of Uriel overcoming Satan. (Photo courtesy Michael Grecco)

Past-life regression and readings are common practices in New Age therapies. However, the collective weaving of past-life narratives as a regular process of intersubjectivity may be unique to Unarius. As a consensus-making procedure, it succeeds because the student must constantly reaffirm his or her relationship to the whole narrative in class sessions. As an interpretive innovation, past-life therapy creates a space for every potential member and binds the long-term student to the duty of keeping the mythos alive.

THE UNARIUS CENTER

The Unarius Center holds classes three times a week for its students. Past-life therapy, the "psychology of consciousness," and art therapy remain the mainstay of the curriculum. Formal instruction consists of the study of "transceived" books of the science. Unarian texts, handsomely illustrated by students, are produced at the in-house print shop located next to the center.

Student artwork graces their books. Unarians take their literary offerings quite seriously, for they believe the art and words come from "Higher Intelligence." The Unarian Academy itself resembles a small public library, although students remind us that it is actually the remanifestation of the long-lost Alexandrian Library of antiquity.

Besides classes, the center hosts a number of celebrations throughout the year. For example, Interplanetary Confederation Day, held around October 12th each year, commemorates the union of the planets under the guidance of Uriel. Begun in the mid eighties, Interplanetary Confederation Day features a parade of colorful banners of the spiritual planets held by costumed participants. Festivities include harp and piano music, choral singing, an art show, intergalactic proclamations, and the annual release of the white doves of peace from a flying saucer replica. The evening program brings a lesson in the science, a film about the arrival of the spaceships, testimonials by students, and a special transmission from the Space Brothers via channeling.

During a recent two-day celebration, a student delivered a proclamation on behalf of the organization. It is excerpted here:

We, therefore, as representatives of the planet Earth, do, in the Name, and authority of the good People of this planet, solemnly publish and declare our intentions to participate in the preparation of our Home Globe, Planet Earth, for the alighting of interstellar vehicles and the resulting contact and alliance with an advanced

race of intelligent souls in the year 2001, for the purpose of enlight-
enment, the exchange of cultural heritage, and the much needed
technical knowledge and physical evidence proving the evolution of Homo Sapiens into Homo Spirtualis! (from leaflet for 9th
Annual Interplanetary Confederation Day, October 10th and 11th,
1992, Unarius)

The Unarius Center reached its heyday in the eighties. Uriel was
still robust despite her advanced age. At that time, it seemed likely that
she would live to be one hundred years old and greet the Space
Brothers when they arrived in their fleet of flying saucers. Wearing one
of her many costumes, she would vigorously lead celebrations such as
Interplanetary Confederation Day. She forcefully directed the center
with the help of Antares. A continuous stream of past lives were
revealed and immortalized under her guidance and encouragement.

By 1989, Uriel's health began to slip. During her hospitalizations,
Unarian students met to discuss how they had tortured her when she
was Dalos in the Orion cycle. Not withstanding the therapeutic confessions of her students, Uriel suffered the increasing pain of advanced
age and osteoporosis.

Sadly, another transition faced Unarians. In a letter dated
December 8, 1991, Uriel wrote her students that she may die before the
landing in 2001. She had contacted the Space Brothers for guidance.
The Brothers affirmed that her mission was completed and she could
leave at anytime.

Mostly bedridden, Uriel still kept track of her students through
videotapes of classes, letters, and phone calls. A few attended her medical needs at her bedside. On Valentine's Day in 1993 she received all
her students individually and blessed them. Each student had a photograph taken with her as a keepsake. Many wept as they realized it
might be the last time they would see her in her earthly form. On July
12, 1993, Uriel died quietly in her sleep. During the reading of her will,
students learned that she would return in 2001 with the Space Brothers.
Despite her passing, Unarians carry on the mission at the center as they
did before her death.

CHARACTERISTICS OF MEMBERSHIP

Unarius claims thousands of members. Its mailing list numbers
five thousand, but actual involved participation remains more modest.
In 1989, the Unarian Academy of Science listed forty-four full-time stu-

FIGURE 5. The Cosmic Generator

The Unarius librarian tends to the "Cosmic Generator" display. The Cosmic
Generator costume was constructed for Uriel by her students. The dress is made
of black velvet, embellished with planets and stars that are electrically illumi-
nated. The costume celebrates Uriel who as the Cosmic Generator "supplies
life-force energies to the earth worlds." (Photo courtesy Michael Grecco)

dents on its membership list, nineteen men (43 percent) and twenty-five women (57 percent). The membership list for 1990 recorded forty-eight people, twenty men (42 percent) and twenty-eight women (58 percent). By 1992, forty-seven students were numbered, which includes twenty-one men (45 percent) and twenty-six women (55 percent). For important events about sixty-five people show up. Home study remains an option for students who live at a distance from the center. No figures are available on the current number of home-study students. Unarius itself does not keep a separate list of them.

The general picture of core membership remains stable at slightly under fifty members. The numbers suggest a very small replacement mobility. For example, the difference between 1990 and 1992 lists reflects addition of five new members and the attrition of seven members: one through death, two through expulsion, one who left without stating a reason, and three who opted for home study. The two who were expelled and told not to return had sent a letter to Uriel in which they disputed the channeling which prompted the December 8, 1991, announcement.

In the first phase of the study, an availability sample of twenty followers filled out a survey in 1986 with the help of the organization. These respondents completed the portion of the questionnaire which asked basis demographic information. They rejected a battery of questions about their personal beliefs and their relationship to Uriel. These questions were labeled as "containing too many negatives."

We report here data from the 1986 sample and from subsequent yearly membership lists where indicated. Women, 65 percent of the 1986 sample, outnumber men, but not overwhelmingly so. This is consistent in ensuing years as indicated above. A little over half the students (55 percent) were under forty years old, unlike Buckner's (1968) group which appeared to be elderly. In 1986, all the students in San Diego were white. Unarius seems to primarily interest whites. Some exceptions have been noted. By 1989, a black woman moved to an apartment near the center after having been a home-study student since 1961. In 1992, she died of cancer. One student who became full-time in 1992 is Hispanic. One home-study student, featured in the Unarian newsletter, lives in Nigeria.

The students of Unarius are adamant that their pursuit is a science and "not a religion." In 1986, when asked if they had a religion, or religious preference, 90 percent stated that they did not have a religion. However, two respondents (10 percent) identified Unarius as their religion.

The members are fundamentally apolitical and report little interest in politics except for the part of Unarius philosophy which focuses on world peace. In 1986, 35 percent responded that they had little or no interest in politics. Only 10 percent said they were very interested in politics. Eighty percent reported that they did not contribute to political campaigns and only 10 percent always voted in local elections. Twenty-five percent said that they always voted in national elections. Fifty-five percent stated that they rarely or never voted. Political ideology seems to play no guiding role in the Unarian practice. An equal number of Democrats and Republicans were found, 25 percent each in the sample. Another 25 percent have no political affiliation. Two members were affiliated with the Peace and Freedom Party. Only two members (10 percent) said they were members of any community or voluntary organizations.

Occupationally, the majority of Unarius devotees can be classified as having working-class jobs, such as floral arranger, carpenter, secretary, hair stylist, nurse, and nurse's aide. Their incomes in 1986 seemed to match their occupational status with 50 percent making less than $1600 a month, around $19,000 a year in 1986. Unarius members display little or no status symbols from American society.

Significantly, 85 percent of the 1986 sample were single. A full 30 percent of those who were single had never married. By 1992, 78 percent of the students on the membership list were unmarried. Unarians who marry are most likely to marry another member. A typical Unarian is single and has no young children. Both observational and quantitative data indicate that Unarius serves as a primary group for the dedicated members. Eighteen percent regularly work for the center. Almost to the person, practically every member donates time for maintenance, clerical, or other types of volunteer work.

Interviews indicate that students spend long hours on Unarius-related activities, such as classes, reading, homework, and volunteer service. From all indications, Unarius acts as a substitute family, therapist, and occupational group for its members. Even those members who hold white-collar jobs like journalist and film-maker work part-time in order to devote extra hours of service to Unarius.

Using the 1992 membership list, we have established data on recruitment. Of the 1992 members ($N=47$), 62 percent of students made their first contacts with Unarius through self-initiated encounters. Those who initiated contact with Unarius either: walked in off the street, received information from a mailer, found a Unarius book in a library or New Age store, looked in the phone book, or encountered ads for Unarius on leaflets, on TV or radio, or through magazines. Two self-initiators found Unarius at a UFO conference. The smaller percentage of members (38 percent) were influenced by personal contacts with acquaintances, friends, relatives, or co-workers. Typically Unarians do not engage in zealous recruitment practices. Rather they take part in appropriate conferences and advertise regularly.

Balch and Taylor (1978) distinguish recruitment from conversion. Strictly speaking, Unarians are not converts. Potential members have already adopted the alternative worldview of the New Age philosophy, particularly acceptance of reincarnation and psychic awareness, much like the group studied by Balch and Taylor (1978). Repeatedly, those interviewed in Unarius describe themselves as "seekers." They view themselves as having "found" Unarius after a lifetime of searching. Many report joining at first sight, either from reading a book or from seeing Uriel. For example,

> I saw Ruth Norman's (Uriel's) picture in the paper with the painting of the Spacefleet Landing. For me it was an immediate inner response of recognition within the oscillations of energy I felt from this One before me on the printed page. My childhood search had ended and my contact with Unarius began. (Norman 1985, 4)

In everyday life Unarius operates as a healing group symbolized by the flying saucer. A noncorporeal orientation to disease and emotional distress characterizes Unarian thinking. In general Unarians are attentive to one another and work cooperatively on a stream of group projects. They are nonaggressive, tolerant, and trusting students. Their sense-making activities involve the discovery of past lives. They account for their present-day healings by telling others who they were in their past lives.

CONCLUSION

Unarius exemplifies how expressive groups make use of innovative practices and emergent narratives to define their present reality and redefine their future directions. The vision of their science and the institutionalization of its therapies evolved over time through the interpretive work of leaders and followers. The qualitative features of the Unarian worldview have unfolded mainly through a process of narrative events which lends credence to the process-oriented perspective of the emergent-norm model.

Unarians now negotiate a new transition as they cope with the death of their beloved leader. Nevertheless, everyday life remains much the same. As for active participants, the numbers have stayed relatively small but have held constant over the years. Newcomers still trickle in.

They come to learn about the science and the great Uriel, "Cosmic Emissary and Goddess of Love." Dedicated students still explore their consciousness by remembering their past lives. By doing so, they work towards their own spiritual evolution. Furthermore, members continue to discover their own place in the Unarian space odyssey as they tell their stories in classes and on film. In their hearts, they also continue to prepare for the landing of Space Brothers and the realization of the Unarian mission in the year 2001.

NOTES

1. Two specific practices, channeling and past-life reading, brought forth much of the body of knowledge called the Unarius Science of Life. Channeling is referred to as "transceiving a message" or "receiving a transmission." "Viewing" or "viewing through the lens" often goes along with transceiving. By viewing, one can see clairvoyantly scenes from other planets and from other periods of time. Past-life reading, or psychic reading, sometimes combines viewing and transceiving. Past-life reading connects the belief in reincarnation to the idea that the events of former lifetimes can be gleaned from an astral document called the Akashic Record.

Transmissions entail an "open channeling" method as opposed to trance channeling or spirit possession. Open channeling (Klimo 1987) involves a "stepping aside" of the conscious mind, in contrast with the stereotypic full trance often portrayed in the media. Uriel has said that the process is like extending an antenna on a car. Thoughts, images, and messages flow through the channeler who is in a relaxed state with closed eyes. Open channeling holds out the possibility that anyone can channel, for it requires no special ability other than receptivity. Psychic reading resembles channeling with emphasis placed upon gaining past-life information.

2. The acronym, Unarius, stands for Universal Articulate Interdimensional Understanding of Science. To become a student of Unarius is to learn "the Science." This lends support to Jurgen Habermas's view that science has become a predominate mode of legitimation for what are essentially symbolically constituted processes. Habermas states, "The reified models of the sciences migrate into the sociocultural life world and gain objective power over the latter's self-understanding" (1970, 113).

REFERENCES

Balch, Robert W., and David Taylor. 1978. "Seekers and Saucers: The Role of the Cultic Mileau in Joining a UFO Cult." In *Conversion Careers*, edited by James Richardson, 43-45. Beverly Hills: Sage Publications.

Buckner, H. Taylor. 1968. "The Flying Saucerians: An Open Door Cult." In *Sociology and Everyday Life*, edited by Marcello Truzzi, 223-31. Englewood Cliffs, N.J.: Prentice-Hall, Inc.

Habermas, Jurgen. 1970. *Toward a Rational Society: Student Protest, Science, and Politics*. Boston: Beacon Press.

Kirkpatrick, R. George, and Diana Tumminia. 1992. "California Space Goddess: The Mystagogue in a Flying Saucer Cult." In *Twentieth-Century World Religious Movements in Neo-Weberian Perspective*, edited by William H. Swatos, Jr., 299-311. Lewiston, N.Y.: The Edwin Mellen Press.

Klimo, Jon. 1987. *Channeling: Investigations on Receiving Information from Paranormal Sources*. Los Angeles: Jeremy P. Tarcher, Inc.

Norman, Ernest L. 1956. *The Voice of Venus*. El Cajon, Calif.: Unarius Academy of Science.

————. 1970. *The Infinite Concept of Cosmic Creation*. Glendale, Calif.: Unarius-Science of Life.

Norman, Ruth. 1985. *Testimonials by Unarius Students: To Help the New Seeker Conceive the Great and Many Benefits of Unarius*. El Cajon, Calif.: Unarius Educational Foundation.

————. 1987. *Preview for the Spacefleet Landing on Earth in 2001 A.D.* El Cajon, Calif.: Unarius Academy of Science.

Norman, Ruth E., and Vaughn Spaegel. 1973a. *The Conclave of Light Beings: or the Affair of the Millennium*. El Cajon, Calif.: Unarius-Science of Life.

————. 1973b. *Tesla Speaks: Scientists*. Volume 1. El Cajon, Calif.: Unarius-Science of Life.

————. 1973c. *Tesla Speaks: Scientists and Philosophers*. Volume 2. El Cajon, Calif.: Unarius-Science of Life.

————. 1974. *Tesla Speaks: Scientists and Presidents*. Volume 3. El Cajon, Calif.: Unarius-Science of Life.

Norman, Ruth E., Vaughn Spaegel, and Thomas Miller. 1974a. *Tesla Speaks: Earth Worlds of the Intergalactic Confederation Speak!* Volume 4. El Cajon, Calif.: Unarius-Science of Life.

————. 1974b. *Tesla Speaks: The Celebration of the Millennium: Crystal Mountains, Cities, and Temples*. Volume 6. El Cajon, Calif.: Unarius-Science of Life.

————. 1974c. *Tesla Speaks: Countdown!!! To Space Fleet Landing*. Volume 7. El Cajon, Calif.: Unarius-Science of Life.

———. 1975. *Tesla Speaks: Earth Worlds Speak to Planet Earth.* Volume 5. El Cajon, Calif.: Unarius-Science of Life.

Norman, Ruth, and Unarian Students. 1979. *The Decline and Destruction of the Orion Empire.* El Cajon, Calif.: Unarius Educational Foundation.

Turner, Ralph H., and Lewis M. Killian. 1987. *Collective Behavior.* Englewood Cliffs, N.J.: Prentice-Hall, Inc.

5

WOMEN IN THE RAELIAN MOVEMENT: NEW RELIGIOUS EXPERIMENTS IN GENDER AND AUTHORITY

Susan Jean Palmer

The Raelian movement appears to be one of the rare examples of a new religious movement (NRM) which promotes in its members a tolerance for sexual ambiguity and encourages homosexual expression. Angela Aidala (1985) has argued that part of the appeal of religious communes to contemporary youth intolerant of the shifting interpretations of masculine-feminine, is their clear-cut, unambiguous gender roles. The Raelian movement is not communal in its organization, but it is millenarian, and radical departures from conventional sexuality are also characteristic of non-communal millenarian groups (Worseley 1976; Balch 1982). Unlike Aidala's religious communes, this NRM deliberately fosters in its members experimental and individualistic approaches to redefining their sexuality. Since Aidala posits a link between the "rigid role divisions" found in communal NRMs and their tendency to promote sexual inequalities, the Raelians' androgynous anthropology and non-traditional gender roles would seem to promise a fertile environment for cultivating feminine authority.

One of the puzzles confronting this researcher, however, is the surprising *scarcity* of women in leadership positions in the Raelian hierarchy. Mary Farrell Bednarowski (1980), in her study of the roles of women in Shakerism, Christian Science, spiritualism, and Theosophy, has proposed four characteristics or common factors found in marginal religions which promote female leadership and sexual equality:

1. A godhead which is androgynous or non-anthropomorphic.
2. A reinterpretation of the doctrine of the Fall.

3. New rules for ordaining clergy.
4. A view of marriage which departs from the traditional emphasis on woman as homemaker and mother.

As this study will attempt to demonstrate, the Raelian movement possesses all four of Bednarowski's characteristics, and yet a study of the 1988 *Raelian Conseil Decisionel* survey on membership reveals that men outnumber women two to one, and that women in the Structure (the fully committed core group) tend to stay at the lower levels. Of the six levels in the hierarchy, which represent degrees of responsibility, self-awareness and proximity to the aliens, women tend to remain in the lowest levels, in level 1 (Assistant Animator), level 2 (Animator), and level, 3 (Assistant Guide). Of the fifteen Priest: Guides (level 4), only four are women, and one of them is actually a transexual (born male). All three level 5 Bishop Guides are men, and Rael, the founder himself, as Planetary Guide represents level 6.

When one considers that, in addition to fitting snugly into Bednarowski's model of a sex-egalitarian religion, the Raelian literature explicitly deplores the subjugation of women and espouses what Allen (1984) terms the "sex unity" view of gender (i.e., the notion that men and women are essentially the same, hence equal), there appears to be no obstacles in terms of ideology, family patterns, or tradition to prevent charismatic women from rising in the hierarchy. So, why don't they? This study will first address this enigma and will then explore the larger significance of this movement in Quebec as providing a forum for experiments in gender and authority for Quebecois youth in an era marked by profound upheavals in the structure of the family.

THE HISTORY

The Raelian movement was founded by the French race-car driver and journalist "Rael" (born Claude Vorilhon in 1946) in 1973 as the result of his alleged encounter with space aliens during a walking tour of the Clermont-Ferrand volcanic mountain range in France. These aliens, whom Rael describes as small human-shaped beings with pale green skin and almond eyes, entrusted him with the "message." This message concerns our true identity: we were "implanted" on Earth by superior extraterrestrial scientists, the "Elohim," who created humanity from DNA in their laboratories. Rael's mission, as "the last of forty prophets" (crossbred between Elohim and mortal women), is to warn humankind that since 1945 and Hiroshima, we have entered the "Age of

Apocalypse" in which we have the choice of destroying ourselves with nuclear weapons or making the leap into planetary consciousness which will qualify us to inherit the scientific knowledge of our space forefathers. Science will enable 4 percent of our species in the future to clone themselves and travel through space, populating virgin planets "in our own image" (Bouchard 1989; *Space Aliens Took Me to Their Planet* 1978).

The movement claims twenty thousand members worldwide, distributed mainly throughout France, Japan, and Quebec, and endeavors through its books and lectures to unite Christians, Jews, and Muslims in a "demythologized" interpretation of Scripture as the true history of a space colonization. Denying the existence of God or the soul, Rael presents as the only hope of immortality a regeneration through science, and to this end members participate in four annual festivals so that the Elohim can fly overhead and register the Raelians' DNA codes on their machines. This initiation ritual, called "the transmission of the cellular plan," promises a kind of immortality through cloning. New initiates sign a contract which permits a mortician to cut out a piece of bone in their forehead (the "third eye") which is stored in ice awaiting the descent of the Elohim. New initiates are also required to send a letter of apostasy to the church they were baptized in.

The "Raelians" are those who have acknowledged the Elohim as their fathers by taking these two steps (initiation and funeral arrangements) and the "Structure" are those who work for the organization and are committed to the two goals of the movement: spreading the message to mankind and building an embassy in Jerusalem by the year 2025 to receive the Elohim. While members of the Structure are committed to making the message available to those who are "already Raelian but haven't realized it yet," they are instructed to avoid pressure tactics and evangelizing. Members who attempt to force their ideas or unwelcome sexual attentions on others are excommunicated from the movement for seven years (the time it takes to replace all their body cells).

The Raelians have a strong millenarian focus in preparing for the descent of the UFOs bearing the Elohim and the thirty-nine immortal prophets (Jesus, Buddha, Mohammed, Joseph Smith, etc.) who, according to Rael's revelation, were born from the union of a mortal woman and an Elohim. The movement might be described as "world affirming" (Wallis 1984) in its orientation towards society. Members are encouraged through summer courses to achieve success in their careers, to have better health through avoiding all recreational drugs and stimulants, and to enlarge their capacity to experience pleasure which Rael claims, will strengthen their immune system and enhance their intelli-

FIGURE 6. Extraterrestrial Embassy

A scale-model of the embassy that the Elohim (visitors from other worlds) requested Rael to build. Once established, the Elohim intend to meet with terrestrial political and scientific leaders, and give the Earth the benefit of their wisdom and technology. (Photo courtesy Raelian Movement)

FIGURE 7. Transmission of the Code

Transmission of the cellular code by a Canadian guide, Bobby Potvin. Raelians regard transmission as the origin of the practice of baptism. (Photo courtesy Raelian Movement)

gence and telepathic abilities. Those who find total self-fulfillment will be immortalized through cloning. Meanwhile, Rael advises Raelians not to marry or exacerbate the planetary overpopulation problem, but to commune with the wonder of the universe by exploring their sexuality with the opposite sex, the same sex, and any other life form—even ETI. To this end, Raelians participate annually in a sensual meditation workshop in a rural setting which features fasting, nudity, sensory awareness exercises, and sexual experimentation, the ultimate goal being to experience the "cosmic orgasm."

RAEL'S PHILOSOPHY OF SEXUALITY

Rael's vision of a perfect society in the future, ruled by the "geniocracy" of intelligent scientists, is based on revelation. As he phrases it, "The Elohim were starting to speak through my mouth, or rather, to write with my hand." He describes his advice on sexual and other matters as "a code of life, a new way of behaving as an evolved being" so as to "open one's mind to infinity and to place oneself in harmony with it. These great rules dictated by the Elohim, Our Creators, our fathers who are in heaven . . . are all here expressed in all their integrality" (Vorilhon 1986a, 122-223).

Rael's recommendations reflect the sexual customs of these space aliens which he observed (and participated in) when they took him to their planet in 1975. As he describes it, Elohim society is composed of ninety thousand quasi-immortal men and women who "can unite themselves freely as they wish, and any form of jealousy is eliminated." They are not allowed to have children, and undergo a small sterilization operation. Consequently, their relationships are "more fraternal and respectful" than ours, and "the unions among them are marvelously pure and high." Rael (1986, 210-13) describes his own encounter with alien sexual mores:

"Would you like some female companions?" asked the robot. "Come, you will make a choice. "
. . . I found myself transported in front of the machine used for fabricating the robots. A luminous cube appeared in front of me. . . . A magnificent young brunette with wonderfully harmonious proportions appeared in three dimensions within the luminous cube. . . . My robot asked me whether she pleased me. . . . Following my refusal to change anything whatsoever about that magnificent woman, a second woman, blond and heady this time,

FIGURE 8. Sensual Meditation

The Raelian movement's advocacy of open sexual expression has attracted the attention of the media, and given the group no little notoriety. The above image is from the cover of one of Rael's books on Sensual Meditation. (Photo courtesy Raelian Movement) appeared in the luminous cube. . . . Finally a third young person, more sensual than the first two and red haired this time, appeared in the strange cube. . . .

At that moment, a magnificent black woman appeared in the cube, then a very slim Chinese woman, and voluptuous oriental woman. The robot asked me which person I desired to have as a companion.

Since Rael was unable to choose between such "magnificent specimens," he retired to his extraterrestrial hotel suite with all six.

There I had the most unforgettable bath I have ever had, in the company of those charming robots, absolutely submissive to my desires. . . . Finally, after a while I went to bed and spent the most extravagant night of my life with my marvelous female companions.

Rael (1986, 237) offers some very decisive guidance on some of the ethical dilemmas which confront contemporary women, such as birth control, abortion, and single parenthood. He condones abortion:

If by mishap you have conceived a being without desiring it, use the means which science puts at your disposal: use abortion. Because a being which was not desired at the moment of conception cannot fully blossom because he was not created in harmony. Do not listen to those who try to frighten you by talking about the physical and especially the ethical after-effects which an abortion can cause.

Conceiving a child should be delayed until "the individual is fulfilled" and this can only be achieved through "the fulfillment of your body" which leads to "the blossoming of your mind." In the interim he recommends birth control. He suggests (Rael 1986, 236) that a kind of eugenics is possible through the psychic control of the parents during the act of conception:

. . . a child cannot be well conceived unless he was truly desired at the moment of conception. . . . this moment must therefore be desired so that the first cell, may be made in perfect harmony, the two minds of the parents being conscious and strongly thinking of the being which they are conceiving. This is one of the secrets of the new man.

Rael (1986, 237) gives women permission to be unmarried mothers, single mothers, and sexually active single mothers:

> To have a child does not necessarily imply being married or even living with a man.
>
> If you wish to have a child without living with a man, do as you wish. Fulfill yourself as you wish, without worrying what others think. . . . Don't think you are condemned because of this to live alone forever: welcome the men you like and they will serve as masculine models for your child. . . . A change of environment is always positive for a child.

He also gives women permission to *dump* their children:

> Thus, if you gave birth to the child you desired . . . and you no longer desire the child, you will be able to entrust him to society so that he may be brought up in harmony necessary for his fulfillment. . . . If the child becomes a nuisance, however slightly, he realises it and his fulfillment is affected. (Rael 1986, 238)

Rael (1986, 329) strongly advises against marriage:

> You will reject marriage which is only the proclamation of ownership of a person. A man or a woman cannot be the property of anyone else. Any contract can only destroy the harmony existing between two beings. When one feels love, one feels free to love, but when one has signed a contract, one feels like a prisoner, forced to love and sooner or later, each one begins to hate the other.

He even advises against trying to maintain a longterm relationship:

> You will live with the person of your choice for only as long as you feel good with them. When you no longer get on well together, do not remain together because your union would become hell. (Rael 1986, 239)

The rationale behind Rael's version of "free love" resembles that of Fourier, John Humphrey Noyes, and Rajneesh. He is concerned that women should not be treated as property:

> . . . we still do not recognize women's right to do with their body as they wish. . . . What is more . . . if we were to kill someone

whom we claim to "love," what is called a "crime passionel," we can get off with sometimes five or six years in prison!

He finds in possessive love the potential for violence:

The one who truly loves hopes his partner will meet someone who will give her even more pleasure. . . . The selfish person prefers to keep "his property." He prefers his companion to be unhappy with him rather than happy with someone else. And if that happens, he takes his gun to kill his "loved one." (Vorilhon 1986c, 64)

He criticizes society for endorsing such violence:

This means we are living in a society which is encouraging its members to kill those they love and let live those they don't love . . . (Vorilhon 1986c, 62-64)

RAEL'S IDEAS ON GENDER

Rael often compares men and women to biological robots who are programmed to give each other pleasure. He quotes the Elohim's explanation of gender:

We saw that it was very easy to create a strain of "sexed" robots, each possessing half a plan so that while "coupling" they would create one complete plan and so allow the "female" to make a "child." We also saw, that to incite our robots to reproduce, we needed to render the act . . . pleasurable . . . by equipping their sexual organs with nerve endings. (Vorilhon 1986c, 65)

Seeing gender as an artificial construct, Rael emphasises its fluidity, resulting from different possible combinations of X and Y chromosomes. This implies that all human beings are essentially androgynous. In one of the testimonials printed at the end of *Sensual Meditation* (1986c, 143) a horticultural technician takes up Rael's argument to explain his homosexual orientation:

Maybe you don't realize it, but one is born as a homosexual, just as one is born with green eyes . . . that is to say, in one's chromosomes, within the nucleus of an individual's cells, the stack of genes carries the characteristics of each person and determines absolutely . . . everything which makes them original. . . . Even in Paris homosexuals are imprisoned, tortured, harassed, hemmed in, and forced to live underground in ghettos by this ignorant society . . . and yet one can understand how such characteristics are determined genetically, thanks to the work of our scientists.

This fluid approach to gender is acted out in one of the most hilarious events in the sensual meditation camp. This is a party in which men dress up as women and women dress up as men, an exercise which encourages participants to experiment with different shades of gender and "choose" the melange of male-female which will best suit them in their everyday life.

WOMEN'S ROLE IN THE MEETINGS

The Mouvement Raelian Canadien has found the English-speaking provinces to be unreceptive, thus far, to the message, but claims to have four thousand members in Quebec. Raelians in Quebec meet on the third Sunday in the month at the local Holiday Inn. These meetings begin with a lively half hour of rapturous greetings before members sit down in the conference room and listen to various announcements and speeches. All participate in a guided meditation called "oxygenation," which involves deep breathing and concentrating on a mental anatomical dissection of the body, arriving at the brain which engages in a visualization exercise of the planet of the Elohim, to the accompaniment of New Age music.

Women are as active as the men in these meetings; they make announcements, give speeches, and they caress their boyfriends and generally behave in an overtly "sensual" fashion. One teenager who is much admired sits through the meetings in a tulle and crinoline skirt, tossing her ponytail and licking lollipops. Men usually outnumber the women and few children attend. The style of feminine dress ranges from elegant *Paris Match*, to punk, to (apparently unconscious) parodies of Brigitte Bardot in her St. Tropez heyday. The male Guides dress in white and wear their hair long, since they believe the hair follicles function as antennae, or telepathics. It is perhaps significant that many of the men I met at the meetings could be described as "effeminate" in their dress and social manner, whereas I did not meet one woman who was "masculine." All Raelians wear large medallions of the swastika inside the star of David, which they believe is an ancient symbol of the integrity of time and space. Between two hundred to four hundred people gather in Montreal at these monthly meetings, and even when Rael spoke at the Montreal December 1991 meeting, there were less than five hundred Raelians present.

Sensual overtures appear to be a common recruitment technique. One of this researcher's more conspicuously ornamental male students (age nineteen) who attended the 1990 Transmission of the Cellular Plan to write a field report, noted that three different women propositioned him outright or tried to arrange a date, and he found this shocking because, "They were at least forty, and old enough to be my mother!" Another student, an eighteen-year-old Jewish girl, received a pep talk on "free love" from one of the Assistant Guides she interviewed, followed by a eulogy on her beauty. She confessed the incident so disturbed her, she was unable to sleep soundly for a week.

One event which illustrates the Raelian disregard for marriage (and for national boundaries) occurred at the 1989 November meeting when two Frenchmen stood up and announced that they were looking for Quebec girls to marry so they could stay in Canada. The group's celebration of sexual adventurism was dramatized in a Guide's announcement in the December 1990 meeting: "Let us congratulate Philador. For one whole year she has been with the same man!" There was a hearty applause. (My student who reported this event commented, "What's the big deal about that? I've had the same girlfriend for three years, and no one ever congratulates me!")

RAELIAN WOMEN: WHO JOINS AND WHY?

This researcher has accessed three sources of information on female membership in the Raelian Movement in Quebec. First, the Raelian Conseil Decisionel released their statistics on Canadian members which were based on a 1988 questionnaire sent to 1400 subjects, of which 399 were returned. Secondly, the author and seven students from Dawson College passed out a questionnaire at the December 1991 meeting in Montreal and received 30 responses (12 women and 18 men) out of 500-odd participants. Thirdly, interviews with 16 Raelians and field notes from participant-observation research at the meetings have been collected by this researcher and her students at Dawson College between 1988 and 1992.

The portrait of a "typical" Raelian woman which emerges from these different sources is as follows: she is likely to be in her late twenties or early thirties, from a Catholic and working-class background but upwardly mobile in a white-collar job; she has an undergraduate degree or is earning one, and lives with her boyfriend with no intention of ever marrying. Also, she is likely to be attractive and have long hair, and to wear flamboyant clothing.

A comparison of the male and female members reveals that twice as many men join as women, and that there is a larger proportion of women in the Structure than among the inactive "Raelians." The sex ratios of members in the Structure, from the beginner level to Rael in level 6 are as follows:

Sex Ratios in the Raelian Structure in Canada

Level	Title	Female	Male
0	Probationer	14	23
1	Assistant Animator	48	52
2	Animator	45	77
3	Assistant Guide	25	34
4	Priest Guide	4	14
5	Bishop Guide	—	3
6	Planetary Guide	—	1

The Raelian survey (which does not distinguish between the sexes) indicates that 59 percent of *membres des structures* are *travailleurs*, 24 percent are students, 13 percent are "other," and only 5 percent are *menageres* or housekeepers. Our Dawson College survey showed that 28 out of 30 members grew up in families in which the mother was a "housewife." It is clear, however, that Raelian women have rejected this traditional role. The average age of members, according to the Raelian survey on 399 respondents, was 35, and the median age was 33.9 for those in the Structure and 32.3 for Raelians. Our Dawson survey (30 respondents) came up with 28 as the average age for women and 33 for men.

Concerning their sexual "lifestyles," or what the Raelian survey terms *le plan sexuel-affectif*, 28 percent of Structure members were *celibataire* or living alone and sexually inactive, 8 percent were living in couples (*ou en trio*) with *plusieurs rencontres extraco*. Thirteen percent were living alone with many sexual encounters, and 40 percent were sexually exclusive (*ou presque*) couples. Members outside the Structure were more likely to be celibate, and, if in couples, less likely to have an "open relationship."

Four of the 12 women in the Dawson College survey were mothers, and these women were older than the average age—between 35 and 41. All of them were single mothers, and had their children before becoming Raelians. Three of them had children who were in their teens and twenties and had recently received the transmission of the cellular plan. (The movement administers a test to children of members to ensure they are free from parental conditioning in their decision to join.) Although one Guide informed me that members of the Structure did not have children, another Assistant Guide assured me it was the individual's decision and, to prove it, pointed to a woman Assistant Guide who was showing off her new baby at the meeting. Unfortunately, we did not think to include a question in the survey form asking *who* they were living with, but our impressions from the meetings is that women and men in the Structure tend to form couples inside the movement.

Of the 30 respondents in the Dawson survey, all but one came from a Catholic background. Their parents (or rather their fathers) were described as fruit vendors, farmers, clerks, janitors, etc., and the respondents themselves tended to hold jobs in technologies or in para-scientific professions, such as lab technician, industrial technician, dental assistant, paramedic or male nurse, and security guard for a psychiatric ward. Also, a surprising number of strippers, both female and male, were encountered by this researcher and her students in the meetings. At one meeting we noted four male strippers present (fully clothed, but they had mentioned their profession in the course of our conversations).

My initial impression of this movement, from observing a great deal of same-sex caressing during the Sunday meetings, is that it attracted a high proportion of "gays" among its following. When I asked an Assistant Guide to give me an estimate of the number of homosexuals in the Quebec movement, he replied rather coldly, "We don't think in such narrow categories. Some of us are unisexual, some are bisexual, some trisexual, and a few of us are even quadrisexual." When I timidly enquired what the last category might represent, he leaned forward and whispered, "With the Elohim!"

Members exhibit a similar fluidity in their views on sexuality, and this was reflected in our Dawson survey. Whereas only two men identified themselves as "bisexual," and one as "homosexual," and all the women ticked the "heterosexual" box, many wrote comments in the margins besides their answers objecting to these "rigid" and "misleading" categories. Many of the women I interviewed described experiences in the sensual meditation camp which an outsider would probably categorize as "lesbian," but which the Raelians themselves would explain as "experimenting with our sensuality."

One twenty-four-year-old stripper explained how sensual meditation had changed her views on sexuality:

I am more open towards people. I used to be only interested in men, chasing the boys. But now, I see the beauty and sensuality of women, of all humans. I am not gay, but I've had experiences at the Sensual Meditation camp I really enjoyed with women, and I don't feel shy about touching my girlfriends anymore.

The conspicuous numbers of strippers, transvestites, and highly expressive homosexuals among the congregation might suggest that this movement is particularly attractive to people who define themselves as sexually marginal. To support this hunch, it should be noted that this researcher observed three transvestites and one transexual at the December 1988 Raelian disco dance. For the sexually "deviant" living in a Catholic culture where they are treated as sinners, the appeal of a community where their sexual experimentation, creativity, and exhibitionism are interpreted as charismatic—as signs of belonging to the elite, the sensually awake who will achieve salvation when the UFOs descend—is a phenomenon which is not difficult to understand.

In addressing the issue of the movement's appeal to women (and the sex ratio indicates it appeals more strongly to men), it could be argued on the basis of the interview data that one of the movement's attractions is its *holistic approach to sexuality*. This is not the only, nor indeed the main reason. Part of the process of "deconditioning" from Catholicism to Raelianism is to adopt a more positive view of the body, and to celebrate one's sexuality, linking it to a more general appreciation of the senses. In the Raelian worldview, human sexuality is aligned with the sacred cosmos and functions as a technique of telepathic communication (with the Elohim) and consciousness expansion (with the whole universe). For working-class Catholic women in Quebec, this religion offers a way out of the miasma of guilt and secrecy surrounding their sexuality, a miasma which clings more closely to woman as the "temptress" who is traditionally identified with nature and the body (Clarke and Richardson 1986).

One woman's testimonial printed in *Sensual Meditation* (1986c, 146) states:

When I discovered Sensual Meditation at twenty four years of age, I had my first orgasm . . . I express one wish, and that is for every woman to be able to discover this, especially as I have learned that 70 percent of women have never experienced an orgasm.

Another woman, an Assistant Guide originally from El Salvador, wrote in her questionnaire that her family had taught her that "sex was a sin," and on joining the Raelians she had come to feel "less guilty."

A thirty-three-year-old secretary and massage therapist, who joined ten years ago while undergoing a divorce, explained how participating in the Sensual Meditation camp had changed her attitudes towards her own sexuality, and she protested that Raelian sexual experimentation was not, as the media portrayed it, an "orgy."

> We have summer camp for two weeks. You don't have to stay for the whole two weeks, the first 5 or 6 days is the sensual meditation seminar that is given every year. This is the meditation technique the extraterrestrials taught Rael when he went on their planet. It's a technique where you can open your mind by opening all your senses. We fast for 24 hours and then we start opening our senses. In the next 24 hours we don't talk or eat or drink anything but water—we really get inside of ourselves. . . . After the 24 hours we start eating again, slowly, and the food! Just the smell of it is great after all that fasting.
>   A lot of people think that [it's an orgy], but most of those people never come to see what really happens. If it was like that I would never have joined the movement, because at first I was so shy! . . . I would just say "Hi!" to someone and I would blush drastically, I was so shy. I'll tell you frankly, if it had been like that I would never have joined, and it's not like that at all. It's funny the way people interpret things . . . they don't really check or ask questions, they just say what they've heard . . . anyways, that's not what happens at all, it's not like an orgy! We do, after 24 hours, have a supper and so on, when you can open up your senses, and if you do find someone appealing, if you feel like going with that person and sharing a beautiful evening or night with him or her . . . it could even be with another woman, but why not? It's beautiful, you're opening your senses, but you don't have to, it's not an obligation. If someone came to you and asked you, "I'd like to sleep with you" and you don't want to, and that person insists, well, that's not right. That person should not insist if he's really sincere with himself, herself. You're allowed to say no, that's part of the respect, the choice you have.
>   It's never happened to me like that, I've never had anybody come up to me and say, "Hey, baby! I'd like to sleep with you." It's not somebody you've never seen before. He's more likely to just come up and say, "I sincerely like you and I find you pretty." They're not going to say they want to sleep with you right away, because it's *sensuality* that comes out of it, not sexuality. Sensuality is when you eat, drink or smell something nice, or when you touch something that's soft, and it's the same thing with a person.[1]

FIGURE 9. Course of Awakening

Attendees at a Raelian "Course of Awakening," where they are taught Sensual Meditation techniques that help them rid themselves "of the repressive and moralistic social inhibitions which paralyse our joy of life." (Photo courtesy Raelian Movement)

The women seemed to be equally active in choosing their partners in sensuality as the men, and also free to refuse overtures from male leaders without suffering loss of status, as an interview with a twenty-four-year-old dancer at the Super Sexe Strip Club reveals:

J. How do you feel about Rael?

G. He has the power of the infinite in his eyes. He is so amazing, so warm. He is the most honest man I know.

J. Have you talked to him personally?

G. Not only was I allowed to talk to him, I was invited to make love with him!

J. Did you?

G. No, he's really not my style.

J. What is your style?

G. Someone I can give pleasure to and receive pleasure from.

J. Rael wasn't attractive enough?

G. It's not that, it just seems he's not my style.[2]

"Francine," one of the four female Bishop Guides and public relations officer for the Canadian movement might be the prototypical Raelian woman. She was interviewed at her apartment by Dawson students Thi Phuong Thao Nguyen and Tosca Rulli (who were somewhat nonplused when she answered the door in a bikini). She is thirty-three, from a "very poor" Catholic farming family near Quebec city; she received Rael's message at the age of twenty, and works as a real estate agent. When questioned concerning her own sexual orientation, she replied, "I'm heterosexual for now, but nothing is constant in the universe. [I] don't know if I might change later on. . . . It's not the sexual habit difference that is the problem, but the lack of respect of another's choice." Her insights into gender roles and authority in the Raelians are worth considering:

They are all considered equal—no discriminations, differences, or favoritism—they're all humans. There are more men guides than women but it's not because they are men, it's because women in our society don't have much chance to expand, but we're getting there! When you reach infinity you don't make differences between man and woman.

Besides noting in members an experimental approach towards their own sexuality, this researcher also observed in several members the assumption that the human body (with a bit of medical assistance) is highly malleable. Plastic surgery, body building, and bleached hair lend a sort of (nordic) Venice Beach glamour to the Montreal meetings. One of the Assistant Guides owes his life to regular kidney dialysis, and one of the Animators (a former Catholic priest) has had a face-lift and hair implant since joining the movement.

The most fluid approach to the body and its gender was found in one of the four woman Priest Guides in Canada, who is a transexual nicknamed "Kiki." She enjoys considerable respect within two international communities: the Raelians and Sexual Minorities. As a transexual, she has achieved a stable and apparently successful family life, which in many respects is closer to a "traditional" marriage than those of many contemporary women; she is a full-time homemaker for her adopted son and common-law husband and has been a volunteer social worker all her adult life. Her special function as a Priest Guide is to counsel Raelians undergoing sexual problems. Kiki is particularly well qualified for this task since she did ten years of volunteer work as a counselor for sexual minorities from her home through a telephone hotline, and Raelians believe her unique status as a transexual enables her to see human sexuality from both points of view. Kiki's first contact with the movement was through the famous transvestite Lana St. Cyr, a colleague in her nightclub circuit. The extract from her interview which follows demonstrates a radically alternative and experimental approach to romantic love and marriage. She began by explaining that her parents had always wanted a girl and proceeded to dress their baby boy in pink dresses until he reached school age and began to wear trousers:

> Kiki: It was very disorienting to have to change sex all of a sudden as a child, and it caused a total disequilibrium in me, so that between the ages of 4 to 27 I didn't really live, I vegetated. Then, at 27, I met my lifelong companion, Horace, who loved me for who I was, not for the sex which I happened to be in. There is no need to say that completely changed my life. With him I was able to realise my greatest fantasy: to become a wife and a mother. . . . So, [I] decided at the age of 32 to undergo the operation. I had my doubts, because I wondered about my husband; suppose he were homosexual, he would no longer be attracted to me. Also, what effect would it have on our son? I explained it to Horace and he was very understanding; he said it would make no difference, that he loved me for my mind and not for my cock and balls, and so I went in. . . . When I woke up from the operation he was standing there and he was holding a bouquet of roses and he said, "I

love you and now I can ask you to be my wife!" I was very
touched, but I laughed and answered, "If we love each other, what
difference would a contract make? I will live with you, but I will
never marry!"

    . . . I travel a lot for the movement and to the International
Transexuals Association. . . . Yes, my husband misses me, but he is
very occupied, he works for VIA RAIL, and we have an agreement that we can have pleasure with other people if the other is
not around. He trusts me, he knows I love him and I always use a
condom. Often when I travel on the airplane I will meet a man I
like and I am always honest and tell them this night is only for
pleasure, and I am also a lesbian, and sometimes I meet a woman
who attracts me.

It is perhaps significant that the most charismatic woman in the
Canadian movement is a transexual. No mere woman could choose to
refashion her own sexual lifestyle in such an impressive act of faith in
science. In an age critical of the ecological problems caused by science, in a religion which exalts the individual's power of choice, she
is a living testimony to the magic of scientists and the shamanic
power and mobility resulting from an experimental approach to sexuality.

REASONS PROPOSED FOR
WOMEN'S MINIMAL PART IN LEADERSHIP

    The rejection of marriage, the de-emphasis on motherhood and
the consensual support for women as *travailleurs* rather than
menageres—these values seem to augure power and authority for
women. Moreover, Rael preaches a kind of "feminization of millenarianism" which awards the role of world savior to women—and to men
who cultivate feminine qualities. Thus, there appear to be no obstacles
in terms of ideology, tradition, or sexist attitudes to prevent charismatic
women rising in the hierarchy. So what is stopping them?
    The reasons I propose are as follows:

1. A (male) gender bias in the language.
2. The central myth of the movement, which is one of male initiation, the
   hero's quest for his true father.
3. Rael's own "sexual lifestyle."

A Gender Bias in the Language

The Elohim are always referred to as "our *Fathers* from Space" who created *men* in their own image. The first aliens Rael encountered in 1973 were male, and the great scientists of Genesis who came to Earth to "implant" *mankind* are men in the illustrations. The renegade scientists of the "Fall" who interbred with mortal women must, presumably, have been males, as were the space alien fathers of the forty prophets (who also happen to be male): "When the Sons of Elohim had intercourse with the daughters of men and had children by them, the Nephelin (mighty men) were on earth, they were the heroes of old, men of renown" (Vorilhon 1986b, 3-4). While non-inclusive language is, perhaps, not sufficient in itself to undermine female leadership (Rajneesh's discourses, for example, are in British Raj prose, and yet he strongly encourages female leadership), the absence of female role models could represent a more serious obstacle to Raelian women.

The Myth of Male Initiation

Rael writes of his visit to the planet of the Elohim where he had an emotional encounter with an alien called "Yahweh," who responds to Rael's question concerning his own origins by addressing him as "*tu*" rather than as "*vous*," and then proceeds to relate the events leading up to Rael's birth:

> After the explosion at Hiroshima we decided that the time had come for us to send a new messenger on Earth. . . . We then selected a woman, as we had done in the time of Jesus. This woman was taken aboard one of our ships and inseminated as we had done with the mother of Jesus. Then she was freed after we had totally erased from her memory all traces of what had happened. (Vorilhon 1986b, 105)

(Having related this tale, Yahweh turns to Rael, who sees in his eyes "a great emotion and feeling of love" and says to him, "From this moment on you may call me father, because you are my son"—and Rael notes of his half-brother, "Jesus too seemed to be moved by the same feelings. Then I kissed my father and my brother for the very first time.")

It is tempting to use this material to concoct what Jon Wagner (1986) deplores, a "capsule psychobiography" of a religious founder: Rael, who experienced a long and difficult birth in a Vichy clinic, whose mother pretended he was not her child; Rael, who grew up in a small French village as an illegitimate and fatherless child, brought up by his adoring grandmother and aunt; Rael, who heard his biological father was a Jewish refugee; this child grows up and proceeds to create an original religion based on the central myth of the mighty fathers from space descending to claim their sons who are undergoing the dangerous process of coming of age. Women in this myth—and in Rael's life on planet Earth—appear shadowy and interchangeable, and their loving attentions are taken for granted.

Women are not powerful in this Creation myth. There was no question of "choice" when the Virgin Mary was selected for her "virgin DNA"—not even the opportunity to deliver a "handmaid of the Lord" speech. She and Rael's mother were impregnated as unceremoniously as laboratory animals. There was no "meaningful relationship" between Yahweh and these mortal women; they were not included in the ecstatic family reunion when Rael "kissed my father and brother for the first time." (While it is tempting to dabble in pop psychology in this case, and to explore the Oedipal content of Rael's reported conversations with his spacefather, there is an element of hubris involved in the sociologist's attempt to plumb the psychological motivations of a complex and creative genius like Rael—or any religious innovator—since this kind of analysis tends to reduce or trivialize the religious content of their visions.) Aside from these issues, Raelian mythology speaks to men more than to women.

Rael's Personal Lifestyle

Whereas Rael makes it clear that everyone should choose their *own* sexual lifestyle, it appears reasonable to assume that—as in any charismatic community—the leader's intimate relationships are carefully scrutinized by his/her followers, and provide (perhaps unconsciously) a model for conducting their own relationships. Rael was married and a father when he began his charismatic career in 1973, but he has since separated from his wife (who with his kids has joined his movement). For several years he has travelled in the company of his "Japanese girlfriend"—who is not necessarily the *same* Japanese girl every year. Although Rael appears to be exclusively heterosexual, he advocates homosexual experimentation and wrote a love song about lesbian spiders. He eschews the macho image and is often described as "gentle" and "feminine" by his followers. When Rael was grilled in a television interview by an aggressive journalist who ask him outright if he had sex with several different partners everyday, Rael replied with self-deprecating humor, "I am 44 years old. Sometimes it is difficult for me to make love even once a day!" His photographic image, however, resembles that of Hugh Heffner. Photographs of Rael appearing in the movement's magazine, *Apocalypse*, nearly always show him surrounded by young, scantily clad beauties—and they are always different beauties. A film made by Radio Canada (*They're Coming!*) features a scene with Rael surrounded on a Mediterranean terrace by four beauties who, because of their racial diversity and bared left shoulders, might be candidates for the Miss Universe contest. While they did not actually peel grapes, they did offer Rael a bowl of fruit.

While this kind of publicity tells us nothing of substance about Rael's private life (except that he seems to enjoy being photographed with beautiful women), and his insensitivity regarding gender-specific language can be excused in one who claims to be from another planet, it appears reasonable to assume that women who define themselves as feminists, on first encountering this literature, might be slightly put off by the sexy biological robots, the alien-inseminated, amnesic virgins, and Rael's bevy of Oriental playmates. Outsiders unfamiliar with the feminist dimensions and complexity of his philosophy of sexuality might even dismiss his organization as "sexist" in the same way that journalists, on seeing the symbol of the swastika and hearing Rael's theory of Jews as descendants of space aliens, have (unjustly) accused him of neo-Nazism. These initial impressions might influence the recruitment of women into the movement.

These three reasons (the language, the mythology and Rael's example), therefore, appear to be deep-seated and unconscious barriers to women's claiming authority in the Structure—at least during the present phase. In a movement so committed to experimentation and individualism, however, it is not unlikely that the situation might change. One of the four women Priest Guides of Canada has just been appointed to head the Raelian movement in the United States, which has begun to respond positively to the message, and the Korean leader is also female.

The Raelians' patterns of authority suggest that "equality" is not a good enough place to start for women aspiring to religious leadership. After all, leaders in charismatic communities must exhibit special (as opposed to equal) qualities. Two NRMs which favor feminine leadership—the Brahmakumaris and the Rajneesh—espouse a view of gender that Rosemary Reuther (1983) has labelled "radical romantic feminism," the view that women possess unique spiritual qualities superior to those of men.

EXTRATERRESTRIALS AND CHARISMA

How does charisma operate in the Raelian movement and how does the authority of the Elohim invested in Rael percolate down through the structure? What is the extent of the influence Rael exerts over members' lives, and what degree of commitment does the movement demand? Our Dawson College survey at the November, 1992, meeting attempted to address these questions. Nine Dawson students passed out fifty questionnaire forms, and managed to receive thirty-three responses. Question six asked: (a) Had you read science fiction books before joining; (b) Were you already interested in UFO sightings and contactees? (c) Had you ever seen a UFO or felt the presence of extraterrestrials before? As the results below indicate, it appears the majority of members were interested in aliens and UFO lore before encountering the movement, but had not realized the personal, emotional, or religious implications of this interest until meeting Rael himself.

Dawson College "Raeliens and Charisma" Survey Form

Previous Interest	Negative	Positive
Read Sci Fi	11	22
Aware UFOs, contactees	8	25
Seen UFO, felt ETs	20	13

As the table above demonstrates, there is no evidence that "joiners" were necessarily more deeply versed in science fiction than their contemporaries. Although twenty-two (22) respondents claimed they had read science fiction, the responses to question nine, indicated they had apparently not read very much; most were familiar with only the most popular "golden age" writers like Asimov, but had watched a lot of Star Trek and seen sci fi movies. In contrast, their interest in UFO sightings and contactee reports was deeper; they had read widely, and kept clippings. Whereas only eight (8) had felt the presence of extraterrestrials before encountering the movement, five (5) claimed to have actually seen UFOs.

The Raelians' attitude to other UFO cults and contactees is ambiguous. While they are quick to point to reports of UFO sightings in the news as corroborating Rael's story, they are inclined to dismiss the claims of career contactees as erroneous. Thus, while many members were interested in the possibility of communication with extraterrestrials before encountering the message, they now disassociate themselves from ufologists, and play down the numinous quality of encounters of the third kind. One Priest Guide declared it had always been obvious to him there was intelligent life outside this planet, but only when he met Rael could he say, "I found something . . . and it fitted!" He outlined the movement's position on UFOs as follows:

> We often encounter ufologists or UFO addicts similar to 'trekkies,' who are interested in nothing but UFOs, but we're not interested in UFOs *per se*, just the Message and those people who might be *inside* the UFOs.

A key to understanding how charisma operates in the movement was found in the responses to question ten. Question ten was worded as follows:

> When (if ever) do you feel in mental communication with extraterrestrials?
>
> a) During Sensual Meditation?
> b) In the presence of Rael?
> c) Through the guides?
> d) Other occasions?

The majority (17) of respondents claimed they felt in touch with the Elohim in the Sensual Meditation, whereas only six (6) felt in contact through Rael's presence, and only one (1) respondent felt. in contact through a guide. In response to question eleven, regarding the initiation ritual ("Describe how you felt during the transmission of the Cellular Plan"), only four (4) initiates felt a sense of communication with the Elohim. Three (3) respondents reported feeling "nothing," two (2) felt joy in belonging to *la belle famille Raelien*, nine (9) expressed feelings of happiness and satisfaction, two (2) were "set free," and four (4) reported intense or dramatic experiences. "I felt filled up to the brim, enlightened"; "My emotions were so strong, I wept"; "I felt waves of electricity from Rael's hands," and "Nothing at the time, but then all night I was having visions of criss-cross hexagonal forms."

Members are encouraged to practice a guided meditation/visualization technique daily, the aim being to transmit love to and telepathic links with the Elohim and to achieve harmony with infinity. This technique involves relaxation, situating the self in relation to the surrounding world, and expanding one's frame of reference until the self becomes a tiny atom in the galaxy. Next, through body consciousness, sensitivity, and sensual stimulation, the bones and organs are visualized and, finally, the atoms of the body. Through making this mental leap from microcosm to macrocosm, Raelians seek to achieve harmony with the infinite and with their Creators. Responses to the questionnaire revealed that experiences as varied as sensations of physical well-being, psychic abilities, enjoying the beauty of nature, and sexual arousal were all interpreted as signs of establishing telepathic communication with the Elohim. The responses to questions ten and eleven, therefore, suggest that Raelians undergo an educational process whereby they learn to contact and recognize the charisma of aliens through practicing this meditation ritual, in which Rael himself was instructed when he visited the planet of the Elohim.

Rael creates the impression of being a gentle, unpretentious and reasonable man. He usually underplays his prophetic role ("Do not look at my finger, look at what it's pointing to"), but at other times seems to employ charisma-building strategies. He tends to drop into meetings as if he just fell to Earth. In his last appearance in Montreal, for example, he crept in during the oxygenation ritual while peoples' eyes were shut, and took over the microphone. Hearing his voice, the Raelians opened their eyes and cheered, and he stood smiling in his heavily padded white "spacesuit," his long hair and beard disheveled as if he had just removed a space helmet. A guide who had been lying on the ground oxygenating then stood up and declared, "I had my eyes shut, but suddenly I felt a violent storm of serenity and peace, and I knew Rael must be near!"

Only Rael's own communications with the Elohim are recognized as authentic. The former National Guide of Canada, Victor Legendre, resigned his position and left the movement in August, 1992, because his girlfriend was a "mystic" and claimed she had received a message from aliens and that Rael was not the only prophet of our time. She was in level 3 of the Structure, but began to challenge Rael's scientific materialism by announcing she was a reincarnation of a seventeenth-century French prophetess, and by exhibiting telekinetic powers in lifting tables—and Legendre supported her claims. He was confronted by Rael at the summer Sensual Meditation Camp and asked to choose between the movement and his girlfriend. At first he renounced her, but later admitted he was too much in love and chose to resign instead. The Raelians appeared to enjoy this drama, and the National Guide exited not as one in disgrace, but rather as a romantic hero. "He was torn between the movement and his love for a woman. . . . His love was stronger than the message," one female Assistant Guide commented approvingly.[3]

In spite of Rael's bouts of house cleaning, his claim to be half alien, and his millenarian message, he conforms more closely to Weber's

FIGURE 10. Rael

Publicity photo of Rael, founder of the Raelian movement, addressing a gathering. Rael claims that his mother was inseminated in a UFO, and that he is the offspring from this union. (Photo courtesy Raelian Movement)

model of an exemplary prophet than to the more exalted and demand-
ing ethical type of prophet (Gerth and Wright 1946). Members interviewed tended to stress the appeal of the message and of the Raelian
community rather than the lure of Rael's charisma in describing how
they joined. It appears that discipline over the outer circle of members is
weak, for many Raelians interviewed confessed to not paying their
tithing, and to indulging in wine and cigarettes. Members of the core
group or Structure, on the other hand, appear to be scrupulous in paying their tithing, and in refraining from reproducing and from recreational drugs—and they are more likely to view Rael as an ethical
prophet. Rael's speeches constantly emphasize the importance of choice,
individuality, and freedom. Raelians tune in to their inner voices of
authority through the ritual breaking of taboos and therapeutic cathar-
sis and seem to emerge with clearer sense of identity and direction.
When they look to Rael, it is not to be told how to live their lives, but
rather for inspiration—as a living example of the self-made, self-realized
man of the future.

SOCIAL CHANGE AND NEW RELIGIOUS SEXUAL EXPERIMENTATION

The striking contrast between the young Raelians and their
Catholic working-class parents' values echoes the dramatic upheavals
occurring in the structure of the family in Quebec, particularly since the
1960s. Baker (1990) notes that the early inhabitants of New France exhibited a "phenomenal rate of population growth" with a birth rate of 50 to
65 per 1,000—one of the largest fertility rates in the world. The typical
family produced eight children, and girls married as early as twelve or
thirteen. Local priests exerted authority over fertility issues and family
life. The father ruled over the domestic sphere, his wife obeyed, and
"children" up to age thirty had to receive his permission to marry.
Quebec's family law is different from the rest of Canada. The Civil Code
of 1886 gave women no control over their own property, and any wages
she received were to be handed over to her husband. Voting rights were
not granted to women until 1940. Since 1967, however, the province has
witnessed the diminishing authority of priests and fathers. Due to the
forces of secularization, urbanization, and the feminist movement, the
birth rate in Quebec has declined sharply. By 1986 it was 13.1 per 1,000—
the lowest in the country. Since 1977 Quebec's divorce rate has been
close to the national figure, and yet its marriage rate is the lowest. In
1985, Quebec's marriage rate was only 560, contrasting with Canada's of

730. These statistics point to the forces of secularization within Quebec society, and Hobart (1989, 64-66) found Francophone youth to be more permissive than an Anglophone sample regarding premarital sex.

Considered within this social context, the Raelian Mouvement Canadien might be regarded as an extreme version, almost a parody, of Quebec "sexual lifestyles." Quebecois youth investigating this new religious movement find a forum for experimenting with sexuality. As Robbins and Bromley (1992) point out, one of the most significant contributions of NRMs is in providing laboratories for experimentation in economic patterns and gender roles. Participants in the two-week Sensual Meditation seminars discover a playing field within which they can engage in a process of radical self-reconstruction and try out new forms of authority and new modes of self-other relating.

Angela Aidala (1985) has argued that part of the appeal of religious communes to contemporary youth intolerant of the shifting interpretations of masculine-feminine, is their clear-cut, unambiguous "traditional" gender roles, which she views as a reaction against and rejection of the ongoing experimentation surrounding gender issues occurring in the larger society. Unlike Aidala's religious communards, the Raelians are flamboyantly experimental and innovative in the area of sexuality and sex roles. Nevertheless, it could be argued that the Raelians' almost militant tolerance of bisexuality and pluralistic sexual experimentation is just another route towards resolving the confusion and ambiguity surrounding gender in our modern world. Thus, young Raelians might be experiencing the same sense of anomy which was reflected in Aidala's sample (1985), and the same need for authority and certainty. In Rael they have found an outspoken advocate of sexual freedom who just so happens to validate their life choices. Within the context of the Raelian cosmology, non-procreative polymorphous sexual expression is defined as an ecologically sound and even mystical endeavor, leading to telepathic communication with the aliens, promoting world peace, and enhancing individual intelligence. Raelians participate through the ritual breaking of sexual taboos in forging a new code of sexual ethics which is quite as "ideologically rigid" and "morally absolute" (in its own way) as the neo-conservative family roles developed in Aidala's communes. I would argue, therefore, that young Raelians are *also* responding to moral ambiguity and cultural crisis, but that what is attractive about this particular NRM is that it offers a forum for experimenting with gender that is even *more intense* and extreme than is possible in the larger society. This degree of freedom and intensity is possible only within the boundaries of an organization based on charismatic authority.

NOTES

1. Interview conducted by Dawson student, Jerry Evangelista.

2. Interview conducted by Dawson student, Jackie Hermann.

3. An account of this crisis in leadership was related to me by three Animators on different occasions, and their stories "jived." They explained in a down-to-earth fashion that rival contactee claims could not be tolerated, as they would give rise to schism.

REFERENCES

Aidala, Angela. 1985. "Social Change, Gender Roles, and New Religious Movements." *Sociological Analysis* 46, no. 3:287-314.

Allen, Prudence. 1987. "Two Mediaeval Views on Woman's Identity: Hildegarde of Bingen and Thomas Aquinas." *Studies in The Religion/Sciences Religeuses* 16, no. 1:21-36.

Apocalypse. Bulletin de Liaison du Mouvement Raelien International.

Balch, Robert. 1982. "Bo and Peep: A Case Study of the Origins of Messianic Leadership." In *Millennialism and Charisma*, edited by Roy Wallis, 13-22. Belfast: The Queen's University.

Barker, Eileen. 1989. *New Religious Movements*. London: HMSO.

Bednarowski, Mary Farrell. 1980. "Outside the Mainstream: Women's Religion and Women Religious Leaders in Nineteenth Century America." *Journal of the American Academy of Religion* 48:207-31.

Bouchard, Alain. 1989. "Mouvement Raelien." In *Nouvel Age . . . Nouvelles Croyances* (sous la direction du Centre d'Information sur les Nouvelles Religions). Montreal: Editions Pailines and Mediaspaul.

Braun, Kirk. 1984. *Rajneeshpuram: The Unwelcome Society*. West Linn, Oreg.: Scouts Creek Press.

Clark, Elizabeth, and Herbert Richardson. 1977. *Women and Religion*. New York: Harper and Row.

Foster, Lawrence. 1981. *Religion and Sexuality*. New York: Oxford University Press.

Kanter, Rosabeth Moss. 1972. *Commitment and Community: Communes and Utopias in Sociological Perspective*. Cambridge, Mass.: Harvard University Press.

Palmer, Susan J. 1990. "Moon Sisters, Rajneesh Lovers, Krishna Mothers: Women's Roles in New Religious Movements." In *Gender in World Religions*, vol. 1:19-56. Montreal: McGill University.

Reuther, Rosemary Radford. 1983. *Sexism and God Talk*. Boston: Beacon Press.

Vorilhon, Claude. 1977. *La Geniocratie*. Brantome: l'Edition du Message.

————. 1986a. *Extraterrestrials Took Me to Their Planet*. Brantome: l'Edition du Message.

————. 1986b. *Let's Welcome Our Fathers from Space: They Created Humanity in Their Laboratories*. Tokyo: AOM Corporation.

————. 1986c. *Sensual Meditation*. Tokyo: AOM Corporation.

Wagner, Jon. 1986. "Sexuality and Gender Roles in Utopian Communities: A Critical Survey of Scholarly Work." *Communal Societies* 6:172-88.

Wallis, Roy. 1979. *Salvation and Protest*. London: Francis Pinter.

Weber, Max. 1946. *Essays in Sociology*. Edited by H. Gerth and C. Wright Mills. New York: Oxford University Press.

Worseley, Peter. 1968. *The Trumpet Shall Sound*. New York: Schocken Books.

6

WAITING FOR THE SHIPS: DISILLUSIONMENT AND THE REVITALIZATION OF FAITH IN BO AND PEEP'S UFO CULT[1]

Robert W. Balch

In September of 1975 a mysterious couple known as "the Two" gave a public lecture about UFOs at a resort in the seaside community of Waldport, Oregon. A few days later over thirty people suddenly vanished without a trace, and their disappearance swelled into one of the biggest media sensations of the year. Almost every day for the next two months, newspapers across the United States regaled the public with stories of starry-eyed seekers who had given up their friends, families, houses, and jobs in hopes of getting "beamed up" to flying saucers that would whisk them away to a higher plane of existence known as "the next evolutionary kingdom." The Two claimed to be from outer space, and their names, Bo and Peep, added a touch of absurdity to the story.

Bo and Peep turned out to be the leaders of a messianic UFO cult, and the people who disappeared in Oregon were among those hoping to be onboard when the ships left Earth for the "level above human." Reporters called the group "HIM," short for "human individual metamorphosis," which was Bo and Peep's name for the process of overcoming human attachments. In fact, the cult had no name for itself, and to members it was known only as "the group." Like many new religious movements in the 1970s, the cult was a totalistic, millenarian movement that appealed mainly to idealistic young seekers whose dreams of a new age had been dashed by the collapse of idealism at the end of the sixties (Foss and Larkin 1976).

Shortly after the Waldport meeting, David Taylor and I infiltrated the group to discover what had become of the Oregon recruits. Several months later we interviewed defectors to find out why they had joined and what led to their leaving. In two subsequent papers (Balch and Taylor 1977a; Balch 1980), we argued that the UFO people joined voluntarily without pressure to convert. Our observations indicated that some of the most dramatic changes in their behavior, such as giving away their possessions and enthusiastically espousing the group's beliefs, occurred *before* they were integrated into the group. Our data also showed that many new members who outwardly appeared to be true believers spent much of their time struggling with doubts and debating with themselves about whether to stay or leave. Based on these observations, we concluded that actions which outsiders took as evidence of brainwashing and sudden conversion could be explained more simply and more adequately as anticipatory socialization and voluntary role playing.

As a result, we soon found ourselves characterized as partisans in the ideological war over cults. Our papers were cited as evidence against the popular brainwashing argument, but as I followed developments in the UFO cult over the next few years, I began to wonder if we had overstated our case by focusing on the recruitment process without describing what happened after people joined. In fact, most members dropped out within a few months. The group was so disorganized, and its socialization techniques were so undefined, that the group could not sustain the commitment of its members. It was not until Bo and Peep radically restructured the group that the defection rate declined.

Lofland and Stark (1965) were among the first to call attention to the difference between joining a cult and becoming committed to it. In their study of conversion to the Divine Precepts cult (a pseudonym for the Unification Church), they contrasted "verbal converts," who merely professed belief, with "total converts" who "put their lives at the disposal of the cult." They found that personal and situational factors were sufficient to create verbal converts, but that intensive, daily interaction with members was required to transform recruits into deployable agents who could be counted on to make the sacrifices and investments expected of true believers. Similarly, Long and Hadden (1983) hypothesized that *recruiting* members involves different processes than *keeping* them, and the history of the UFO cult bears them out. Although voluntary affiliation was accompanied by outward displays of conviction, it was not enough to create a committed, deployable membership.

In this chapter I will argue that genuine commitment did not develop until Bo and Peep introduced social influence processes that are usually associated with the brainwashing model, such as the regimentation of daily life and the use of mental exercises to eliminate independent thinking. To do this, I will trace the early history of the UFO cult, focusing on changes in the group's socialization techniques and the commitment of its members. But first I need to describe the study itself.

STUDYING THE UFO CULT

I first encountered the UFO people six weeks after the Waldport meeting, when about twenty-five members presented "the message" at a similar meeting at Yavapai Community College in Prescott, Arizona. They were on their way to California where they expected to meet up with the Two and the rest of the group. Since I was on leave from the University of Montana and had no commitments at the time, I thought about asking if I could come along to document their final days on the planet. However, it quickly became obvious that it would be impossible to study the cult using conventional sociological methods. The reason was the group's obsession with "spirits."

Spirits were attachments to the "human level" that took the form of doubts, desires, old habits, and memories of friends and relatives who had been left behind. Only when these "influences" had been overcome would members be eligible to enter the "next kingdom." To protect their followers from these spirits, Bo and Peep had created an encapsulated environment where outsiders of any kind were unwelcome. Members typically stayed in isolated campgrounds, and if anyone asked who they were, they usually identified themselves as a Bible-study group on a retreat or adopted some similar cover to conceal their identity.

Even during public meetings, members insulated themselves from outsiders. Contact with the audience was limited to a formal presentation followed by a question-and-answer period. Afterwards they took the names and phone numbers of those who wanted more information, and then, making sure they weren't followed, they would slip away to a secret campsite where they wouldn't be bothered by spirits or outsiders who might harass them for their unusual beliefs.

Once I understood the concept of spirits, I decided not to identify myself as a sociologist. I left my number and that night got a call telling me the location of another meeting the next afternoon. It was during the follow-up meeting that I decided to infiltrate. Afterwards I called David Taylor, then a graduate student at the University of Montana, who agreed to join me when I got to California. We spent the next two months posing as new members. During that time we came into contact with about 100 members, roughly half the people who belonged to the group at its maximum size.

It was relatively easy to play the role of committed believers because group norms discouraged members from forming friendships or revealing their true feelings. The people we observed generally kept to themselves, devoting their energy to overcoming their "humanness," so most of the time we had little trouble taking part in the group without committing ourselves. Recording observations was another matter. We had to write our notes in bathroom stalls or get up before dawn when we could write while everyone else was still asleep.

The ethical problems of undercover research did not occur to us until we were inside the group. Instead of the mindless converts portrayed in the media, we discovered ordinary people searching for truth and struggling with doubt. Beneath the facade of uniformity that members presented to the public, we found a range of personalities at least as wide as what I routinely encounter in a large university class. In fact, aside from their beliefs, most members were indistinguishable from ordinary college students. These were revealing but disconcerting revelations—revealing because they called into question the popular concept of brainwashing; disconcerting because we were deceiving people who in many ways weren't much different from ourselves.

In March of 1976 we started interviewing ex-members. Taylor eventually left the study to work on his Ph.D., but I continued collecting data until 1983, interviewing defectors who had left the group as late as 1981. Using a snowball technique to locate informants, we interviewed forty-three dropouts, including Bo and Peep's first follower who helped put me in touch with people who had known the Two before their "awakening." Considering that the group probably never had more than two hundred members at its largest point, the sample is relatively large, and based on our observations, it appears to be a good representation of the group as a whole. Only eight of our informants had defected after June, 1976, but they proved to be especially important because they described a group that was radically different from the cult Taylor and I observed in 1975.

I was surprised to find that dropouts were willing to be interviewed even after we explained our deception. Only four people refused, and none expressed any hostility. Several informants told us that the only way anyone could have understood the UFO cult was by becoming part of it. The inside knowledge we acquired as members turned out to be invaluable during our interviews. Since we already understood the group's structure and beliefs, we could concentrate on the details of our informants' experiences. In many cases we could check the validity of their accounts by comparing what they said with what we had recorded in our field notes. Contrary to the argument that retrospective accounts can't be trusted (Taylor 1976), our informants turned out to be quite reliable.

The greatest inconsistencies were in the interviews I had with members who left the group after 1975. While their accounts of what happened in the group were very similar, they often disagreed about dates, the sequence of events, and the size of the group at different times. I think the inconsistencies stem from the group's increased isolation and focus on the present after 1975, which I will describe later. These changes cut members loose from the conventional anchors of calendar-based time. Whatever the reason for the inconsistencies, my chronicle is only an approximation of the group's history. It may contain some factual errors, but I believe the overall picture is accurate.

EARLY HISTORY: FROM TEXAS TO OREGON

The UFO cult was started by a middle-aged Texas couple named Marshall Herff Applewhite and Bonnie Lu Nettles (Balch 1982a). Herff, as he was known to friends, was a former music professor, and Bonnie had been a nurse in a Houston hospital. Although raised as a Baptist, Bonnie was a member of the Houston Theosophical Society, and she belonged to a meditation group that channeled messages from discarnate spirits. Herff's background was more conventional. The son of a Presbyterian minister, he had studied for the ministry and later got a music degree at the University of Colorado. After a brief stint on the music faculty at the University of Alabama, he was hired by St. Thomas University in Houston to establish a Fine Arts program.

Despite appearances, Herff's former friends reported that he was a troubled person. Though married with two children, Herff secretly had numerous homosexual affairs. He felt guilty about his double life, and confided to at least one of his lovers his longing for a meaningful, platonic relationship where he could develop his full potential without sexual entanglements. After getting divorced, Herff vacillated between homosexual and heterosexual identities, never feeling comfortable with either.

At St. Thomas Herff quickly became a charismatic teacher and successful fundraiser for the university. His musical productions won rave reviews in the Houston press. Then in 1970, at the peak of his career, Herff was abruptly dismissed following a scandal involving a relationship with one of his students. Herff was devastated. Friends described him as bitter, confused, and deeply depressed. Not long afterwards he reportedly began hearing voices, which only added to his confusion.

Bonnie entered the picture in 1972. After a chance meeting in the hospital where she worked, Herff and Bonnie became inseparable. In Bonnie, Herff finally found the platonic "helper" he had longed for all his life. It was Bonnie who introduced Herff to the world of metaphysics. Later that year they embarked on a short-lived venture called the Christian Arts Center where Bonnie offered classes in astrology, mysticism, and Theosophy, and Herff taught the performing arts. Although the Center closed in a few months, Herff and Bonnie continued holding classes in a house they called "Knowplace." Gradually they withdrew from their friends, becoming absorbed in a private world of visions, dreams, and paranormal experiences that included contacts with space beings who urged them to abandon their worldly pursuits.

Then in 1973 Herff and Bonnie suddenly left Houston. Convinced they had an important mission together, they set out to discover their higher purpose. After months of traveling and doing odd jobs to support themselves, they set up camp along the Rogue River near the Oregon coast in an isolated spot they called "Hideaway." Six weeks later, in a revelation Herff compared to taking a "whiff of smelling salts," the pieces of the puzzle fell into place. They realized they were the two witnesses prophesied in Revelation 11. After spreading God's word, they would be assassinated and their bodies would lie in the street for three and a half days. Then they would rise from the dead and "ascend up to heaven in a cloud" (Rev. 11:12). Herff and Bonnie believed the cloud referred to a spacecraft.

It was well over a year before Herff and Bonnie came across a group of people who wanted to follow them (Balch 1982b). The location was Los Angeles. In the spring of 1975 a metaphysical teacher named Clarence Klug asked them to speak to his students. By then Herff and Bonnie had stopped using their human names. Instead they introduced themselves as Guinea and Pig, a humorous comment on their role in what they described as a cosmic experiment.

Twenty-four people, including Clarence, decided to join. To symbolize their role as space-age shepherds, Herff and Bonnie changed their names to Bo and Peep. Two weeks later they led their flock back to the Oregon coast where the UFO cult began taking shape. The structure Bo and Peep created was designed to lead members through an awakening similar to their own. They put men and women together in platonic partnerships where each was expected to help the other in the overcoming process. Members spent most of their time alone with their partners "tuning in" to the "next level," just as Bo and Peep had done during their six weeks on the Rogue River.

SPREADING THE MESSAGE

The next phase began in the summer of 1975 when Bo and Peep sent their followers out on the road to be tested by the next level. Except for a few trusted believers who stayed with Bo and Peep, each partnership traveled alone. The Two claimed "members of the next kingdom" would guide them through the experiences they needed to complete their overcoming. One of the most important was the experience of being "rejected of men." Members had to "test the churches," which meant asking ministers for food and gas money. Besides the obvious purpose of surviving day to day, "testing" provided preachers with an opportunity to demonstrate their Christian commitment, and it helped Bo and Peep's followers overcome their human pride.

During this phase, the group's most important objective was to tell others about Bo and Peep's message. By the time of the Waldport meeting the members had gathered momentum and found a successful way of delivering their information about the next level. They advertised the meeting with posters from Portland to northern California. On September 14 about two hundred people gathered to hear Bo and Peep explain how to gain eternal life in the "level above human." Bo and Peep sat at the front of the room, flanked by members known as "buffers" whose job was to absorb "negativity" from the audience.

They explained that "the Father's kingdom' is not a spiritual realm as Christians believe, but the "literal heavens," meaning the entire universe, and the only way to get there is in a spacecraft. Earth is just one of countless heavenly "gardens" that members of the next level planted with the seeds of consciousness millions of years ago. Now, they said, this garden is being prepared for its first and possibly last "harvest." Only by escaping the planet's spiritually poisoned atmosphere could humans expect to break the endless cycle of death and reincarnation. Once seekers reached the next level, they would become immortal, androgynous beings living in a state of perpetual growth.

Bo and Peep compared the seekers in the audience to caterpillars striving to become butterflies. To transform themselves into heavenly beings, the seekers would have to enter a chrysalis state, separating themselves from the world and turning all their energy inward, a process they called "human individual metamorphosis." The first step was to "walk out the door of your life." This meant giving up all attachments to the human level.

The Two claimed the harvest was drawing to a close. Within a few months, possibly weeks, they would fulfill the prophecy of Revelation 11 by being assassinated. They called the event "the demonstration" because their death and resurrection would demonstrate the truth of the message. After their ascension, their followers would be taken to the Father's kingdom in spaceships. This time thirty-three people decided to join.

After Waldport the Two held another meeting in Denver and then headed to Illinois. There, however, two men infiltrated the group in hopes of finding a friend who had joined in Oregon. When they were discovered, Bo and Peep abandoned plans to hold a meeting in Chicago. Fearing assassination before all the "ripe fruit" could be harvested, they announced they were "withdrawing into the wilderness" to prepare for the demonstration. They split the cult into small groups, each headed by two "spokesmen" consisting of a trusted partnership, and sent them in different directions to spread the message. Then Bo and Peep disappeared.

BECOMING A MEMBER

Even without its leaders, the UFO cult continued to grow. Most members joined in the West, but some joined as far away as Massachusetts and Florida. Although ages ranged from fourteen to seventy-five, most members were in their early twenties. Males slightly outnumbered females, and except for two blacks, one of whom left within a week, everyone was white.

Nearly every member joined at a meeting like the one in Waldport. In almost every case the format was the same: a formal presentation followed by a question-and-answer period, and then a follow-up meeting a day or two later. Aside from these brief encounters, people who were interested in joining had no contact with members. The procedure protected members from spirits and allowed seekers to make up their minds without pressure to join. Bo and Peep emphasized the importance of free choice. Seekers had to want membership in the next kingdom more than anything else. Those who had to be persuaded obviously weren't ready to leave the planet.

I was surprised at how quickly people decided to join. The day after the Prescott meeting, about fifteen people came to the follow-up session. Eight had already decided to join, and one more made up her mind later in the day. They acted so much like people who already belonged to the group that during the follow-up meeting I had trouble distinguishing them from actual members. Their conversations were peppered with terms and expressions from the message, and they talked excitedly about the demonstration. Within two days they had given away all their possessions, except for cars and camping gear, and they were on their way to California to meet Bo and Peep. Even more dramatic were a few new members who decided to join based on nothing more than what they heard in sensationalized news stories. I met one couple who had traveled seven thousand miles to find the group, but who decided not to join because they would have had to give up their children, who were too young to decide for themselves if they wanted to be "on the process."

Most of the people who joined the UFO cult were spiritual seekers who shared a worldview where reincarnation, lost continents, flying saucers, and psychic phenomena were taken for granted (Balch and Taylor 1977a). Today this worldview is called New Age, but in the 1970s, before that term became commonplace, people were more likely to say they were "into metaphysics."

With few exceptions they could be grouped in two categories based on their relationship to the dominant culture. The first included most of the people who joined in Los Angeles with Clarence Klug. Like Bonnie Nettles, they had middle-class jobs and led conventional lives, rejecting both drugs and anti-war protests. The only thing setting them apart from mainstream American culture was their involvement in metaphysics. However, most of Bo and Peep's followers, including nearly all the Oregon recruits, belonged to the second category. They were younger and more likely to have been involved in the hippie counterculture. Though the majority came from middle-class backgrounds, they lived on the margins of society, living simply and working sporadically at lowpaying jobs.

While the news media played up the sacrifices people made to join the group, most of the new members from either category had little to lose. On the whole they were young, single or divorced, highly mobile, and free of serious commitments. Those who had full-time jobs usually were bored with their work. Reporters often exaggerated what members had given up. For example, a married couple who reportedly gave away a farm after the Waldport meeting actually had sold their property and moved into a commune long before Bo and Peep entered the picture. "We were already on the path of giving things up," the husband explained, so joining the UFO cult was "just another step."

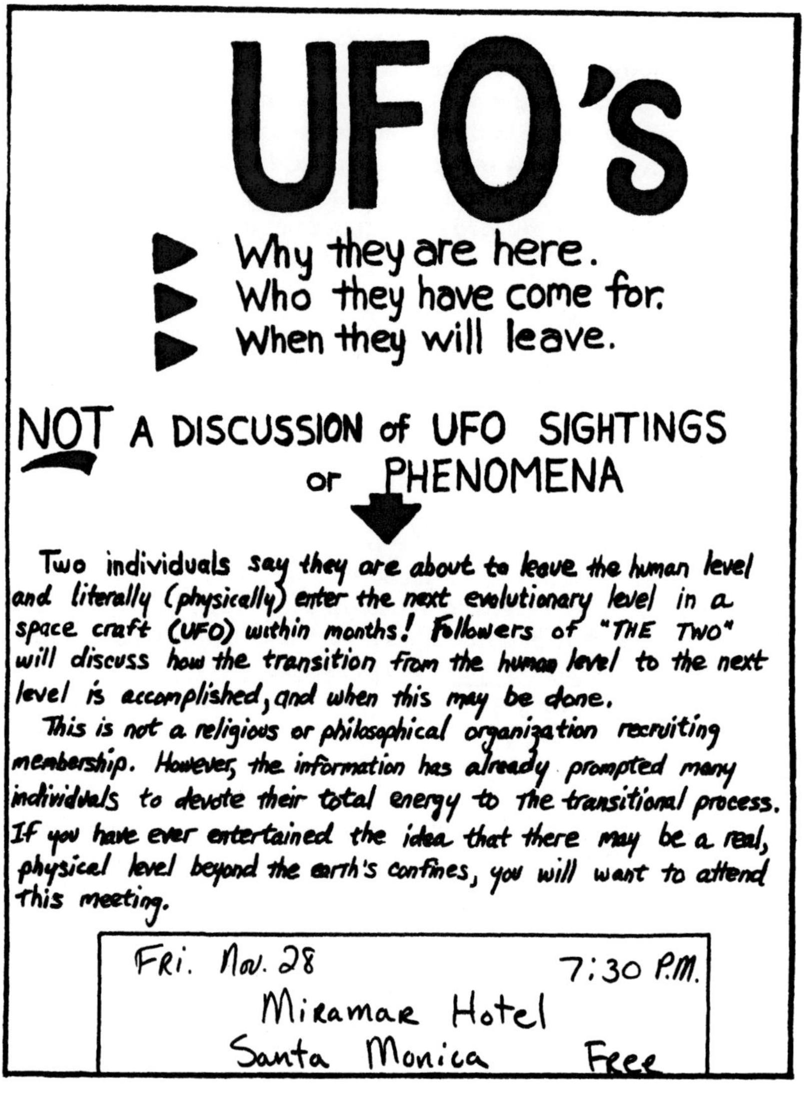

FIGURE 11. UFO Flyer.

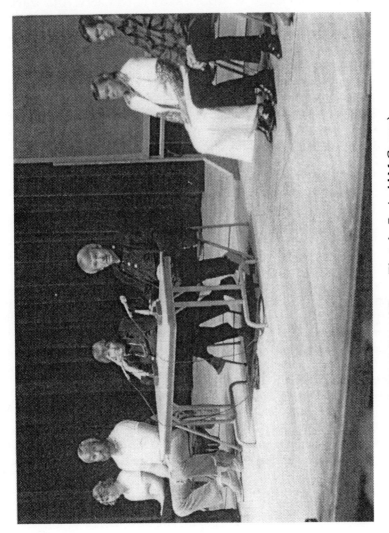

FIGURE 12. Bo and Peep. (Photo by Reginald McGovern)

Most new members had experimented with a wide variety of spiritual "paths" in an unfulfilling quest for truth. One member described their lives as "a bumper car ride through a maze of spiritual trips." A young woman who joined in Arizona told a typical story. After leaving home at fifteen, she had tried LSD, witchcraft, born-again Christianity, anti-war protests, holistic healing, and the Unity Church. "I could get high so many ways," she said, "drugs, music, scenery, people, but I still felt an emptiness. I never felt that fullness, that rock-bottom solidness I was looking for."

Robert Lifton (1970) coined the term "protean man" to describe individuals whose lives are characterized by weak commitments and constant flux. The name comes from the Greek god Proteus who could change his form at will:

> The protean style of self-process is characterized by an interminable series of experiments and explorations—some shallow, some profound—each of which may be readily abandoned in favor of still new psychological quests. (Lifton 1970, p. 319)

Lifton's words might have been written about the UFO people I met. Although members claimed that joining the group was a logical step in their spiritual growth, their decisions were tempered by a tentative, experimental attitude toward participation (Lofland and Skonovd 1981). Some new members even set personal deadlines for the demonstration. For instance, a young couple who left their two preschool children with a friend after the Waldport meeting said they would return in three months if "the process" didn't live up to their expectations. Three months and one week later they were back.

In short, joining the UFO cult may have been a radical step, but it was not out of character. The people who joined gave away their possessions, left their friends, and changed the way they talked and acted around others, but not because they had been brainwashed. Instead, they joined because they wanted to investigate what the Two were offering.

SOCIALIZING NEW MEMBERS

Formal socialization took place in an isolated location known as a "buffer camp." Sometimes the camp was hundreds of miles away from where they joined. The Oregon recruits, for example, were expected to meet the Two at a campground in Colorado almost eight hundred miles from Waldport. Getting to the buffer camp was their first test. Those who didn't make it either didn't want what the next level was offering or they weren't ready for it. In contrast to the high-pressure socialization techniques used by some of Bo and Peep's more notorious contemporaries, such as Synanon (Ofshe 1980) and the Unification Church (Taylor 1978), socialization in the buffer camp was a casual process lasting only a few days. In a series of informal campfire meetings, group leaders would assign partners, answer questions, and explain the fine points of the message. If the Two were present, new members might be invited to their tent for individual meetings. Beyond the sacrifices they had to make to get to the buffer camp, new members were not expected to make any special commitments. Bo and Peep did not require testimonies, confessions, or other tests of membership. Anyone willing to play by the rules was welcome.

Although members claimed the group had no rules, there were many "guidelines" designed to help people overcome their attachments to the human level, much like Alcoholics Anonymous teaches its members to avoid situations that might draw them back into drinking. Some guidelines discouraged contact with the outside world: Don't read newspapers or watch TV; don't call your parents; don't visit old friends; don't pick up hitchhikers. Other rules were designed to eliminate old habits and identities: Quit using drugs; change your name; shave your beard; get rid of clothing and jewelry that symbolize your old self. Still others were intended to prevent the formation of interpersonal attachments within the group: no sex, no human-level friendships, no socializing on a human level. Aside from daily meetings, usually once in the morning and again in the evening, group activities were virtually nonexistent.

Some of these guidelines came directly from the Two, but others reflected a tendency to turn Bo and Peep's suggestions into rigid rules, and without the Two to clarify matters, there was some confusion about what some of the guidelines meant. For example, most of the members I observed were unclear about when their relationships were becoming "too human," and for many the uncertainty was a constant source of anxiety.

The socialization process became increasingly haphazard after Bo and Peep disappeared. When I joined in Arizona, members were in such a hurry to get to California that the buffer camp was skipped altogether. A few days after the Prescott meeting, Taylor and I met about seventy-five UFO people from all over the country in a campground north of San Francisco. The Two failed to show up because the meeting turned out to be a hoax publicized by a local newspaper, and Bo and

Peep's whereabouts remained a mystery. In the confusion, new members were left to themselves. During my first day in camp I had complete freedom to wander about asking questions. Some of the new people were smoking marijuana, an obvious violation of the rules, and most appeared to have little understanding of the message.

Later that day the new members, including Taylor and myself, were assigned partners, an unceremonious process of drawing names two at a time out of a pair of plastic bowls, but even then we were left to our own devices. At my partner's suggestion, we walked from one campsite to the next, asking "older" members (meaning those who had been in the group the longest) what was expected of us. The only event approximating formal socialization occurred one evening when someone played a tape of the Two delivering the message at a public meeting in California.

The next day the UFO people divided into new groups and prepared to leave. My partner and I joined a group of sixteen that was heading south. Were it not for the tape of Bo and Peep and our own inquisitiveness, our first encampment would have passed without any indoctrination whatsoever. Already several of the newer members had dropped out, including two from the Prescott meeting.

THE COLLAPSE OF COMMITMENT

Taylor and I became part of the UFO cult at a critical time. It had only been three weeks since Bo and Peep had disappeared, but members were already becoming demoralized. According to Kanter (1972), commitment is reflected in three aspects of social organization: group cohesiveness, social control, and the retention of members. By every indicator, commitment in the people I observed plummeted during the next two months. However, the decline was an uneven process punctuated by periods of elation and despair.

The first signs of disillusionment in our group emerged within a week after Taylor and I joined. Picking up on the somber mood in camp, an older member asked us to say whatever was on our minds. Since sharing doubts was discouraged because of how it might affect others, I was surprised by the frankness of the remarks. One by one members expressed their concerns, using terms like "darkness" and "limbo" to describe their feelings. Then the man who opened the discussion dropped the bombshell: "I had a flash," he said, "that the Two aren't who they say they are." Several people laughed nervously, but none appeared shocked by what he said.

Eventually we decided to split up for a few days and meet again in southern California. Ideally my partner and I would have traveled alone, but because neither of us had a car, we had to ride with another couple. Life on the road was rejuvenating. Since we had no money, we had to test the churches to eat and keep our car running. In fact, we got help in many places: sanitary napkins for my partner from a hospital, poison ivy medicine for myself at a drugstore, gas for our car from a Catholic mission, and a meal and Bibles for all of us from the Salvation Army.

My companions took our good fortune as a sign that the next level was taking care of us. When we "tested" for gas at the Catholic mission, we also got a free quart of oil. We hadn't asked for the oil, but afterwards we discovered our car was exactly one quart low. As our driver pointed out, "The Father is the best mechanic there is." By the time we reached our destination, faith in the message had been restored.

That changed as soon as we rejoined our group. We found ourselves stranded in a cold, windswept expanse of desert with broken-down cars and almost nothing to eat. Shortly after we arrived, an outspoken member named Aaron received a "revelation" that split the group into factions. Aaron argued that the final step in the process of ridding ourselves of attachments was overcoming our dependence on the Two. Only by transcending our need for spiritual teachers could we expect to enter the next kingdom.

Aaron's revelation provided the perfect rationale for defection. Members could leave even while professing allegiance to the message. In less than a week three-fourths of the group had adopted Aaron's point of view. Some were smoking marijuana and drinking beer with other campers, and Aaron reportedly was having sex with his partner. Aaron justified this behavior by arguing that we could smoke, drink, and have sex as long as we had overcome our *need* for drugs and intimacy.

All but four members decided to leave. They were packing up their camping gear when two people from another group of followers arrived with dramatic news. They claimed the Two had "emerged from the wilderness" and were heading to southern California. Our visitors wanted to hold a huge public meeting in Los Angeles, and they speculated that Bo and Peep would show up to present the message. Citing the angry apostate stories that were starting to appear in the press, they claimed the Two might even be assassinated at the meeting. Once again the demonstration seemed imminent, and almost immediately our group reunited. Even Aaron returned to the fold. By the next day his divisive revelation appeared to have been forgotten.

Over sixty members gathered in a campground north of Los Angeles to plan the big meeting, but their enthusiasm quickly evaporated. Bo and Peep's reappearance turned out to be an unfounded rumor, and without strong leadership, decision making was almost impossible. Aaron reemerged as a divisive force and factionalism increased. At one point some of the more committed members decided our camp had been invaded by spirits. They laid the blame on a low-ranking Colorado recruit, claiming he had been possessed by Beelzebub. They warned the rest of us to stay away from him, but spirits of doubt and dissension continued to grow. People were leaving. Sometimes they left for only a few days to reassess their commitment, but in many cases they never came back.

It took ten days to organize the Los Angeles meeting. Once we found a place to present the message, we began blanketing the city with posters advertising the event. At the time, brush fires were raging through the mountains north of Los Angeles. As we drove south into the smoke, the sky darkened and the sun turned red, at one point disappearing almost completely. Ashes fell like snowflakes while my partner read from the Bible:

> And I will show wonders in heaven above, and signs in the earth beneath; blood, and fire, and vapor of smoke:
> The sun shall be turned into darkness, and the moon into blood, before that great and notable day of the Lord come. (Acts 2:19,20)

The portents were striking, even for me. What better place for the demonstration than Los Angeles, the Babylon of the modern age?

Despite the portents, the meeting turned out to be a disaster. Not only did the Two fail to appear, but the members chosen to present the message did such a poor job that the audience repeatedly erupted in hoots and jeers. Out of a crowd of at least six hundred, only eight people decided to join.

The buffer camp was even worse. Located in an empty stretch of desert in southern Arizona, the site was chosen because of its isolation to prevent the intrusion of spirits. However, it was only a matter of days before trouble started again. The most disruptive influence was the unexpected arrival of two members who told us about a meeting the Two recently held in Salt Lake City. Supposedly Bo and Peep had said that the demonstration might not happen after all. This announcement sent shock waves through the group because the demonstration had been fundamental to the message since the group began. For many members, denying the demonstration meant rejecting the Bible and everything the Two had said. The news split the group into new factions. Some members accepted the new information, while others denounced Bo and Peep as frauds. But most were confused and didn't know what to believe.

For the first time, the discussion of doubts became widespread. Doubts had been expressed in group meetings before, but members usually were vague about their feelings. They might just say they were having trouble staying "in tune," or that they were being "bombarded" by spirits. What distinguished the Los Angeles buffer camp was members' willingness to speak openly about what was bothering them and to debate the authenticity of the Two in group meetings. Not surprisingly, two of the eight Los Angeles recruits dropped out even before the buffer camp ended.

Other members were leaving too. Despair pervaded the camp. Everyone felt confused, demoralized, and cut off from the next level. Within a few days the buffer camp disintegrated. Some members left to join other groups of followers, while the rest went off with their partners to decide on their next move. Most members dropped out soon afterwards. What happened in Arizona was typical. All over the country, members were dropping out for similar reasons. By February of 1976 at least half of Bo and Peep's followers had left (Balch 1984, 1985).

REVITALIZING THE CULT

When Taylor and I left the group at the end of 1975, it was hard to believe anyone would still be on the process six months later. What we hadn't counted on was the reappearance of the Two. Two months after returning to Montana, I learned that two members had scheduled a public meeting in Spokane, Washington. I attended to find out if anything new had developed and was shown a photocopy of a letter from two members of Bo and Peep's inner circle. The letter said the Two could be reached at a post office box in Gulfport, Mississippi. Anyone still on the process was urged to write for information. That letter, passed along in chance encounters across the country, marked the beginning of Bo and Peep's effort to revitalize their following.

Somewhere between ninety to one hundred members eventually were reunited with the Two. During the next year Bo and Peep made sweeping changes that reversed the trend toward disintegration. The first important change occurred at a public meeting in the Midwest. After struggling with hecklers throughout the presentation, Peep suddenly stood up and announced that "the doors to the next level are closed." Efforts to share Bo and Peep's message ended abruptly. Peep's declaration not only eliminated a major point of contact with the outside world, but it reinforced the group's sense of specialness. The harvest was over. Out of billions of people worldwide, less than one hundred were considered eligible to enter the next kingdom.

More changes occurred in the summer of 1976 when the Two took the group to a remote camp in the mountains near Laramie, Wyoming. Bo and Peep started by announcing that the demonstration had been canceled. They claimed their followers weren't ready to enter the next kingdom. Members had spent too much energy thinking about the demonstration and not enough working on their own growth. The most important thing was not getting off the planet, but learning to serve the next level. The emphasis on service was a new theme designed to get members to focus on the present rather than worrying about the future.

Bo and Peep also took steps to reinforce their authority by clarifying their connection with members of the next level. Before Wyoming, members believed guidance came directly from the next level in the form of intuitive hunches and flashes of insight. This belief had proved disruptive because members like Aaron used it to justify breaking the rules. When others challenged their actions, the deviants would claim they were acting on instructions from the next level. Without Bo and Peep's leadership, factions emerged and confusion set it.

The Two solved the problem by eliminating any possibility of individual revelation. They explained that all information from the next level was channeled through a "chain of mind" linking the next kingdom to individual members through Bo and Peep. The only valid information about the process flowed in a direct line from the Father to Peep to Bo and then to their followers.

The chain of mind was consistent with Bo and Peep's past behavior. Bo had always acted as their spokesman, doing most of the talking in public and private meetings, whereas Peep played the role of clarifier, stepping in only when she thought Bo's remarks might be misconstrued. Bo always deferred to her superior knowledge. The chain-of-mind concept solidified their roles, but more importantly, it made Bo and Peep necessary intermediaries between members and the next level.[2]

The Wyoming encampment was intended to prepare members for life in space. Bo and Peep divided the group into several camps known as "star clusters" that were named after constellations. Each camp consisted of a circle of identical tents surrounded by a perimeter of sticks and logs laid end to end. Inside each tent the Two required members to arrange their camping gear in a particular way to maximize efficiency. Each star cluster included two members of Bo and Peep's inner circle, known as "helpers," who were rotated from camp to camp. The helpers relayed information from the Two and reported back to them on a regular basis. Bo and Peep lived nearby in a small camp trailer at the edge of a larger circle called "Central." Every camp was connected to Central by a trail marked off the same way the star clusters were. Similar trails led to the parking area, known as the "docking zone," and a remote circle called the "decontamination zone" where members went when they were being bothered by spirits. Except for special jobs, such as collecting firewood or doing laundry, which had to be done in town, all activities took place within these boundaries.

In addition to the normal tasks demanded by camping in the mountains, daily life was taken up with countless drills and exercises. One of the earliest was the use of the "A tone," which was designed to help members stay in tune with the next level by eliminating human thoughts. Members would put a vibrating tuning fork against their temples and concentrate on the note it produced, learning to focus on the sound while eating, washing cars, doing laundry, and taking care of other chores. Another exercise was called the "smooth whirlwind." For about a month everyone rotated from one camp to the next, being paired with a different partner in a different tent every day. The plan worked in such a way that members only returned to their permanent partners every Friday when the cycle ended. The whirlwind had two functions. It forced members to get better acquainted with each other, and it helped them become comfortable with change. Bo and Peep said humans instinctively avoid change, but that change is constant at the next level and candidates for the next kingdom needed to get used to it.

Some exercises were designed to help members overcome the need for verbal communication. In one, known as "tomb time," members spent several days without talking, except to say "yes," "no," or "I don't know" in response to brief questions. Any other communication was handled with written notes. Afterwards members entered a period where they spoke to each other only when verbal communication was absolutely necessary. Bo and Peep explained that talking would not be needed after the lift-off since members of the next level communicate simply by putting their thoughts into the "ethers." Candidates for the next level, they said, should strive to emulate members of the next kingdom in everything they do.

Members also started wearing uniforms. Although styles changed, the typical outfit included a nylon windbreaker, a hood with cloth-mesh eyes and gloves in winter. The uniforms eliminated the distinctiveness of their human "vehicles," and the hoods in particular reduced nonverbal communication during periods of silence. To make sure outsiders didn't stumble across the group while members were wearing their uniforms, sentries were posted in the hills to watch for approaching cars or hikers.

Bo and Peep referred to these exercises as "games." They were meant to be challenging and fun. Sometimes the Two explained their purpose in advance, but most of the time the reasons did not become evident until later. Members learned to accept Bo and Peep's innovations without question, always assuming there was a valuable lesson to be learned.

Compared to the chaotic period in 1975, the summer of 1976 was marked by incredible regimentation. As one ex-member described it, there was "a procedure for every conscious moment of life," including cooking, eating, bathing, washing clothes, and sleeping. The best example was a routine known as "the docket." Every twelve minutes throughout the day a different partnership reported to the "service desk" under an awning in Central where two or four members, depending on the program, stepped onto a platform and silently asked the next level, "What can I do to serve?" They might be told to perform a chore such as gathering firewood or washing a car, or they could be dismissed if nothing needed to be done. It was virtually impossible to follow the routine without being totally focused on the present. Members who were excused from checking in after being assigned particular tasks were said to be "out of orbit."

Although the group had always been insulated from the outside world, the UFO people became even more isolated after moving to Wyoming. The Two had members practice tearing down the camp and packing their cars until they were able to be ready to leave in less than fifteen minutes. I know of two times when this drill was put into practice. Once was when a disillusioned member took a car without permission and drove into Laramie, and the other was when the Two discovered that someone had secretly sent a letter to his family.

Paradoxically, some members had to get jobs for awhile when money ran short. This happened sometime after the group moved to a campsite near Salt Lake City in the fall of 1976. Despite being thrust back into the human level, members maintained their detachment with various mental exercises. For example, Bo and Peep encouraged them to keep to the camp routine by watching the clock and mentally asking the next level how they could be of service every twelve minutes. Members also had to write reports describing their personal feelings while working among humans. Even more surprising was the introduction of a television, which could be plugged into a car cigarette lighter. The Two wanted members to "watch humans" and understand their behavior, but family-oriented shows, such as "Little House on the Prairie" were not part of the program because they "vibrated on the human level."

Despite these measures, some people continued to harbor doubts. The Two often encouraged weaker members to leave, once even drawing a line in the sand and asking members to step over it if they wanted to stay, but a few doubting Thomases hung on through the fall. Then late in the year Bo and Peep singled out nineteen of the least committed members and sent them to Phoenix, Arizona. Their instructions were to get jobs and wait for further information. Bo and Peep kept in touch by telephone for a few weeks, but eventually they stopped calling, leaving the prodigals to fend for themselves. Without the Two and the disciplined structure they created, the Phoenix group quickly fell apart and members scattered in different directions.

The camping phase ended soon afterwards because Bo and Peep suddenly came into money. Although the sources and amounts are unclear, one ex-member who was close to the Two told me that two members received inheritances totaling at least $300,000. With the money Bo and Peep were able to rent houses for the group, first in Denver and later in the Dallas-Fort Worth area. Since the Denver houses were located in a suburban neighborhood, members moved in secretly at night, and Bo and peep covered the windows so the neighbors would not catch a glimpse of someone in uniform. Only a few people ever went outside, and then only for brief jobs like mowing the yard.

Each house was called a "craft," and every activity was designed to prepare members for life at the next level. Every member was expected to adhere to a fixed routine where activities were prescribed minute by minute. A woman who left the group in 1981 showed me the schedule she followed during a brief period in one of the Denver houses. Her first of four daily rest periods began at 3:36 P.M. and ended exactly two hours later. At 5:57 she bathed. Twenty-four minutes later she took a vitamin pill, one of thirty-two consumed every twenty-four hours. At 6:36 she drank a liquid protein formula, and one hour later she ate a cinnamon roll. By 9:54 she was back in bed for another two hours. During her waking moments she wore a uniform at all times. Free periods were devoted to "fuel preparation" (i.e., cooking), classes on astrology or "brain exercises" such as working jigsaw puzzles. Because she never left the house, the only way she knew what the weather was like was by watching the sky through a clerestory window—the only window in the house that wasn't covered. She wasn't sure how long this phase lasted because she lost track of time. However, another dropout who was allowed outside during this period estimated that it lasted about six months.

To insure conformity after the Two dispensed with partnerships, members took shifts as "eyes" to monitor each other's behavior. Although one informant admitted that the practice "sounds like the Gestapo," he added that "We all wanted to quickly change our behavior . . . [so] 'eyes' wasn't a threat but an aid to overcome areas that we alone wouldn't recognize within ourselves." The Two also required members to submit detailed written accounts of their thoughts and feelings, once including a "spirit list" describing the influences they still needed to overcome. The ultimate sanction was expulsion, and a few members were asked to leave, but Bo and Peep always bought them bus or plane tickets so they could get home.

The changes that occurred in Wyoming, Colorado, and Texas can be characterized as a continuous attempt at resocialization. Bo and Peep introduced one exercise after another, always seeking to improve on the previous one. Even when members spent months following rigid schedules, the Two constantly varied activities to keep members engaged in a continuous process of learning and overcoming. Everyone I interviewed who went through these changes talked about the "intensity" of life in the group after the move to Wyoming, which one defector contrasted with the "dark ages" of 1975.

ASSESSING THE IMPACT OF
BO AND PEEP'S RESOCIALIZATION TECHNIQUES

The effects of these changes can be assessed by using Kanter's (1972) three indicators of commitment: group cohesiveness, social control, and the retention of members. Group cohesiveness clearly increased during the Wyoming encampment. Morale improved, conflicts between members were eliminated, and the group became tighter than ever before. According to one of the helpers, "The harmony day in and day out was truly amazing." Social control ceased to be a problem, partly because the least committed members had been sent to Phoenix, but also because the remaining members made a deliberate effort to do what the Two called "the most right thing" in their everyday lives. This meant acting like members of the next level, or in other words, doing exactly what Bo and Peep said. The most direct measure of the effectiveness of the changes introduced by the Two is the defection rate. Unfortunately, I can only provide rough estimates. During the turbulent period in 1975, there was no membership list and Bo and Peep's followers were scattered all over the country without any reliable way of keeping track of each other. Taylor and I had trouble enough counting defections on the West Coast where we knew most members by name. To assess the defection rate after 1975, I have had to rely on estimates provided by defectors, but they were often unsure of numbers and dates.

Given these limitations, I will hazard some guesses about changes in the defection rate. Between ninety and one hundred members reunited with the Two in the spring of 1976, less than a year after Bo and Peep gathered their first group of followers in Los Angeles. Assuming the Two had two hundred followers at the group's peak in 1975, the defection rate was at least 50 percent in the group's first year. If we add in those who left before the group reached its maximum size, as well as those who dropped out a few days after hearing the message, the defection rate would have been much higher, maybe as much as 70 or 80 percent. According to two informants, eighty-eight members were present when Bo and Peep gathered the group together in Wyoming, and then nineteen were sent to Phoenix, leaving sixty-nine members. According to my most reliable informant, a former member of Bo and Peep's inner circle, forty-eight were left by the end of 1978. This means the defection rate dropped from at least 50 percent in the year after the Two recruited their first group of followers, to roughly 30 percent in the next two and a half years, or about 12 percent per year. Not only did the defection rate decline, but the attitude of defectors changed. Members who left after the Wyoming phase typically remained loyal to Bo and Peep. Most had to be persuaded to talk about their experiences, and even then they refused to divulge information about the group's location. Instead of dropping out because of disillusionment, they left because they no longer had the determination to endure the discipline that being on the process required.

These findings can be interpreted different ways. I believe they show the effectiveness of Bo and Peep's use of social psychological principles to enhance the commitment of their followers. The military uses similar techniques for building commitment (Dornbusch 1955), and some ex-members actually compared their experience in the Wyoming encampment with being in the army. However, the matter of cause and effect is ambiguous because there are alternative explanations for the data. One is that commitment increased simply because Bo and Peep were again available to answer questions, settle disagreements, and provide a focal point for the group. After months without leadership, the mere presence of the Two clearly boosted morale.

Another explanation is that the longer members stayed in the cult, the fewer alternatives they saw for themselves outside the group. While this happened, it was not emphasized by any of my informants. The most persuasive alternative explanation is that the least committed members either defected shortly after joining or were expelled, leaving only true believers in the group. Several informants said there was a noticeable increase in the overall level of conformity after the departure of the Phoenix group.

I don't see these explanations as mutually exclusive. Commitment in the Bo-Peep cult definitely increased after 1975, probably for all the reasons I've suggested, but members themselves attributed most of the increase to the changes introduced by the Two. The more they immersed themselves in the routines and exercises designed by Bo and Peep, the more real the message seemed. For example, two dropouts remarked on the physical sensations they experienced during the silent periods known as tomb time, usually around 3:00 A.M. when the ships were suspected to be in close range. These included ringing in the ears, "body rushes," and a general feeling of "incredible energy." Both informants said these experiences helped keep them on the process when they were struggling with doubt. As one put it, "I would be going, yes! This is happening! This is real!"

IMPLICATIONS FOR THE STUDY OF COMMITMENT

The changes that occurred in the UFO cult have important implications for the study of commitment to new religions. To restore their followers' commitment, the Two felt it necessary to create a highly regimented lifestyle where personal freedom was not permitted and independent thinking was replaced with what a member characterized as "crew-mindedness." The fact that people had joined the group willingly and enthusiastically was not enough to sustain their commitment in the face of the hardships of being on the process.

Long and Hadden (1983) classified conversion models into two categories. The first is the brainwashing model. This approach focuses on social influences that persuade recruits to adopt a new belief system. The second is the "social drift" model, a term borrowed from Matza's (1964) research on juvenile delinquency. In the drift model, recruits flirt with commitment, joining tentatively and moving on if the group fails to meet their needs. The first model emphasizes the power of social forces to shape behavior and beliefs, whereas the second stresses the ability of potential recruits to pick and choose among competing belief systems.

Long and Hadden argued that the models are not as contradictory as they appear because each focuses on a different aspect of the conversion process. The drift model provides a good description of recruitment, while the brainwashing model describes processes that strengthen commitment once people have joined.

My research on the UFO cult supports Long and Hadden's hypothesis. The drift model fits the recruitment phase in 1975, but the brainwashing model is a better description of what happened afterwards. My only objection to Long and Hadden's argument is their choice of terms. Because "brainwashing" has negative, misleading connotations, I will use the term "social influence model" instead (Cialdini 1993).

The influence model clearly does not apply to the recruitment process Taylor and I observed in 1975. Bo and Peep were good salesmen, but people shopping for new cars routinely encounter much more pressure and manipulation (Cialdini 1993). People joined the UFO cult with virtually no pressure to convert, and they enthusiastically adopted group norms even before the socialization process began. Indoctrination was brief and unsystematic. There was no deception and little social pressure. Even when the buffer camp procedure was abandoned, recruits took it upon themselves to find out what was expected of them. Bo and Peep's followers were clearly willing participants in the conversion process.

However, it soon became obvious that most members were unable to sustain their enthusiasm. Without the Two to help them stay focused, they became confused, demoralized, and fragmented by internal disputes. Commitment fluctuated wildly as moments of elation inevitably were followed by deepening troughs of despair.

The new phase that began in Wyoming was marked by the introduction of systematic social influence processes as Bo and Peep embarked on a concerted effort to shore up the sagging faith of their followers. By the end of 1976 the UFO cult bore little resemblance to the hapless group we observed a year earlier. The changes included regimentation, deindividuation, and mental techniques designed to eliminate any thoughts that weren't related to the process. The UFO cult became an extreme case of religious totalism where activities were prescribed literally down to the minute.

I don't want to imply that members were coerced. After months of chaos, most followers welcomed the new rules. They remained free to leave at any time, and some did. Although the tuning fork exercise sounds like classic mind control (Hassan 1988), the Two could not force members to concentrate on the sound. Their followers continued to be willing participants, but in the context of their increasingly encapsulated, regimented lives, Bo and Peep's message became ever more plausible. Opposing views lost credibility, seeming less and less real as the lessons behind each new exercise were revealed.

It is not necessary to venture into the philosophical debate over free will and determinism to see the appropriateness of the social influence model. While there is no evidence that members lost their ability to make free choices, it appears that the introduction of systematic resocialization techniques reversed the trend toward group disintegration. The level of commitment in the UFO cult increased sharply after the summer of 1976. Factionalism disappeared, conformity increased, and the defection rate dropped precipitously.

In short, the changes that occurred in the UFO cult are consistent with Long and Hadden's argument that the social drift and social influence models are both correct. Each model accurately describes the UFO people, but neither is complete. The drift model helps us understand why people joined, but the social influence model explains how Bo and Peep were able to transform their followers into highly committed believers. The evidence should temper the extremism of social scientists on both sides of the brainwashing controversy. Instead of devoting their energy to discrediting their opponents, they should follow Long and Hadden's lead and begin looking for ways to integrate their competing models of commitment.

EPILOGUE

I stopped collecting data on the UFO cult in the early 1980s. I was involved in other projects, and the group had become so secretive that keeping track of it would have been almost impossible without another leave of absence, which I couldn't afford. In 1982 I attended a meeting of parents whose children belonged to the cult. It had been seven years since any of them had seen their sons and daughters, and almost that long since anyone had received a letter or postcard. Most had no idea if their children were even alive.

The picture changed suddenly the next year when many members unexpectedly came home for brief visits on Mother's Day. In most cases, parents were surprised to discover that their children, now in their late twenties and early thirties, were able to function normally in the outside world. One mother I interviewed was astonished when her son, once an aimless drug user, turned out to be a mature, helpful, enjoyable person. He stayed for two weeks, helped around the house, visited old friends, and then disappeared without leaving an address or phone number, saying only that he would get in touch again sometime. During these visits members hinted that they were learning computer technology and experimenting with innovative diets, but beyond that they revealed almost nothing about the group or their daily lives.

In 1993, under the name of Total Overcomers Anonymous, the group ran a full-page advertisement in *USA Today* entitled "'UFO Cult' Resurfaces with Final Offer." The ad focused primarily on the group's beliefs, which appeared to have changed little in the last eighteen years. However, it had an apocalyptic tone that was much more dramatic than anything I had heard in 1975:

> The Earth's present "civilization" is about to be recycled—"spaded under." Its inhabitants are refusing to evolve. The "weeds" have taken over the garden and disturbed its usefulness beyond repair.

Then in 1994, believing the lift-off might happen in a year or two, the group started holding public meetings again, including one in my hometown. A few days before the meeting two members, Sawyer and Evan, unexpectedly stopped by my office to talk, and the next day I met two more. Except for their beliefs and the way they dressed (long-sleeved shirts buttoned to the top and worn over their belts), there was nothing unusual about them. They were pleasant, good humored, and much more open about their lives than members had been in 1975. Until the end of 1993 they had been supporting themselves by working at conventional jobs, although keeping their identities secret from fellow employees. They said there were just twenty-four members left at the first of the year when they resumed public meetings. After deciding to go on the road again, they had quit their jobs, liquidated most of their assets, and split into three groups to spread their message around the country one last time. As in 1975, they were living off donations, although occasionally some members took part-time jobs doing computer work. Despite their willingness to talk, there remained an aura of secrecy about them. They were reluctant to tell me where they were staying, and instead of giving me the phone number for their motel, they gave me a temporary voice mail number in Seattle where I could leave messages while they were in town.

The meeting followed the same format I had seen many times in 1975, although here too members were more willing to answer questions about their personal lives. As in 1975, there was no hard-sell, no effort to recruit, only a desire to make people aware of the message. Of the nine members present at the meeting, at least three had joined the group in the last year. I was told that a total of twelve people had joined since the "final offer" began, but nobody in the audience at this particular meeting was receptive. By the end of the presentation, only myself and two others were left, but the UFO people didn't seem discouraged.

During the meeting the speakers talked about the Two as if they both were still physically present in their lives. However, Peep had died of cancer in 1985, or as their followers put it, she had "left her vehicle" because her work on the human level was finished. I had learned about Peep's death from her daughter, who said Bo had sent her a tape explaining what had happened. Despite the group's emphasis on overcoming human attachments, she said Bo seemed to be crying when he talked about her mother. When I asked the members about this, they didn't see a contradiction. After all, they explained, even Jesus had wept in the garden of Gethsemane, but that didn't mean he was attached to the human level. Yet I still had to wonder about Peep. After her death, two members delivered her only possessions to her daughter, including, ironically, a teddy bear.[3]

NOTES

1. I would like to thank Sawyer and Evan, two current members of the UFO cult, for making comments on an earlier draft of this chapter just as it was about to go to press. While I have followed most of their suggestions, they asked me to include the following disclaimer:

> Although we edited this, per Mr. Balch's request, we do not support its content as an accurate picture of what we represented in 1975 or represent to date. Certain of the facts are accurate and we tried to correct misconceptions or inaccuracies as we found them throughout. We respect this work as Mr. Balch's best attempt to portray his own experience and interpretation of our group's history and purpose.

2. About this time Bo and Peep changed their names to Do and Te (sic), after the musical notes. Later they became known simply as TeDo. For the sake of consistency, however, I will continue to refer to them as Bo and Peep.

3. Additional information about the UFO cult can be found in the references. The papers by Taylor and myself deal with the following topics: Bo and Peep's awakening and the origins of their belief system (Balch 1982a); the beginnings of the cult in Los Angeles (Balch 1982b); recruitment, conversion, and commitment (Balch 1979, 1980, 1982b; Balch and Taylor 1977a, 1978); disillusionment and defection (Balch 1984, 1985); and the changes introduced by Bo and Peep early in 1976 (Balch and Taylor 1977b).

The most informative nonacademic sources are Phelan's article (1976), which provides a revealing portrait of the Two, and the book by Hewes and Steiger (1976) which summarizes events in the first five months after the Waldport meeting.

Although the Hewes and Steiger book is based largely on information from newspaper articles, it offers a valuable look at the sensationalism surrounding the UFO cult. It also includes excerpts from an interview with Bo and Peep, as well as portions of a written statement the Two prepared especially for the book. During their time in the "wilderness," Bo and Peep were preparing this statement while living in a cabin near Oklahoma City. They hoped the book would reach a wider audience than their public meetings, but they repudiated the project after the publisher cut substantial portions of their statement. The book also turned out to be too sensational for their taste.

REFERENCES

Balch, Robert W. 1979. "Two Models of Conversion and Commitment in a UFO Cult." Paper presented at the annual meeting of the Pacific Sociological Association. Anaheim, Calif.

———. 1980. "Looking Behind the Scenes in a Religious Cult: Implications for the Study of Conversion." *Sociological Analysis* 41:137-43.

———. 1982a. "Bo and Peep: A Case Study of the Origins of Messianic Leadership." In *Millennialism and Charisma*, edited by Roy Wallis, 13-71. Belfast: The Queen's University.

———. 1982b. "Conversion and Charisma in the Cultic Milieu: The Origins of a New Religion." Paper presented at the annual meeting of the Association for the Sociology of Religion. Providence, R.I.

———. 1984. "The Social Construction of Reality in Religious Defection: A Conversational Analysis." Paper presented at the annual meeting of the Pacific Sociological Association. Seattle, Wash.

———. 1985. "When the Light Goes Out, Darkness Comes: A Study of Defection from a Totalistic Cult." In *Religious Movements: Genesis, Exodus, and Numbers*, edited by Rodney Stark, 11-63. New York: Paragon Press.

Balch, Robert W., and David Taylor. 1977a. "Seekers and Saucers: The Role of the Cultic Milieu in Joining a UFO Cult." *American Behavioral Scientist* 20:839-60.

———. 1977b. "The Metamorphosis of a UFO Cult: A Study of Organizational Change." Paper presented at the annual meeting of the Pacific Sociological Association. San Diego, Calif.

————. 1978. "On Getting in Tune: Some Reflections on the Process of Making Supernatural Contact." Paper presented at the annual meeting of the Pacific Sociological Association. Spokane, Wash.

Cialdini, Robert B. 1993. *Influence: The Psychology of Persuasion*. New York: William Morrow.

Dornbusch, Sanford N. 1955. "The Military Academy as an Assimilating Institution." *Social Forces* 33:316-21.

Foss, Daniel A., and Ralph W. Larkin. 1976. "From 'The Gates of Eden' to 'Day of the Locust': An Analysis of the Dissident Youth Movement of the 1960s and Its Heirs of the Early 1970s—The Postmovement Groups." *Theory and Society* 3:1-44.

Hassan, Steven. 1988. *Combatting Cult Mind Control*. Rochester, Vt.: Park Street Press/Inner Traditions.

Hewes, Hayden, and Brad Steiger. 1976. *UFO Missionaries Extraordinary*. New York: Pocket Books.

Kanter, Rosabeth Moss. 1972. *Commitment and Community: Communes and Utopias in Sociological Perspective*. Cambridge, Mass.: Harvard University.

Lifton, Robert Jay. 1970. "Protean Man." In *History and Human Survival*, edited by Robert Jay Lifton, 311-31. New York: Random House.

Lofland, John, and Norman Skonovd. 1981. "Conversion Motifs." *Journal for the Scientific Study of Religion* 20:373-85.

Lofland, John, and Rodney Stark. 1965. "Becoming a World-Saver: A Theory of Conversion to a Deviant Perspective." *American Sociological Review* 30:862-75.

Long, Theodore E., and Jeffrey K. Hadden. 1983. "Religious Conversion and the Concept of Socialization: Integrating the Brainwashing and Drift Models." *Journal for the Scientific Study of Religion* 11:1-14.

Matza, David. 1964. *Delinquency and Drift*. New York: Wiley.

Ofshe, Richard. 1980. "The Social Development of the Synanon Cult: The Managerial Strategy of Organizational Transformation." *Sociological Analysis* 41:109-127.

Phelan, James S. 1976. "Looking For: The Next World." *New York Times*, magazine section. February 29:12, 58-59, 62-64.

Taylor, Bryan. 1976. "Conversion and Cognition: An Area for Empirical Study in the Microsociology of Religious Knowledge." *Social Compass* 23:5-22.

Taylor, David. 1978. *The Social Organization of Recruitment in the Unification Church*. Unpublished master's thesis. Missoula, Mont.: University of Montana.

7

SPIRITUALISM AND UFO RELIGION IN NEW ZEALAND: THE INTERNATIONAL TRANSMISSION OF MODERN SPIRITUAL MOVEMENTS

Robert S. Ellwood

Spiritualism and UFO movements, like many forms of alternative or New Age religion, have been quite successful in New Zealand. (Although conventional church attendance in New Zealand is, according to surveys, around 10 to 12 percent of the population in an average week—far below the 40 percent Gallup finds for the U.S. and in the dismal west European range—census and membership figures put the number of Theosophists and spiritualists in New Zealand per capita at some twenty-five times the U.S. figure.[1]) The transmission of UFOism to the island nation in the twentieth century has striking parallels to that of spiritualism in the nineteenth. In both cases, the heart of the transmittal process was visiting speakers, from Emma Hardinge-Britten for spiritualism to a UFO "contactee" like George Adamski. Most of the visiting speakers came from Britain or America, evoked great media publicity, and left behind them much controversy and small but enthusiastic groups of believers. Both endeavored to indigenize the new faith to New Zealand by finding parallels in Maori or settler folklore, and both appealed to motifs deeply engrained in the New Zealand experience.

Understanding the relative success of spiritualist and UFO lecturers in New Zealand will, I think, shed light on the appeal and transmittal of new spiritual movements in other settings as well, especially comparable nineteenth- and twentieth-century English-speaking settler societies, such as Australia and the American West, where such movements have also been exceptionally successful. Such societies have a number of common characteristics relevant to this receptivity:

1. Religious needs are less well provided than in the sending societies; churches are fewer, and clergymen not always of the best quality or prepared to adapt to colonial conditions.
2. Many immigrants came as isolated individuals (usually male) or at best as nuclear families, and felt less social pressure for conventional religious participation than at home. Moreover, they often came from classes already quasi-alienated from. conventional religion, as was the case with many British working-class immigrants.
3. Often immigrants experience a "sea-change" suggesting that, with the immigration experience, they and the world could be different from how they had known it. Especially in the case of New Zealand, this was put in the form of idealistic, even utopian, dreams of building a new and far better society—with the implication that it could also have new spiritual underpinnings. Motifs characteristic of nineteenth-century spiritualism, such as its alliance with reformism, the equality of women, the romantic dream of transcending prior limits of human achievement, and sympathy for indigenous shamanistic religion, Native American or Maori, made it appealing to this mood.
4. On the other hand, the hardness and isolation of pioneer life, often pressing one toward pragmatic solutions and appreciation of immediate results, *also* contributed to the appeal of spiritualism in settler societies, for it could easily be a non-clerical do-it-yourself religion offering immediate contact with the Other World.

Yet a new and isolated colony is also going to have some diffidence about setting itself against the wisdom of the Old World on its own. In its isolation, it will be hungry for ideas brought in from outside which represent themselves as on the cutting edge of the latest scientific and spiritual thought, especially if they also conform to deep and barely articulated yearnings on the part of those who have shared the settler experience. Here is where the role of the visiting lecturer comes in. He or she will stir up controversy, win ardent fans and foes, and probably leave no more than a mustardseed following. But the speaker will be appreciated for the diversion she or he has brought, and will be talked about. In New Zealand the relative rise and fall of spiritualism and UFOism can be closely linked to the coming and going of outside speakers, who give the novel faith an impetus that gradually wears off as local mediums or UFO enthusiasts are generally unable to equal the phenomena presented, or reported by the international visitor—only to be renewed with the next outside lecturer.

As examples I would like to present three or four 1870s spiritualist visitors to New Zealand, and then the 1959 visit of the Polish-American UFO "contactee" George Adamski. As a preliminary I would only like to point to the claims of nineteenth-century spiritualism, like that of later UFOism, to accord with the frontline of science and unfettered thought—thus the sympathy, if not belief, shown the new faith by Sir Robert Stout, caustic editor, prominent Rationalist, and sometime prime minister of New Zealand in the last century. Spiritualism encapsulated, and in some respects paradigmed, the century's increasingly bitter liberal versus conservative battles in religion. While claiming to be the "oldest religion in the world," one with the faith of the paleolithic shaman, and sometimes proclaiming Jesus and the prophets as "great mediums," the spirit-faith displayed no high reverence for contemporary religious institutions. Instead, it anticipated issues and perspectives soon to be raised in more respectable circles by "modernism": universalism, religious empiricism, insistence that Scripture be examined critically and reinterpreted to harmonize with current scientific and social realities.

It must be emphasized that, in its own time and terms, spiritualism was a strongly liberal movement both religiously and socially. It saw itself on the side of progress and reform in virtually all the great causes: abolition of slavery, women's rights, universal suffrage, and opposition to "privilege" whether in church or state. As we shall see, New Zealand spiritualism as early as the 1870s was in uneasy but definite alliance with the burgeoning Rationalist movement, both mediums and freethinkers opposing the "ignorance" and "superstition" of the past. Spiritualists even called their educational centers lyceums like the Rationalists to contrast them with the Christian Sunday schools.

Spiritualism came to New Zealand after it had already experienced its first rise and fall in the U.S. and Britain. It first appeared in the late 1860s in Otago, the intellectual center of the new colony. Indeed, in 1869 debate on spiritualism in the *Otago Daily Times* was transcended only by the vociferous correspondence concerning the new Church of England Bishop of Dunedin, Henry Jenner.[2]

But by 1870 the novel spirit-faith was the most burning religious issue in Dunedin, provoking among other responses the establishment of a Spiritual Investigation Society.[3] This was the context of rapid immigration, the establishment of Otago University (among the first in the world which women were allowed to attend, even as spiritualism was among the few faiths in which women exercised leadership), and vigorous discussion of the relation of the colony to the home government. (There were voices in favor of virtual independence, or even of transfer of allegiance from Queen Victoria to the United States of America, and much discontent with the current colonial status.) On May 28, 1870, an article in Robert Stout's Dunedin *Echo* presented spiritualism as growing, gaining converts worldwide in the millions. Fifteen years ago, readers were told, spiritualists were laughed at, but "Now who laughs at them?"

This observation was followed on June 11 by a piece borrowed from *Queen* (England) entitled "Extraordinary Spiritual Phenomena," about the celebrated medium D. D. Home and his alleged levitation perceived by Lord Adare; the tone hovers evenhandedly between belief and skepticism.

But on June 15 notice was given in the *Echo* that five or six "spirit circles" were meeting in Dunedin with "successful results." These were countered by accounts of lectures by ministers against spiritualism. The spiritualist camp, however, benefited from the publication ten days later of an article by Emma Hardinge (later Hardinge-Britten), the famous Anglo-American spiritualist who was subsequently to visit New Zealand and write about the faith there. Her June 25, 1870, contribution was "Rules to be Observed When Forming Spiritual Circles." The rules were apparently well received, for shortly after, on July 9, the same paper reported of spiritualism that, "That subject still monopolises a large share of public attention, and nothing is heard of but the formation of 'Spirit Circles.'"

However, an amusing incident took place, we are informed, at one such circle recently formed by some young gentlemen. The table they were trying to tilt would not move, notwithstanding a strict compliance with "Emma Hardinge's Rules." Every participant, except one, had asked it to be good enough to stir, but the piece of furniture remained immobile. The one recalcitrant gentleman was, it seems, a "skeptic." But at last he was prevailed upon to ask the table to oblige him by moving. Then suddenly—from whatever cause—that object suddenly lunged forward with violent, abrupt motion. This so shocked the "skeptic" that he fainted, and had to be restored by his friends.

The same issue of the *Echo* also contained news of the controversial Davenport brothers, whose stage-magic spiritualist performances were arousing much interest, and much debunking, in both Europe and America.

On July 30 the *Echo* noted sympathetically the appearance of the third issue of a sister publication, the *Day Star*, which contained articles on natural theology, women's rights, and spiritualism, together with "strictures on the clergy of Dunedin." This eclectic collection of interests was typical not only of the company which spiritualism kept, but also of the man behind the *Echo*, Robert Stout. Stout was then an energetic young editor, and soon would become both an outspoken Rationalist and an important political figure. One suspects he gave spiritualism such vivid publicity less out of personal faith than to keep his paper lively, and no doubt also because the subject annoyed the orthodox churchmen he loved to bait.

Stout was clearly fascinated by spiritualism. His book and pamphlet collection (now in the Beaglehole Room of the Victoria University Library, Wellington) offers a treasury of early spiritualist works. But there is no evidence here that he was ever seriously convinced, even though, as we shall see, he was later to marry the spiritualist daughter of a couple famous in spiritualist history. Yet it says much for the level of religious tolerance and ferment in the colony that he could, as it were, get by with both Rationalism and open-minded sympathy toward spiritualism, while retaining enough popularity to send him to parliament and later to the premiership.

Other Dunedin journalists evidenced less enthusiasm for the high-spirited new faith. A series of pieces in the *Otago Witness* in 1870 treated the burgeoning spiritualist lectures and phenomena to lighthearted satire. But an account on August 13 of a speaker who treated Christianity, Socialism, Positivism, Darwinism, spiritualism, and Mormonism, all in one lecture, indicated that the remote outpost was alert to the issues facing the intellectual world in the 1860s and '70s. In the past, listeners were told, Christianity had often been assailed but few substitutes were proposed. But now spiritualist tracts—as well as those of Mormons, Socialists, and the rest—could be seen everywhere.

The lifeblood of spiritualism itself, in this pluralistic society, was the visiting lecturer. An early example was James Smith, who came over from Australia to Dunedin April to May 1872. Smith (1820-1910) had emigrated from England to Melbourne in 1854, and became a spiritualist about 1870. He contributed to the *Harbinger of Light* (founded in 1870), the long-influential Australian spiritualist journal.[4]

In 1873, the year following his New Zealand visit, Smith predicted the imminent destruction of the world. This led to his condemnation by the Victorian Association of Progressive Spiritualists; the controversy caused many defections. Smith later attracted mixed attention with his alleged attempts to educate his children by transmitting the wisdom of deceased scholars "magnetically" to their receptive minds.

In 1872, however, Smith was. in high form, lecturing in New Zealand not only on spiritualism but also on Shakespeare and Venice.

His spiritualism generated heated debate, but apparently won friends. At a farewell function on May 13, the Australian was given a purse of fifty sovereigns.[5]

Even more excitement was produced the following year, 1873, by the arrival of two Americans, J. M. Peebles and "Dr." E. C. Dunn. The *Otago Daily Times* (Jan. 29, 1873) limned Peebles as "an elderly gentleman, of intellectual countenance and patriarchal mein," and added, "we will not say that he is an eloquent speaker, but he is fluent, earnest, and impressive."[6] Another account made him "an elderly gentleman, rather tall, somewhat eccentric—wearing long hair and beard, with a distinct and fluent utterance" (*Otago Daily News*, Feb. 3, 1873). (This characterization may be compared to Alfred Deakin's portrayal of Peebles as "a very amiable, composed, kindhearted and truthful man."[7]

The Rev. Mr. Peebles, a sometime Universalistic minister, had, like several others of that denomination, moved on to spiritualism in the 1850s. Characteristically, he combined a wide set of progressive activities with his already-liberal Universalism and spiritualism; his admiring biographer tells us he was "an earnest and unflinching friend and apostle of temperance," and also espoused "the anti-slavery reform, Odd Fellowship, the dress-reform, and woman's rights" (Barrett 1878:37). Support for causes like these was typical of spiritualists generally, whether in the U.S., Britain, or New Zealand.[8]

Even as he aligned himself with the righteous on Earth, Peebles also acquired the patronage of a notable band of spirit communicators, including Mozart, several American Indians, a sister of Louis XIV, and John, the beloved disciple of Jesus. After some vicissitudes, including several church ministries and a brief term as U.S. consul in the exotic city of Trebizond, he fell into a world-wandering career as itinerant lecturer. He possessed a this-worldly traveling companion in the form of Dr. E. C. Dunn. Although Peebles was married to a Bostonian art teacher, one gets an impression that that relationship was less than ardent, and it was Dunn who joined the spiritualist advocate on his wide-ranging expeditions.

According to Peebles's biography, the frontier-born Dunn had been kidnapped at an early age by a band of thieves who trained him as their servant and scout. But he escaped and subsequently worked in a circus as a ventriloquist. He later settled in Battle Creek, Michigan, where Peebles was a Universalist minister. Dunn then had a reputation as a wild and "dissipated" youth. But Peebles, seeing him perform as subject in a traveling hypnotist's show in 1858, recognized remarkable mediumistic talent and became determined to cultivate the hulking, uncouth young man. Under the minister's tutelage, Dunn reportedly reached remarkable heights of clairvoyant ability. Despite considerable community criticism of the relationship, Peebles then took him as a companion and co-worker in the ministry. As he moved into spiritualism, Dunn served as medium and healer, Peebles as teacher and interpreter.

So it was in Dunedin, where Dunn exhibited his mediumship, while Peebles was content mainly to lecture and display the trance skills of his colleague, though he also did some healing as a specialist in the "magnetic passes" popular in mesmeric circles. Dunn received negative comment from one letter-writer in the *Otago Daily Times* for his "Yankee twang" and bad grammar, and his professional credentials—allegedly from an "Eclectic College of Medicine" in Cincinnati—occasioned some skepticism on the part of other correspondents.[9] Finally, the *Otago Daily Times* seemed to find it necessary to vouch for this spiritual pair, that "their relations were those of acquaintances, friends, and traveling companions—nothing more" (*Otago Daily Times*, Jan. 29,1873).

The *Otago Daily News* announced a typical Peebles lecture in this manner:

Notice: Spiritualism
A Lecture on the Above Subject
will be delivered in the
Lower Hall of the Atheneum
by the Rev. J. M. Peebles
This evening, Tue., 28 Jan. [1873], at 8 o'clock
Admission 1s

This address was reported the next day at considerable length in the press. "Delivered before a crowded and most respectable audience," it dealt with the "origin of the present Spiritual Wave, and the rapid dissemination of the principles of Spiritualism." The lecturer spoke of the modern "wave" as "'new' to our conceptions and experiences," yet also as old, for it is but a new scientific perspective on phenomena as ancient as human records: "prophecy, premonitions, dreams, visions, angel visitations, and spiritual gifts." Peebles learnedly presented a host of witnesses, commencing with Zoroaster and Socrates, and climaxing in the the recent "Rochester rappings" and the spirit-explosion they incited.

Peebles and Dunn maintained their popularity. At a farewell soiree for them in March, some two hundred men and women were present, the hall was eloquently decorated with evergreens and flowers, and the two Americans were presented the sum of £100, plus "a greenstone pendant, mounted in gold" for each. In his remarks, Peebles referred to Dr. Dunn's "levitation and immunity while in a trance state from the effects of fire." Peebles said he had seen Dunn "lying on a sofa entranced, and saw him raised by some unseen force of power, and floating in the atmosphere" (*Otago Daily Times*, March 21, 1873). On this note they set sail.

A response to the visiting spiritualists worth mentioning is a strikingly intelligent article in the *Otago Daily News* (Jan. 30, 1873) on current trends in religion. It perceives a broad falling away from "orthodoxy" worldwide, gauged by the growth of Positivism and scientism, but sees almost sectarian responses to the loss of consensus orthodoxy in such conservative movements as Anglican "ritualism" and Roman Catholic papalism (this was of course the age of Pius IX, and just after the first Vatican Council had defined papal infallibility), and another sort of response to the crisis of faith in spiritualism.

"Orthodoxy" was far from defanged, however. A further consequence of the Peebles-Dunn visit was the ecclesiastical trial of one John Logan, a deacon of Knox Presbyterian Church in Dunedin, who was haled before the church session for appearing on the platform with the visiting Spiritualists, thus countenancing an occasion where "blasphemy was being uttered against Christianity." It was one thing, the clergyman advancing the charges said, to go to such an event only to listen "for the purpose of learning what was said," thereby the better "to oppose what was advanced." But in this case the errant believer was "on a plafform backing up one who attacked the very foundations of their faith" (*Otago Daily Times*, March 6, 1873). But Robert Stout, in an editorial entitled "A Heresy Hunt in Otago," made clear his contempt of the whole matter (*Dunedin Echo*, March 8, 1873).

Logan was convicted and excommunicated, but he was not forgotten. In her classic account of spiritualism around the world, *Nineteenth Century Miracles*, the formidable Emma Hardinge-Britten—who traveled to New Zealand in 1879 and met the Logans—spared nothing to paint the embattled deacon as a victim of ruthless bigotry against the faith of the future. Logan's wife was at his side during the trial, Hardinge-Britten relates, but to her poignant plea, "Is there no one here to speak a word for John Logan?" the churchmen's only answer was stony silence. Not surprisingly, after this ordeal both Logans became active spiritualists, Mrs. Logan developing mediumship though she had showed little interest in spirit-communication before (Hardinge-Britten 1884: 270).

Emma Hardinge (1823-1899) was born in England, but came to the United States in 1855, where she performed as a singer for ten years and also became active in the new spiritualist religion. She returned to her homeland at the end of the Civil War, but was back in America in 1869. She married an American, William Britten, in 1870, the same year her famous rules for a spiritual circle were published in Dunedin. She was a founding member of the Theosophical Society in 1875, but Spiritualism remained her main commitment and her relations with Helena Blavatsky were not always smooth. (Both women, however, dramatized the power of these new faiths to liberate persons of their sex for careers in the realms of the spirit on a global scale, a possibility scarcely then imaginable in the conventional churches.)

Hardinge-Britten and her husband lectured widely on behalf of spiritualism in the late seventies, including during the Australia-New Zealand visit of 1879 in which she met the Logans. She settled permanently in England in 1882. Deakin described her as a woman "of large proportions, excellent appetite and unshakable self-confidence." She was "theatrical," and though possessing "a large share of egotism, was also a sincere believer in spiritualistic principles." (Deakin, *Autobiographical Notes*: 433-44, cited in Smith 1965:253-54).

Hardinge-Britten's 1879 visit was the next major event in New Zealand spiritualism after Peebles-Dunn, and one exceptionally significant because it became the basis of a chapter in her *Nineteenth Century Miracles*, with its survey, drawn largely from her own travels, of spiritualism around the globe.

The New Zealand chapter begins with a look at spirit phenomena in Maori shamanism, an important move not only because of spiritualism's general role as a revitalization within "civilization" of such primordial religious motifs, but also because New Zealand was (from the European perspective) a new country in which both the primordial and the revitalized faced each other. There might be hope for a fresh level of mutual understanding between the most archaic and the most recent efflorescences of the human spirit. As we shall see, this was not entirely a forlorn expectation.

Mrs. Harding-Britten's Dunedin lectures were in the Princess Theatre on Sunday evenings and at the Atheneum on weekdays. They aroused heated controversy in the isolated colony over the several months of her stay. The combination of Mrs. Hardinge-Britten's imposing presence, a new religion with sensational new claims, and a high-spirited challenge to Otago's well-entrenched and always-combative believers obviously set the city on its ear. In a day before the rival diversions of film or automobile, seeing the champions of rival sects having a go at each other was clearly prime entertainment.

Hardinge-Britten writes that no sooner had she begun her lecture-hall skirmishes than "the irrepressible M. W. Green," a "minister of the

Church of Christ," arrived from Melbourne with a sheaf of counter-lectures. It was apparently not the first match between these two combatants, for Britten tells us that her rival disembarked "just in time to hurl his javelin once more at Spiritualism, in the height of its success and popularity." Now the gauntlet was down, and we read of halls packed with hooting and stamping supporters of both sides, as though it were a sporting event.[10]

But spiritualism was not the only sword the devil had to wield against Otago's embattled orthodoxy, and the question was whether two seemingly disparate swords could be forged into one. Hardinge-Britten's lectures were under the auspices of the "Free Thought Committee" chaired by Robert Stout, by then also an M. P., Attorney General, and in conspicuous opposition to the use of the Bible in government schools. This clear-cut alliance of spiritualism with Rationalism was of great, and revealing, importance to Mrs. Hardinge-Britten. She wrote, "The day has never come-and heaven grant that it never may!—when sharp lines of demarcation will be drawn, for the purpose of dividing the ranks of 'Freethinkers' and Spiritualists." As is well-known, however, those lines were soon enough to be drawn, for the Rationalists were not convinced the spiritualists were sufficiently rational, nor the latter that their sometime allies spiritual.

This divide was a foretaste of spiritualism in the 1890s, when the movement essentially split between those whose interest was in the scientific study of the paranormal phenomena it allegedly produced, and those whose main concern was spiritualism as a faith able to meet their religious needs. The former generally went into such bodies as the burgeoning Society for Psychical Research; the latter into the spiritualist churches and denominations which first appeared as full-fledged religious institutions, with ministers, Sunday services, and governing boards, in that decade.

Very much the same split can be seen some six decades later in the UFO movement, which has been no less rent between those professing a "scientific" interest in the mysterious aerial phenomena, and those clearly most engaged by their ability to meet religious needs for contact with transcendent cosmic powers. For them the beings riding the flying saucers, and deigning from time to time to speak to mortal men and women, become, in Carl Jung's term, "technological angels," the gods, masters, and descending saviors of old, now garbed in spacesuits. In New Zealand this split was remarkably exacerbated by the lecture-visit in January and February 1959 of George Adamski, who both galvanized and deeply divided the UFO community, until now centered in Harold Fulton's CSI (Civilian Saucer Investigation).

George Adamski (1891-1965) was Polish-born but lived most of his life in the U.S. He was the most famous of all the early "contactees," for whom the beings riding the UFOs bore divine wisdom to their earthly disciples. Those privileged ones, like Adamski, in turn dispensed it in books and from the lecture platform, together with lively accounts of their interworldly meetings and often their journeys in the UFOs to distant planets.

At the time of his adventure Adamski was the proprietor of a hamburger stand on the road to Mt. Palomar, site of the famous observatory. He claimed that on November 20, 1952, he saw a UFO land and met Orthon, a man from Venus, on the California desert. More contacts followed, together with tours in space ships and elevated discussions with beings from various planets. All this was reported in books, especially *Flying Saucers Have Landed* (with Desmond Leslie, who contributed learned material on UFOs through the ages), and *Inside the Space Ships* (Adamski 1955; Adamski and Leslie 1953). These works were quite successful, giving Adamski celebrity status and innumerable opportunities for lectures, interviews, and TV appearances.

By 1954, a year after the initial publication of *Flying Saucers Have Landed*, the Adamski enthusiasm reached New Zealand. His book sold well, was serialized in magazines, and advertisements appeared inviting interested people to write the author in California. In late 1954 Fred and Phyllis Dickeson inaugurated a long UFO career by establishing the Australasian Adamski Flying Saucer Group, later the Adamski Correspondence Group. At their request Adamski agreed to make tapes, which were played at meetings in Timaru and Christchurch. (The tapes originally made for Timaru by Adamski and Desmond Leslie later became part of his permanent stock and were distributed worldwide.) In the meantime, the Adamski Correspondence Group became successful and competed with Fulton's CSI for membership. In 1957 the Dickesons arranged with a newly formed Henderson group, under the Dutch-born Henk Hinfelaar, to organize North Island work, while Timaru would continue to manage South Island activities. Henk and Brenda Hinfelaar had been members of CSI since 1954, and were experienced UFO activists, but clearly they were moving in an Adamskian direction. The Hinfelaars produced a small newsletter independent of CSI for North Island Adamski Correspondence Group people, and the Dickesons did a southern version of the same. All this helped prepare for Adamski's visit to New Zealand, but it also paved the way for disillusionment.[11]

Already Adamski's critics were numerous, though perhaps the extent to which he and his claims struck most level-headed people as outrageous was not yet appreciated in faraway New Zealand. The far-fetched tale, the dubious look of the UFO photographs that adorned his publications, the insouciant self-contradictions, and the lack of the most elementary astronomical knowledge in much of what he said, repelled many. Reports surfaced that this was not the man's first foray into the profitably mysterious. During the 1930s he had operated an esoteric school called the "Royal Order of Tibet." The "cosmic philosophy" of his UFO contacts was allegedly no more than a rehash of what he had retailed as that occult lodge's instruction. He was even said to have once submitted to editors as fiction an earlier version of the Venusian encounter he now, amid the UFO mania, managed to get published as fact.[12]

Despite the rivalry with the Dickesons' overtly Adamskian groups, Harold Fulton's early reaction to the Californian was reasonably tolerant.[13] But as time went on, and especially after Adamski himself actually appeared on the scene, the tone was much more critical. In the September 1959 issue of *Space Probe* (as the CSI magazine was now called; this was the final issue before it went into "recess"), Harold Fulton presented devastating attacks on Adamski's claims. The contactee still had his enthusiasts, however, and in any event he made news. Let us look at the accounts of his New Zealand tour.

January 1959 was an interesting month for news. Fidel Castro triumphed in Cuba, Pope John XXIII called his climactic ecumenical council, the Polaris missile found the Earth to be pear-shaped. A Canterbury University professor was quoted as saying that there may be conscious beings on other worlds, though they would not be people like us. We should be prepared to meet them. Tucked among these items were stories about the visit to New Zealand of a man who said he *had* met them and they *were* like us.

The *Evening Post* of January 21, 1959 (p. 8), headlined the story, "Mr. Adamski Alights in N.Z.—From Conventional Plane." He was here, readers were told, for a four-week lecture tour. He was greeted by news of a letter found in a bottle that had just washed up. The decanter had allegedly been thrown to sea by the crew of the *Joyita*, a ship that had disappeared without a trace in 1955, and the missive reported that all hands had been forced on board "a strange circular metallic object." Although the note may well have been a hoax, Adamski took it seriously and said the account was "feasible."

The contactee then went on to talk about Venusian culture and religion (a "science of life" without temples), and their desire to communicate with us, at least "through our minds." "But they say earthmen are so preoccupied with our own thoughts we are unable to receive impressions when they do send them." On Venus, however, religion is conveyed in educational institutions rather than churches, has to do with the power of the mind over the body and relationships with the cosmos, and is put into practice daily rather than once a week.

Adamski had other thoughts as well about the space friends. To sold-out lecture halls in the major New Zealand cities, he spoke of the Venusians as "exactly like us," but once added, "I have not been to Venus. If I do I will not come back. The ladies there are too beautiful." The Venusians, he said, have come to Earth to observe, not to support any political or religious movement, though they are concerned about negative developments on the third planet (*Evening Post* [Wellington], Jan. 23,1959:14).

Adamski's reception was decidedly mixed. His films of space-ships were declared "unconvincing," and he sometimes met frank laughter and only moderate applause. But, for whatever reason, halls continued to be packed until his departure.

The January 31 *Post* juxtaposed the running Adamski story with an article on Carl Jung's work, *Flying Saucers: A Modern Myth of Things Seen in the Sky*. As we have noted, the great analytic psychologist opined that the saucer vogue was due to deep-level fears engendered by the atomic bomb and the cold war, and a corresponding desire to be rescued by "technological angels," a modern version of the heaven-descended gods and saviors of old. UFOs give us a golden opportunity to see how a legend is formed and how in a difficult and dark time for humanity a miraculous tale grows up of an attempted intervention of extra-terrestrial 'heavenly' powers" (*Evening Post*, Jan. 31,1959:7 and 16).

An editorial, "Visitors from Outer Space," was skeptical of Adamski's human-like Venusians but liberal on extraterrestrials and UFOs generally. The tone was remarkably reminiscent of the *Otago Daily Times* editorial which four decades before had greeted another sensational lecturer from overseas, calling his own beliefs a bit excessive and dogmatic, but endorsing more open-minded research in the areas of which he spoke. It was therefore appropriate that this editorial, without apparently being aware of the parallel, ended with a quote from Arthur Conan Doyle: "The wisdom of man is small, and the ways of Nature are strange, and who shall put a bound to the dark things which may be found by those who seek for them?" (*Evening Post*, Feb 2, 1959:7).

On February 6 a Tokoroa man reportedly took a clear picture of a UFO, and said he would probably forward the photo to George Adamski, "who would no doubt be pleased to study it to determine whether or not it would add confirmation to his theories." On the 9th the picture was reproduced in the paper. It was slightly hazy, but did look like a UFO. The *Post* asked, somewhat facetiously, if the flying saucer people are following Mr. Adamski around.

Adamski himself avowed that they were in his own account of his New Zealand tour, found in his last major book, *Flying Saucers Farewell.* He said that UFOs were sighted over Lake Taupo during his visit, seen by a Mr. W. Miller, "the local leader of the George Adamski Group," just after he had parted from Adamski. The lecturer added, "The spacecraft sightings seemed always to come at the right time to awaken public interest. This was one of the reasons we enjoyed over-flow crowds at all the New Zealand lectures." Like earlier spiritual vis-itors to New Zealand, Adamski showed interest in Maori legend and faith. At Napier he spoke of the Pania statue and story, which we referred to in connection with the spiritualistic Mrs. Cottrell. Adamski was excited to learn that several Maori boys had been taken on a ride in a spacecraft. (The *New Zealand Herald*, however, claimed he had con-fusedly taken an old Maori legend for current fact.)

Adamski found his New Zealand tour more successful than sub-sequent efforts in Australia and the United Kingdom, which were trou-bled by debate and alleged efforts to stop the showing of his film. Like Conan Doyle, Adamski contrasted his New Zealand reception favorably with the rougher treatment he got across the Tasman, and (also like his predecessor) put New Zealand number one among nations, saying "If I were a young man, choosing a new land in which to live, I believe I would select New Zealand" (Adamski 1961:121-33).

For all its oddity, the Adamski script contains the essential ele-ments of a viable UFO religious movement, and indeed of standard new religions generally. As C. G. Jung recognized, for the spiritually minded, UFOs can represent age-old otherworldly hopes (or, as for John Stuart, terrors), now ensconced in gleaming metallic vessels. Like cargo cults, they are classic religious eschatologies revamped to meet the fears and dreams of the modern world. Adamski took pains to distinguish between his contact experience and psychic, mediumistic, or ouija-board communication with the UFOnauts. Both sides, however, were there, as they must be: the initial definitive revelation and the ongoing, more subjective commerce with supernatural reality it launches.

There is also in Adamskism the important religious theme of a link with the past, that shows that though the new faith may appear frail and precarious, it is really legitimated by a rich lineage. Thus Desmond Leslie, in his chapters on *Flying Saucers Have Landed*, makes much of saucers in Atlantis, ancient India, and medieval Europe, often using Theosophical texts like *The Secret Doctrine* as resources. In the

New Zealand context, Adamski does much the same in referring to Maori lore, however inappropriately. Finally, Adamski's vaguely utopian evocations of life on Venus and elsewhere and the "cosmic" philosophy that underlie them offers some semblance, at least, of a prophetic message for earthlings. What is missing—and this no doubt explains why Adamskism never became a real religion—is any regular rite or institutional structure to give the faith vehicles for the long haul. But other UFO religions, all more or less inspired by Adamski's hour in the sun, have created these requisites, most often in the form of spiritualistic mediums and "circles" through which UFO messages are continually received. As we shall see, certain of these group continue in New Zealand to the present.

Adamski came and went, but New Zealand saucerism continued. The year of his visit and of Harold Fulton's departure, 1959, was understandably a watershed year for the movement. First, after the Adamski tour the Adamski Correspondence Groups, apparently at the instigation of the much-disappointed Dickesons, changed their name to New Scientific Space Research Groups (NSSRG). The Adamski tour at least benefited UFO study; by 1961 there were some twenty-five NSSR groups, from Kaikohe to Invergargill.

But in 1961 to 1962 a rift emerged between the Hinfelaars and the Dickesons over allegiance to Adamski. The Timaru group produced evidence that the California contactee's alleged photographs of Venusian spacecraft had been faked. The Henderson Adamski loyalists rejected such heresy, suggesting among other things that the Dickesons "had not taken the refractive properties of Venusian glass into account."

In a personal letter, Phyllis Dickeson explained the appeal and the consequences quite effectively. On June 11, 1988, she wrote to me:

> The War [World War II] had highlighted man's inhumanity to man. Suddenly the F/S furore spread from the United States to the rest of the world. The George Adamski crusade hit New Zealand. We were confronted with G. A. and Desmond Leslie's book in 1954 . . . wherein readers were told of beautiful space friends coming from other planets, and living in peace and harmony, with love and understanding. To us the concept sounded wonderful to say the least. (How gullible we were.) However, apparently, as you well know, this book aroused world wide interest. It did stir the hearts of many like ourselves . . .
>
> But, in 1962 we were instrumental in doing an exposure of George Adamski, because we found our research had taken a new

direction. Rather shattering at the time, but it was necessary, as we wished to find only the TRUTH in all matters concerned. Glaring inconsistencies were suddenly detected, when we saw for the first time . . . past photographs of spacecraft included in his two books. Careful study set us wondering d indeed we had been too gullible and conditioned into believing and accepting all we had been told by G. A. as gospel truth. No. 18-19 of SATCU mags go into great detail of scientific tests we carried out. Incidentally we had both been photographers in the RNZAF and experience had taught us many things . . .

After the schism, the southern group changed its title to New Zealand Scientific Approach to Cosmic Understanding (SATCU), and slowly set out to build a UFO network based on a middle ground between "hard" science and the contactee enthusiasts. For a time the Henderson camp dominated the New Zealand UFO world. But as the 1960s wore on, its uncritically pro-Adamski stance tried the credulity of many followers. For one thing, Adamski had forcefully maintained that the moon, Mars, and Venus were all inhabited by human-like beings of superior accomplishments. The mid sixties Mariner probe of Mars and lunar landings made those claims exceedingly difficult to maintain, despite Hinfelaar's heroic efforts to reconcile them to Adamski and keep the faith. By the end of the decade NZSSRG had notably declined (it was disbanded in 1974), while SATCU's fortunes were soaring.

This group published New Zealand's leading UFO periodical after the fifties *Satcu*, called *Zenolog*, 1973 to 1981. (It ceased publication in 1981.) *Satcu-Zenolog* presented UFO news, articles, and reviews representing diverse responsible points of view. Bruce Cathie's theories, for example, received considerable discussion. Early issues contained anti-Adamski, pro-scientific astronomy material.

During the late sixties and early seventies several other New Zealand UFO groups appeared, but most lasted only a few years. One exception is the Tauranga UFO Investigation Group, headed over many years by Harvey Cooke. Founded as an Adamski Correspondence Group in 1957, it has since become intellectually much more diversified, and it organized New Zealand UFO conventions in 1972 and 1975.[14] The Cosmic Centre, in Whangarei, run by Ron Birch, has published *Kosmon News* since 1971. This interesting paper combines UFO and spiritualistic perspectives freely, interpreting the UFOnauts essentially as spirit-communicators (Quast 1975).

Again we see that the visiting lecturer is best able to generate enthusiasm, but is ill-prepared to sustain a movement over the long haul. The transcendence of ordinary rationality, both in message and format, excites but does not wear well. Yet the recurrence of such episodes as Peebles and Dunn, or Adamski, has kept New Zealand alive to alternative spirituality. This is a land where conventional religion has also failed to sink deep and enduring roots.

NOTES

1. My findings support the contention of Roy Wallis that British settler societies, and egregiously New Zealand, lead among comparable first-world societies in receptivity to new religious movements. Roy Wallis, "Figuring Out Cult Receptivity," *Journal for the Scientific Study of Religion* 25, no. 4 (Dec. 1986):494-503.

2. This prelate, after being consecrated in England for the southern see, arrived in January 1869, but was disapproved by the first synod of his new diocese on the grounds that he was a "ritualist," and eventually returned home.

3. The controversy is suggested by a pamphlet by "A Spiritualist" in the Robert Stout collection in the library of Victoria University, Wellington, dated 11 January 1870, and entitled "Spiritualism, To the Reverend the Synod of the Presbyterian Church of Otago and Southland." The anonymous author presents his vigorous defence of his faith "because some of your number are enquiring after the subject of Spiritualism," and (if we take him at his word) he goes so far as to offer a 1,000 guinea wager that spiritualism is true.

4. This periodical lasted until 1956, when it became the *Psychic Science News-Magazine*. New Zealand spiritualists contributed to the *Harbinger* and received much of their working information on spiritualist affairs from it.

5. On James Smith's lecture tour, see *Otago Daily Times* April-May 1872 passim. For published lectures see James Smith, "Spiritualism; or the Magnetic Teaching, Its Method and Its Objects; Being Three Lectures, Delivered in Dunedin, April 25, May 5, and May 12, 1872" (Dunedin: *Daily Times*). (In the Stout Collection, Victoria University.) For his life see *Australian Dictionary of Biography*, vol. 6, 1851-1890, p. 146.

6. Actually James M. Peebles (1822-1922) was no more than fifty at the time, only half-way through a life of a hundred years. (In 1884 he confidently published, amid his spiritualist and travel books, *How to Live a Century and Grow Old Gracefully*, and in 1912, as though to keep tabs on his own progress in this respect, *Ninety Years Young and Healthy: How and Why*.)
On January 1, 1897, he arrived in Auckland for a second visit to New Zealand, described in a 1898 account eventually collected in his *Five Journeys Around the World, or Travels in the Pacific Islands, New Zealand, Australia, Ceylon, India, Egypt and Other Oriental Countries* (Los Angeles: Peebles Publ. Co., 1910).

Unfortunately, the first 1872 visit to New Zealand is given scant notice, cited only as part of a trip around the world "not alone to see, but to teach as I travelled" (p. 5), and while the second affords much rather pedestrian general discussion of New Zealand climate, geography, and so forth, not much of religious interest is present, apart from a fierce and ill-informed attack on the Christian eucharist as "cannibalism," apparently sparked by an encounter with Christchurch Anglicanism. Then, summoning his usual animus against Christianity and his readiness to idealize anything else as pure and noble, he discourses favorably on the Maori religion, pointing especially to its equivalents to spiritualist seances (pp. 51-54). But while there is certainly much to admire in Maori religion, one is left in this case with a displeasing sense of a liberal mind as narrow and bigoted in its liberalism as any reactionary in his views. Probably this crotchetiness came as he approached his young and healthy nineties, though, since the 1870s accounts of Peebles depict a kindly and admirable personality.

Interestingly enough, Peebles, now "Doctor Peebles," has emerged as a major spirit-guide and cult figure in contemporary American spiritualism. Not a few important mediums communicate out of trance his gruffly spoken but often apt advice to their clients, though for some reason (also not entirely clear) this American-born divine sometimes turns into a Scottish doctor and acquires a Scots accent. But, though seance-room trails are often murky, it seems beyond doubt that the name of this current mentor from the other side derives from the opinionated Victorian who became a patriarch of his faith.

7. Alfred Deakin, later Prime Minister of Australia and architect of Federation, was an enthusiastic spiritualist as a young man, becoming President of the Victorian Association of Progressive Spiritualists, the leading Australian organization, in 1878. Since most of the world-traveling spiritualist lecturers combined their visit to New Zealand with an Australian tour, Deakin was familiar with them. His remarks make it clear that these visits were a necessary but mixed blessing. Highly touted spiritualist lecturers from abroad were the main source of publicity and income for local groups, but the wandering stars who presented them, Deakin indicates, were hard to manage and likely to leave squabbles over the mantles and the receipts in their wake. Peebles, for all his amiability, left dissension and a schism in Melbourne behind him (Alfred Deakin, *Autobiographical Notes*, p. 44; unpublished material in the care of Prof. J. A. La Nauze, University of Melbourne; cited in F. B. Smith, "Spiritualism in Victoria in the Nineteenth Century," *Journal of Religious History* 3, no. 3 [June, 1965] [Sydney University Press], pp. 252-53).

8. For Britain, see Logie Barrow, *Independent Spirits: Spiritualism and English Plebians, 1850-1910* (London and New York: Routledge and Kegan Paul, 1986). For the U.S. with special reference to feminism, see Ann Braude, *Radical Spirits: Spiritualism and Women's Rights in Nineteenth-Century America* (Boston: Beacon Press, 1989).

9. Perhaps rightly so. Barrett, Peebles's biographer, does not even mention the Cincinnati school, but states only that Dunn's medical training was by spirit-

teachers, and that he was "Dr. E. C. Dunn" by virtue of his being "duly diplomatized in the medical school of the spirit-world" (Barrett, *The Spiritual Pilgrim*, p. 70).

10. Hardinge-Britten, *Miracles*, p. 271. For Green's assault see M. W. Green, "Mrs. Hardinge-Britten in the Crucible, Being a Lecture Delivered . . . in Dunedin . . . July 9, 1879, in Reply to 'Spiritualism Vindicated, and Clerical Slanders Refuted'" (pamphlet, Dunedin: G. T. Clark, 1879); and his, "The Devil's Sword Blunted; or Spiritualism Examined and Condemned" (pamphlet, Dunedin: G. T. Clark, 1879). Both pamphlets are in the Stout Collection, Victoria University.

11. This paragraph follows Henry Quast, "A History of the UFO Movement in New Zealand," *Zenolog* 100 (Sept.-Oct. 1975).

12. See articles on Adamski in J. Gordon Melton, *Biographical Dictionary of American Culiand Sect Leaders* (New York and London: Garland Publishing, 1986, pp. 2-4); and Ronald D. Story, *The Encyclopedia of UFOs* (Garden City, N.Y.: Doubleday, 1980, pp. 2-4). For a more sympathetic treatment, see Lou Zinnstag and Timothy Good, *George Adamski: The Untold Story* (Beckenham, Kent: Ceti Publications, 1983).

13. Thus his CSI journal, *Flying Saucers* 5, no. 1 (3rd quarter, 1957): 21, reproduced a 1953 letter to the editor of a London publication by Adamski's coauthor, Desmond Leslie.

14. In a personal letter of May 26, 1988, Harvey Cooke told me that over the years the Tauranga group has come to a deepening understanding of the spiritual meaning of their UFO experience. The UFO idea, and reading books of the Adamski sort, from the beginning somehow helped them to fully realize there is intelligence and purpose behind the universe, and that we can draw on the cosmic mind to handle problems here and now. One gets a feeling that, in some sense, the UFOs and space beings are but triggers of transcendence that have enabled people to break through to what, in the end, was more important, this kind of spiritual awareness. But most of the Adamski-era spiritual/contactee groups have by now faded. The Tauranga groups is one that, thus far, has not.

REFERENCES

Adamski, George. 1955. *Inside the Space Ships*. New York: Abelard-Schuman.

——. 1961. *Flying Saucers Farewell*. New York and London: Abelard-Schuman, pp. 121-33.

Adamski, George, and Desmond Leslie. 1953. *Flying Saucers Have Landed*. New York: British Book Centre. London: Werner Laurie.

Barrett, J. O. 1878. *The Spiritual Pilgrim: A Biography of James M. Peebles*. Boston: Colby and Rich.

Hardinge-Britten, Emma. 1884. *Nineteenth Century Miracles*. New York: Lovell.

Quast, Henry. "A History of the UFO Movement in New Zealand," *Zenolog* 100 (Sept.-Oct. 1975).

Smith, F. B. "Spiritualism in Victoria in the Nineteenth Century," *Journal of Religious History* 3, 3 (June 1965) (Sydney University Press).

8

EXO-THEOLOGY: SPECULATIONS ON EXTRATERRESTRIAL LIFE

Ted Peters

Astronomer and exobiologist Carl Sagan has written: "Space exploration leads directly to religious and philosophical questions."[1] Just what are these questions? Unfortunately, some of the first questions typically asked are very misleading. At the top of the list is a question posed all too frequently by skeptical scientists and tabloid journalists. The question goes like this: If we discover living beings in outer space as intelligent or more intelligent than we, will the Christian religion collapse? Physicist and popular science author Paul Davies provides an example. In his *God and the New Physics* he lays down the gauntlet:

> The existence of extra-terrestrial intelligences would have a profound impact on religion, shattering completely the traditional perspective on God's relationship with man. The difficulties are particularly acute for Christianity, which postulates that Jesus Christ was God incarnate whose mission was to provide salvation for man on Earth. The prospect of a host of "alien Christs" systematically visiting every inhabited planet in the physical form of the local creatures has a rather absurd aspect. Yet how otherwise are the aliens to be saved?[2]

Ted Peters received his Ph.D. from the University of Chicago and is now Professor of Systematic Theology at Pacific Lutheran Theological Seminary and the Graduate Theological Union in Berkeley, California. He is editor of *Dialog, A Journal of Theology*. He is also author of *UFOs—God's Chariots? Flying Saucers in Politics, Science and Religion* (1977); *GOD—The World's Future: Systematic Theology for a Postmodern Era* (1992); and *SIN: Radical Evil in Soul and Society* (1994).

What is misleading here is the assumption that the Christian religion is fragile, that it is so fixed upon its orientation to human beings centered on Earth that an experience with extraterrestrial beings would shatter it. An alleged Earth centrism renders Christianity vulnerable. Yet, I find little or no credible evidence that such a threat exists. To the contrary, I find that when the issue of beings on other worlds has been raised it has been greeted positively. Nevertheless, it is important to observe that the issue has only seldom been raised; and so to Davies credit it is not crystal clear how theologians would react should extraterrestrial intelligence (ETI) suddenly become part of our everyday world. So I believe the theological community should view the Davies challenge as an opportunity to think more deeply about the matter. I advocate *exo-theology*—that is, speculation on the theological significance of extraterrestrial life.

In what follows it will be my task to show that theologians following philosophers in the ancient and medieval periods consciously confronted the prospect of life on other worlds and on more than one occasion actually integrated such thinking into their theological understanding. Then I will survey examples of contemporary religious and theological spokespersons who represent Roman Catholic, evangelical Protestant, liberal Protestant, and Jewish theological perspectives. Here we will find that the topic of extraterrestrial intelligence is seldom raised; but when it comes up it seems to present no significant difficulty. Nevertheless, such study would not be complete without examining the fundamentalist literature of the 1970s that may have contributed to the misunderstanding alluded to above. This literature sought to demonize the UFO phenomenon—presuming that UFOs are associated with extraterrestrial intelligence—and this literature might have given the impression that the Christian faith is more fragile than it in fact is. To this agenda we now turn.

HISTORICAL THEOLOGY:
MIGHT GOD CREATE MANY WORLDS?

The question of the existence of extraterrestrial intelligent life as we pose it today was, in the ancient world, subsumed under a slightly broader question: Are there many worlds or only one? The story begins prior to the Christian era. It begins during the rise of philosophy in Greece in the fourth century before Christ.

Yes, there are many worlds, said the atomistic philosophers Democritus (460-370 B.C.) and Epicurus (341-270 B.C.). The basic assumption of atomism is that the things we know in the world are the result of chance. They are formed by the chance coalescence of atoms moving about within the void, within empty space. Atoms are in constant motion, colliding, sticking together, and forming things. This is how our world came into existence. And because the number of atoms is infinite, it follows that there is an infinite number of other worlds (*aperoi kosmoi*) resulting from the same cause and effect chance formations. A Roman disciple of these earlier Greeks, Lucretius (98-54 B.C.), wrote in his famous *On the Nature of Things*: "since there is illimitable space in every direction, and since seeds innumerable in number and unfathomable in sum are flying about in many ways driven in everlasting movement," the existence of other worlds must be admitted, "especially since this world was made by nature."[3] Just as there are many kinds of fish, there are many earths. Just as there are many kinds of life on earth, there are many kinds of worlds.

What about life in those other worlds? Epicurus and Lucretius positively asserted the existence of plants and living creatures on other worlds. Speculation on this question sometimes focused on the moon. One late Greek source known as pseudo-Plutarch says that "the moon is terraneous, is inhabited as our earth is, and contains animals of a larger size and plants of a rarer beauty than our globe affords."[4] Note the assumption that we live on a global, not a flat, earth. Note also the hint of utopianism: the "rarer beauty than our globe affords."

No, answered the towering giant of ancient philosophy, Aristotle (384-322 B.C.); there is only one world and not many. He rejected the arguments of the atomists, especially the idea of chance formation. Aristotle's primary argument was based on his belief that all things naturally seek their proper place. The motions of the four simple elements which make up reality—earth, air, fire, and water—were governed by two principles. They would move toward their natural place by nature, or they would move away from their natural place by violence. The natural place for the Earth is the center of the world, and the other elements are oriented accordingly. Fire seeks its natural place by ascending to the heavens, while water and air seek their places in between. What results is a cosmological vision of a single reality with the Earth at its center. Extending out from the center we find concentric spheres until we reach the one and only heaven. The heart of the argument is what we might call a "natural centrism" toward which all of nature tends. And, of course, there can exist but one center. Therefore, there can exist one and only one world.[5]

It is well known that Aristotle's philosophy made a significant impact on Christian theology. It dominated the medieval tradition of scholasticism. Perhaps this accounts for the assumption made by Paul Davies and others that Christian theology thinks of the earth or humanity as the center of the universe. Although Aristotle's influence was doubtless formidable, nevertheless, it would be simplistic to say that Christians say it just because Aristotle says it. There was a good deal more flexibility and even controversy than we might assume.

St. Thomas Aquinas (1224-1274) of the University of Paris is the best known and most influential of the scholastic theologians; and, to be sure, he was dedicated to reconciling the Christian faith with Aristotelian philosophy. The particular question he confronted which leads into our topic here was this: Is God's omnipotence compromised if God creates only one world? The counter assumption seems to be that an omnipotent God could, if he so desired, create an infinite number of worlds. Thomas's position is that "it is necessary that all things should belong to one world."[6] The key premise is that perfection is found in unity. One world which is constituted of everything that exists would be perfect, a definition which, by the way, derives from Plato. In sum, it would be more in accord to say that God has created a single perfect world than a great number of necessarily imperfect worlds. Hence, divine omnipotence and the existence of only one world are compatible.

Note what is missing here. Thomas is not arguing according to some principle of Earth chauvinism that the Earth must be the center because it is the best. He is not arguing that the human race is the be-all and end-all. Rather, he is exploring where the logic of certain premises might take him. He is agreeing with Aristotle that our world is ordered, not by chance as Democritus and the atomists said, but by the principle of unity tending toward perfection. Be that as it may, the Thomistic view is definitely in favor of one world, not many.

But Thomas was not the only one to consider this issue. Others did with other opinions. John Buridan (1295-1358), also at the University of Paris, said, ". . . we hold from faith that just as God made this world, so he could make another or several worlds."[7] Note that Buridan's position is based upon faith, not philosophy. Yet Buridan did not want to fly in the face of Aristotle's arguments. So, he added a premise. Different elements which operate according to different laws could be produced in other worlds. Other worlds, then, would not have to obey what we earlier identified as Aristotle's law of natural centrism. This would permit God to create another world; and he could order the things in it to that world and not to the center of ours. Thus, Buridan could meet the demands of both faith and philosophy.

Nicole Oresme (1320-1382), Bishop of Lisieux, extended Buridan's thinking in his treatise, *De coelo de mundo*. But rather than make peace between faith and Aristotle, Oresme simply repudiated Aristotle. To do so he reformulated the definitions of "up" and "down," the directional indicators for the movement of light and heavy things. Heavy things go down, toward the center of the earth. According to Oresme's reformulation, however, no longer do "up" and "down" refer only to the center and circumference of our world alone. Another world with another center could have its own version of up and down. All things do not have to orient themselves to our world's center. There could exist a plurality of centers. This denies the position of both Aristotle and Thomas that all things in the same universe must have a relation to one another. Two worlds sufficiently removed need not have a relation to one another, but only relations between their own respective parts. In the fourteenth century it was easier to disagree with Aristotle than it would be later when Aristotle's metaphysics became almost a criterion of Christian orthodoxy.

So Steven Dick can unravel a litany of medieval theologians prior to the Copernican Revolution who could accept the many worlds idea, including Albertus Magnus, John Major, Leonardo da Vinci, and Spanish Jewish scholar Hasdai Crescas. With some theologians, such as Nicholas of Cusa (1401-1464), we not only get a plurality of worlds but also extraterrestrial life.

> Life, as it exists here on earth in the form of men, animals and plants, is to be found, let us suppose, in a higher form in the solar and stellar regions. Rather than think that so many stars and parts of the heavens are uninhabited and that this earth of ours alone is peopled—and that with beings perhaps of an inferior type—we will suppose that in every region there are inhabitants, differing in nature by rank and all owing their origin to God, who is the center and circumference of all stellar regions.[8]

This is what we find in the medieval period. What happened at the dawn of the modern period? What happened to religious thinking about life on other worlds in the wake of the Copernican Revolution and the heliocentric theory of the universe where each planet, including Earth, has its own center of gravity?

This heliocentric view, of course, met with resistance from some church leaders. Not all church theologians objected, of course, only those who had committed themselves to Aristotelian metaphysics. We recall here that heliocentrism was condemned in 1616. Yet it is important to note that this condemnation was not based directly on the issue of many worlds. In his defense of Galileo, Tommaso Campanella in effect gave support to the many worlds point of view. He made it clear that the idea of multiple worlds violated no decrees of the Roman Catholic Church and certainly was not contrary to Scripture. It was contrary only to the opinion of Aristotle. Then, lifting the argument to a higher level, he pointed out that Galileo's heliocentric view does not actually posit a plurality of worlds; rather, it discloses one world, the universe, with many subsystems within it.

Theological accommodation to the new science and the vast view of the universe opened up by astronomy moved sufficiently rapidly so that Arthur Lovejoy could write, "by the first or second decade of the eighteenth century not only the Copernican theory of the solar system but also belief in other inhabited planets and in the plurality of worlds seems to have been commonly accepted even in highly orthodox circles."[9]

In his important study on the history of Protestant thought and natural science, John Dillenberger reports how the debate over many worlds continued in the Reformation churches. "The debate hung on the assumption that human life existed on other planets," writes Dillenberger. A second and more troubling assumption was that Scripture nowhere mentions extraterrestrial life. In the event that life on other planets is discovered through science, then this significant truth about our universe would be revealed apart from Scripture. The recognition of this possibility could mean a shift in the focus of Christian theology toward creation; creation would be thought to be more extensive than redemption. In the tradition of the Two Books—Scripture and Nature—nature seemed to be revealing more about creation than Scripture about redemption. "Now creation, interpreted as the wisdom of God in His works, was more significant than redemption . . . there was an entire realm where science was valid and where the Biblical tradition had nothing to say."[10] The significance of this historical observation for our study here is that, although a theological debate took place, the theologians did not deem it important to reject the notion of other worlds with living creatures.

So Steven Dick can list numerous natural theologians of the seventeenth and eighteenth centuries, following the Copernican Revolution, who could affirm many worlds such as Richard Bentley, John Ray, William Derham, Immanuel Kant, and others. Similar to Nicholas of Cusa, Richard Bentley, a theologian and contemporary colleague of Isaac Newton, posited the existence of ETI. As he did so, he anticipated contemporary ethical concerns regarding the centrality or non-centrality of the human race on our planet. He was preparing to combat what we might today call "earth chauvinism."

... we need not nor do not confine and determine the purposes of God in creating all mundane bodies, merely to human ends and uses ... all bodies were formed for the sake of intelligent minds: and as the Earth was principally designed for the being and service and contemplation of men; why may not all other planets be created for the like uses, each for their own inhabitants which have life and understanding?[11]

In sum, during the formidable period of medieval scholasticism, despite the forceful impact of Aristotelian philosophy, Christian theology was by no means wedded to the idea that God created only one world. An honest debate raged that carried on well past the Copernican Revolution into the modern era. More than one position was put forth. Some of our best minds not only affirmed the idea of multiple worlds, some even spoke positively regarding the existence of extraterrestrial life.

CONTEMPORARY THEOLOGY: WHAT ABOUT ETI?

The period of history following World War II is the space age in many respects. We have been putting satellites in orbit and astronauts on the moon, and we have been sending probes to Venus, Mars, and beyond. We have been searching for extraterrestrial life with radio telescopes.[12] Budgetary arguments regarding space exploration rage annually in the U.S. Congress. Our theaters have been showing sci-fi films depicting interplanetary space travel and even wars between extraterrestrial civilizations. Nine percent of the U.S. population claims to have seen what they believe to be a UFO, and half the people who think of UFOs as a reality believe they come from outer space.[13] Our culture is shot through and through with space consciousness.

One would expect, therefore, that theological leaders would want to respond to the rise in space consciousness by providing some intellectual guidance. Yet, surprisingly, relatively little is being done. The subject is too widely ignored, in my judgment.[14]

Be that as it may, in those instances during the post-World War II period when the subject has been seriously taken up, the possibility of the existence of ETI is positively affirmed. Beginning with the Roman Catholics, a theologian of the Manualist tradition which extends scholasticism down to the present day, George van Noort, has held that it is not in the least incompatible with faith to admit that rational beings exist on other heavenly bodies.[15] Fr. Theodore Hesburgh, past president of the

University of Notre Dame, served on a NASA commission and argued that he could legitimately accept the possibility of life on other planets. His argument was that because God is infinite in intelligence, freedom, and power, we cannot take it upon ourselves to limit what he might have done.[16] Notorious German theologian Hans Küng, while making an argument to decenter the place of humanity on planet earth, says "we must allow for living beings, intelligent—although quite different—living beings, also on other stars of the immense universe."[17] And Karl Rahner, whom many see as the theological giant of Catholicism in the twentieth century, refers to "the many histories of freedom which do not only take place on our earth."[18] Francis J. Connell, C.S.S.R., dean of the School of Sacred Theology at the Catholic University of America during the 1940s and 1950s, sums the matter up: "it is good for Catholics to know that the principles of their faith are entirely compatible with the most startling possibilities concerning life on other planets."[19]

Turning to the conservative wing of Protestantism, evangelical preacher Billy Graham welcomes both the prospect of ETI and UFOs. "I firmly believe there are intelligent beings like us far away in space who worship God," he told an interviewer. "But we would have nothing to fear from these people. Like us, they are God's creation."[20] In his book on angels, Graham writes,

> Some . . . have speculated that UFOs could very well be part of God's angelic host who preside over the physical affairs of universal creation. While we cannot assert such a view with certainty . . . nothing can hide the fact that these unexplained events are occurring with greater frequency around the entire world. . . . UFOs are astonishingly angel-like in some of their reported appearances.[21]

Moving a bit more to the center of mainline Protestant theology, we find New Testament scholar Krister Stendahl, former Bishop of Stockholm and former dean of Harvard Divinity School. At a NASA-sponsored symposium in 1972, Stendahl was asked about communication with ETI. "That's great," he said. "It seems always great to me, when God's world gets a little bigger and I get a somewhat more true view of my place and my smallness in that universe."[22]

A. Durwood Foster poses the very question central to this chapter. Given the prospects of contact with extraterrestrial intelligent beings, "is faith in any way threatened by the possibilities here in view? Why should it be?" He answers that a faith already steeped in God's mystery should be prepared for the unexpected and even affirmatively open to it. He goes on to cite the New Testament recognition that there are other sheep of which we know not (John 10:16). Then he concludes, "The love of God manifest in Jesus Christ has surely not remained unknown wherever there is spiritual receptivity."[23]

Paul Tillich would agree. Tillich, the renowned systematic theologian with one foot in neo-orthodoxy and the other in liberal Protestantism, takes the question of ETI quite seriously. The prospects of extraterrestrial life raise important issues for the doctrines of creation, anthropology, and Christology.

> . . . a question arises which has been carefully avoided by many traditional theologians, even though it is consciously or unconsciously alive for most contemporary people. It is the problem of how to understand the meaning of the symbol "Christ" in the light of the immensity of the universe, the heliocentric system of planets, the infinitely small part of the universe which man and his history constitute, and the possibility of other worlds in which divine self-manifestations may appear and be received.
>
> . . . our basic answer leaves the universe open for possible divine manifestations in other areas or periods of being. Such possibilities cannot be denied. But they cannot be proved or disproved. Incarnation is unique for the special group in which it happens, but it is not unique in the sense that other singular incarnations for other unique worlds are excluded. . . . Man cannot claim to occupy the only possible place for incarnation.[24]

The issue Tillich debates here is the one cynically referred to as "absurd" by Paul Davies. The issues is this: Does the existence of multiple worlds of intelligent life require multiple divine incarnations and multiple acts of redemption? Tillich seems to be answering in the affirmative.[25] Tillich so conflates the doctrines of Creation and Redemption that he believes God's saving power would already be at work regardless of the situation in which ETI find themselves. One implication of this position is that we earthlings would not necessarily need to send missionaries to initiate aliens into God's plan of salvation.

Returning to the Roman Catholics for a moment, two contemporary scholars have tackled this issue and, at some variance from Tillich's position, argued for the universal efficacy of the Christ event on earth. In an interview, Jesuit journalist L. C. McHugh was asked: What would be the relation of intelligent beings inhabiting a far corner of the cosmos to Jesus Christ? McHugh responded saying, such people "would fall under the universal dominion of Christ the King, just as we and even the angels do."[26] Similarly, J. Edgar Bruns, a New Testament scholar and president of Notre Dame Seminary in New Orleans, writes that ". . . the significance of Jesus Christ extends beyond our global limits. He is the foundation stone and apex of the universe and not merely the Savior of Adam's progeny."[27] This position would probably imply that, should ETI be discovered, missionaries would be called for much as they were when Europe discovered the Western hemisphere.

This is not the case for Roman Catholic Karl Rahner, who seems to side more with Tillich. Rahner, as mentioned earlier, argues that the possibility of extraterrestrial intelligent life "can today no longer be excluded." Then he raises the question of "Christ as head of all creation." He speculates: "In view of the immutability of God in himself and the identity of the Logos with God, it cannot be proved that a multiple incarnation in different histories of salvation is absolutely unthinkable." He concludes that theologians on Earth will "not be able to say anything further on this question," because they are limited by revelation. The purpose of Christian revelation is limited to "the salvation of humankind, not to provide an answer to questions which really have no important bearing on the realization of this salvation in freedom."[28]

In this debate over the need for multiple incarnations, we need to keep one item in mind. Even though there are slight differences of opinion regarding the relationship between ETI and the historical event of redemption here on Earth, what is important is the common assumption that possible ETI belong within the realm of God's creation and are well worth serious theological consideration.

Back to the Protestants. Moving a step in the liberal direction on the spectrum, German theologian Wolfhart Pannenberg affirms at least the vague possibility of intelligent life living in other solar systems in our own or in remote galaxies. With regard to redemption, however, he differs from Tillich. Pannenberg understands Jesus Christ to be the incarnation of the eternal *logos*, and the eternal *logos* is the medium through which the whole of creation has come into being. The significance of Jesus Christ extends to the farthest reaches of the universe, because through Christ God has promised to draw the whole of time and space into a consummate unity.[29]

The issue of the universality of Earth's Christ event is taken up as well by Lewis Ford, a spokesperson for the school of process theology. Disciples of the philosophy of Alfred North Whitehead, process theologians usually find themselves on the liberal end of the Protestant spectrum. Ford begins by stating that "salvation is not just limited to men but applies to all intelligent beings wherever they may dwell."[30] Ford embraces the concept of evolution, applies it to every location in the universe, and then asserts that God is always and everywhere drawing the evolutionary process toward greater complexity and higher value.

> . . . we may define God as that dynamic source of values which lures the evolutionary process to an ever-richer complexity productive of increasing freedom and intensity of experience. As such, God is necessarily operative in the development of every life and in every culture, whether terrestrial or extraterrestrial.[31]

The Ford position is close to Tillich's. It virtually collapses salvation into creation. As with Tillich, Ford affirms multiple manifestations of the divine, each one appropriate to the species for which redemption is aimed. Jesus Christ constitutes the incarnation aimed at the human race on Earth. Other parallel incarnations are then possible for other intelligent races. In every instance, however, operative is the same creative and redeeming work of the same God.

Although I wish more theologians would take the matter of other worlds and ETI seriously, I still find the spectrum of theological considerations of ETI and even UFOs impressive.[32] Yet the above-mentioned theologians are all Christians. When researching this topic, I began to wonder what a Jewish theologian might say. So I telephoned my friend and colleague, Rabbi Hayim Perelmuter. Dr. Perelmuter is former president of the Chicago Board of Rabbis and a professor at the Catholic Theological Union in Chicago. He is one of those renaissance people who covers the waterfront: he is an author, a Scripture scholar, knowledgeable about the history of intellectual thought, experienced in Jewish-Christian dialogue, up to date on the politics of Israel, and most apt to know the broad sweep of current Jewish thinking. I described the issue on which I was working. His response was forthright and clear. Contemporary Jewish theology would have no difficulty whatsoever in accepting new knowledge regarding the existence of extraterrestrial life. In fact, it would simply broaden the scope of our understanding of God's creation. Then he added a note of tragic humor. "We Jews have had to adjust to all kinds of things in history, including Nazi Germany and the difficulties with Israel. I am sure we could adjust to space beings emerging from flying saucers as well."[33]

FUNDAMENTALIST LITERATURE: UFOS AS CHARIOTS OF SATAN

During the decade of the 1970s numerous magazine articles and books appeared that dramatically challenged the alleged existence of

UFOs and depicted the entire phenomenon as a Satanic plot. This literature sought to frighten Christian readers into disbelief in ETI, and in doing so to capitalize on the fascination that usually accompanies fright. The literature influenced many conservative and evangelical clergy and eventually found its way into sermons and Christian education programs. This approach was most likely stimulated by the wide publicity given to the Pascagoula, Mississippi abduction of Charles Hickson and Calvin Parker on October 11, 1973, as well as the extremely large sales of books such as *Chariots of the Gods?* by Erich von Däniken. A brief upsurge in fright publications followed the release of Spielberg's movie, *Close Encounters of the Third Kind* in December 1977, but then it died down. In the 1980s and 1990s anti-New Age and then anti-Satanism literature seems to have rushed in to fill the gap in Christian terror literature.[34]

Puzzled at such extremism at a time when Billy Graham had spoken so favorably about ETI, I engaged these proponents in conversation. As best I can reconstruct it, their theological argument follows three steps that lead us to the question of biblical authority. First, there can be no life on other planets because the Bible has not revealed this to be the case. Because the Bible does not anywhere mention life on other worlds, belief in ETI is anti-biblical.

> If there were intelligent beings with origins in outer space, we would expect the Bible to support the fact. However, the Bible takes no such position . . . the Bible doesn't even mention the existence of other planets . . . the person of Jesus Christ and His redemptive work underscore the uniqueness of life to the planet earth. He came to die for man's sins, exclusively.[35]

Note how blatantly this argument commits the fallacy of *argumentum ex ignorantia*, the argument from ignorance: because the Bible ignores UFOs and ETI, therefore, UFOs and ETI do not exist. This is fallacious because no one has ever claimed that the Bible constitutes the exhaustive supply of all knowledge that can be known. It is logically possible for things to exist that are not mentioned in the Bible. Toyotas and Swiss watches and Big Mac hamburgers exist indisputably, but they are not mentioned in the Bible.

Note also the Earthcentrist assumption here. Perhaps this shows that Paul Davies has some grounds for predicting a radical challenge to Christian belief—at least this brand of Christian belief—should the existence of ETI be empirically confirmed.

The second step in the fundamentalist fright argument is to acknowledge that belief in ETI seems to presuppose the theory of evolution. This observation is correct. The UFO phenomenon and the concept of evolution converge in our culture to form a kind of mythical view of reality.[36] Since the 1950s and perhaps even before, a myth has been under construction in our society that pictures Ufonauts as coming from a civilization in outer space that is further advanced than ours—further advanced in science, technology, and morality. This means they have evolved further than we on Earth. According to this emerging myth, the Ufonauts are traveling to Earth to teach us how to evolve faster, to save ourselves from disaster as we cross the nuclear threshold. The space beings constitute our own future coming back in time as well as space to rescue us, to save us.[37] What the fundamentalist interpreters believe they see in this emerging UFO myth is the human imagination gone wild. By presuming validity to the theory of evolution, earthling imagination has projected evolutionary advance to the point of developmental salvation onto imaginary civilizations in outer space. What we find here, complain the fundamentalists, is a subversive plot to convince our people to believe in evolution and, of course, then to deny the authority of the biblical account of Creation in the book of Genesis.

The third step in the argument is to declare all this demonic. Scientists who propound the theory of evolution have with some frequency in the past been denounced by fundamentalists as enemies of the Bible. Indirectly this denouncing is repeating itself between the lines of anti-UFO literature. Further and more decisively, the UFO phenomenon with its accompanying evolutionary myth provides a temptation for earthlings to look for salvation in someone other than the biblical Jesus Christ. Responding specifically to the movie *Close Encounters of the Third Kind*, as well as to the generic cultural UFO myth, Frank Allnutt considers the implications of believing in a race of ETI who are "smart enough to have outlawed crime and war." He goes on,

> That line of reasoning sees the possibility that these extraterrestrials have become masters over those things which cause death and that they hold the key to the mysteries of immortality. And, maybe, they intend to teach us the secret way to obtain eternal life.[38]

Allnutt can only conclude, then, that "the UFO phenomenon is being caused by Satan and his demons. Their purpose is to confuse people about the true source of salvation, the Lord Jesus Christ."[39]

It seems to me that the fundamentalist interpreters perceive with accuracy the salvific structure inherent to the developing UFO myth in our society and, further, that this myth stands at some variance with what Christians want to teach. For this the appropriate response is Christian apologetic theology, to be sure. Yet, the apologetic argument as actually raised here is unnecessarily confused with fallacious appeals to the exclusive authority of the Bible.[40]

CONCLUSION

In sum, although there are partial grounds for thinking the Christian faith is so Earth centrist that it could be severely upset by confirmation of the existence of ETI, an assessment of the overall historical and contemporary strength of Christian theology indicates no insurmountable weakness. The Aristotelian metaphysical tradition within medieval theology and recent fulminations by fundamentalists have admittedly propounded versions of Earth centrism that might give one pause in this regard. Despite St. Thomas's use of Aristotelian arguments against many worlds, however, Christian theologians have routinely found ways to address the issue of Jesus Christ as God incarnate and to conceive of God's creative and saving power exerted in other worlds. This applies, of course, to historic Christianity in its contemporary Roman Catholic, evangelical Protestant, and liberal Protestant forms. Although Paul Davies' challenge does apply to some expressions of fundamentalism, we must note that, in the giant storybook that constitutes the two-thousand-year history of the Christian religion, fundamentalism makes up at best one tiny subchapter. It would be a mistake to take the fundamentalist fright as representative of Christianity as a whole.

At this point in time we can only speculate. The UFO mystery remains unsolved. The question of the actual existence or non-existence of ETI remains open. Should contact between terrestrials and extraterrestrials occur, we cannot predict with certainty how hitherto earthbound society will react. Some scenarios present themselves as likely. In the event that the ETIs appear rich, friendly, and benevolent, we will at first greet them with open arms. In the event that the ETIs appear to be warlike conquerors or disease-ridden contaminators or in some other way a threat, we may see the diverse peoples of Earth uniting together in a common defense. In the event that the ETIs appear to be much like us, we can expect both of the above reactions initially, and then we will eventually see the development of alliances and counteralliances between segments of both Earth and ETI populations. In all three cases, alert Christian theologians will attempt to extrapolate on the basis of existing knowledge of earthling behavior and try to guide us all toward a peaceful and fraternal bond of friendship. Such theologians would affirm with St. Thomas that "all things should belong to one world," and this one world would include both earthlings and extraterrestrials. In the meantime, while we wait for contact, I recommend that some scholars take up Paul Davies' challenge and engage in a preliminary form of exotheology.

NOTES

1. Carl Sagan, *The Cosmic Connection* (New York: Dell, 1973), p. 63.

2. Paul Davies, *God and the New Physics* (New York: Simon and Schuster, Touchstone, 1983), p. 71.

3. Lucretius, *On the Nature of Things*, Book 2, lines 1052-66. See the overall account of the development of the idea of many worlds by Steven J. Dick, *Plurality of Worlds: The Origins of the Extraterrestrial Life Debate from Democritus to Kant* (Cambridge: Cambridge University Press, 1982); hereinafter abbreviated PW. For his citing of Lucretius, see p. 11. After the rediscovery of Lucretius's book in medieval Europe in 1417, there was considerable Christian opposition raised against atomism. The heart of the opposition did not stem from the many worlds theory per se, but rather from Lucretius's overt atheism.

4. Cited by Dick, PW, p. 19.

5. Aristotle, *On the Heavens* books 8 and 9. Dick wants to argue that in only one place does Aristotle commit himself to one world only (PW, p. 193, n. 18). But the texts he gives as evidence of variation (*Physics* II:196a:25-30; III:203b:20-30; IV:218b:4-10; VIII:250b:20-23) do not, in my judgment, support Dick's claim. In fact, what Aristotle says in *Metaphysics* XII:1073a:33-40 reiterates what he said in book 9 of *On the Heavens*.

6. Thomas Aquinas, *Summa Theologica*, First Part, Question 47, Article 3. Shortly before his death, Thomas wrote a commentary on Aristotle's *On the Heavens*. It is *Aristotelis libros de caelo et mundo, generatione et corruptione, meteorologicorum expositio* (Rome, 1952).

7. John Buridan, *Quaestiones super libris quattuor de caelo et mundo*, cited by Dick, PW, p. 29.

8. Nicholas of Cusa, *On Learned Ignorance*, trans. Fr. Germain Heron (New Haven: Yale, 1954), pp. 114f., cited by Dick, PW, p. 41. It was Nicholas, in discussing the boundlessness of God's universe, who gave us the line which Carl Jung likes so well: its "center is everywhere and its circumference is nowhere."

9. Arthur O. Lovejoy, *The Great Chain of Being* (New York: Harper and Row, 1936), p. 130.

10. John Dillenberger, *Protestant Thought and Natural Science* (New York: Doubleday, 1960), p. 136.

11. Richard Bentley, *A Confutation of Atheism from the Origin and Frame of the World* (London, 1693), reprinted in *Isaac Newton's Papers and Letters on Natural Philosophy*, ed. by I. B. Cohen (Cambridge, Mass.: Harvard University Press, 1958), pp. 356-58.

12. The US NASA project known as SETI (Search for Extraterrestrial Intelligence) under the leadership of Frank Drake at the University of California at Santa Cruz began using radio telescopes in 1960 to listen for signals coming from various locations in our galaxy. So far no contact. On October 12, 1992, NASA added new channels and upgraded its technical listening capabilities by a factor of 10,000. SETI has also been renamed the High-Resolution Microwave Survey. See "SETI Faces Uncertainty on Earth and in the Stars," *Science* 258, no. 5079 (October 2,1992): 27.

13. In his fascinating study of the UFO phenomenon in terms of the classical mythical structure of human experience, Keith Thompson recognizes the already widespread public acceptance of the idea of extraterrestrial intelligence.

> The main significance of UFOs for society may well rest not so much in their extraterrestrial origins, or lack thereof, as in the fact that a sizable segment of society believes and behaves as if they are real, regardless of the available evidence. Public opinion surveys show an increasing willingness of Americans to believe we are not alone in the universe.

Angels and Aliens: UFOs and the Mythic Imagination (Reading, Mass.: Addison-Wesley Publishing Co., 1991), pp. 244-45.

14. There are some exceptions, of course. Jack Finegan and later A. Durwood Foster, both theological professors at the Pacific School of Religion in Berkeley, California, tried to provide such guidance in their respective books, *Space, Atoms, and God* (St. Louis: Bethany Press, 1959) and *The God Who Loves* (New York: Collier-Macmillan, Bruce, 1971), esp. pp. 118-26. Jack A. Jennings, a Presbyterian campus minister, contends that both UFOs and ETI should become items of theological debate; but, unfortunately, the debate is not being carried on in the learned journals. Because the church ignores the topic, we find it being considered in the marketplace. Jennings recommends that the main bodies of orthodox Christian believers begin getting ready ("UFOs: The Next Theological Challenge?" *Christian Century* [Feb. 22,1978], pp. 184-89).

15. The fifth edition of Msgr. Van Noort's *Tractatus de Vera Religione* comes in nine volumes. In the English rendering, he points out that we can expect progress in Christian theological thinking if we grant one fundamental principle: "dogmatic progress, i.e., progress in faith, can go in only one direction: a deeper, fuller explanation of one and the same revealed truth, without any change in the essential meaning of a dogma" (*Dogmatic Theology*, Volume III

[Westminster, Md.: Newman Press, 1961], p. 394). Applied to the question of ETI, we may expect progress insofar as it is a deepening of our essential apprehension of the fullness of God's creation.

16. Reported by Alan Lightman, "In His Image: Reflections on Other Worlds," *Books and Religion* 13, no. 6 (September 1985): 1.

17. Hans Küng, *Eternal Life?* (New York: Doubleday, 1984), p. 224.

18. Karl Rahner, *Foundations of Christian Faith* (New York: Crossroad, 1978), p. 446. See Denis Edwards, *Jesus and the Cosmos* (New York: Paulist Press, 1991), p. 89.

19. Francis J. Connell, C.S.S.R., "Flying Saucers and Theology," in *The Truth About Flying Saucers*, by Aime Michel (New York: Pyramid Books, 1967), p. 258.

20. *National Enquirer* (November 30,1976).

21. Billy Graham, *Angels: God's Secret Agents* (Garden City, N.Y.: Doubleday, 1975), pp. 9-14 passim. In an article on the social implications of UFOs and ETI, James M. McCampbell comments skeptically on the Graham book. If the primary duty of both angels and UFOs is to protect the faithful, he says, then they are not doing a very good job. "Unfortunately, they seem to be off playing golf during wars, earthquakes, famines, epidemics, tidal waves, tornadoes, hurricanes, volcanoes, murder, and airplane accidents. Perhaps somebody should fire about 200,000,000 angels and hire some reliable replacements." ("Significance for Society If UFOs Are Extraterrestrial," unpublished paper, 1988, p. 12).

22. *Life Beyond Earth and the Mind of Man*, ed. by Richard Berendzen (Washington: NASA Scientific and Technical Information Office, 1973), p. 29. Even God-is-dead theologian William Hamilton agrees that there may be ETI. But Hamilton says so minus the "that's great!" enthusiasm of Stendahl. He writes, "I see no objection to saying that God may have created other worlds than this one. I see no objection to saying that a savior may have visited other places in other times. I see no objection, but neither do I see a point" (William Hamilton, "The Discovery of Extraterrestrial Intelligence: A Religious Response," in *Extra-Terrestrial Intelligence: The First Encounter*, ed. by James L. Christian [Buffalo: Prometheus Books, 1976], p. 108).

23. Foster, *The God Who Loves*, p. 125. A century earlier Albrecht Ritschl approached the matter similarly. Ritschl announced his acceptance of the Copernican Revolution and the decentering of planet Earth and then speculated about "the development of a spiritually-endowed race of organisms" living on other worlds. "Thus it is possible that the earth is not the only scene of the history of created spirits" (*The Christian Doctrine of Justification and Reconciliation*, Vol. 3 of *The Positive Development of the Doctrine*, tr. by H. R. Mackintosh and A. F. Macaulay [Clifton, N.J.: Reference Book, 1874, 1966],

pp. 614-15). The continuity here is the notion that there could exist on multiple planets spiritual beings who are receptive to divine grace.

24. Paul Tillich, *Systematic Theology* (3 volumes: Chicago: University of Chicago Press, 1951-63) 2:95f.

25. Positions taken on this issue vary. William of Vorilong, a contemporary of Nicholas of Cusa, could affirm many worlds but only one Christ event. The death and resurrection of Jesus Christ on Earth is sufficiently efficacious for the redemption of extraterrestrial civilizations. Jesus would not have to die again (*Sentences*, book 1). Philip Melanchthon, sixteenth-century Reformer and compatriot of Martin Luther, would deny the existence of many worlds on the ground that there could be only one redemptive event. "Therefore it must not be imagined that there are many worlds, because it must not be imagined that Christ died and was resurrected more often, nor must it be thought that in any other world without the knowledge of the Son of God, that men would be restored to eternal life" (*Initia doctrinae physicae* [Wittenberg, 1550] fol. 43. See Dick, PW, pp. 42f., 87f.).

26. "Life in Outer Space? An Interview with Rev. L. C. McHugh, S.J.," *Sign* 41, no. 5 (December 1961): 29. In this interview Rev. McHugh uses the term 'exotheology' for what is to my knowledge the first time it has appeared in print. A similar term, 'exochristology', appears in an article by Andrew J. Burgess, "Earth Chauvinism," *Christian Century* (December 8,1976), 1098-1102.

27. J. Edgar Bruns, "Cosmolatry," *The Catholic World* 19, 1 (August 1960): 286.

28. Karl Rahner, "Natural Science and Reasonable Faith," in *Theological Investigations* (22 vol. [New York: Crossroad, 1961-1988], vol. 21:51-52).

29. Wolfhart Pannenberg, *Systematische Theologie* (3 vol. [Göttingen: Vandenhoeck und Ruprecht, 1988-1993], vol. 2).

30. Lewis S. Ford, "Theological Reflections on Extra-Terrestrial Life," *Raymond Review* 3, no. 1 (Fall 1968): 2.

31. Lewis S. Ford, *The Lure of God* (Philadelphia: Fortress Press, 1978), p. 63; pp. 54ff. John Hick, a liberal Protestant though not of the process school, believes similarly that "God could become incarnate more than once—and indeed, in principle, an indefinite number of times—for the sake of separate groups of people . . . on other planets of other stars" ("A Response to Hebblethwaite," in *Incarnation and Myth: The Debate Continues*, edited by Michael Goulder [Grand Rapids, Mich.: Eerdmans, 1979], p. 192).

32. Some theology is more serious than others. A book widely ignored in theological circles yet fascinating to a large number of readers in other circles is Barry Downing's *The Bible and Flying Saucers* (New York: Avon, 1968 and Berkeley, 1989), wherein Downing acknowledges the hermeneutics of existen-

tialist and death-of-God theology and then proceeds to interpret the Bible in such a way as to discern repeated ETI visits in UFOs. Less serious is the spate of literature that tried to superimpose a scientific naturalism upon the scriptural witness, turning God into a technologically advanced Ufonaut. See: R. L. Dione, *God Drives a Flying Saucer* (New York: Bantam, 1969) and *Is God Supernatural? The 4,000 Year Misunderstanding* (New York: Bantam, 1976). See also the notorious Erich von Däniken, *Chariots of the Gods?* (New York: Bantam, 1970), *Gold of the Gods* (New York: Bantam, 1972) and *Gods from Outer Space* (New York: Bantam, 1972).

33. This theme of creative survival under the worst imaginable conditions unites the various chapters of Jewish history for Perelmuter, whether this be the rise of Rabbinic Judaism in the ancient world or survival under the Nazi assault in the twentieth century. See his epilogue to *This Immortal People: A Short History of the Jewish People* by Emil Bernhard Cohn, revised and expanded by Hayim Goren Perelmuter (New York: Paulist Press, 1985) and the book he authored, *Siblings: Rabbinic Judaism and Early Christianity at Their Beginnings* (New York: Paulist Press, 1989).

34. A relevant example is William M. Alnor, *UFOs in the New Age: Extraterrestrial Messages and the Truth of Scripture* (Grand Rapids: Baker, 1992). Alnor cannot make up his mind as to whether or not ETI exist. He is waiting for more facts. Yet he is confident that a combined UFO-New Age conspiracy seeks to entice us away from orthodox Christian beliefs into a vague mystical and universalistic religion. "Their foremost concern seems to be to change the way we think about God. They are almost equally interested in changing God's Word, the Bible, and inserting in its place a type of universalism that says it really doesn't matter what one believes in matters of religious faith as long as one is sincere. Truth is irrelevant" (p. 133; see p. 15).

35. Frank Allnutt, *Infinite Encounters: The Real Force Behind the UFO Phenomenon* (Old Tappan, N.J.: Fleming H. Revell, 1978), p. 80. In the same genre see John Weldon with Zola Levitt, *Encounters with UFOs* (Irvine, Calif.: Harvest House, 1975) reprinted as *UFOs: What on Earth is Happening?* (New York: Bantam, 1975); Clifford Wilson and John Weldon, *Close Encounters: A Better Explanation* (San Diego, Calif.: Master Books, 1978).

36. I outline this emerging myth in Ted Peters, *UFOs—God's Chariots?: Flying Saucers in Politics, Science, and Religion* (Louisville: Westminster/John Knox Press, 1977). The thesis I develop in this book follows the trail blazed by Carl Jung in *Flying Saucers: A Modern Myth of Things Seen in the Sky* (Princeton: Princeton University Press, 1973) and expanded by incorporating the methods of Mircea Eliade, Paul Tillich, and Langdon Gilkey so as to uncover the covert religious dimensions of an otherwise apparently secular phenomenon. The previously mentioned work by Keith Thompson, *Angels and Aliens: UFOs and the Mythic Imagination*, follows a different path. Thompson's fascinating thesis is that the very unsolvability of the split between surface appearance and myste-

rious underlying reality of UFOs provides the driving energy that keeps the UFO myth alive and generates its ongoing symbolic power.

37. New Age spirituality is also cultivating evolution in mythological ways. In contemporary literature we find an interesting synthesis of UFOs and evolutionary spirituality in the work of psychologist Kenneth Ring. Ring compares and contrasts UFO experiences with near-death experiences and suggests that both are precipitated by what philosopher Michael Grosso calls the "Mind at Large." UFO aliens enter our imagination through the Mind at Large, and our imagination becomes an "objectively self-existent" reality with a purpose, namely, to transform human consciousness. To what end? In order to persuade the human race to take responsibility for the ecological health of the planet. This leap in human consciousness constitutes a psychospiritual evolutionary advance, says Ring. "We are in the midst of an evolutionary spurt toward greater spiritual awareness and higher consciousness—and the occurrence of UFOEs and NDEs is an integral part of that progression" (*The Omega Project: Near-Death Experiences, UFO Encounters, and Mind at Large* [New York: William Morrow, 1992], p.186. In contrast to the contactees of the 1950s for whom UFOs would save us from nuclear destruction, Ring says the UFOs will save us from ecological destruction (p. 180). And, because Ring incorporates an eschatological vision of a new heaven and a new earth (pp. 235f.), I believe he represents a nuanced example of the celestial savior model of UFO interpretation I outline in *UFOs—God s Chariots?* chapter 7.

38. Allnutt, *Infinite Encounters*, p. 72.

39. Ibid., p. 122.

40. I am not challenging the authority of the Bible here. I am challenging the fallacious form of arguing for application of biblical authority to UFO-ETI claims.

9

UFO CONTACTEE PHENOMENA FROM A SOCIOPSYCHOLOGICAL PERSPECTIVE: A REVIEW

John A. Saliba

Reports of human encounters with extraterrestrial life forms have a long history, as has been amply documented by George Eberhart's massive bibliography (1986). Over the last forty years personal testimonies by individuals who claim they have had contacts and communications with space beings have increased (Melton and Eberhart 1990). These contacts have often contained religious messages and moral instructions that pertain both to the material and spiritual well-being and destiny of humankind.

At times, those who have experienced the presence of intelligent beings from other worlds have interpreted that experience in religious terms. George Adamski (1891-1965), for instance, the first contactee of the modern era who elicited veneration from his followers, may have seen himself as a latter-day space prophet. Heroic stories about him hint that he was not an ordinary person from this planet and that, after his apparent "death," he went on to other planetary missions. Several UFO contactees have attracted disciples and established religious organizations. Movements like the Aetherius Society, the Cosmic Circle of Fellowship, Human Individual Metamorphosis, and Unarius Academy of Science can be characterized by the definite prophetic and/or mystical leadership roles assumed by their founders and can be cited as typical examples of new religious movements.

One of the main difficulties encountered in the study of UFO reports is that they are not open to the same process of investigation that has become the normal procedure in the modern scientific world. First of all, UFO phenomena cannot be analyzed directly, immediately, and thoroughly by the scientific community. Second, UFO phenomena cannot be easily categorized—they do not fall into one of the established areas of academic study and there are no universally acknowledged specialists who can be entrusted with the task of verification. Third, the scientific world may not be able to deal with reports that combine both empirical data with the religious and psychic overtones that permeate many UFO reports and accounts of contacts with, and visitations from, alien beings. Four, there is a mysterious quality about UFOs which leaves the door wide open for all kinds of interpretations, both plausible and far-fetched. It is, thus, understandable, if unfortunate, that many natural scientists have been unreceptive to the need of studying the flying saucer phenomenon with an open mind.

Given these inherent problems in studying UFOs and confirming their existence as an objective reality by the proven methods of the natural sciences, two major alternative explanations have been advanced.[1] One tries to understand UFO experiences in terms of psychic phenomena. In this approach the seemingly bizarre and irrational events linked with UFO encounters are associated with psychic events, like telepathy and clairvoyance, which are not part of conventional science (Andrews 1980; Schwarz 1983). This same approach is related to the opinion that UFO contacts are religious events comparable to visions and apparitions of spiritual beings that have been reported in many different traditions (Evans 1984,1987a).

The other method treats UFO phenomena from the point of view of the behavioral sciences. The focus here is directed to the social and cultural factors that accompany UFO reports, to the psychological states of those who experience them and believe in their presence and mission, and to the effects that such encounters might have on the mental health of UFO sighters. In this chapter the major social, psychological, and psychiatric attempts to explain the UFO phenomenon will be outlined.

THE MYTH OF FLYING SAUCERS

Among the more common interpretations of flying saucers, an interpretation shared by many social and behavioral scientists, is that UFO narratives are basically a form of modern mythology (Bartholomew 1989; Goran 1978; Cohen 1967). In other words, they have to be treated as legendary stories involving supernatural beings and must be considered as cultural creations that come into being to explain phenomena for which no complete scientific explanation has yet been proposed.

gious language that expresses the perennial human quest for mean-
and relevance in an uncertain and often unpredictable universe.

Since a UFO report originates with the perception of an anoma-
s event, which is then interpreted, it is not easy to distinguish
ween what actually caused the UFO contactees' experiences and the
erpretations given to the experiences themselves. This explains, in
t at least, why the numerous debates about whether flying saucers
lly exist have not changed much in nature or content over the last
y decades; nor have they persuaded many people to change their
ws. In spite of the overtly negative stance of some scholars, the
jority of social and behavioral scientists are not concerned with mak-
judgments about the physical reality of extraterrestrial visitors and
ntacts, but are rather interested in identifying and examining the con-
ts in which UFO encounters occur.

SOCIOLOGICAL APPROACHES

Sociological studies of UFOs start with the premise that the source
UFO sightings and contacts has to be located in the culture or society
which the encounters occur. The tendency of most sociologists and
thropologists is to see a necessary link between social phenomenon
d belief systems. This approach, theoretically speaking, does not eval-
te the evidence for the existence of UFOs nor does it comment on
e validity and plausibility of the belief in flying saucers and their
eged mission.

Os and Sociocultural Traditions

One of the most common approaches in sociology and anthropol-
y is to examine UFO accounts as integral parts of society and/or cul-
re. The underlying assumption is that UFO beliefs come into being
d flourish in a culture that is congenial to their existence and draw
eir materials from already existing traditions. UFOs must be related to
e matrix in which they occur and thrive. Culture, it is maintained,
ays a key role not only in spreading the ideology behind UFO narra-
ves, but also in influencing those who report UFO sightings of, and
ntacts with, their alien occupants. To what extent this influence actu-
ly determines UFO phenomena is a debatable issue. Attempts to show
at a relationship exists between UFO phenomena and some cultural
ements, such as contemporary technology and folklore, are common
sociological literature.

The basic elements of the story and its meaning can be summarized as follows: based on alleged visual UFO sightings and contacts by
sincere and reliable people and on investigations by noted ufologists, it
is concluded that intelligent beings, either from planets in our solar
system or from remote regions of outer space, have been, possibly for
many centuries, watching us and contacting select people. In UFO literature one comes across four basic types of encounters based on their
level of intensity: (1) close encounters of the first kind, in which a flying
saucer is seen at a distance of a few hundred feet; (2) close encounters of
the second kind, when the spacecraft has left some tangible sign of its
presence, such as a scorched area on the ground where it landed; (3)
close encounters of the third kind, where contact with aliens has been
reported; and, more recently, (4) close encounters of the fourth kind,
namely those that involve abductions.[2]

Since these alien beings could not have visited the Earth unless
they had developed a technology suitable for space travel, they are
assumed to be vastly superior to us in many respects. Speculations
about the nature and appearance of the "ufoauts" themselves, their
technological achievements, and their spiritual and psychic powers
abound. Various scientific and/or religious speculations about their
friendly or hostile presence, and reasonable explanations of why not
everybody sees them and why their occupants do not land and make
contact with the human race, have been devised. As we have seen in
earlier chapters some people have stressed the spiritual or religious
elements in UFOs and have committed themselves to the mission
revealed by the aliens, who are judged to be spiritually mature beings
who have come to deliver important messages that affect the destiny of
the human race.

Many social scientists take it for granted that there is no conclusive
empirical evidence to support the myth of flying saucers as outlined
above. They maintain that the belief in UFOs can be compared to
ancient beliefs that assigned natural phenomena, like thunder and the
eruption of a volcano, to different gods. The legends about flying
saucers have developed into complex stories that are fed on the one
hand by misinterpretations of quite natural terrestrial objects and, on
the other, by science fiction literature.

Among the most articulate critics of both UFO reports and
research are Philip Klass (1989) and Donald Menzel (Menzel and Taves
1977). They declare unambiguously that UFO accounts are untrue stories (myths) that cannot be substantiated by solid evidence. They carefully refute the instances of alleged UFO sightings and assert that all
UFO close encounters are subject to natural explanations. Because UFO

legends are part of the current popular Western culture and figure prominently in the media, people are conditioned to be receptive to the possibility of extraterrestrial visitations. But such myths are nothing but "insidious" falsehoods that delude people and lead them astray by encouraging them to rely on fanciful desires. People who believe in UFOs or claim to have seen, or been contacted by, an alien craft are individuals who are maladjusted, prone to hallucinations, alienated, foolish, or vulnerable to mystical phenomena. Klass denounces abduction stories as psychologically dangerous accounts. Menzel is particularly disparaging of those who dedicate their time and effort trying to prove the existence of UFOs and goes so far as to call ufology a "pathological science."

Other scholars appear to have a more benign view of the myth of flying saucers. Elizabeth Bird (1989), for instance, advances the view that psychological explanations are sufficient to explain UFO sightings. She concedes, however, that those who claim to have seen a flying saucer or been abducted by aliens are not unstable individuals who suffer from psychosis or some serious personality dysfunction. Rather they are fantasy-prone, suggestible people who are easily influenced by cultural patterns. She sees similarities between stories of witches flying on broomsticks and accounts of abductions by UFOs. From a psychological point of view, therefore, believers in UFOs are not psychologically "normal" individuals. However, mythological accounts of UFO encounters, including those that describe abduction experiences, are not harmful, but perform some useful psychological functions.

One of the most developed treatments of UFOs as a modern myth is that of Carl Jung (1970), who examined the pervasive presence of UFOs not only in reports but also in dreams and modern paintings. Jung finds UFO phenomena interesting because they contribute to our knowledge of the human psyche. He relates close UFO encounters to collective stress or perceived danger. In other words, human beings project a threatening situation into an image of a flying saucer. Because UFOs more often appear as round objects, they are symbols of totality. The myth of flying saucers is a meaningful expression of human nature and deserves the attention of scholars.

Another interpretation of accounts of flying saucers has been influenced by Claude Lévi Strauss's structural study of myth (1963). Ashworth (1980), for example, makes an interesting comparison between two mythologies: (1) accounts of UFOs as expressed by writers such as Erich von Däniken (1969,1976), and (2) stories about Atlantis (De Camp 1975). He argues that religion, science, and popular science are all myths in the sense that they raise questions about ultimate meaning.

Religion and science, however, have nothing t inexplicable phenomena like UFO sightings, co The myth of flying saucers belongs to popular being to resolve these contradictions. One cou that contemporary Western culture has created religion and science, assigning to them oppo views of the universe and of the role humans UFO myth attempts to unite religion and sci framework, thus resolving the contradictions an

While many interpreters of the UFO myth itly or implicitly, that the accounts of sightings, tions are not empirical events, the approach take more cautious. Hilary Evans (1983), for examp ined the evidence for the existence of flying s more open attitude and does not rule out the pos ings might be based on some objective phenom unknown to modern science. While stressing the in UFO stories, Evans suggests that they may nomenon and that "there is a real probability, des tions, that a great many UFOs *are structured art origin*" (1983, 150).

Others prefer a phenomenological approac judgment with regard to whether flying saucers e ers argue that belief in them is a modern way of ra ultimate concerns that are not answerable by mod an approach common in the academic study of 1989, 68ff.; Schmidt 1988, 181ff.), they state that the mystery element inherent in the universe ar UFO myths are, consequently, a suitable way of beliefs and values in a metaphor that is more adap scientific speculations about the nature and struc and the human potential to conquer space.

Keith Thompson (1989), for instance, provide both psychological and sociological interpretations prefers an approach which is more in line with the He has been influenced by the works of Joseph C Carl Jung (1970) and links the UFO myth with impo The reality of UFO visions and abductions as phy secondary to their reality as vehicles of meaning. U on UFOs, Thompson opts for a multidimensional a into consideration the social, political, and archety phenomena. Stories about UFO sightings and con

John Spencer (1987, 328), enlarging on this theme, observes that "the apparent development of UFO has tended to very closely mirror the development of our own technology." He speculates that there are five possible reasons why this is the case: (1) UFOs are extraterrestrial vehicles visiting the Earth for some yet unknown reason and their technology is slightly ahead of our own; (2) UFOs are real flying saucers from other planets and their presence has the advantage of stimulating our own technological advancement; (3) UFOs are invaders from space who are more advanced technologically than we are, but who have no desire to expose themselves and their scientific secrets; (4) UFO descriptions reflect the current trend in UFO research and, as our technology advances, so does that of our alien visitors; and (5) the manner in which UFOs are conceived depends on the ways the media (particularly the movie industry and television) depict them. Spencer observes that, for instance, by the early 1950s, movies about UFOs began to display the fears of a nuclear war. He concludes that the possible relationship between our technology and that of alien beings explains why the study of the cultural influences on contactees is at least as important as their reports.

Another cultural element that must be taken into account when dealing with UFO reports is contemporary science fiction. The theme of scientifically advanced extraterrestrial creatures who visit the Earth for various purposes is common both in literature and in the cinema. Nigel Watson (1987, 337), reviewing the movies that are based on flying saucers and alien beings, complains:

> Unfortunately ufologists have tended to ignore the influence of the cinema on our perception of UFO phenomena, whilst filmmakers have largely ignored the wealth of material within the UFO literature that could bring new insights into the human conditions on the screen.

One of the advantages of this theory is that it simplifies matters by relating the UFO phenomenon to one important and pervading cultural item, be it technology or science fiction. Its main weakness is that it fails to realize that UFOs present a more complex problem. Science fiction stories, unlike so many UFO contacts, rarely have religious and/or philosophical implications. In some instances, particularly in religious movements like the Aetherius Society, UFO technology is interwoven with the religious messages and spiritual techniques that the aliens are believed to impart.

Herbert Hackett (1948), in one of the earliest essays discussing the matter, endeavors to show how the concept of "flying saucers," once formulated, becomes a stereotyped cultural idea, which is transmitted through the news media and buttressed by new experts and authorities in the field. Conceptions about unidentified flying objects and their pilots are part of a worldview that has both emotional and intellectual implications. They become slogans and social constructs and are disseminated through the usual sociocultural channels.[3] Hackett compares the concept of UFO to those of "Jew" in Hitler's time and "Communism" in America during the 1950s. Belief in UFOs, therefore, does not necessarily depend on actual sighting or contact nor on indisputable empirical evidence.

The emergence and popularity of UFO sightings and contacts are analogous to other beliefs and convictions in Western culture. Evans (1987b), who has made important contributions to the study of anomalous phenomena, compares the modern interest in flying saucers to the witchcraft craze of the fourteenth to the seventeenth centuries and thinks that they serve both a psychological and cultural purpose. He outlines several principal responses to UFOs, responses that are embedded in culture. The skeptic's rebuttal of the claims of many ufologists is just one type of reaction that can be labeled the "negative obsession of the unbeliever," which is a widespread phenomenon in the West. Evans observes that there are different cultural responses to UFOs and concludes that UFOs reflect public preoccupations. The study of flying saucers is important because, whether they exist or not, they are a mirror of modern culture.

A different, though related, approach is pursued by Phyllis Fox (1979), who questions the reasons why people believe in UFOs. She insists that the UFO phenomenon is not related to social status but is rather consistent with contemporary Western culture, which supports belief in flying saucers. She points out that UFO reports are not to be confused with empirical evidence for the existence of flying saucers. Further, she stresses the need to explore the part played by rumor in disseminating UFO reports and outlines the cultural and social "predictors" of belief in UFOs.

UFO and Marginality

One possible sociological approach argues that the social status of individuals is the main element that must be explored in order to understand UFO reports and contacts. One variety of this interpretation is known as the status inconsistency theory. This hypothesis is based on the observation that in highly stratified societies individuals may occupy incompatible statuses or roles. Four important social statuses are distinguished: income, occupational prestige, education, and ethnicity. A person, for example, may occupy a position of little prestige, while having the educational background that qualifies him or her for greater respect from the community. In this case the individual experiences discrepancy and contradiction between education and public consideration. This may lead to resentment and to the desire for change in one's social condition or private life. Status inconsistency, which is a form of marginality and alienation, can result, therefore, in the lack of predictable behavioral reactions, as well as in psychological stress and cognitive dissonance.

Donald Warren, in a seminal article on flying saucers, discovers a regular pattern in UFO sightings and argues that "UFO sightings are linked to status frustration and, especially, to perceived status deprivations relative to one's position on the social ladder" (1970, 600). After examining the social conditions of UFO contactees, he concludes that reports of these mysterious extraterrestrial aircraft are ways in which some individuals break out of the social order which, in their estimation, is not giving them the place and attention they deserve and is, thus, a source of frustration. UFO encounters are, consequently, a form of escape "into unrealized and perhaps unrealizable consistent situations," an escape that reflects the rejection of the established order and its values.

The above study relates UFO sightings to the social marginality of those who have actually seen or made contact with a UFO. It fails, however, to explain why those who are in a position of status inconsistency see flying saucers rather than, say, join an established religious sect or a marginal, nontraditional religious group. Warren's theory has been indirectly challenged by Troy A. Zimmer (1984), who compares the social psychological attributes of UFO sighters and nonsighters among college undergraduates enrolled in an introductory course in sociology at a California public university. Those taking part in the questionnaire were examined for their interest in science fiction, their mystical experiences, their rejection of culture, their pessimistic view of the world, their personal well-being, and their backgrounds (age, sex, and college major). The author concludes that the UFO sighters were, in general, similar to nonsighters. They were more likely to know someone else who has had a UFO experience and to believe in occult phenomena. They were, further, usually reluctant to talk about their UFO encounters and tended to regard the government as being dishonest about the UFO phenomenon. But apparently, no sign of status inconsistency was detected. "It is evident," Zimmer (1984, 204) unhesitatingly states, "that they [i.e., the sighters] are no more alienated, distressed, or maladjusted than nonsighters."

UFOs and Folklore

Related to the above approach is the position of several scholars (Bullard 1988, 1989; Lowe 1979; Rojcewicz 1986) who have studied the UFO phenomenon as part of folklore traditions. They point out that UFO occupants, for instance, exhibit the physical appearance, character, behavior, and concerns that elves and fairies have done in folktales. UFO abductions are remarkably similar to narratives of kidnaping by fairies, initiation ordeals, and journeys to the land of the dead. The same kind of evidence is adduced to buttress both stories about UFOs and folklore legends that include extraordinary personages. UFO accounts are, moreover, reported and transmitted by the same processes that all folklore is. Theories about the origin, function, and meaning of folklore are equally applicable to UFO narratives. Linda Degh (1971), for example, in an article outlining the dialectic of belief, has shown how the UFO legend of extraterrestrial creatures and their visits to Earth rests on the departure of content from standard social reality. UFO beliefs are comparable to other religious belief systems because, since they do not fit into the normal ways of perceiving the environment, they elicit uncertainty and contradictory positions.

A good illustration of how folklore is transmitted is provided, for instance, by Ron Westrum (1980), who distinguishes between UFO sightings and reports. He points out that since not all sightings become reports, it is necessary to examine the procedure that transforms the former into the latter. He considers four major steps in the report process (1980, 308): (1) the sighting itself; (2) a discussion of the sighting with family and friends; (3) the communication of the sighting to the press, the authorities, or investigators; and (4) the publication of the sighting.

This process can be lengthy and complex. It involves the reflections of several individuals, the reactions of nonsighters, the writing up of the story in a manner that is communicable to those who have not experienced the sighting and/or contact, and the dissemination of various reports that make comparison possible. It is easy to see how whatever is sighted becomes colored by the perceptions, beliefs, and attitudes of the many individuals who take part in producing a written UFO report. The process itself is valuable because it provides a method for pinpointing those elements that are fictitious.

Another inclusive cultural approach would stress the similarities between the physical appearance of aliens and that of mythological and folkloristic beings. Alvin Lawson (1980a) has shown that the vast majority of descriptions of aliens can be classified into six types—human, humanoid, animal, robot, exotic, and apparition. These categories, he points out, are found in mythology, folklore, science fiction literature, comic books, television serials, movies, and even advertising. He thinks that those who have had close encounters of the third kind are drawing from this cultural source. He further asserts that the "similarities raise the possibility that encounter witnesses unconsciously derive descriptions of alien robots, exotic and other UFO entities from traditional available models" (1980a, p. 32).

In like manner, accounts of UFO sightings and abductions are comparable to many folktales from different parts of the world. Degh (1977) points out that these accounts fall into traditional folklore categories. Legends of superior beings who watch over us and of whom we can expect redemption are hardly novel. In UFO stories, these traditional tales appear in a revised form that is more in harmony with modern society and contemporary human aspirations. Degh also explores the legend-telling chain and suggests that real legend tellers may, at least from a folkloristic viewpoint, be more important than the eyewitnesses and/or believers.

The current interest in abductions, where UFO creatures figure as nefarious beings from other physical or psychic realms, has been investigated by several folklorists. Bertrand Meheust (1987) explores dominant patterns that are detectable in these frightening accounts. He selects four recent records of such abductions and compares them to cases in nonliterate societies. He finds that the motifs, such as the themes of death and rebirth and the isolation of the subject, are the same. In UFO accounts, however, the standard topics have been reworked and expressed in modern language and imagery. The abductees go through a religious experience that is comparable to that of shamans, who also report that they fly to distant lands.[4] One of the more perceptive observations that Meheust makes is that shamans are able to cope with their unusual experience, because their culture provides them both with ways of understanding and dealing with it and with the support of most members of their community. Modern UFO abductees, however, have no way of coming to terms with their experiences. Their culture, instead of offering them sanction or encouragement, exposes them to ridicule. And their experiences, rather than being accepted and admired as one form of genuine encounter with the holy, are considered to be signs of pathology.

In a similar fashion, Valerii Sanarov (1981) has examined nineteenth-century sightings and linked them with the then-budding development of the airship. He draws parallels between flying saucer reports, airship tales, traditional tales of the rope-trick of Indian fakirs, and world-tree fairy tales. Among the common characteristics of these accounts is that they all seem to happen at twilight or at night. Aggressive behavior occurs in all types of folktales. In the case of flying saucer stories, the abductees are usually taken by force and subjected to medical examinations. Sanarov is of the opinion that flying saucers and the little green men that operate them and abduct humans have no objective reality. They are, however, symbolic of the level of social development, the cultural situation, and the beliefs of those who report their experiences.

Stories of "men-in-black," who confront those who have witnessed a UFO with the intention of persuading them to keep their knowledge of space creatures a secret, are also amenable to a folkloristic analysis. They have parallels to strange people who visit those who have come in contact with monsters. Peter Rojcewicz (1987,1989) sees both resemblances and differences between the descriptions of the men-in-black and more traditional appearances of the devil. He raises the question whether the visits of the men-in-black can, at times at least, be considered a kind of psychological drama. Unlike the majority of social scientists and folklorists, Rojcewicz seems willing to consider the possibility that some real experiences may lie behind the bizarre tales of the men-in-black.

UFO Cults and Organizations

Another sociologically oriented line of inquiry looks into the kind of UFO groups, institutions, and organizations that emerge in the wake of UFO encounters. Michael Schutz (1980), for one, has distinguished between three major types of UFO groups—religious cults, platform societies, and investigation groups—that have arisen especially since the early fifties. Most, if not all, members of these groups believe in the existence of UFOs, though they disagree regarding their nature and function.

The first type of UFO group, called a cult or religious movement, is made up of a closely knit community whose leader claims contact with UFO beings, who are believed to be beneficent entities from other planets. Regular messages from these space beings deal with traditional religious topics. Becoming a member of one of these fellowships requires some kind of conversion and initiation process with the concomitant commitment to the group's ideology and lifestyle.

The second type of UFO group, the platform societies, are relatively loose networks. They provide the opportunity for speakers to expound their views on flying saucers and for those who have had a

UFO experience to relate it in a public and sympathetic forum. Many of these associations display a general concern for occult matters and attract people of different interests. They do not, consequently, form a community of believers who share a definite belief system and way of life under one acknowledged leader. Neither do they require the conversion and commitment of their membership.

The final type of UFO group, the investigative associations, are largely made up of research-oriented individuals who are interested in UFOs mainly from an academic standpoint. Although some astronomers have been associated with these societies, their members are largely amateurs who have examined cases of UFO sightings and contacts and reached some conclusion about their authenticity. They are careful not to accept any UFO account as a genuine encounter and do not hesitate to give natural explanations to many UFO phenomena. They allow more open discussions on the UFO problem and tolerate more divergent opinions on the subject. Though some members of these establishments believe that UFOs exist, they do not usually attach religious or spiritual significance to their presence, even though they sometimes exhibit an enthusiasm reminiscent of religious converts and proselytizers.

Sociologists are interested in how these groups emerge, the people they attract, their organizational structures, and the methods they use to proclaim their spiritual message or publicize their findings. They are further interested in the composition of the membership of UFO cults. Gordon Melton (1981) and Shirley McIver (1987) have conducted initial surveys of UFO contactees and UFO groups in the United States and Great Britain respectively. Melton compares over one hundred people who have reported encounters and traces the history of such contacts from Swendenborg to the modern era. He places the UFO experience within the occult (psychic) religious tradition and links it with dissociated states of consciousness. McIver explores British UFO associations partly to find out how religiously oriented groups differ from other UFO organizations. She concludes that UFO research falls into the category of movement organization that differs from contactee cults, the former being interested in anomalies, the latter in mysteries. Like many other scholars she holds that UFO research groups are a reaction to science and reason and form part of the revived interest in the occult. UFO cults are one form of alternative religion.

The study of UFO groups may lead to a better understanding of the reasons why the topic of flying saucers arouses so much interest and why, in several instances, the belief in UFOs is accompanied by dedication and commitment in a community or fellowship. Two types

of studies can be distinguished. The first attempts a general assessment
of UFO groups. The second explores individual movements in some
depth.

General Assessments of UFO Movements. A standard sociological
approach to UFO cultic beliefs is to link them with a broader range of
beliefs common to new religious movements. There is disagreement as
to whether UFOs are genuine religious phenomena. Irving Hexham
(1986), for instance, rejects the opinion that UFOs are extraterrestrial
spacecraft. He sees the rise of UFO reports as another reaction to the secularization and rationalism of Western society. Interest in UFOs is a
sign that people are rejecting a false faith in modern science. It also
indicates that people are returning to a pseudo religious perspective of
the nature and origin of the human species, an outlook that belonged to
an earlier, prescientific era and must be judged to be a degenerative
move towards irrationalism, which can only be held at bay by education.

Others, however, consider UFO reports as an instance of the many
encounters with the supranormal, encounters which, in the past, were
usually interpreted as diabolical. Donald Ward (1977) outlines the
diverse modern interpretations of the supranormal and considers some
of the traits and functions of paranormal experiences. He leans to the
view that such experiences, which may be therapeutic, are innate in
the human psyche and can lead us to understand the nature of "homo
religiosus."

Still others are more insistent that belief in UFOs is religious in
nature and that consequently some UFO organizations can be looked
upon as modern religions. Ronald Story (1977) has made some important contributions to the understanding of UFOs as a religious phenomenon. Though he finds von Däniken's theory to be faulty from both
anthropological and archaeological points of view, he observes that it
carries a certain "von Däniken mystique." He thinks that its appeal lies
in its apparent success at reconciling modern science with a literal interpretation of the Bible, in its offer of a view of salvation that is more in
harmony with modern scientific progress, and in its treatment of the
problem of good and evil in a personal fashion. His view is reminiscent
of Levi Strauss's structural analysis of myth, in the sense that it looks on
mythology as a human effort to deal with the problems and contradictions of life.

In like manner John Saliba (1990) focuses on those qualities that
make the UFO phenomenon religious. He examines seven religious
themes that pervade UFO literature, namely (1) mystery, (2) transcen-

dence, (3) belief in supernatural entities, (4) perfection, (5) salvation, (6) worldview, and (7) spirituality. That many UFO encounters are ascribed religious significance has also been confirmed by the earlier works of Ted Peters (1977a, 1977b).

Studies of UFO Movements. One of the more ambitious overviews of UFO cults and their respective origins and ideological connections has been attempted by David Stupple (1984). In a posthumously published article he traces the rise of interest in UFOs to the Theosophical Society, several of whose leaders acted as mediums through which the Masters from other planets passed on their messages to the human race. The development of the flying saucer movement from the nineteenth century to the present is outlined and some of the differences between the early Theosophists and modern psychic contactees are noted. The author distinguishes between the scientific (rational) and the religious (romantic and utopian) interests and responses to UFOs. Another major distinction made is that between psychic (religious) and non-psychic (folkloristic) contactees, a distinction which, according to the author, is related to class and gender. Besides drawing attention to the need for classifying the variety of interests in UFOs, the author brings into focus some as yet unexplained sociological features, particularly the lack of involvement of American blacks in the flying saucer movement. In spite of its deficiencies (which include some inaccuracies and oversimplifications), this essay draws attention to the complexity and variety of UFO movements, particularly those of modern times.

Less ambitious in its scope is Taylor Buckner's (1961) analysis of the historical development of the UFO movement since 1947. The author examines the process through which a distinct occult philosophy becomes an open-door cult, that is, a movement which has generalized goals and an all-embracing ideology. In such a cult, the members are essentially religious seekers who move on from one occult group to another. The groups the author seems to be referring to are more like platform societies than closely knit religious cults, whose leaders so often claim a monopoly on divine revelation. They are, in the words of Rodney Stark and William Sims Bainbridge (1983), "audience cults." The sociological profile ascribed to the members of a flying saucer movement is hardly complimentary or exciting. It is alleged that those who join the movement are largely older women, widowed or single, who belong to the lower classes, are less educated, and suffer from both physical and mental difficulties.

Kevin McClure (1987) gives a brief description of the following six flying saucer cults: (1) Mrs. Keech's movement; (2) the One Word

Family; (3) the Institute for Cosmic Research; (4) Light Affiliates; (5) Human Individual Metamorphosis; and 6) the Aetherius Society. Some of these groups are now extinct. The group that calls itself Human Individual Metamorphosis is still in existence, though its membership, which was never very high, has dropped sharply since its heyday in the mid 1970s. The Aetherius Society, which the author refers to as "the most famous and long-lived UFO cult," is a well-organized and well-known UFO group and has been in existence since the mid 1950s. In spite of its presence in several continents and its many publications and advertised activities, the Aetherius Society never seems to have attracted a large number of adherents. McClure leans toward a sociopsychological interpretation of all these cults, which he sees as performing the function of fulfilling the respective needs of both their founders and members. His final evaluative statement makes it clear that he sees little significance in these UFO cults, even though they mirror a more common interest in extraterrestrial life and flying saucers and form part of a broader and more widespread occult movement.

Not too many in-depth studies of individual UFO cults exist. The study by Festinger, Riechen, and Schachter (1956) remains probably the best and most-quoted, full-length monograph in the field. Basically, what this book does is to apply the theory of cognitive dissonance to one particular flying saucer cult led by a certain Mrs. Keech, who claimed to have received messages from space beings. The authors provide a thorough account of this movement's ideology, the members' involvement in a flying saucer cult, their preparation for the final flood announced by alien creatures through Mrs. Keech, and their reactions to the failure of the prophecy. This book remains a major source for those studying UFO groups both for its method and theory.

The studies of Robert Balch and David Taylor (Balch 1980, 1982, 1985, and in this volume; Balch and Taylor 1976,1977) on one modern UFO cult are probably unparalleled in sociological literature. These two researchers used the questionable method of covert participant observation to investigate the UFO movement called Human Individual Metamorphosis. The two leaders of this group, who conferred on themselves exotic names, like Bo and Peep, assumed the traditional role of prophets who bring the message of an impending catastrophe or apocalyptic holocaust. In one of his main articles on this UFO cult, Balch (1980) focuses on the conversion process of its members. Rejecting the brainwashing explanation of cult conversion, he applies the role model theory to show how new converts start acting like members and only later become convinced of the belief system of the cult. He suggests that cult members actually play two roles—the stage role in front of outsiders, where they appear as ardent believers, certain and secure in their belief system and religious expectations, and the normal role among themselves, where they express the differences, doubts, and fears that are common within any religious community. Balch thinks that the members' "zombie look," which has popularly been interpreted as a sign that they have been brainwashed, is actually a front and is purposely put on to ward off evil spirits.

A typical sociological approach to a UFO religion is Roy Wallis's unique essay (1974) on the Aetherius Society. Although short summaries on the Aetherius Society are occasionally included in encyclopedias, articles, and books on UFO phenomena,[5] this interesting group's historical roots, ideology, ritual practices, and organizational structure remain virtually unexplored. Wallis, besides providing a concise sketch of this society's history, beliefs, and practices, advances an analysis based on Max Weber's (1956) theory of religion. Weber contrasted the mystagogue with the prophet and concluded that the former defined his source of legitimation in magical rather than ethical terms. George King, the founder of the Aetherius Society, is, in Wallis s view, a mystagogue who performs magical and/or sacramental actions to promote salvation and who, in Weber's words, differs from the average magician in degree, "the extent of which is determined by the formation of a special congregation around him" (1956, 54).

Wallis (1975) has also compared the founders of two UFO groups, namely Mrs. Keech and George King. Applying once again Weber's distinction, Wallis sees the former as a prophet, the latter as a mystagogue. Because the prophet often announces a definite future event, the failures of his or her prophecies to come to fruition are bound to create turmoil among the membership. The group that centered around Mrs. Keech is a typical example of a cult, which by nature is a precarious institution. George King, however, has never announced dates of impending human disasters. His society is sectarian in structure and has developed a stable organization, which accounts for the fact that it has survived for over three decades. A similar Weberian interpretation has been applied to Uriel (Ruth Norman), one of the founders and present leader of Unarius Academy of Science, a flying saucer cult in southern California (Kirkpatrick and Tumminia 1992; and in this volume).

Many flying saucer associations, however, are not led by prophetic or mystagogic figures and have not developed into well-defined systems of beliefs and practices that demand conversion and commitment. David Stupple and Abdollah Dashti's essay (1977) describes one such fluid network, which binds its members by a common source of information rather than by a common credal statement and ritual practice. Flying saucer clubs and societies of this nature are not, strictly speaking, religious cults and movements since they do not advance one specific ideological and ritual system. They further have no social networks to transmit religious beliefs nor do they encourage mystical experiences to confirm them. Their members are transient with no strong roots in the organization. United largely by their interest in stories of close encounters with flying saucers, they do not break away or distance themselves from society as, for instance, the members of the Human Individual Metamorphosis are required to do. Flying saucer organizations like the Saucerian Press enable people to become integrated to some degree within the flying saucer subculture without, however, abandoning their religious and social ties to mainstream culture.

Sociological Rejection of Psychological Interpretations

The tendency among sociologists and anthropologists alike is to question or reject psychological and psychiatric explanations of UFO phenomenon. Social scientists differ from many psychologists and psychiatrists in that the former dismiss as unsatisfactory the view that flying saucers are simply anomalistic phenomena and that, consequently, UFO beliefs and experiences belong to the field of pathology. The argument implicitly advanced in sociological studies is that, because so many cultural and social factors accompany flying saucers, their appearance cannot be adequately interpreted with reference to individual, aberrational psychological traits. It is, therefore, not surprising to find that sociologists and anthropologists are less likely to conclude that UFO sighters and contactees are unbalanced individuals and to categorically state that UFO vehicles are illusions.

An excellent example of this approach is Robert Hall's essay (1972) on the sociological dimensions of UFOs. The author does not focus on the arguments for and against the existence of flying saucers or on whether those who report UFO sightings and contacts are mentally competent people. He rather draws attention to the ways UFO reports affect group behavior. He points out that observing the way people react to ambiguous phenomena is essential for understanding accounts of UFOs and that UFO stories tend to be easily assimilated into a belief system. Reflecting on the major debate as to whether a UFO sighting is a physical event or a case of "motivated misconception," Hall is inclined to believe that some physical stimulus must have triggered the UFO experience. The negative reaction to the evidence brought forth to support belief in UFOs is subjected to a similar sociological analysis. Even scientific knowledge can function as a belief system that is reluctant to accept new ideas and to reconsider its fundamental assumptions.

Another scholar, J. Blake (1979), who is interested in why ufology has not been accepted as a natural science, reaches similar conclusions. He looks at the three theoretical elements—conceptualization, scope, and methods—that are part of any scientific endeavor. He observes that three social contexts, namely the journalistic press, the reports of the U.S. Air Force, and the scientific community, have contributed to the present intellectual plight of ufology. The serious study of flying saucers has been initiated not by the intellectual elite of modern science but by ardent believers in the existence in UFOs. The deficiencies of ufology as a science are partly due to the scientific reaction which ignores it or condemns it as a bogus science.

The sociological stance that adopts a less judgmental position with regard to the existence of flying saucers is clearly demonstrated by Bainbridge (1978), a sociologist of religion. His attitude towards von Däniken's UFO theory differs radically from that expressed by writers like Ronald Story (1977). Instead of attacking the theory, Bainbridge seeks to understand why it is so popular. Rejecting the strain and control theories, both of which include psychological deviance as an integral part, the author applies the cultural deviance and trait theories and finds them helpful in showing why so many people find in von Däniken's books (1969,1976) a plausible explanation of ancient human artifacts. He concludes that the idea of ancient astronauts is part of a generalized occult and prescientific subculture. People believe in extraterrestrial visitations not because they are intellectually deficient and gullible, but because they fall under the influence of an inferior type of intellectual response that permeates the occult subculture in America. Consequently, belief in UFOs does not represent a childish return to the irrational or prelogical thought process.

In like fashion, Troy Zimmer (1985) rejects those theories that dismiss UFO sighters as alienated, deprived individuals. He supports the view of those who believe that the UFOs are alien spaceships, at least in the sense that UFO encounters are based on some external stimulus. He argues that the majority of those who believe in flying saucers do not ascribe to them a religious meaning or import. Disagreeing with Bainbridge, he asserts that belief in UFOs is related to science fiction and not to mysticism and the occult. UFO cults have probably contributed to a negative evaluation of UFO enthusiasts, whom the author sees as quite normal people.

PSYCHOLOGICAL APPROACHES

No matter what the sociocultural background to UFOs might be, the people who have close encounters describe them in terms of individual experiences. As such, they fall in the province of the psychological disciplines. Besides interest in the types of personality of those who come in touch with UFOs and alien creatures, the psychological sciences are concerned both with the reactions to UFO-related events and the mental health implications, particularly on those individuals who are convinced that they have been abducted by alien invaders. Why is it that only a relatively few number of people have UFO experiences? Do these individuals, for instance, have a history of encountering strange creatures? Do they have UFO experiences when they are under stress or suffering from some specific psychological problem? Are their experiences a result of perceptual impairment or memory distortion? Or are they symptomatic of more serious pathological conditions? Both psychological and psychiatric evaluations of people who report UFO contacts have been largely negative. UFO experiences are said to be indicative of some psychological weakness and/or mental handicap.

The reason why relatively few psychologists have dedicated little serious effort to the study of UFO experiences may be due, in part, to the anomalous nature of the phenomenon itself. Armando Simon (1984) complains about this lack of interest. He thinks that studies of perception and of the attitudes and personalities of UFO sighters and contactees express a typical psychological viewpoint, namely that reports of UFO encounters tell us more about the contactees than about flying saucers themselves. After reviewing the psychological literature on UFOs, he warns his readers of the problem of the "experimenter bias." He makes the following conclusions that reflect some common psychological positions:

1. There is a strong indication that those UFOs whose existence can be objectively verified, and are usually blobs of light in the sky, are the physical equivalent of Rorschach inkblots. They will be reported according to the reporter s mental set.
2. Belief in flying saucers and extraterrestrial life is correlated with youth, high income, increased education, and being male.
3. To believe that UFOs are piloted by "little green men" is the cultural norm in North America, and not, as is put forth, a minority viewpoint. It is not a sign of mental illness.
4. There is a strong indication that the rate of flying saucer sightings fluctuates according to the amount, as well as the quality, of coverage by the mass media.

5. The "contactee" cult groups, mostly based in California, are composed primarily of senile and schizoid members. They tend to be religious and low-key.

6. Due to (3) and (4), there appears to be a cultural consensus of what a "UFO" is supposed to look like and what "aliens" are supposed to look like.

Psychological Functions of UFOs

One popular psychological explanation of UFO encounters is that they come into being to satisfy deep emotional needs. They occur when the contactees are under individual or social stress. Patrick Moore (1970, 1001) explains it as follows:

> One reason for this sort of belief [i.e., in UFOs] is the feeling that we of the present day are in danger of destroying ourselves. . . . Unfortunately, the danger is very real indeed; weapons capable of wiping out our civilization actually exist, and could be unleashed. Subconsciously, the flying saucer believers are trying to give us a warning and their advice is eminently sound. . . .

This is essentially the theory of Carl Jung (1970), who observed that the fears generated by the cold war of the late 1940s and early 1950s could easily have led to people projecting their tensions into flying saucers in the sky. UFOs are expressions of human anxieties and of the need humans feel for being saved from their earthly woes.

The same view is elaborated by Otto Billig (1982, 115) who points out that "despite occurrences of their appearances in different periods of history, extraterrestrial objects sighted in the sky by the aborigine, the prophet of Biblical times, and by twentieth-century man show remarkable similarities." The encounter usually takes place when the contactees are alone or in an isolated place, especially when they are in some kind of altered state of consciousness. In all cases the experiences leave the persons with a feeling of being helplessly overpowered by a supernatural power or force. Emerging from this unusual state of consciousness, they are frightened or excited and announce that they have seen certain apparitions in the sky. Further, many of them feel chosen to deliver a special message or warning to the human race. Billig holds that these experiences get isolated from the total functioning of the individual and become imbued with the character of independent, emotionally charged, and magical events. He interprets these similarities in sky apparitions as a confirmation of "man's universal need to create supernatural forces when he feels incapacitated by threatening stress situations" (1982, 116). Since neither the individual nor society can dissipate these overwhelming amieties, the human mind falls back on mythological avenues to find peace of mind and emotional tranquility.

There is some evidence, however, that UFOs may create more anxiety than they relieve. Mark Moravec (1987) has explored the psychological and physiological repercussions of UFO experiences and has come to the conclusion that "the most common psychological reactions to UFO events are fear, followed by curiosity." He suggests that "the fact that fear alone is generated in many individual UFO experiences makes a powerful reason, in itself, for the continued study of UFO experience" (1987, 295). While there is some evidence that supports the correlation between UFO sightings and periods of personal and/or social unrest and anxiety, it is not clear whether, or to what extent, belief in UFOs is the direct result of these conditions.

UFOs and Wishful Thinking

Belief in flying saucers has also been viewed as a form of wishful thinking or fantasy. "The subconscious wish," writes Moore (1970, 1003), "to believe in friendly beings watching over us is too strong to be dismissed so easily." The myth of UFOs is a form of escapism from the unsettling and unpleasant nature of world news. It not only arouses feelings of mental and emotional security, but provides people with hope for the future. It serves the convenient emotional function found in many myths, that is, it satisfies deep-seated human desires.

Another psychologist, Robert Baker (1987), contends that those who have close encounters with flying saucers are, like mediums, psychics, and religious visionaries, "fantasy-prone individuals." Their belief in UFOs is a reaffirmation of the human need for order and hope. The majority of these people are normal. They "function as well as others" and are as "well-adjusted, competent, satisfied or dissatisfied as everyone else" (1987, 154).

Whether, and to what degree, "fantasy-proneness" is indicative of a psychopathological condition has been the subject of debate in psychological literature (Rhue and Lynn 1987; Lynn and Rhue 1988). Fantasy-proneness is generally used in a pejorative sense, implying both unreality and pathology. Kenneth Ring (1989b) has suggested that it should, consequently, not be used to describe the psychological state of UFO contactees. He argues that the interpretations of UFO abductions may not fall under the categories of either empirical fact or fantasy. A new category of "imaginal" realities may describe more accurately what happens. He states:

Individuals that score high on measures of fantasy-proneness may in fact be highly gifted persons who have a privileged means of access to imaginal reality. Thus, they may be closer to visionaries than to schizophrenics. Rather than being disdained, their experiences should be studied carefully for the information they may contain concerning the nature and dynamics of the realms to which such persons are sensitive. (1989b, 21-22)

Ring's suggestion seems to identify UFO encounters with traditional religious visions. His view is not easily harmonized with the conviction of both contactees and many ufologists that flying saucers originate from other planets. Whatever opinion one adopts, it is clear that the tendency to fantasize and project one's most cherished desires cannot provide a complete explanation of UFO contacts. Such a theory still leaves unanswered the question: Why are flying saucers selected as the medium for such projection and fantasy? The wishful-thinking hypothesis must have recourse to some other theory to show why UFOs are sometimes the chosen symbols or vehicle of meaning.

UFO and Worldview

The belief in UFOs can also be seen as a useful psychological tool in that it fulfills some human intellectual needs. Several intellectual functions assigned to myth are applicable to the belief in flying saucers. Myths are explanatory devices that satisfy the human quest for knowledge. They often account for the origin of the universe and of a people's cultural traditions. Consequently, they give meaning to the universe at large and specify the place and role of humans in the cosmos. They assign an unambiguous purpose to human life and designate the ultimate goal of human existence. And further, they stamp it with the aura of divine authority. The answers given by myths are rarely questioned because they start with postulates, like the belief in gods, that are taken for granted.

The biblical cosmology, which placed human beings at the center of the universe and at the peak of creation, received a serious setback with the Copernican Revolution and with Darwin's theory of evolution. Modern astronomy and space travel have challenged even further the worldviews that underlie creation stories, not only in the Judeo-Christian tradition, but also in other religions, past and present. They have altered the way people think about the universe and their relationship to it. Von Däniken's cosmological reconstructions are intellectually attractive because they provide an organized framework for a new conception of the universe, a framework buttressed by allegedly empirical, and hence irrefutable, evidence. More specifically, the question of human origins—a perennial one that repeatedly appears in many mythological stories—is still being asked in the twentieth century. By postulating that space beings played a crucial part in human origins on earth, von Däniken supplies us with the raw materials for linking human beings more directly with the cosmos and for elevating human nature to a higher status than that provided by the scientific theory of evolution.

In general, this functional approach seems to argue that UFO encounters can be a normal way people who live in a space age relieve their anxieties, express their unconscious desires, and construct a meaningful worldview. Such encounters, functioning as traditional religious experiences, may in the long run be more beneficial than harmful.

PSYCHIATRIC APPROACHES

Psychiatric explanations of UFOs differ from psychological ones in that they frequently consider the UFO myth a serious psychological aberration rather than an unusual way by which human beings come to grips with their problems. UFO encounters, particularly those in which people believe they have made contact with, or been abducted by, aliens, are indices not of fairly common psychological problems but of serious pathology. In other words, while wishful thinking, lapses of memory, and mistakes in perception may be mild temporary disorders, close encounters of the third and fourth kinds are experienced by unquestionably pathological individuals who require treatment.

Psychological Processes in UFO Experiences

One of the main axioms in psychiatry is that psychological and psychopathological processes play a significant role in experiences involving flying saucers and encounters with allen creatures. Moravec (1987) has conducted a thorough analysis of such processes. His chart (1987, 310) outlining them and the contexts in which they occur is worth reproducing, because it covers all the areas discussed by psychologists and psychiatrists who have studied the UFO phenomenon.

Process	Context	Experience
Misperception	Insufficient knowledge of natural/manmade phenomena	Spurious UFO sighting reports

Process	Context	Experience
Hoax	Attention-seeking	Fabricated sightings and physical traces
Psychosis	Stress/personal crisis/ predisposition	Reports involving mental communications/ apparitions/paranoia
Folie a Deux	Psychosis plus dominance/ subordinance/ relationship	Reports with false consensus of two or more percipients
Conversion hysteria	Fear/intense emotions/ bodily predisposition	Physiological symptoms of psychosomatic nature
Altered state of consciousness	Reduction of overload of stimuli/history of ASCs, etc.	Reports involving time distortion/dreamlike elements, etc.
Hypnopomic/ Hypnagogic imagery	Sleep/Awake interface	Reports involving communications/ apparitions/entities
Amnesia/Fugue	Stress/trauma	Reports featuring time lapses/disorientation/ physical wandering
Possession/ Multiple personality	Stress/trauma disposition	Reports featuring "invading entities"/ messages from same
Automatic writing	Personal crisis/ spiritualistic beliefs/ predisposition	Reports featuring written written messages
Autohypnosis/ Hypnotic regression	Concentration for long periods/leading questions/desire to please hypnotist	Trancelike states/ fantasized abductions/ abduction by UFO entities

Moravec's outline contains unmistakable references to several cases of serious psychopathology among UFO witnesses. Altered states of consciousness (which involve trance), multiple personality (which includes possession by alien entities), and conversion hysteria (in which a psychic conflict is changed into somatic form) are classic examples of pathology in psychiatric literature. But Moravec notices that only a very small percentage of UFO experiences can be attributed to psychological disorders. He states that "there is no firm evidence to support the hypothesis that UFO witnesses tend to be psychologically disturbed or socially maladjusted as a group" (1987, 298). His view is supported by others (e.g., Sprinkle 1988) who argue that, while believers in UFOs are normal individuals, there is a need for psychotherapeutic services to help them cope with their unusual experiences.

Not many psychiatrists would agree with this optimistic assessment. Joost Meerloo (1968), for example, has argued that flying saucer sightings and contacts are an expression of the human need for miracles. He links the UFO phenomenon with the eight following disorders, some more serious than others: (1) memory distortions; (2) the personal search for magic; (3) optical illusion; (4) psychological perceptual distortion; (5) physical distortion of images; (6) anxiety; (7) mass paranoia (as seen in flying saucer cults); (8) rumor and propaganda, linked with alienation and panic about a world headed for atomic disaster. While memory and perceptual distortions are not necessarily pathological, Meerloo strongly maintains that involvement in UFO cults is a sign of severe pathology.

Many psychiatrists agree with Meerloo that UFO experiences are linked to either serious disorders of perception and hallucinations or personality problems. The fact that there is a clear relation between UFO experiences and psychic phenomena[6] is taken as corroborative evidence of the psychopathological nature of UFO encounters. Moreover, alleged encounters with UFOs can precipitate emotional states like anxiety, depression, and dissociation. The negative reaction of outsiders can also influence the mental and psychological state of contactees.

UFOs and Human Perception

One common theory advanced to explain UFO sightings is that they are the result of human perception, which can distort ordinary celestial objects into something strange, mysterious, or alien. Perception is the process by which coherence and unity are given to sensory input. It synthesizes human sensations into an intelligible form. It, therefore, includes not only physical, physiological, neurological, and sensory components, but also cognitive and affective ones. Because so many UFO sightings occur at night, the chances of misinterpreting common aspects of the night sky are increased. Anticipation, motivation, knowledge, and belief are also important contributors to the way people perceive objects.

Both physiological and psychological factors that are linked with perception can lead to inaccurate reports by eyewitnesses. The event itself can contain unusual elements, such as an extremely bright light, that make it difficult for the observer to determine what the object is. Further, the individual characteristics of the eyewitness can limit his or her ability to notice some details and to embellish and exaggerate others, thus easily leading to a misidentification of the object seen. The emotional shock of seeing something strange in the skies inevitably affects human perception. If one were to add the eyewitness's cultural background, upbringing, and previous knowledge about UFOs, then it is quite possible that reports of many UFO sightings are not simple and exact descriptions of objective phenomena (Menzel and Taves 1977).

While human perception has its weaknesses and limitations, it does record at least some accurate information. The issue is whether, in the case of UFO close encounters, perception so distorts outward data and stimuli that the eyewitness is psychologically impaired to such a degree that he or she must be judged to be suffering from illusions and/or hallucinations. The men-in-black (MIB) phenomenon[7] may be an illustration of the hallucinatory nature of UFO experiences. Evans (1984, 145), who compares these alien apparitions with those of the Blessed Virgin and ghosts, thinks that they are hallucinations "projected as a result of the percipient's private fears, and given a specific shape or form based on prevalent notions of the CIA and other such agencies." The question raised by Evans's reflections is whether some UFO encounters are triggered by persecution mania, a form of paranoid schizophrenia, in which the patient's intellectual functions are impaired.

In general the tendency of psychiatrists is to treat UFO encounters as subjective rather than objective experiences. This does not necessarily imply that UFO contactees are willfully fabricating the stories, but rather that they are either suffering from some kind of chemical imbalance[8] or else succumbing to their personal hopes and fears and relieving them by creating imaginary encounters with alien creatures. Evans is "persuaded that all of the subjects do believe that something strange did occur—but conviction can, as we saw with witches who were so sure that they had attended a sabbat, be founded on hallucination" (1987a, 167).

Lawson (1980a), in a lengthy essay evaluating the experiences of UFO abductees, points out that UFO abductions differ from imaginary and hallucinatory experiences. He asserts:

Witnesses *really perceive* images—from whatever source—such as bright and pulsating lights, lattice-textured forms moving randomly in the sky, lighted tunnel, humanoid figures, etc. These abduction constants are combined with data from the imagina-

tion, memory, and existing UFO data known by witnesses to create a "real" UFO encounter. The subjective reality of the intense
hallucinatory structure convinces the witnesses that the entire
experience is a physically real event. Subsequently they may
report the "truth" as they experience it, although the actual occurrences remain unclear. (1980a, 196)

A more cautious approach is adopted by Mark Rhine (1969) who, in
one of the earlier psychological essays on UFO reports, pursues an
approach that he himself labels "benevolent skepticism." He dwells not
on the psychological make-up of UFO sighters, but rather on the nature of
the phenomenon itself. He suggests that errors in perception, which may
result from psychopathology and/or disturbed emotional states, could
influence what an individual sees. In other words, the UFO sighter may
actually see an obscure natural phenomenon and interpret it as a flying
saucer. Perception is partly subjective and, therefore, the sighting of a
UFO is to some degree determined by the psychological condition of the
witness. Rhine agrees with many psychologists and psychiatrists that
both the lie detector test and hypnosis are unreliable instruments for
studying and recording of UFO experiences. He thinks, however, that
the perceptual distortion of UFO sighters cannot be labeled pathological.

UFOs and Personality Problems

UFO experiences have also been interpreted in terms of psychoanalytic theory (Moravec 1987, 297). UFO visions and contacts are a result
of powerful unconscious processes, which are externalized in symbolic
form. Because the shapes of flying saucers can be reduced, in most cases,
to two types, the circle and the cigar, Freudian psychoanalysts' read
UFO encounters as expressions of unconscious preoccupation and anxiety about sex. The fact that several reports of UFO abductions contain
reference to rape and/or perinatal imagery (Lawson 1984) can be
adduced to support this analysis. Further, several psychoanalysts, such
as Lester Grinspoon and Alan Persky (1972), maintain that UFO encounters are clear instances of regression to a more primal, magical mode of
thinking. This return to childish fantasy could only take place in chron-
ically disturbed individuals or in people suffering from milder, transient periods of mental or psychological imbalance. Close encounters
with UFOs should be, therefore, treated as a type of personality disorder.

Another psychoanalytic approach would consider encounters
with UFOs a form of dissociative disorder, which is characterized by a
breakdown in the usually integrated functions of consciousness, self-

perception, and sensory behavior. Multiple personality, amnesia, and fugue are examples of such disorders. Abductee accounts are especially subject to be interpreted as fugues, which are psychiatric disabilities wherein an individual experiences a sudden and unexpected leaving of home and adopts a new personality elsewhere. Several studies of UFO abductees, however, found no evidence of such disorders. But the same studies concluded that some subjects who have UFO experiences manifest, under stressful conditions, "the potential for transient psychotic experiences involving a loss of reality testing along with confused and disordered thinking that can be bizarre, peculiar or very primitive and emotionally charged" (Moravec 1987, 303).

A more moderate view is adopted by some, like Aphrodite Clamar (1988), June Parnell (1988), and James Gordon (1991), who assert that those who have had UFO experiences are relatively average and ordinary individuals. Contactees are not suffering from severe pathology. They are not paranoid or schizoid individuals, crazy people, or social misfits. But these authors seem to indicate that those who report encounters with UFOs have more psychological problems than those who do not. Clamar (1988, 147) observes that contactees suffer from a degree of identity disturbance and mild paranoia. Parnell (1988, 163), on the other hand, thinks that they have "a greater tendency to endorse unusual feelings, thoughts, and attitudes," to be "suspicious and distrustful," and "to be creative, imaginative, or possibly have schizoid levels." And Gordon (1991, 92), commenting on studies that show that those individuals who have UFO experiences are more likely to have been abused as children, states that "it is possible that they have an as yet undescribed form of multiple personality disorder."

UFOs and Birth Trauma

Some psychoanalysts have also interpreted UFO encounters, particularly abduction cases, as a form of regression which, in psychoanalysis, has a negative connotation. Otto Rank (1952, 117ff.) held that the original problems of the human psyche began when the individual was expelled from the comfort of one's mother's womb into a hostile, nongratifying world. Vivid remembrance of one's birth experience is a sign that the individual cannot cope with the real world and has not quite grown up. Rank interpreted many religious beliefs, Christian and non-Christian alike, as infantile returns to the womb. This *regressus ad uterum* is a sign of pathology.

UFO encounters may be a sign of such regression because of their parallels with remembered birth traumas. Lawson points out that the newly born infant's outside world, like the spacecraft in which UFO abductees are taken, has strange beings, bright lights, unusual sounds, and even physical examinations. He adds:

> There may be a relationship between the tunnel images of the UFO encounters and the vaginal tunnel through which most of us pass during birth. The tunnel/tube image recurs in reports of cylindrical UFOs, tube-shaped rooms, and especially in weird, flat-ended tubes of light through which witnesses are allegedly levitated into craft. (1980b, 35)

Since abductee experiences contain perinatal imagery, they can be interpreted as memories of the birth trauma (Lawson 1984). The abductee, due to stress and anxiety, finds it increasingly difficult to come to terms with the problems of life and, through the abduction experiences, attempts to run away from reality and seek refuge in a more infantile stage.

UFOs and Altered States of Consciousness

Because contacts with aliens from UFOs so often occur when the contactees are in a state of trance, or when they are in a hypnagogic (near sleep) or hypnopompic (near waking) state, and because such contacts are more readily recalled when the subject is under hypnosis, UFO encounters have been linked with altered states of consciousness.

Even though the psychological disciplines have tended to neglect the study of altered states of consciousness, there seems to be a general tendency in the field to regard certain forms of these states, particularly trance, as dissociative and hence pathological.[10] Further, the connection between UFO experiences and extrasensory perception tends to confirm the negative psychological evaluation of these close encounters with extraterrestrial entities.[11]

One form of trance or altered state of consciousness that is frequently discussed when dealing with close encounters, particularly of the third or fourth kinds, is hypnosis. And, since "the most outstanding characteristic of the hypnotic state is the suggestibility of the subject" (Small 1977, 56), psychiatrists are inclined to look negatively on reports of UFO encounters and descriptions of aliens extracted during hypnosis. Because suggestion is the process of inducing an uncritical acceptance of knowledge, emotion, or behavior, the hypnotized UFO contactee is open to accept without much evaluation any ideas about flying saucers that are brought up in the hypnotic session.

Baker (1987), for instance, takes up one of the more important psychiatric issues by exploring the central place of hypnotism in the recalling of the UFO experience. He dismisses the current claims by enthusiastic UFO researchers and argues that the accounts of UFO contactees and abductees can be explained by anomalistic psychology. He stresses the unreliability of hypnosis and hypnotic regression and adduces evidence to show how both do not lead to an accurate remembrance of events. Confabulation, inadvertent cueing by researchers, psychological needs, and fantasy-proneness all play a part in the recalling of a UFO experience.

It is Baker's view that, although people who have contacts with UFOs have a different psychological make-up than those who do not, they are rational and perfectly sane individuals. They do not suffer from any abnormalities that can be discovered by psychiatric tests. As one reads Baker's essay, however, one is lead to the conclusion that UFO sighters and contactees are very impressionistic individuals who might benefit from counseling. Baker seems to blame the researchers, for they should know, for instance, that hallucinations that occur when a person is about to fall asleep or wake up could easily be a major cause of UFO experiences.

Berthold Schwarz (1979), a well-known contributor to the study of UFOs, agrees with Baker and is highly critical of the tendency to evaluate UFO witnesses as psychologically abnormal or mentally ill individuals. His contribution lies in his detailed outline of what the psychiatrist's role should be in the investigation of UFO encounters. He insists on the need to conduct a physical examination of a UFO witness. Disagreeing with Baker's devastating critique of the validity of reports extracted under the influence of hypnosis, he attributes some value to contactees' accounts given under this induced state of altered consciousness. Schwarz, in fact, offers a balanced psychiatric approach, which combines both cultural factors and psychological states without, however, giving a negative assessment of the personalities of UFO contactees. Unlike Baker, however, Schwarz leaves open the possibility that both objective and psychological elements might account, in part at least, for some UFO experiences. He is, consequently, unwilling to subscribe to the view that anomalistic psychology or abnormal psychiatry provide sufficient explanations of UFO reports and contacts.

The Conflict Between Social Scientists and Ufologists

Social and psychological interpretations do not question the possibility that life might exist elsewhere in the cosmos.[12] They do, however, provide alternative explanations of UFO contactee phenomena that conflict with the major presuppositions of ufologists, whether these are religiously inclined or not. The flying saucer theory does not enjoy much favor among sociologists, psychologists, and psychiatrists alike. Thomas McDonough expresses the opinion of most scientists when he writes:

> I don't know of any absolutely reliable evidence that we have been visited by beings from another world. Most famous UFO cases can be explained by mundane phenomena, and the few remaining ones are filled with uncertainties and lack of physical evidence. (1987, 190)

The disagreement between sociologists, psychologists, and psychiatrists on the one hand, and ufologists and UFO contactees on the other, is both theoretical and methodological. Like natural scientists, behavioral scientists cannot accept the flying saucer theory because it has not been verified by or subjected to definite empirical and objective tests. In other words, they can study UFO reports and analyze human psychological conditions, but not the objects and sightings that are said to have triggered the experiences and led to the reports. Ufologists do not follow the rigid procedures that are universally accepted in the scientific world. They unfortunately leave the impression that they are relying more on the individual's subjective experience, which tends to eschew or minimize the need for empirical testing and confirmation.

It is a basic principle in the academic disciplines that efforts to explain UFO phenomena by natural means should receive priority, and that the introduction of a mystery element in the proceedings does nothing but hamper the investigations and/or place the matter beyond the reach and scope of science. Ufologists and contactees, on the other hand, have at times created an aura of mystery by talking about the secret activities and plots of aliens and/or government agents. Ufologists tend to examine anomalous phenomena as if these fall under the province of the natural sciences that are conceived to be broader in scope and content than they actually are. Although many ufologists today judge a large number of UFO reports to be spurious, if not downright hoaxes, there is still the tendency, in some quarters at least, to mystify the UFO phenomenon. Ufologists and scientists are at odds with one another because they approach paranormal events from different perspectives and with diverse presuppositions.

The conflict about method can be illustrated with reference to Budd Hopkins's recent book (1987) that relates the story of a series of UFO abductions of one individual. Hopkins's account purports to provide evidence that aliens are watching us and conducting genetic experiments on the human species. The author starts with a note to the readers, in which he correctly, though quite unashamedly, assures them that his "book will almost certainly strain your credulity to the breaking point" (xi). He draws an analogy with Walter Laqueur's (1980) book on the Holocaust, in which the author describes the early (1943) reaction of unbelief to the evidence that Nazi Germany had been executing a plan to exterminate the Jews. Hopkins's argument is that, just as people at that time found it hard to believe that the revelations about Nazi Germany were true, so too will those who read his own descriptions of what the aliens are doing find them hard to believe. Hopkins indirectly admits that his analogy limps and goes on to assure his readers that "an analogy exists only in the methods we use to avoid such disturbing testimony" (1987, xii). But, as one reads the book, it becomes increasingly clear that Hopkins is comparing the evidence for the existence of UFO abductions to that for the atrocities against the Jews during World War II. He states:

> In this book I will present new and compelling evidence that an ongoing genetic study is taking place—and that the human species itself is the subject of a breeding experiment. I am fully aware that this idea is so outrageous that one's natural response upon reading it is to echo Justice Frankfurter's remark about the Holocaust and simply announce that one cannot believe it, period, regardless of the evidence. But I ask that you hear me out. If what I report in these pages is true, as I believe it is, our view of the cosmos and our place within it will be forever changed. With the stakes that high the evidence must be attended to. (1987, 27)

The main point, surely, is not whether people's initial response to unpleasant and frightening testimonies or events is one of unbelief, but, rather, whether these happenings can be confirmed by incontestable evidence. The real issues are whether UFOs exist or not as physical phenomena and whether the Earth is being invaded by superior space creatures who pose a threat to human life. Since Hopkins makes a comparison with the reaction to, and evidence for, the Holocaust, he is suggesting that UFOs are not just psychic or spiritual, but also physical phenomena. Hence, the kind of evidence or proof for UFOs must be similar to that adduced to confirm the mistreatment of the Jews by the Nazi rulers of Germany.

At the present time, the only reliable methods we have at our disposal to verify the alleged empirical existence of flying saucers are those of empirical science. And it is precisely at this juncture that the analogy with the Holocaust breaks down completely. Within a few years after the revelations recorded by Laqueur, the descriptions of the Nazi treatment of the Jews were confirmed beyond a shadow of a doubt, not only by innumerable eyewitness reports, but by information that was open to the scrutiny of everybody, namely documentation, indisputable photographic materials, court trials, concentration camps, and mass graves. Different explanations and interpretations of the Holocaust are possible, but these basic facts cannot be even remotely questioned.[13] Yet, after forty years of UFO reports and alleged encounters, we still have no comparable evidence. The UFO phenomenon has remained a mystery about objects flying in the skies. Hopkins, in fact, requests his readers to make something more than the "leap of faith." He is asking them to accept the empirical reality of UFOs without providing the empirical evidence to support it. The negative reactions of both natural and social scientists should not come as a surprise.

It would, therefore, have been more appropriate and logical if Hopkins had compared the evidence for and human response to UFOs to the proofs for and reactions to other anomalous phenomena, like the Loch Ness Monster and Big Foot, spiritual entities (spirits, ghosts, angels, and demons), apparitions of the Virgin Mary, and medieval traditions about the witches' Sabbath (Evans 1984; Fuller 1980, 313-18).

The theories proposed by some ufologists have tended to widen the gulf between them and social and behavioral scientists. Jacques Vallée (1975, 1979, 1988), for instance, has proposed such an alarming view of the presence and intentions of UFOs that it has been rejected as paranoia (McKenna 1989, 24-25). In Vallée's opinion, a politically orientated group of people are behind the UFO phenomenon. Armed with an advanced technology, this group is able to fool and will ultimately control everybody else. The empirical data to support such a hypothesis is hardly self-evident. Such theories are more likely to discredit ufology than elevate it to a respectable science.

Whether sociological and psychological studies can ultimately and satisfactorily account for close encounters with unidentified flying objects and their alien pilots will certainly be debated for a long time. Since the sincere beliefs of contactees, the reports of investigators, and the rebuttals of skeptics all contribute to the UFO myth, it is difficult to sort out the fantasies, misperceptions, and predisposed opinions from the facts. Moravec has accurately summed up the nature of the problem. He points out that:

> As we follow the chain beginning with the UFO event, we find that the percipient, the investigator, and the skeptic can all input

their sometimes biased views and thereby change the UFO event as reported. The sensational distortions by the mass media and the overall social beliefs about UFOs can further transform the data. The result is that published UFO reports may be very different from what actually happened. The investigator must ensure objectivity is maintained in his or her investigation, and the researcher must remain aware of the potential biasing influences of people's beliefs. (1987, 306)

CONCLUSION

The sociopsychological literature on the UFO phenomenon is bound to leave many readers disappointed because it does not succeed in solving the riddle of the flying saucers. It prefers not to dwell on the type and reliability of the evidence that has been adduced to prove the existence of UFOs, nor on the counterarguments that have repeatedly appeared in both scientific and popular literature. Moreover, sociopsychological writings appear to be reductionistic, in the sense that the existence of UFOs is explained with reference not to objective stimuli but to social and psychological factors.

Social and behavioral scientists have, however, raised several issues regarding the meaning of UFO sightings and encounters, issues which have hardly surfaced in popular literature and are usually ignored or downplayed by ufologists. They have changed the more customary focus of UFO investigations—which is to verify UFO reports—by suggesting that, since the UFO problem is not likely to be resolved in the near future, there is more to be gained by examining their sociopsychological significance. The meaning of the flying saucer phenomenon might lie more in its social and psychological dimensions than in whether extraterrestrials exist or not, or in what the aliens themselves are supposedly saying and doing. In other words, belief in flying saucers and alleged encounters with their occupants might reveal something important about human nature, the study of which is, in fact, central to the social, psychological, and psychiatric disciplines.

NOTES

1. Many theories have been proposed to account for this unusual phenomenon. Unidentified flying objects have been said to be products of natural phenomena, such as weather, visible planets, gases, and balloons, or largely

hoaxes. They have also been linked with earthquakes by Michael A. Persinger and his colleagues who, over the last decade, have written over sixty articles on the subject (see, e.g., Persinger 1980, 1981, 1984; Mattsson and Persinger 1986; Persinger and Derr 1990). One theory explains them as a form of psychic projection, while another as spacecraft from a different space/time dimension. More daring speculations hold that UFOs come from underwater civilizations on Earth or from inside the Earth itself (the Hollow Earth theory). See, for instance, Michael Avery (1989, pp. 48ff.) for different opinions and their rebuttals. Brad Steiger (1986) lists eighteen possible, sometimes overlapping, explanations of UFO phenomena. Martin Gardner (1987, p. 34) suggests that the psychic theory of UFOs has been proposed by ufologists who, faced with the fact that no definitive physical evidence o f UFOs has been found, have taken refuge in the safe, untestable theory that flying saucers exist in some higher plane of reality.

2. Condon (1969) standardized the first three types. The fourth type is a relatively new addition necessitated by the recent increase in abduction stories (see Gordon 1991).

3. This is known as the social construct theory (cf., e.g., Best 1989; Schneider 1985).

4. Ring (1989a) finds that near-death experiences and UFO encounters are similar to shamanic initiations. He identifies the following related elements: (1) "separation"; (2) "appearance of the cosmic shaman"; (3) "dismemberment ordeals"; (4) "death-and-rebirth motifs"; (5) "esoteric knowledge"; (6) "return to the physical world with a special sense of purpose."

5. Melton's (1989) encyclopedia gives short sketches of these and other UFO movements.

6. For a brief overview of the connection between psychic phenomena and UFO experiences see Andrews (1980). One of the most original theories regarding this connection has been advanced by Jacques Vallée (1987, p. 318) who states that "the UFO phenomenon is the product of a technology that integrates physical and psychic phenomena and primarily affects cultural variables in our society through manipulation of physiological and psychological parameters in the witnesses."

7. Gray Barker (1956) is credited with having introduced the legend of the "men-in-black." See Rojcewicz (1986, 1987, 1989) and Ward (1977) for recent studies on these stories of alien intervention.

8. This area of psychiatry remains virtually unexplored. McKenna (1989, p. 25) states: "We have ascertained by questionnaire that UFO contact is perhaps the motif most frequently mentioned by people who take psilocybin recreationally, using fifteen-milligram-range doses sufficient to elicit the full spectrum of psychedelic effects. They encounter another space with UFOs and

aliens—classic little green men." This, of course, does not mean that all UFO contactees are under the influence of psychedelic drugs.

9. Hitching (1979, p. 188) gives thirty-one drawings of reported UFOs, most of which are shaped like circles or cigars that, in Freudian theory, are sexual symbols.

10. For studies on altered states of consciousness, see Gowan (1978-79) and Tart (1990).

11. For a summary of the psychological approach to ESP, see Rao (1984).

12. The question of extraterrestrial life is a topic of frequent discussion and speculation, particularly among astronomers. See, for examples, Asimov (1979), Ashpole (1989), Hoyle and Wickramasinghe (1987), McDonough (1987), and Horowitz (1986). Baird (1987) presents a somewhat critical reaction to human attempts to contact aliens.

13. For an overview of the Holocaust one can consult Robinson's (1971) essay which includes photographic documentation.

REFERENCES

Andrews, Arlan K. 1980. "Psychic Aspects of UFOs." In *The Encyclopedia of UFOs*, edited by Ronald Story, 286-89. London: New English Library.

Ashpole, Edward. 1989. *The Search for Extraterrestrial Intelligence*. London: Blandford Press.

Ashworth, G. E. 1980. "Flying Saucers, Spoon-Bending, and Atlantis: A Structural Study of New Mythologies." *Sociological Review* 28:353-76.

Asimov, Isaac. 1979. *Extraterrestrial Civilizations*. New York: Crown Publishers.

Avery, Michael. 1989. *UFOs: Opposing Viewpoints*. San Diego, Calif.: Greenhaven Press.

Bainbridge, William Sims. 1978. "Chariots of the Gullible." *Skeptical Inquirer* 3, no. 3:33-48.

Baird, John C. 1987. *The Inner Limits of Outer Space*. Hanover, N.H.: University Press of New England.

Baker, Robert A. 1987. "The Aliens Among Us: Hypnotic Regression Revisited." *Skeptical Inquirer* 12:147-61.

Balch, Robert. 1980. "Looking Behind the Scenes in a Religious Cult." *Sociological Analysis* 41:137-43.

———. 1982. "Bo and Peep: A Case Study of the Origins of Messianic Leadership." In *Millennialism and Charisma*, edited by Roy Wallis, 13-72. Belfast: Queen's University Press.

———. 1985. "When the Light Goes Out, Darkness Comes: A Study of Defection from a Totalist Cult." In *Religious Movements: Genesis, Exodus, and Numbers*, edited by Rodney Stark, 11-55. New York: Paragon House.

Balch, Robert, and David Taylor. 1976. "Salvation in a UFO." *Psychology Today* 10, no. 5:58, 61-62, 66, 104.

———. 1977. "Seekers and Saucers: The Role of the Cultic Milieu in Joining a UFO Cult." *American Behavioral Scientist* 20:839-60.

Barker, Gray. 1956. *They Knew Too Much About Flying Saucers*. New York: University Books.

Bartholomew, Robert E. 1989. *Ufolore: A Social Psychological Study of a Modern Myth in the Making*. Stone Mountain, Ga.: Arcturus Book Service.

Best, Joel, ed. 1989. *Images and Issues*. New York: Aldine de Gruyter.

Billig, Otto. 1982. *Flying Saucers—Magic in the Sky: Psycho-history*. Cambridge, Mass.: Schenkman.

Bird, Elizabeth. 1989. "Invasion of the Body Snatchers." *Psychology Today* 23, no. 4:64-66.

Blake, J. 1979. "Ufology: The Intellectual Development and Social Context of the Study of UFOs." In *On the Margins of Science*, edited by Roy Wallis, pp. 315-37.

Buckner, H. Taylor. 1961. "The Flying Saucerians: An Open Door Cult." In *Sociology in Everyday Life*, edited by Marcello Truzzi, 223-30. Englewood Cliffs, N.J.: Prentice-Hall.

Bullard, Thomas E. 1988. "Folklore Scholarship and UFO Reality." *International UFO Reporter* (July/August):9-13.

———. 1989. "UFO Abduction Reports: The Supernatural Kidnap Narrative Returns in Technological Guise." *Journal of American Folklore* 102:147-70.

Campbell, Joseph. 1974. *The Mythic Image*. Princeton, N.J.: Princeton University Press.

Clamar, Aphrodite. 1988. "Is It Time for Psychology to Take UFOs Seriously?" *Psychotherapy in Private Practice* 6:143-49.

Cohen, Daniel. 1967. *Myths of the Space Age*. New York: Dodd, Mead.

Condon, Edward U. 1969. *Final Report of the Scientific Study of Unidentified Flying Objects*. New York: Dutton.

Däniken, Erich von. 1969. *Chariots of the Gods?: Unsolved Mysteries of the Past.* New York: Berkley Publishing.

———. 1976. *Gold of the Gods.* New York: Putnam.

De Camp, L. Sprague. 1975. *Lost Continents: The Atlantis Theme in History, Science, and Literature.* New York: Ballantine.

Degh, Linda. 1971. "The 'Belief Legend' in Modern Society: Form, Function, and Relationship to Other Genres." In *American Folk Legend: A Symposium,* edited by Wayland Hand, 55-68. Berkeley: University of California Press.

———. 1977. "UFOs and How Folklorists Should Look at Them." *Fabula* 18:242-48.

Eberhart, George. 1986. *UFOs and the Extraterrestrial Contactee Movement.* 2 vols. Metuchen, N.J.: Scarecrow Press.

Evans, Hilary. 1983. *The Evidence for UFOs.* Wellingborough, UK: Aquarian.

———. 1984. *Visions, Apparitions, and Alien Visitors.* Wellingborough, UK: Aquarian Press.

———. 1987a. *Gods, Spirits, and Cosmic Guardians: A Comparative Study of the Encounter Experience.* Wellingborough, UK: Aquarian Press.

———. 1987b. "UFOs as Social and Cultural Phenomena." In *UFOs, 1947-1987: The 40-Year Search for an Explanation,* edited by Hilary Evans and John Spencer, 359-63. London: Fortean Press.

Festinger, Leon, Henry W. Riechen, and Stanley Schachter. 1956. *When Prophecy Fails.* Minneapolis: University of Minnesota Press.

Fox, Phyllis. 1979. "Social and Cultural Factors Influencing Beliefs About UFOs." In *UFO Phenomena and the Behavioral Scientist,* edited by R. F. Haines, 20-42. Metuchen, N.J.: Scarecrow Press.

Fuller, Curtis G., et al., eds. 1980. *Proceedings of the First International UFO Congress.* New York: Warner.

Gardner, Martin. 1987. "Science-Fantasy Religious Cults." *Free Inquiry* 7, no. 3:31-35.

Goran, Morris. 1978. *The Modern Myth: Ancient Astronauts and UFOs.* New York: A. S. Barnes.

Gordon, James S. 1991. "The UFO Experience." *The Atlantic Monthly* (August):82-92.

Gowan, John Curtis. 1978-79. "Altered States of Consciousness: A Taxonomy." *Journal of Altered States of Consciousness* 4:141-56.

Grinspoon, Lester, and Alan Persky. 1972. "Psychiatry and UFO Reports." In *UFOs—A Scientific Debate*, edited by Carl Sagan and Thornton Page, 233-46. Ithaca, N.Y.: Cornell University Press.

Hackett, Herbert. 1948. "The Flying Saucer: A Manipulated Concept." *Sociology and Social Research* 32:869-73.

Hall, Robert L. 1972. "Sociological Perspectives on UFO Reports." In *UFOs—A Scientific Debate*, edited by Carl Sagan and Thornton Page, 213-23. Ithaca, N.Y.: Cornell University Press.

Hexham, Irving. 1986. "Yoga, UFOs, and Cult Membership." *Update: A Quarterly Journal on New Religion Movements* 10, no. 3:3-17.

Hitching, Francis. 1979. *The Mysterious World: An Atlas of the Unexplained*. New York: Holt, Rinehart, and Winston.

Hoyle, Fred, and Chandra Wickramasinghe. 1978. *Lifecloud: The Origin of Life in the Universe*. New York: Harper and Row.

Hopkins, Budd. 1987. *Intruders: The Incredible Visitations at Copley Woods*. New York: Random House.

Horowitz, Norman. 1986. *To Utopia and Back: The Search for Life in the Solar System*. New York: Freeman and Co.

Jung, C. G. 1970. "Flying Saucers: A Modern Myth of Things Seen Flying in the Sky." In *The Collected Works of C. G. Jung*, edited by Herbert Mead, Michael Fordham, and Gerhard Adler, vol. 10, pp. 307-33. Princeton, N.J.: Princeton University Press.

Kirkpatrick, R. George, and Diana Tumminia. 1992. "California Space Goddess: The Mystagogue in a Flying Saucer Cult." *Syzygy: Journal of Alternative Religion and Culture* 1:159-72.

Klass, Philip. 1989. *UFO Abductions: A Dangerous Game*. Buffalo, N.Y.: Prometheus Books.

Laqueur, Walter. 1980. *The Terrible Secret: Suppression of the Truth about Hitler's "Final Solution."* Boston: Little, Brown.

Lawson, Alvin H. 1980a. "Hypnosis and Imaginary UFO 'Abductees'." In *Proceedings of the First International UFO Congress*, compiled and edited by Curtis G. Fuller, 195-238. New York: Warner.

———. 1980b. "Archetypes and Abductions." *Frontiers of Science* 2, no. 6:32-36.

———. 1984. "Perinatal Imagery in UFO Abduction Reports." *Journal of Psychohistory* 12:211-39.

Lévi-Strauss, Claude. 1963. "The Structural Study of Myth." In *Structural Anthropology*, by Claude Levi-Strauss, 206-31. New York: Basic Books.

Livingston, James C. 1989. *Anatomy of the Sacred*. New York: Macmillan.

Lowe, Virginia A. P. 1979. "A Brief Look at Some UFO Legends." *Indiana Folklore* 12:67-79.

Lynn, Steven Jay, and Judith W. Rhue. 1988. "Hypnosis, Developmental Antecedents, and Psychopathology." *American Anthropologist* 43:35-44.

Mattsson, Dan, and Michael A. Persinger. 1986. "Geophysical Variables and Behavior: XXXV. Positive Correlations Between Numbers of UFO Reports and Earthquake Activity in Sweden." *Perceptual and Motor Skills* 63:921-22.

McClure, Kevin. 1987. "UFO Cults." In *UFOs, 1947-1987: The 40-Year Search for an Explanation*, edited by Hilary Evans and John Spencer, 346-51. London: Fortean Press.

McDonough, Thomas R. 1987. *The Search for Extraterrestrial Intelligence: Listening for Life in the Cosmos*. New York: Wiley and Sons.

McIver, Shirley. 1987. "UFO (Flying Saucer) Groups: A Look at British Membership." *Zetetic Scholar*, nos. 12/13:39-57.

McKenna, Terence. 1989. "A Conversation over Saucers." *Revision: Journal of Consciousness and Change* 11, no. 3:29-30.

Meerloo, Joost. 1968. "The Flying Saucer Syndrome and the Need for Miracles." *Journal of the American Medical Association* 203 (March 18): 170-72.

Meheust, Bertrand. 1987. "UFO Abductions as Religious Folklore." In *UFOs, 1947-1987: The 40-Year Search for an Explanation*, edited by Hilary Evans and John Spencer, 352-58. London: Fortean Press.

Melton, J. Gordon. 1981. "The Contactees: A Survey." In *The Spectrum of UFO Research: Proceedings of the Second UFO Conference, 1981*, edited by Mimi Hynek, 99-108. Chicago: J. Allen Hyneck Center for UFO Studies.

———. 1989. *The Encyclopedia of American Religions*. 3rd ed. Detroit: Gale Research.

Melton, J. Gordon, and George M. Eberhart, compilers. 1990. *The Flying Saucer Contactee Movement: 1950-1990*. Santa Barbara, Calif.: Santa Barbara Centre for Humanistic Studies, 1990.

Menzel, Donald H., and Ernest Taves. 1977. *The UFO Enigma: The Definitive Explanation of the UFO Phenomenon*. New York: Doubleday.

Moore, Patrick. 1970. "Flying Saucers." In *Man, Myth, and Magic*, edited by Richard Cavendish, 1000-1003. New York: Marshall Cavendish.

Moravec, Mark. 1987. "UFOs as Psychological and Parapsychological Phenomena." In *UFOs, 1947-1987: The 40-Year Search for an Explanation*, edited by Hilary Evans and John Spencer, 293-312. London: Fortean Press.

Parnell, June. 1988. "Measured Personality Characteristics of Persons Who Claim UFO Experiences." *Psychotherapy in Private Practice* 6:159-65.

Persinger, Michael A. 1980. "Earthquake Activity and Antecedent UFO Report Numbers." *Perceptual and Motor Skills* 50:791-97.

———. 1981. "Geophysical Variables and Behavior: III. Prediction of UFO Reports by Geomagnetic and Seismic Activity." *Perceptual and Motor Skills* 53:155-22.

———. 1984. "Geophysical Variables and Human Behavior: XVIII. Expected Perceptual Characteristics and Local Distributions of Close UFO Reports." *Perceptual and Motor Skills* 58: 951-59.

Persinger, Michael A., and J. S. Derr. 1990. "Geophysical Variables and Behavior: LXII. Temporary Coupling of UFO Reports and Seismic Energy Release Within the Rio Grande Rift System: Discriminative Validity of the Tectonic Strain Theory." *Perceptual and Motor Skills* 71 (1990): 567-72.

Peters, Ted. 1977a. *UFOs—God's Chariots?: Flying Saucers in Politics, Science, and Religion.* Atlanta: John Knox Press.

———. 1977b. "UFOs: The Religious Dimension." *Cross Currents* 27:261-78.

Rank, Otto. 1952. *The Trauma of Birth.* New York: Robert Brunner.

Rao, K. R. 1984. "Parapsychology." In *Encyclopedia of Psychology*, edited by Raymond J. Corsini, vol. 2, pp. 478-82. New York: John Wiley and Sons.

Rhine, Mark W. 1969. "Psychological Aspects of UFO Reports." In *Final Report of the Scientific Study of Unidentified Flying Objects*, edited by Edward U. Condon, 590-98. New York: E. P. Dutton.

Rhue, Judith W., and Steven Jay Lynn. 1987. Fantasy Proneness and Psychopathology." *Journal of Personality and Social Psychology* 53:327-36.

Ring, Kenneth. 1989a. "Near-Death and UFO Encounters as Shamanic Initiations: Some Conceptual and Evolutionary Implications." *Revision: A Journal of Consciousness and Change* 11, no. 3:14-22.

———. 1989b. "Toward an Imaginal Interpretation of 'UFO Abductions'." *Revision: Journal of Consciousness and Change* 11, no. 4:17-24.

Robinson, Jacob. 1971. "Holocaust." In *Encyclopedia Judaica*, edited by Cecil Roth, Geoffrey Wigoder, et al., vol. 8, pp. 829-906. New York: Macmillan.

Rojcewicz, Peter M. 1986. "The Extraordinary Encounter Continuum Hypothesis and Its Implications for the Study of Belief Materials." *Folklore Forum* 19:131-52.

———. 1987. "The 'Men in Black' Experience and Tradition: Analogues with Tradition Devil Hypothesis." *Journal of American Folklore* 100:148-60.

———. 1989. "The Folklore of the 'Men in Black': A Challenge to the Prevailing Paradigm." *Revision: A Journal of Consciousness and Change* 11, no. 4:5-16.

Saliba, John A. 1990. "Religious Dimensions of UFO Phenomena." Paper presented at the conference on The UFO Phenomenon in the 1990s, held at Santa Barbara, California, November 24.

Sanarov, Valerii I. 1981. "On the Nature and Origin of Flying Saucers and Little Green Men." *Current Anthropology* 22:163-67.

Schmidt, Roger. 1988. *Exploring Religion.* 2d ed. Belmont, Calif.: Wadsworth.

Schneider, Joseph W. 1985. "Social Problems Theory." *Annual Review of Sociology* 11:209-29.

Schutz, Michael. 1980. "Sociological Aspects of UFOs." In *The Encyclopedia of UFOs*, edited by Ronald Story, 339-41. London: New English Library.

Schwarz, Berthold Eric. 1979. "Psychiatric and Parapsychiatric Dimensions of UFOs." In *UFO Phenomena and the Behavioral Scientist*, edited by R. F. Haines, 113-24. Metuchen, N.J.: Scarecrow Press.

———. 1983. *UFO Dynamics: Psychiatric and Psychic Dimensions of the UFO Syndrome.* 2 volumes. Moore Haven, Fla.: Rainbooks.

Simon, Armando. 1984. "Psychology and UFOs." *Skeptical Inquirer* 8:355-67.

Small, Alice, ed. 1977. *Concise Encyclopedia of Psychology and Psychiatry.* New York: Franklin Watts.

Spencer, John. 1987. "UFO and the Public." In *UFOs, 1947-1987: The 40-Year Search for an Explanation*, edited by Hilary Evans and John Spencer, 328-32. London: Fortean Press.

Sprinkle, R. Leo. 1988. "Psychotherapeutic Services for Persons Who Claim UFO Experiences." *Psychotherapy in Private Practice* 6:151-57.

Stark, Rodney, and William Sims Bainbridge. 1983. "Concept for a Theory of Religious Movements." In *Alternatives to American Mainline Churches*, edited by Joseph Fichter, 3-25. New York: Rose of Sharon Press.

Steiger, Brad. 1986. "Eighteen Theories on UFOs." *UFO: A Forum for Extraterrestrial Theories and Phenomena* 1, no. 1:16-17.

Story, Ronald. 1977. "Von Däniken's Golden Gods." *Zetetic* 2 (Fall/Winter):23-35.

Stupple, David. 1984. "Mahatmas and Space Brothers: The Ideology of Alleged Contact with Extraterrestrials." *Journal of American Culture* 7:131-39.

Stupple, David, and Abdollah Dashti. 1977. "Flying Saucers and Multiple Realities: A Case Study in Phenomenological Theory." *Journal of Popular Culture* 11:479-93.

Tart, Charles T. 1990. *Altered States of Consciousness*. Revised and updated edition. San Francisco: Harper and Row.

Thompson, Keith. 1989. "The Mythic Dimensions of the UFO Phenomenon." *Revision: A Journal of Consciousness and Change* 11, no. 3:31-47.

Vallée, Jacques. 1975. *The Invisible College: What a Group of Scientists Have Discovered About UFO Influences on the Human Race*. New York: Dutton.

——. 1979. *Messengers of Deception: UFO Contacts and Cults*. Berkeley, Calif.: And/Or Press.

——. 1987. "The Psycho-Physical Nature of UFO Reality: A Speculative Framework." In *The Encyclopedia of UFOs*, edited by Ronald Story, 317-19. London: New English Library.

——. 1988. *Dimensions*. Chicago: Contemporary Books.

Wallis, Roy. 1975. "Reflections on When Prophecy Fails." *Zetetic Scholar* 4:9-14.

——. 1974. "The Aetherius Society: A Case Study of a Formation of a Mystagogic Congregation." *Sociological Review* 22:27-44.

Ward, Donald. 1977. "The Little Man Who Wasn't There: Encounters With the Supranormal." *Fabula* 18:212-25.

Warren, Donald I. 1970. "Status Inconsistency Theory and Flying Saucer Sightings." *Science* 170 (November 6):599-603.

Watson, Nigel. 1987. "The Day Flying Saucers Invaded the Cinema." In *UFOs, 1947-1987. The 40-Year Search for an Explanation*, edited by Hilary Evans and John Spencer, 333-37. London: Fortean Press.

Weber, Max. 1956. *Sociology of Religion*. Boston: Beacon Press.

Westrum, Ron. 1977. "Social Intelligence About Anomalies: The Case of UFOs." *Social Studies of Science* 7:271-302.

——. 1980. "Reporting UFO Sightings." In *The Encyclopedia of UFOs*, edited by Ronald Story, 308. London: New English Library.

Zimmer, Troy A. 1984. "Some Psychological Correlates of Possible UFO Sightings." *Journal of Social Psychology* 123:199-206.

——. 1985. "Belief in UFOs as Alternative Reality, Cultural Rejection, or Disturbed Psyche." *Deviant Behavior: An Interdisciplinary Journal* 6:405 19.

10

THE FLYING SAUCER CONTACTEE MOVEMENT, 1950-1994: A BIBLIOGRAPHY

J. Gordon Melton and George M. Eberhart

INTRODUCTION

During the last several centuries an increasing number of individuals have claimed to have had direct contact with extraterrestrial entities. During the modern flying saucer era which began in 1947, these claims of contact have generally been classified into three rather distinct varieties. Close encounters of the third kind (CEIII) are UFO reports which include the claim of sighting and usually some interaction with a humanoid extraterrestrial entity. The CEIII is characterized by its mundaneness, i.e., the simple sighting of something unusual. Closely related is the second type of extraterrestrial contact, the abduction report. This second type of report centers upon the report of an individual who claims that they have been abducted by UFO entities, taken aboard a spacecraft, and frequently subjected to some kind of medical procedure. In distinction from the more mundane CEIII, people reporting abductions express great emotional upset and a sense of being violated. Many of the reports are far from common memories, being initially uncovered in a clinical situation, often accessible only with the aid of hypnosis.

The present chapter is concerned with neither the classic CEIII nor the abduction cases. It deals with the contactee, the third type of people who claim contact with extraterrestrials. Like the abductee expe-

This chapter is an updated version of a booklet published by the Santa Barbara Centre for Humanistic Studies in 1990 as "The Flying Saucer Contactee Movement: 1950-1990."

rience, the contactee experience differs from CEIII reports by the unusual nature of the contactee claims; however, the contactee experience radically differs from the abductee experience in the positive nature of the contact. It is quite common for the contactee to claim a familiarity with extraterrestrials occasioned by long-term contact and the reception of numerous communications from them. Contactee reports also differ in that they frequently lead to the formation of spiritual/religious groups of an occult or metaphysical nature.

Ufology, the scientific study of UFOs and UFO reports, has generally dismissed the contactees. Ufologists have been embarrassed by the questionable activities of some of the more controversial contactees, especially some of the original ones in the 1950s. A few ufologists, most prominently R. Leo Sprinkle, have devoted a major portion of their time to studying contactees, but in general their work has yet to be integrated into the main literature of ufology.

Reports of the contactee experience have been marred by counterclaims of lying and hoaxing by contacts, the most prominent ongoing case being that of Swiss contactee Eduard "Billy" Meier. While the overwhelming majority of contactees have never been accused of hoaxing, those few hoaxes which have been documented have frequently been used as an excuse to ignore the rest. Possibly more at the heart of the issue between ufology and contactees, the typical contactee report includes as an integral aspect of the account interaction between extraterrestrial and earthling by various paranormal (psychic-occult) processes. Reports of telepathy, teleportation, dematerializations, and psychokinesis abound. Those contactees who report long-term contact are usually "channels" (mediums) who regularly "channel" information for the extraterrestrials. The contactees are the source of the term "channeling" now popular in the New Age movement. Thus the serious study of the contactee in any positive way would automatically leAd ufology toward parapsychology, thus complicating the ufologist's life with further controversy and more obstacles to having their research given its due consideration.

Whatever one might think of the contactee phenomenon, it has persisted as a topic of interest within the larger community of people interested in UFOs. However, anyone wishing to study the phenomenon immediately encounters a major problem in that most of the material concerning the contact experience is published informally in rather limited editions. Thus even before researchers tackle the problem of finding someone from whom to purchase material, they have the more pressing problem of discovering what material exists. This bibliography attempts to provide a comprehensive list of contactee literature, both primary and secondary. It continues the prior attempts by Melton in 1981 and 1982, Eberhart in 1986, and Eberhart and Melton in 1990, and adds to while updating the previous lists of contactee monographs produced since 1952.

The chapter is meant to be exhaustive of literature produced by and about contactees since 1950 and the exception of the periodicals produced by contactee groups, articles in UFO movement periodicals on contactees, and newspaper articles (thought a few outstanding examples of the latter are mentioned). Anyone knowing of material which needs to be added to this list for future editions is invited to be in touch with the compilers. The only large collection of contactee material known to exist in a publicly accessible location is in the Special Collections Department of the Davidson Library of the University of California-Santa Barbara, where it has become an integral part of the American Religions Collection. A copy of the great majority of the items listed below can be found there.

OUTLINE OF REFERENCES MATERIALS

I. **General Sources**

II. **Contactees in the 1950s**

A. The Major Contactees

> George Adamski
> Cedric Allingham
> Orfeo Angelucci
> Truman Bethurum
> Dana Howard
> Dino Kraspedon
> Gloria Lee (Cosmon Research Foundation)
> Howard Menger
> Buck Nelson
> George Hunt Williamson

B. Major Contactee Groups

> Aetherius Society (George King)
> Borderland Sciences Research Foundation
> Cosmic Circle of Fellowship (William Ferguson)
> Human Individual Metamorphosis (The Two; Bo and Peep)
> L/L Research
> Mark-Age MetaCenter

Unarius-Science of Life (Ruth Norman)
Understanding (Daniel Fry)
Universariun Foundation
George Van Tassel and the Ashtar Command

C. Additional Contactee Literature

III. Contact Since 1960

A. The Contactee Personalities

Michael X. Barton
Uri Geller
Eduard "Billy" Meier
Brad Steiger
Frank Stranges

B. Additional Contactee Literature

GENERAL SOURCES

Material in this first section attempts to analyze and understand the phenomenon of UFO contactees from both academic and journalistic perspectives. Some is quite polemic, dismissing the contactees as religiously and/or psychologically aberrant. In spite of the interest in new spiritual and religious groups during the last two decades, the flying saucer contactee movement has received relatively little attention, and the work that has been done has been scattered through an array of journals. One major book, now a classic sociological study (Festinger et al.) was produced from the observation of a contactee group in Oak Park, Illinois. A very helpful addition to the literature is an anthology compiled by Saliba which includes the most significant of the psychological and sociological material. A broad survey of contactee groups is found in Melton.

Through the 1980s in recent years R. Leo Sprinkle and June O. Parnell have led an annual conference for contactees, the proceedings of which have been published. These proceedings provide a most valuable source for beginning to understand the contactee phenomenon. though the space given to critical reflection has been quite limited.

1. Alnor, William M. *UFOs in the New Age: Extraterrestrial Messages and the Truth of Scripture*. Grand Rapids, Mich.: Baker Book House, 1992. 293p. *Note:* An Evangelical Christian response to contactee claims.

2. Ashworth, C. E. "Saucers, Spoon-Bending, and Atlantis: A Structural Analysis of New Mythologies." *Sociological Review* 28 (1980): 353-76.

3. Baird, John. *The Inner Limits of Outer Space*. Hanover, N.H.: Dartmouth College/University Press of New England, 1987. 226p.

4. Blake, Ian. "Channeled ETs Wax Shallow." *UFO* 6, 6 (1991): 31-32.

5. Buckner, H. Taylor. "The Flying Saucerian Books: A Lingering Cult." *New Society* (September 9, 1965): 14-16. Reprinted as "The Flying Saucerian Books: An Open Door Cult." In Marcello Truzzi, ed., *Sociology and Everyday Life*. Englewood Cliffs, N.J.: Prentice-Hall, 1968, 223-30.

6. Burge, Weldon. *The UFO Cults*. Cincinnati, Ohio: Pamphlet Publications, 1979, 39p.

7. Catton, William R. "What Kind of People Does a Religious Cult Attract?" *American Sociological Review* 22 (1957): 561-66.

8. Clark, Jerome. *The Emergence of a Phenomenon: UFOs from the Beginning through 1959*. Detroit, Mich.: Omnigraphics, Inc., 1992. *Note:* Volume 2 of *The UFO Encyclopedia*. This important volume includes entries on many of the 1950s contactees with extensive bibliographical listings, including numerous articles in the UFO periodicals of the period.

9. ———— . *UFOs in the 1980s*. Detroit, Mich.: Apogee Books, 1990. 234p. *Note:* Volume 1 of *The UFO Encyclopedia*.

10. ———— . "Waiting for the Space Brothers." *Fate* Part 1: 39, 3 (March 1986): 47-54. Part 2: 39, 4 (April 1986): 81-87. Part 3: 39, 5 (May 1986): 68-76.

11. Cohen, Daniel. *UFOs: The Third Wave*. New York: M. Evan's and Co., 1988. 173p.

12. Ellwood, Robert S. *Religious and Spiritual Groups in Modern America*. Englewood Cliffs, N.J.: Prentice-Hall, 1973, 131-56.

13. Ellwood, Robert S., and Harry B. Partin. *Religious and Spiritual Groups in Modern America*. 2d ed. Englewood Cliffs, N.J.: Prentice-Hall, 1988, 111-33.

14. Evans, Christopher. *Cults of Unreason*. London: George Harrap, 1973; New York: Farrar, Straus and Giroux, 1974, 135-75. Paperback ed., St. Albans, Herts: Panther, 1974, 137-79. American paperback ed., New York: Delta, 1975, 135-75.

15. Evans, Hilary. *Gods, Spirits, Cosmic Guardians: A Comparative Study of Encounter Experience*. Wellingborough, Northamptonshire, UK: Aquarian Press, 1987.

16. Festinger, Leon, Henry W. Riecken, and Stanley Schachter. *When Prophecy Fails: A Social and Psychological Study of a Modern Group that Predicted the*

Destruction of the World. Minneapolis: University of Minnesota, 1956. 256p. Paperback ed., New York: Harper Torchbook, 1964. 253p. *Note:* The pseudonymous contactees described in this work are actually Dorothy Martin (more recently known as Sister Thedra, head of the Association of Sananda and Sanat Kumara) and Charles Laughead. Melton and Wallis offer responses to this study.

17. Flammonde, Paris. *The Age of Flying Saucers: Notes on a Projected History of Unidentified Flying Objects.* New York: Hawthorne, 1971. 288p.

18. ———. "What the Flying Saucer Cult Really Means." *Cavalier* (March 1967): 55-56, 82-87.

19. Greer, Steven M. "Alien Motives May Be Non-Hostile." *UFO* 6, 6 (1991): 26-30.

20. Hexham, Irving. "Yoga, UFOs, and Cult Membership." *Update: A Quarterly Journal of New Religious Movements* 10, 3 (1986): 3-17.

21. Holzer, Hans. *The UFO-nauts.* Greenwich, Conn.: Fawcett Publications, 1976. 304p.

22. Horn, Jack C. "The UFO Cult Revisited: Waiting for the Next Spaceship." *Psychology Today* 11 (October 1977): 25, 30-31.

23. Hudson, Jan. *Those Sexy Saucer People.* Canterbury, N.H.: Greenlead Classics, 1967. 176p.

24. Jackson, John A. "Two Contemporary Cults." *The Advancement of Science* 23 (June 1966): 60-64.

25. Jacobs, David, *The UFO Controversy in America.* Bloomington, Ind.: Indiana University Press, 1975.

26. McClure, Kevin. "UFO Cults." In Hilary Evans and John Spencer, eds., *UFOs, 1947-1987: The 40-Year Search for an Explanation.* London: Fortean Times, 1987, 346-58. Reprinted in America as John Spencer and Hilary Evans, eds. *Phenomenon: Forty Years of Flying Saucers.* New York: Avon Books, 1988. 413p.

27. Manas, John H. *Flying Saucers and Space Men.* New York: Pythagorean Society, 1962. 124p.

28. Melton, J. Gordon. "The Contactees: A Survey." In Mimi Hynek, ed., *The Spectrum of UFO Research: Proceedings of the Second UFO Conference.* Chicago: Center for UFO Studies, 1975, 99-108.

29. ———. *The Encyclopedia of American Religions.* 2 vols. Wilmington, N.C.: McGrath, 1978. Vol. 2, pp. 87-89, 119, 120-21, 131-33, 155-65, 188-89, 198-213, 243. 2d ed. Detroit: Gale Research Company, 1983. 4th ed. Detroit: Gale Research Company, 1992. 1100p.

30. ——— . "Spiritualization and Reaffirmation: What Really Happens When Prophecy Fails." *American Studies* 26, 2 (Fall 1985): 17-29.

31. ——— . "UFO Contactees: A Report on Work in Progress." In Curtis Fuller, *Proceedings of the First International UFO Congress.* New York: Warner, 1980, 378-95.

32. Milton, James T. *Take Me to Your Leader.* Cottonwood, Ariz.: Esoteric Publications, 1979. 89pp.

33. Mishlove, Jeffrey. *Preliminary Investigation of Events which Suggest the Possible Allied Psi Abilities of Mr. Ted Owens.* San Francisco: Washington Street Research Center, December 1977. 48p. 2d ed., Washington Research Center, January 1978. 52p.

34. Nebel, Long John. *The Way Out World.* Englewood Cliffs, N.J.: Prentice-Hall, 1961, 28-89. Paperback ed., New York: Lancer, 1962, 22-84.

35. Rasmussen, Richard Michael. *The UFO Literature: A Comprehensive Annotated Bibliography of Works in English.* Jefferson, N.C.: McFarland, 1985. 263p.

36. St. Clair, David. *The Psychic World of California.* New York: Bantam Books, 1973, 320-26.

37. Sagan, Carl. "The Saucerian Cult: An Astronomer's Interpretation." *Saturday Review* 49 (August 6, 1966): 50-52.

38. Saliba, John A., ed. *Flying Saucer Contactees: A Sociopsychological Perspective.* Detroit: Apogee Books, 1990.

39. Sanarov, Valerii I. "On the Nature and Origin of Flying Saucers and Little Green Men." *Current Anthropology* 22 (1981): 163-76.

40. Schwarz, Berthold Eric. "UFO Contactee Stella Lansing: Possible Medical Implications of Her Motion Picture Experiments." *Journal of the American Society for Psychosomatic Dentistry and Medicine* 23 (1976): 60-68.

41. Shepherd, Leslie. *Encyclopedia of Occultism and Parapsychology.* 2 vols. Detroit, Mich.: Gale Research Company, 1978. 2d ed. 3 vols. 1985.

42. Spencer, John. *The UFO Encyclopedia.* London: Headline Book Publishing, 1991. 340p.

43. Story, Ronald D., ed. *The Encyclopedia of UFOs.* Garden City, N.Y.: Doubleday and Company, 1980.

44. Stupple David. "Mahatmas and Space Brothers: The Ideologies of Alleged Contact with Mahatmas and Space Brothers." *Journal of American Culture* 7 (1984): 148-60.

45. Stupple, David, and Abdollah Dashti. "Flying Saucers and Multiple Realities: A Case Study in Phenomenological Theory." *Journal of Popular Culture* 11 (1977): 479-93.

46. Tassi, Dan. *The Mind and Time and Space*. Philadelphia: Dorrance, 1962. 114p.

47. Wallis, Roy. "Reflections on 'When Prophecy Fails.'" *Zetetic Scholar* 4 (1975): 9-14.

48. Wilhelm, John L. *The Search for Superman*. New York: Pocket Library, 1976, 35-45.

49. Zusne, Leonard, and Warren H. Jones. *Anomalistic Psychology: A Study of Extraordinary Phenomena of Behavior and Experience*. Hillsdale, N.J.: Lawrence Erlbaum Associates, 1982. 528p.

THE ROCKY MOUNTAIN CONFERENCES ON UFO INVESTIGATION

Held since 1980 in Laramie, Wyoming, under the leadership of R. Leo Sprinkle and June O. Parnell, the Rocky Mountain Conferences on UFO Investigation have welcomed contactees to an open meeting for sharing, research, and inquiry into the nature of the reality of the contactees' experience. Parnell has completed a Ph.D. dissertation from her work on the contactees who have attended. As a whole the conferences have emphasized the reporting of experiences rather than research, but the future conferences offer hope of producing a significant amount of insightful data.

50. Parnell, June O. "Personality Characteristics on the MMPI, 16PF, and ACC of Persons Who Claim UFO Experiences." Laramie, Wyo.: Ph.D. dissertation, University of Wyoming, 1986. 96p.

51. ——— . *Proceedings: Rocky Mountain Conference on UFO Investigation, Ninth Annual Contactee Conference*. Laramie, Wyo.: Paranormal Research Organization for UFO Studies, 1988. 135p.

52. ——— . *Proceedings: Rocky Mountain Conference on UFO Investigation, Seventh Annual Contactee Conference*. Laramie, Wyo.: Paranormal Research Organization for UFO Studies, 1986. 110p.

53. ——— , ed. *Proceedings: Rocky Mountain Conference on UFO Investigation, Eighth Annual Contactee Conference*. Laramie, Wyo.: Paranormal Research Organization on UFO Investigation, 1987. 35p.

54. Sprinkle, R. Leo. *Proceedings: Rocky Mountain Conference on UFO Investigation (Second UFO Contactee Conference)*. Laramie, Wyo.: Paranormal Research Organization for UFO Studies, 1981. 286p.

55. ———— . *UFO Contactees and New Science*. Laramie, Wyo.: The author, 1990. 13p.

56. Tipton, Doug., ed. *Rocky Mountain Conference on UFO Investigation (Sixth UFO Contactee Conference)*. Laramie, Wyo.: Paranormal Research Organization and UFO Studies, Institute for UFO Contactee Studies, 1985. 99p.

CONTACTEES IN THE 1950S

The Major Contactees

The modern era of the extraterrestrial contact movement began on November 20, 1952, with George Adamski's alleged encounter in the California desert with a long-haired man from Venus named Orthon. Adamski soon became the first contactee to achieve national fame. His three commercially published books became best sellers and brought him a following that still flourishes over two decades after his death.

Fame brought Adamski not only loyal followers but determined critics. He was attacked by people questioning his credibility, first by ufologist James Moseley in the pages of *Nexus* and *Saucer News* and then by former colleagues Jerrold E. Baker and Carol A. Honey. Critics claimed that Adamski had (1) faked his photographs of UFOs and their occupants; (2) used the same phraseology in his allegedly true *Inside the Space Ships* that he had used in his much earlier science fiction book, *Pioneers of Space*; and (3) reprinted his 1936 *Questions and Answers by the Royal Order of Tibet* as his *Science of Life Study Course* in 1964, substituting the words "Space Brothers" and "Cosmic Brotherhood" where the words "Royal Order of Tibet" had appeared in the former work.

The reaction to a 1979 attempt to conduct a sympathetic appraisal of Adamski by sociologist David Stupple showed the strong opinions, pro and con, that Adamski could still generate. Sifting out the fraud and fantasy from what George Adamski really believed and experienced may well be impossible.

Whether prophet or faker, possibly both, Adamski inspired a number of others who also claimed contact with extraterrestrials. Characteristic of the contactees of the 1950s were encounters facilitated by some means of psychic phenomenon, usually the reception of telepathic messages over a period of time (what is today called channeling) and a subsequent call for a religious response to the content of the channeled messages. Most of the contacts also resulted in the formation of a spiritual group which resembled either a spiritualist or theosophical organization.

The first decade of contact can be said to have ended with the death of Gloria Lee who succumbed to a fast she had started in a quest to have officials in Washington, D.C. listen to her messages from a Jupiterian space brother.

GEORGE ADAMSKI

57. Adamski, George. *Answers to Questions Most Frequently Asked About Our Space Visitors and Other Planets.* [Valley Center, Calif.]: The author, 1965. 30p.

58. ———— . *A Challenge to Spiritual Leaders.* [Valley Center, Calif.]: The author, [1965]. 3p.

59. ———— . *Cosmic Consciousness.* N.p., n.d. *Note:* Not seen; mentioned by Winfield Brownell.

60. ———— . *Cosmic Philosophy.* [San Diego, Calif.]: The author, 1961. 87p. Reprint, Freeman, S.D.: Pine Hill, 1972; [Valley Center, Calif.: UFO Education Center, 1975?]. 87p.

61. ———— . *Cosmic Science Newsletters.* Northboro, Mass.: International Cosmic Council, n.d. 21p. *Note:* Collection of letters from his *Cosmic Science Newsletter*, 1961-1963.

62. ———— . *Cosmic Science Questions and Answers.* 2 parts. [Anaheim, Calif.: Carol A. Honey], 1958. Series 1, part 2, [25p.]. *Note:* Part 1 not seen.

63. ———— . *Flying Saucers Farewell.* New York: Abelard-Schuman, 1961. 190p. Reprinted as *Behind the Flying Saucer Mystery.* New York: Paperback Library, 1967; Warner Paperback Library, 1974. 159p.

64. ———— . *Gravity and the Natural Forces of the Universe.* N.p., n.d. 3p. *Note:* From an informal talk given in Vista, Calif., in the early 1960s. Adapted from a tape recording.

65. ———— . "I Photographed Space Ships." *Fate* 4 (July 1951): 64-74. *Note:* (Letters), Frank Scully, W. K. Butler, Lonzo Dove, Richard McMahon, George Adamski (October 1951): 116-22; George Adamski (November-December 1951): 122.

66. ———— . *In My Father's House Are Many Mansions.* Detroit: Interplanetary Relations, 1955. 14p. Reprinted as *Many Mansions.* Willowdale, Ont.: SS&S, [1974, 1983]. [18p.] *Note:* From a press conference with the ministers of Detroit in September 1955.

67. ———— . "Inside a Flying Saucer." *Real Adventure* (July 1956): 40-43, 84-97. *Note:* Condensation of his book, *Inside the Space Ships.*

68. ———— . *Inside the Space Ships.* [Ghostwritten by Charlotte Blodgett.] New York: Abelard-Schuman, 1955. 256p. British ed., London: Neville

Spearman, 1956, 1966, 1971. 236p. Reprinted, New York: Fieldcrest, 1966. Revised ed., with a portion of *Flying Saucers Have Landed*, Vista, Calif.: George Adamski Foundation, [1980]. 296p. Reprinted as *Inside the Flying Saucers*. New York: Paperback Library, 1967; Warner Paperback Library, 1974. 192p.

69. ———— . *Latest Fascinating Experiences*. N.p., n.d. *Note:* Not seen; listed in Catalog no. 8 published by R. Michael Rasmussen.

70. ———— . *The Law of Levitation*. N.p., n.d. *Note:* Not seen; mentioned by Winfield Brownell (706).

71. ———— . *Petals of Life: Poems*. Laguna Beach, Calif.: Royal Order of Tibet, 1937. 16p.

72. ———— . *Pioneers of Space: A Trip to the Moon, Mars and Venus.* [Ghostwritten by Lucy McGinnis.] Los Angeles: Leonard-Freefield, August 1949. 259p.

73. ———— . *Press Conference with Detroit Ministers*. Detroit, Mich.: The Interplanetary Foundation, 1955. 10p.

74. ———— . *Private Group Lecture for Advanced Thinkers*. N.p., [1955?]. 17p. *Note:* Lecture, Detroit, May 4, 1955.

75. ———— . *Questions and Answers by the Royal Order of Tibet*. Wisdom of the Masters of the Far East, vol. 1. [Laguna Beach, Calif.]: Royal Order of Tibet, 1936. 67p. Reprinted, Mokelumne Hill, Calif.: Health Research, 1974. 67p. Revised by Adamski as *The Science of Life Study Course* in 1964.

76. ———— . *Religion and Saucers*. Detroit: Interplanetary Relations, 1955. 22p. *Note:* Transcript of public lecture in Detroit, September 19, 1955.

77. ———— . *The Space People*. N.p., n.d. *Note:* Not seen; mentioned by Winfield Brownell (706).

78. ———— . *Special Report: My Trip to the Twelve Counsellors Meeting That Took Place on Saturn, March 27-30th, 1962*. Vista, Calif.: Science of Life, 1962. 9p. Reprinted, Jane Lew, W.Va.: New Age, [1983?]. 11p.

79. ———— . *Telepathy: The Cosmic or Universal Language*. 3 parts. N.p.: The author, 1958. 31 + 32 + 42p. Reprinted, Vista, Calif.: George Adamski Foundation, [196-]. 17 + 18 + 19p. Reprinted, [Valley Center, Calif.: UFO Education Center], [197-]. 31 + 32 + 42p.

80. ———— . "Who Is Trying to Stop the Truth Coming Out?" *Flying Saucer Review* 5, 1 (January/February 1959): 18-19.

81. ———— . *The World of Tomorrow*. Detroit: Interplanetary Relations, 1956. 19p. *Note:* Transcript of public lecture given in Detroit, September 20, 1955.

82. "Are the Flying Saucer People Physical Like Ourselves?" *Bright Horizons* 2, 3 (April 1954): 14-17.

83. Baker, Jerrold E. "Adamski's Answer to Baker." *Mystic* 10 (June 1955): 96-97.

84. Barker, Gray. *The Adamski Papers.* Jane Lew, W.Va.: New Age, 1983. 100p.

85. ———. *Gray Barker's Book of Adamski.* Clarksburg, W.Va.: Saucerian Books, [1966]. 78p.

86. ———, ed. *The Adamski Documents: Part One.* Clarksburg, W.Va.: Saucerian Books, [1980]. [108p.]

87. Brown, Dulcie. (Letter). *Caveat Emptor* 7 (Spring 1973): 22-23. *Note:* (Letter), Laura Mundo, 8 (Summer 1973): 28.

88. Buckle, Eileen. *The Scoriton Mystery: Did Adamski Return?* London: Neville Spearman, 1967. 303p.

89. Collins, Robert Perry. *George Adamski: A Closer Look.* [Bridgeport, Conn.]: The author, [1982]. [27p.]

90. Cramp, Leonard G. *Space, Gravity and the Flying Saucer.* London: T. Werner Laurie, 1954; New York: British Book Centre, 1955, 166-79.

91. Dove, Lonzo. (Letter). *Fate* 5 (January 1952): 114.

92. ———. (Letter), "Claims Saucer Knowledge." *Fate* 5 (June 1952): 126-27.

93. "George Adamski Dies." *Fate* 18 (October 1965): 45.

94. "George Adamski: Pioneer of Space." Washington, D.C.: National Investigations Committee on Aerial Phenomena, 1965. 1p. Information sheet.

95. Grant, Bob. "George Adamski: The First Ambassador to Outer Space?" *Real* (August 1966): 8-11, 60-62.

96. Heiden, Richard W. "Where to Report UFO Sightings and Where Not To." *Wisconsin Law Enforcement Journal* 17 (Winter 1977): 25, 28.

97. Hewes, Hayden C. "The Man Who Didn't Talk with Venusians." *Fate* 32 (July 1979): 60-62.

98. Honey, Carol A. *Cosmic Science Correspondence Course.* Anaheim, Calif.: Science Publications, 1964-1967. 109p.

99. ———. *The Origins of This World's Religions.* Anaheim, Calif.: Science Publications, May 1964. [33p.]

100.d Johnson, Maud [Lalita, pseud.]. *Transmitted Light*. Laguna Beach, Calif.: Royal Order of Tibet, 1937. 132p.

101. Kenney, Elna E. *Under the Saucer's Shadow*. New York: Vantage, 1974. 44p.

102. Laughead, Lillian. "A Message from the Flying Saucers?" *Mystic* 8 (February 1955): 63-69.

103. Leslie, Desmond, and George Adamski. *Flying Saucers Have Landed*. London: Werner Laurie; New York: British Book Centre, 1953. 232p. Paperback ed., London: Panther, 1957. 237p. Revised ed., London: Neville Spearman, 1970. 281p. Commentary on Adamski added. Paperback ed., London: Futura, 1977. 281p.

104. Melton, J. Gordon. *A Biographical Dictionary of Sect and Cult Leaders*. New York: Garland, 1986. 354pp. *Note:* Includes entry on Adamski.

105. Moore, William L., ed. *FBI "George Adamski" File*. Prescott, Ariz.: The editor, [1983]. [52p.]

106. ———. *Research Working File on Goerge Adamski*. Burbank, Calif.: The editor, [1985]. [122p.]

107. Mundo, Laura {Laura Marxer]. *Belmont*. [Dearborn Heights, Mich.: Laura Mundo Enterprises, 1972]. 178p. *Note:* Autobiographical novel.

108. ———. "The Concept of Living Atomic Being, or How to Survive the Present Times." [Dearborn Heights, Mich.]: Interplanetary Center, [1970?]. 1p. Revised ed., 1981. 11p.

109. ———. *Cosmogony, Genesis and Eschatology*. Dearborn, Mich.: Planetary Space Center, [196-]. 76p.

110. ———. *A Course in Living Electronics*. Dearborn Heights, Mich.: Laura Mundo Enterprises, 1972. 96 + [10]p. *Note:* A separately published introduction to *Nothing New Under the Sun?*

111. ———. *Doomsday . . . Coming Up?* Novi, Mich.: The author, November 1974. 45p.

112. ———. *Earth Woman!* Detroit: Interplanetary Center, November 1967. 108p.

113. ———. *Flying Saucer Up-Day!* Dearborn Heights, Mich.: Interplanetary Center, [1971]. 60p. 2d ed., Novi, Mich.: Mundo Monitor, 1974. [12] + 70p.

114. ———. *Flying Saucers*. Dearborn Heights, Mich.: Planetary Council, [1969]. 22p. 2d ed., 1982. 15 + 2p.

115. ——— . *Flying Saucers and the Father's Plan*. Clarksburg, W.Va.: Saucerian Books, [1963, 1981]. 80p. Revised ed., *The Father's Plan and Flying Saucers*. Detroit: Planetary Space Center, 1964. 48p.

116. ——— . *How to Contact a Space Person*. Novi, Mich.: Flying Saucer Information Center, [1976?]. 3p.

117. ——— . *How to Save the World (Which May Include Yourself!)*. Dearborn Heights, Mich.: Planetary Council, June 1968. 8p.

118. ——— . *Laura Mundo's Telepathic Messages from Outerspace V.I.P.'s on More Advanced Planets*. [Dearborn Heights, Mich.: Flying Saucer Information Center], 1981. 16p. Revised ed., [Pasadena, Md.: Flying Saucer Bureau], 1983. 17p.

119. ——— . *Letter from Laura*. N.p.: The author, 1981. 12p.

120. ——— . *The Mundo UFO Report*. Pasadena, Md.: Flying Saucer Information Center, 1978. 90p. Revised ed., New York: Vantage, 1982. 160p.

121. ——— . *Nothing New Under the Sun?* Dearborn Heights, Mich.: Interplanetary Center Working Committee, May 1972, 1981. 10 + [4]p.

122. ——— . *Open Letter to the Now Generation*. [Dearborn Heights, Mich.: Planetary Council], March 6, 1969. [8p.]

123. ——— . *Our Trip to the Moon and Venus*. Illus. Sandra Sarto. Dearborn Heights, Mich.: Planetary Council, January 1970. 36 + [3]p. *Note*: A children's book for adults.

124. ——— . *Pied Piper from Outer Space*. Los Angeles: Planetary Space Center Working Committee, 1964. 294 + 4p.

125. ——— . *Private Lecture for Flying Saucer Study Groups (Advanced Stinkers!): Dedicated to Myself*. Dearborn Heights, Mich.: Planetary Space Center, [1961]. 22p.

126. ——— . *The Secret of the Sunbeam: or, How to Look Into the Center of the Atom*. Detroit: Planetary Space Center, May 1963. 8p.

127. ——— . *Sex and the Scientist-Mystic*. Dearborn Heights, Mich.: Laura Mundo Enterprises, [1974?]. 35.

128. ——— . *Sex and the UFO*. (Dearborn Heights, Mich.: Interplanetary Center], 1981. 4p.

129. ——— . *Sunspot Countdown!* Inkster, Mich.: The author, [1979]. 8p. Revised ed., [Pasadena, Md.: Planetary Center], [1983]. 4p.

130. ——— . *There Is a Way Out*. Dearborn Heights, Mich.: Planetary Space Center, 1961. 59p.

131. ———— . *"Time of the End."* Detroit: Visitors Plan Committee, April 1958. 32p. Tabloid format.

132. ———— . *The Universal Scientific/Spiritual Symbols of Yesterday and Today.* Pasadena, Md.: Planetary Center, 1983. 14p.

133. ———— . *The Visitor's Plan.* Detroit: Visitors Plan Committee, [1959]. [275p.]

134. Mundo, Laura, and Jim Wales. *Correlations of Radio and Mind Frequencies.* Pasadena, Md.: Planetary Center, 1983. 7p.

135. Norman, Ruth. *Countdown!!! To Spacefleet Landing, or George Adamski Speaks Again from Planet Venus.* Vol. 7 of *Tesla Speaks* series. El Cajon, Calif.: Academy of Parapsychology, Healing and Psychic Sciences, 1974. 186p.

136. Ogden, Richard. *Air Force Evidence Confirms Adamski Story.* n.p., 1958. *Note:* Scheduled for publication in late 1958, according to *Flying Saucer Review*, September/October 1958, but may never have been published.

137. ———— . *The Case for George Adamski's Contacts with Flying Saucers.* 2 vols. Seattle, Wash.: Ufology Publications, [1962]. 138p.

138. Oliver, Norman T. *Sequel to Scoriton.* London: The author, October 1968. 44p.

139. Petersen, Hans C. *Report from Europe.* Skive, Denmark: Skandinavisk UFO Information, 1963. 191p.

140. Pierce, Roger K. *A Truth About Gravity and the Universe (Pierce Gravitational Theory).* [Albuquerque, N.M.]: The author, 1979. 39p.

141. Rondinone, Peter. "UFO Update." *Omni* 6 (October 1983): 171.

142. Sanders, Gilbert F. *Flying Saucers and Planets.* [Denver, Colo.]: The author, [1980]. 28p.

143. Society of Metaphysicians. *Biometric Analysis of the "Flying Saucer" Photographs.* Hastings, Sussex: Metaphysical Research Group, Society of Metaphysicians, 1954, 1968, 1970. 26p. *Note:* Archers' Court Research Group, a subgroup of the society, performed the analyses using an aura biometer developed by Wilfred Earnshaw Benham.

144. Steckling, Fred. *General Information on Extraterrestrial Spacecraft (Flying Saucers, Etc.) and the People Who Pilot Them.* n.p.: The author, n.d. 4p.

145. ———— . *We Discovered Alien Bases on the Moon.* Vista, Calif.: The author, 1981. 191p.

146. ———— . *Why Are they Here? Spaceships from Other Worlds.* New York: Vantage, 1969. 148p.

147. Stupple, David W. "Mahatmas and Space Brothers: The Ideologies of Alleged Contact with Mahatmas and Space Brothers." *Journal of American Culture* 7 (1984): 131-39.

148. ———. "The Man Who Talked with Venusians." *Fate* 32 (January 1979): 30-39. *Note:* (Letters), C. A. Honey, Fred Steckling, Laura Mundo, David Stupple (May 1979): 113-20; Jerri Frint (July 1979): 119; John E. Kraker, George D. Fawcett, Richard W. Heiden (October 1979): 116-18.

149. Thomas, Richard. "George Adamski: The Untold Story: Pioneer or Profiteer?" *Fate* 36 (July 1983): 60-65. *Note:* (Letters), Gilbert and Lorine Glenn (October 1983): 127-28; Timothy Good, Richard Thomas, William T. Sherwood (November 1983): 113-17.

150. Wales, Jim. *Flying Saucer Report.* N.p. 1971? *Note:* Not seen; mentioned in *Saucers, Space and Science,* no. 61, p. 18.

151. Weekley, Maurice, and George Adamski. "Flying Saucers As Astronomers See Them." *Fate* 3 (September 1950): 56-59.

152. Wirth, Diane E. "Adamski on Trial." *Pursuit* 13 (Summer 1980): 103.

153. Zinstaag, Lou. *On George Adamski.* Basel, Switz.: The author, 1959. 5p.

154. ———. *UFO—George Adamski: Their Man on Earth.* Tucson, Ariz.: UFO Photo Archives, 1990. 198p.

155. Zinstaag, Lou, and Timothy Good. *George Adamski: The Untold Story.* Beckenham, Kent: Ceti, 1983. 208p.

CEDRIC ALLINGHAM

156. Allen, Christopher, and Steuart Campbell. "Flying Saucer from Moore's?" *Magonia* 23 (July 1986): 15-18.

157. Allingham, Cedric [Patrick A. Moore, probably author]. "I Met a Man from Mars." *Pageant* (May 1955): 128-33.

158. ———. "I Met the Messenger from Mars." *True Space Secrets* 1 (April 1958): 41, 55-58. *Note:* From his book, *Flying Saucer from Mars.*

159. Hough, Peter A. "The Astronomer and the Flying Saucer from Mars." *Fate* 40, 3 (March 1987): 76-81.

160. Moore, Patrick A., alleged author [Cedric Allingham, pseud.]. *Flying Saucer from Mars.* London: Frederick Muller, 1954; New York: British Book Centre, 1955. 153p.

ORFEO ANGELUCCI

161. Angelucci, Orfeo M. *Again We Exist.* n.p.: The author, 1960. 12p. *Note:* Not seen; mentioned in Rasmussen.

162. ——— . *Concrete Evidence.* Phoenix, Ariz.: Franky G. Miller, 1959. 16p. 2d ed., New York: Flying Saucer News, [1967?]; [Scotia, N.Y.]: Arcturus Book Service, 1983. 15p.

163. ——— . *Million Year Prophecy!* Los Angeles: Golden Dawn, 1959; [Scotia, N.Y.]: Arcturus Book Service, 1983. 33p.

164. ——— . *The Nature of Infinite Entities.* Trenton, N.J.: The author, 1948. Revised ed., Hemet, Calif.: Talk of the Times Press, 1952, 1954, 1955. 6th ed., Los Angeles: DeVorss and Co., 1958. 20p.

165. ——— . *The Secret of the Saucers.* Edited by Raymond A. Palmer. [Amherst, Wisc.]: Amherst Press, 1955. 167p.

166. ——— . *Son of the Sun.* Los Angeles: DeVorss and Co., 1959. 211p.

167. ——— . *20th Century Times.* Los Angeles: The author, 1953. 8p. *Note:* Tabloid format, labeled vol. 1, no. 1; only one issue published.

168. ——— . "Will You Escape This Life Alive?" In *Harmony Grove Lectures: Book 3.* Los Angeles: Golden Dawn, 1963.

169. Angelucci, Orfeo, and Paul M. Vest. "My Awakening on Another Planet." *Mystic* 6 (October 1954): 14-32.

TRUMAN BETHERUM

170. Bethurum, Truman. *Aboard a Flying Saucer.* [Ghostwritten by Mary Kay Tennison.] Los Angeles: DeVorss and Co., 1954. 192p.

171. ——— . *Facing Reality.* Prescott, Ariz.: The author, [1959]. 177p.

172. ——— . "I Was Inside a Flying Saucer." *Saucers* 1, 2 (1953): 4-5.

173. ——— . *The People of the Planet Clarion* [Edited by Timothy Green Beckley.] Clarksburg, W.Va.: Saucerian Books, 1970. 142p.

174. ——— . *Truman Bethurum's Personal Scrapbook.* Edited by Robert C. Girard. [Scotia, N.Y.]: Arcturus Book Service, 1982. [73p.]

175. ——— . *The Voice of the Planet Clarion.* Prescott, Ariz.: The author, [1957?]. 40p. Revised ed., [1961?]. 88p.

DANA HOWARD

176. Howard, Dana. *Diane: She Came from Venus.* London: Regency, [1955]. 90p.

177. ——— . *The Keys to the Citadel of Space.* Los Angeles: Llewellyn, 1960. 203p.

178. ———. *The Kingdom of Space: Are We Going to Survive?* Los Angeles: DeVorss and Co., 1961. 76p.

179. ———. *My Flight to Venus.* London: Regency, [1954]. 64p. American ed., San Gabriel, Calif.: Willing, 1954. 89p.

180. ———. *Over the Threshold.* Los Angeles: Llewellyn, 1957. 140p.

181. ———. *The Strange Case of T. Lobsang Rampa.* Los Angeles: Llewellyn, 1958. 56p.

182. ———. *Up Rainbow Hill.* Los Angeles: Llewellyn, 1959. 159p.

183. ———. *Vesta: The Earthborn Venusian.* Corpus Christi, Tex.: Essene, 1959. 287p. *Note:* Space brother story, disguised as fiction.

184. ———. *Without Figleaves.* Clarksburg, W.Va.: Saucerian Books, 1964. 92p. *Note:* Not seen; ad in *Saucer News,* 63:14.

DINO KRASPEDON

185. Kraspedon, Dino [Aladino Felix]. *My Contact with Flying Saucers.* Translated by J. B. Wood. London: Neville Spearman; New York: Citadel, 1959. 205p. American reprints: Clarksburg, W.Va.: Saucerian Books, 1960. 205p. New York: Fieldcrest, 1966. 205p. Reprinted as *My Contact with UFOs.* London: Sphere, 1977, 1978. 205p. *Note:* Translation of *Meu Contato Com Es Eiscos Voadores.* São Paulo: The author, 1957.

GLORIA LEE (COSMON RESEARCH FOUNDATION)

186. Christina. *Song Consumate.* Palos Verdes, Calif.: Cosmon Research Foundation, 1960. 10p.

187. Comella, Thomas M., Jr. [Peter Kor, pseud.] "The Strange Case of Gloria Lee." *Search* (June 1963):30-31.

188. Lee, Gloria [Gloria Lee Byrd]. *The Changing Conditions of Your World, by J. W. of Jupiter, Instrumented by Gloria Lee.* Palos Verdes Estates, Calif.: Cosmon Research Foundation; Los Angeles: DeVorss and Co., 1962. 213p.

189.. ———. *The Going and the Glory.* Instrumented by Verity. Auckland, N.Z.: Heralds of the New Age, 1963, 1965, 1966, 1968. 73p.

190. ———. *Space People: Are They Angels, or Astronauts?* Auckland, N.Z.: Heralds of the New Age, 1966. 19p.

191. ———. *Why We Are Here. By J. W., A Being from Jupiter Through the Instrumentation of Gloria Lee.* Palos Verdes Estates, Calif.: Cosmon Research Foundation: Los Angeles: DeVorss and Co., 1959. 183p. 2d ed., Mokelumne Hill, Calif.: Health Research, 1974. 183p.

192. Warn, Charles Lathrup. *Today, as in the Days of Noah!* Revised 3d ed. Palos Verdes, Calif.: Cosmon Research Foundation, 1961. 61 + [4]p.

HOWARD MENGER

193. Menger, Connie [Marla Baxter, pseud.]. "Life Form from Outer Space." *Fantastic Universe* 11 (October 1959): 72-79.

194. ———. *My Saturnian Lover.* New York: Vantage, 1958. 72p.

195. ———. *Song of Saturn.* Clarksburg, W.Va.: Saucerian Books, 1968. 116p.

196. Menger, Howard. *From Outer Space to You.* Clarksburg, W.Va.: Saucerian Books, 1959. 256p. Later ed., n.d. 136p. Tabloid reprint, [1981]. 20p. Reprinted as *From Outer Space.* New York: Pyramid, 1967, 1974. 254p.

197. Menger, Howard, Connie Menger, and Milton Selleck. *The Carpenter Returns.* 1959?

198. ———. "Howard Menger's Own Story." *Flying Saucer Review* 4, 2 (March/April 1958): 141-71.

BUCK NELSON

199. Kness, Anna B. (Letter), "In Behalf of Buck Nelson." *Fate* 12 (January 1959): 125-29.

200. Nelson, Buck. "I Visited Mars, Venus and the Moon!" *Search* 18 (December 1956): 6-20. *Note:* Taken from a lecture before the Study Group of Inter-Planetary Relationships, Detroit, July 26, 1955.

201. ———. *My Trip to Mars, the Moon, and Venus.* Grand Rapids, Mich.: Grand Rapids Flying Saucer Club, 1956. 33p. 2d ed., West Plains, Mo.: Quill Press, 1956. 28p + addenda. 3d ed., Parker, Colo.: Stover, October 1957. 38p. 4th ed., Denver, Colo.: Olson Enterprises, [1958?]. 38p. Revised ed., West Plains, Mo.: Quill Press, 1959. 41p. 7th ed., Mopuntain View, Mo.: The author, 1966. 44p.

GEORGE HUNT WILLIAMSON

202. [Laughead, Charles, and Lillian Laughead]. *A Book of Transcripts.* Edited by George Hunt Williamson. Hemet, Calif.: T.O.T.T. Press, [1957]. *Note:* Compiled reprinting of a periodical, *The Abbey Transcripts*; see article in *Saucer News,* no. 48.

203. Williamson, George Hunt. *Other Tongues Other Flesh.* Amherst, Wisc.: Amherst Press, [1957]. 448p. British ed., London: Neville Spearman, 1965, 1969, 1973. 448p. *Note:* Williamson also used his Yugoslavian family name of Michel d'Obrenovic, though most of his writing was done under the anglicized name.

204. ——— . *Road in the Sky*. London: Neville Spearman, 1959. 248p. American ed., New York: Fieldcrest, [1966]. Paperback ed., London: Futura, 1975. 240p.

205. ——— . [Brother Philip, pseud.] *Secret of the Andes*. Clarksburg, W.Va.: Saucerian Books, 1961. 151p. British ed., *Secret of the Andes: Brotherhood of the Seven Rays*. London: Neville Spearman, 1961. 160p. British paperback ed., London: Corgi, 1973. 126p. Later eds.: San Rafael, Calif.: Leaves of Grass, 1976. 144p. New York: Fieldcrest, [1966?]. *Note:* Much material was taken from the Laughead's *Book of Transcripts*.

206. ——— . *Secret Places of the Lion*. London: Neville Spearman, 1958; Amherst, Wisc.: Amherst Press, 1958. 230p. British paperback ed., London: Futura, 1974. 230p. American paperback ed., New York: Warner Paperback Library, 1977. 269p. Later eds.: New York: Fieldcrest, [1966?]. New York: Destiny Books, 1983. 230p.

207. Williamson, George Hunt, and Alfred C. Bailey. *The Saucers Speak! A Documentary Report of Interstellar Communication by Radiotelegraphy*. Los Angeles: New Age, 1954. 127p. Later editions list Williamson as sole author. Revised ed., London: Neville Spearman, 1963. 160p. Later eds.: New York: Fieldcrest, [1966?]. Mokelumne Hill, Calif.: Health Research, [1985].

208. Williamson, George Hunt, and John O. McCoy, Jr. *UFOs Confidential!* Corpus Christi, Tex.: Essene Press, 1958. 100p.

The Major Contactee Groups

AETHERIUS SOCIETY (GEORGE KING)

209. Aetherius Society. *The Aetherius Society Calendar with the Annual Commemoration Dates for 1985*. Hollywood, Calif.: Aetherius Society, 1985. [10p.]

210. ——— . *Close Encounters of the Fourth Kind*. London: Aetherius Society, [1978]. 2p.

211. ——— . *Physical Space Contact at Aetherius Society*. Hollywood, Calif.: Aetherius Society, 1966. 2p.

212. ——— . *The Story of the Aetherius Society*. Hollywood, Calif.: Aetherius Society, n.d. 20p.

213. Bond, Bryce. "Our Man Bond Interviews Dr. George King." *Psychic Observer* 36 (October 1975): 330-35, 364-70.

214. ——— . "Our Man Bond Interviews George King, Founder, Aetherius Society." *Psychic Observer* 34 (June 1973): 310-19; (July-August 1973): 434-39, 457-62.

215. *How to Become an Absolutely First Class Aetherius Society Member*. London: Aetherius Society, 1967. 7p.

216. King, George. *The Atomic Mission*. Detroit: Aetherius Society, [1973?].

217. ———— . *Become a Builder of the New Age*. Hollywood, Calif.: Aetherius Society, [1965?]. 12p.

218. ———— . *Book of Sacred Prayers*. Los Angeles: Aetherius Society, [1966?].

219. ———— . *Contact Your Higher Self through Yoga*. London: Aetherius Society, 1955; Hollywood, Calif.: Aetherius Society, 1966. 20p.

220. ———— . *A Cosmic Message of Divine Opportunity*. Hollywood, Calif.: Aetherius Society, [1964]. 9p.

221. ———— . *The Day the Gods Came*. Los Angeles: Aetherius Society, 1965. 72p.

222. ———— . *Destruction of the Temple of Death and Rescue in Space*. Hollywood, Calif.: Aetherius Society, 1984. 28p.

223. ———— . *Eternal Recognition of Operation Sunbeam*. Hollywood, Calif.: Aetherius Society, n.d.

224. ———— . *The Festival of Carrying the Light*. Hollywood, Calif.: Aetherius Society, 1984. 22p.

225. ———— . *The Five Temples of God*. Los Angeles: Aetherius Society, 1967. 72p. Revised ed., 1975. 72p.

226. ———— . *The Flying Saucers: A Report on the Flying Saucers, Their Crews and Their Mission to Earth*. London: Aetherius Press, n.d. 12p. Reprinted, Los Angeles: Aetherius Society, 1962, 14p., and 1964, 16p.

227. ———— . *The Holy Mountains of the World*. Hollywood, Calif.: Aetherius Society, n.d.

228. ———— . *The Importance of Commemoration. Spiritual Happiness*. Hollywood, Calif.: Aetherius Society, 1962. 9p. *Note:* Two brief messages combined in a single volume.

229. ———— . *Join Your Ship: A Helpful Transmission from the Cosmic Masters with Commentary*. Hollywood, Calif.: Aetherius Society, [1964]. 16p.

230. ———— . *Karma and Reincarnation*. Hollywood, Calif.: Aetherius Society, 1962. Revised ed., 1986. 22p.

231. ———— . *Life on the Planets*. London: Aetherius Press; Hollywood, Calif.: Aetherius Society, 1959. 24p. Revised ed., Detroit: Aetherius Society, January 1980. 29p.

232. ———— . *My Contact with the Great White Brotherhood*. Los Angeles: Aetherius Society, 1962. 14p.

233. ———— . *The Nine Freedoms.* Los Angeles: Aetherius Society, 1963. 200p.

234. ———— . *Operation Space Magic: The Cosmic Connection.* Hollywood, Calif.: Aetherius Society, n.d.

235. ———— . *Operation Sunbeam: God's Magic in Action.* Hollywood, Calif.: Aetherius Society, 1979. 24p.

236. ———— . *The Practices of Aetherius.* London: Aetherius Press, [1961?]; Hollywood, Calif.: Aetherius Society, 1964. 28p.

237. ———— . *Space Contact in Santa Barbara.* Los Angeles: Aetherius Society; London: Aetherius Press, n.d. 9p.

238. ———— . *A Special Assignment.* Hollywood, Calif.: Aetherius Society, [1965?]. 8p.

239. ———— . *Spiritual Happiness.* Los Angeles: Aetherius Society, [1966?]. *Note:* Not seen; mentioned in *The Five Temples of God.*

240. ———— . *This Is the Hour of Truth.* Los Angeles: Aetherius Society, [1965?]. *Note:* Not seen; mentioned in *The Day the Gods Came.*

241. ———— . *The Three Saviours Are Here!* Los Angeles: Aetherius Society, 1967.

242. ———— . *The Truth about Dynamic Prayer.* Los Angeles: Aetherius Society, 1980. 5p.

243. ———— . *The Twelve Blessings: The Cosmic Concept.* London: Aetherius Press, [November 1958]. 59p. Revised ed., 1961. 63p.

244. ———— . *Wisdom of the Planets.* Los Angeles: Aetherius Society, [1960?].

245. ———— . *You Are Responsible!* London: Aetherius Press; Hollywood, Calif.: Aetherius Society, 1961. 173p.

246. King, George, and Kevin Quinn Avery. *The Age of Aetherius.* Hollywood, Calif.: Aetherius Society, 1975. Revised ed., 1982. 96p.

247. King, George, and Mary King. *Cosmic Voice: Mars and Venus Speak to Earth.* New Brunswick, N.J.: ESP Library, [1965?]. 22p.

248. Stupple, David. "Notes on Mystagoguery: Notes on Roy Wallis' Study of the Aetherius Society." *The Zetetic* 3, 2 (June 1975): 6-8.

249. Wallis, Roy. "The Aetherius Society: A Case Study in the Formation of a Mystagogic Congregation." *Sociological Review* 22 (February 1974): 27-44. Reprinted in Roy Wallis, *Sectarianism.* London: Peter Owen, 1975, 17-34.

BORDERLAND SCIENCE RESEARCH FOUNDATION

250. Crabb, June, and Riley Crabb. *The Fourth Way: The Way of the Sly Man or Adept*. Vista, Calif.: Borderland Sciences Research Foundation, n.d. 70p.

251. Crabb, Riley Hansard. *An Attempt at Cosmic Fellowship*. Vista, Calif.: Borderland Sciences Research Foundation, 1964. 39p.

252. ———. *Communication with Flying Saucers: A Detailed Analysis of the Problem of Understanding the Visitors from Outer Space*. Vista, Calif.: Borderland Sciences Research Associates, [1960]. 30p.

253. ———. *ESP: The Space Travel Problem and How We'll Solve It*. Vista, Calif.: Borderland Sciences Research Foundation, 1964. 47p.

254. ———. *Flying Saucers and America's Destiny*. Vista, Calif.: Borderland Sciences Research Associates, [1959]. 28p. Revised ed., Vista, Calif.: Borderland Sciences Research Foundation, [1972]. 37p.

255. ———. *Flying Saucers and the Coming Space Probes*. Vista, Calif.: Borderland Sciences Research Associates, 1958, 1963. 28p. Revised ed., Vista, Calif.: Borderland Sciences Research Foundation, [1964, 1974]. 40p. *Note:* From a talk in Vista, Calif., November 29, 1958.

256. ———. *Flying Saucers and the New Consciousness*. Vista, Calif.: Borderland Sciences Research Associates, 1958, 1963. 27p. Revised ed., Vista, Calif.: Borderland Sciences Research Foundation, 1973. 48p.

257. ———. *Flying Saucers and the Polar Flip*. San Diego, Calif.: Borderland Sciences Research Associates, [1958?]. 30p. *Note:* Not seen; ad in *Search*, October 1959.

258. ———. *Flying Saucers at Edwards AFB, 1954*. Vista, Calif.: Borderland Sciences Research Foundation, [1973]. 39p.

259. ———. *Flying Saucers on the Moon*. Vista, Calif.: Borderland Sciences Research Associates, [1962].

260. ———. *Flying Saucers Uncensored*. Vista, Calif.: Borderland Sciences Research Foundation, [1965]. 49p. *Note:* Lecture to the San Francisco Interplanetary Club, September 24, 1965.

261. ———. *Meeting on the Moon: At the Mars Stronghold, Flying Saucers 1959-1969*. Vista, Calif.: Borderland Sciences Research Foundation, 1969, 1980. 48p. *Note:* Lecture to the San Francisco Interplanetary Club, November 22, 1968.

262. ———. *Spacecraft from Beyond the Sun*. Vista, Calif.: Borderland Sciences Research Associates, [1966]. 48p. *Note:* From a talk at the Tenth Annual Northern California Spacecraft Convention, Berkeley, Calif., October 30, 1966.

263. ———— . *Who Flys* [sic] *the Saucers?* Vista, Calif.: Borderland Sciences Research Foundation, [1967]. 47p. *Note:* Lecture to the San Bernardino Unit of Understanding Inc., August 27, 1967.

264. Layne, Meade. *Associates of Borderland Sciences Research . . . To His Excellency the President of the United States . . . Your Attention Is Respectfully Drawn to a Matter of Urgent and Critical Importance.* San Diego, Calif.: Borderland Sciences Research Associates, August 1952. 4p.

265. ———— . *The Coming of the Guardians.* San Diego, Calif.: The author, [1950]. 38p. 2d ed.?, 1953. 72p. 3d ed.?, 1954? 4th ed., 1958. 89p. 5th ed., Vista, Calif.: Borderland Sciences Research Foundation, 1964. 72p. 6th ed., 1972. 72p. 7th revised ed., 1978. 78p., with material by B. Ann Slate.

266. ———— . *The Ether of Space.* San Diego, Calif.: Borderland Sciences Research Associates, 1953. 27p. 2d ed., Vista, Calif.: Borderland Sciences Research Foundation, 1963. 3d ed., 1980. 27p.

267. ———— . *The Ether Ship Mystery and Its Solution: Flying Discs.* San Diego, Calif.: Borderland Sciences Research Associates, 1950, 1954. 38p. Reprinted as *The Flying Saucer Mystery and Its Solution.* Vista, Calif.: Borderland Sciences Research Foundation, [1962]. 40p.

268. ———— . "The Etheric or '4-D' Interpretation of the Aeroforms." San Diego, Calif.: Borderland Sciences Research Associates, March 1954. 1p.

269. ———— . *The Mystery of the Etherians.* N.p., n.d. *Note:* Not seen; mentioned in Allen Manak's *Flying Saucer Ventures* (1970).

270. ———— . *The UFOs.* San Diego, Calif.: Borderland Sciences Research Associates, [1955]. 5p. *Note:* Not seen; mentioned in *Clips, Quotes and Comments,* March 1, 1955.

271. ———— , ed. *The Mystery of the Flying Discs.* [San Diego, Calif.]: Talk of the Times, 1948. 42p.

272. Millard, Lindy. *The Ether-Vortex Concept.* San Diego, Calif.: Borderland Sciences Research Associates, [1957]. 15p.

273. Palmiverian Fellowship. *The Last Days: or, Years of Destiny 1952 to 1958.* San Diego, Calif.: Borderland Sciences Research Associates, [1953?]. 32p. *Note:* Issued by the Palmiverian Fellowship, Panajacel, Guatemala.

274. Telano, Rolf [Ralph M. Holland]. *The Flying Saucers.* San Diego, Calif.: Borderland Sciences Research Associates, 1952. 11p.

COSMIC CIRCLE OF FELLOWSHIP (WILLIAM FERGUSON)

275. Diroll, Cloe. *Alpha and Omega: Revealed to William Ferguson.* Potomac, Md.: Cosmic Study Center, 1984. 15p.

276. ——— . *The Comforter Speaks*. Potomac, Md.: Cosmic Study Center, 1977. 27p.

277. ——— . *Overall View of Biblical Prophecies of the Book of Revelation and Decoded in "The New Revelation by the Revelator Himself*. Potomac, Md.: Cosmic Study Center, 1983. [20p.] *Note:* Paper presented to the First World Multidisciplinary Congress on Prognostication and Prediction for the Year 1984, Jerusalem Hilton, December 11-15, 1983.

278. ——— . *Science of Cosmic Creation*. Washington, D.C.: Miracle Hour, 1963. 32p.

279. ——— . *True Art of Creation Revealed to William Ferguson: Blends Scientific and Religious Perspectives*. Potomac, Md.: Cosmic Study Center, 1983. 71 + [7]p.

280. ——— . *UFOs Unveiled*. Potomac, Md.: Cosmic Study Center, 1974. 6p.

281. Ferguson, William. *Five Hours with the Oligarchs of Venus*. Chicago: Cosmic Circle of Fellowship, 1955; New York: Flying Saucer News, [1964?]. 12p. 2d ed., Potomac, Md.: Cosmic Study Center, n.d. 4p.

282. ——— . *Illumination of My Consciousness*. Washington, D.C.: Miracle Hour, 1954; Santa Venetia, Calif.: Marjorie Hensen, n.d. 2p.

283. ——— . *A Message from Outer Space*. Oak Park, Ill.: Golden Age, 1955 [54p.]

284. ——— . *My Trip to Mars*. Chicago: Cosmic Circle of Fellowship, September 1954. 13p. Reprinted, Clarksburg, W.Va.: Saucerian Books, 1955, 13p. Kitchener, Ont.: Galaxy, 1973, [15p.]. Potomac, Md.: Cosmic Study Center, n.d. 13p.

285. ——— . *The New Revelation by the Revelator Himself*. n.p., 1959. 107p.

286. ——— . *Relax First*. 4th ed., Chicago: [Cosmic Circle of Fellowsh, 1956]. 79p. *Note:* First edition apparently published in 1937.

287. *Regarding the Space Phenomena*. Chicago: Cosmic Circle of Fellowship, October 1, 1958. 3p.

HUMAN INDIVIDUAL METAMORPHOSIS (THE TWO, BO AND PEEP)

288. Balch, Robert W. "Looking Behind the Scenes in a Religious Cult: Implications for the Study of Conversion." *Sociological Analysis* 41 (Summer 1980): 137-43.

289. Balch, Robert W., and David Taylor. "Salvation in a UFO." *Psychology Today* 10 (October 1976: 58-62, 66, 106.

290. ——. "Seekers and Saucers: The Role of the Cultic Milieu in Joining a UFO Cult." *American Behavioral Scientist* 20 (1977): 839-60.

291. Benedict, W. Ritchie. "The UFO Cult of 'The Two.'" *Fate* 37 (October 1984): 50.

292. "Flying Saucery in the Wilderness: New Revelations from the Sheep of Bo and Peep." *Time* (August 27, 1979): 58.

293. Hewes, Hayden C. (Letter), "What the Media Missed." *Fate* 29 (May 1976): 111-12. *Note:* (Letter), Lee Walsh, 30 (January 1977): 116-17.

294. Hewes, Hayden, and Brad Steiger. *UFO Missionaries Extraordinary.* New York: Pocket Books, 1976. 173p.

295. Joachim, Leland. "The Two: A Pair of Prophets or a Couple of 'Space Cadets'?" *Probe the Unknown* 4 (January 1976): 12-15, 60. *Note:* (Letter), Orion E. Hubbard (November 1976): 8.

L/L RESEARCH

296. Elkins, Don T. *Telepathy Data Collected by Extraterrestrial Communication.* Clarksburg, W.Va.: Saucerian Books, [1963]. 79p.

297. Elkins, Don T., and Carla Rueckert. *The Crucifixion of Esmeralda Sweetwater.* Louisville, Ky.: L/L Research, 1986. 200p.

298. ——. *Secrets of the UFO.* Louisville, Ky.: L/L Company, 1977. 103p.

299. Elkins, Don T., Carla L. Rueckert, and James Allen McCarty, eds. *The Law of One.* Louisville, Ky.: L/L Research, 1981. 164p. Reprinted as *The RA Material: An Ancient Astronaut Speaks.* Norfolk, Va.: Donning, 1984. 229p.

300. ——. *The Law of One: Book 2.* Louisville, Ky.: L/L Research, 1982. 95p.

301. ——. *The Law of One: Book 3.* Louisville, Ky.: L/L Research, 1982. 137p.

302. ——. *The Law of One: Book 4.* Louisville, Ky.: L/L Research, 1983. 144p.

MARK-AGE METACENTER

303. Mark-Age MetaCenter [primarily messages received through the mediumship of Nada-Yolanda, Pauline Sharpe]. *Action and Reaction.* Miami: Mark-Age MetaCenter, [1963]. *Note:* Not seen.

304. ——. *Angels and Man.* Miami: Mark-Age MetaCenter, 1974. 138p.

305. ——. *Ask and Receive: Mark-Age Correspondence.* Miami: Mark-Age MetaCenter, [1966]. 40p.

306. ——. *Begin Anew.* 3 vols. Miami: Mark-Age MetaCenter, 1972. *Note:* Not seen.

307. ———— . *Birth of Astrid.* Miami: Mark-Age MetaCenter. [1969]. 56p.

308. ———— . *Birth of The Christ.* Miami: Mark-Age MetaCenter, [1964]. *Note:* Not seen.

309. ———— . *Book of Knowledge: Manual of Instruction for Light Workers.* Miami: Mark-Age MetaCenter, [1968]. 128p.

310. ———— . *Breakthrough.* Miami: Mark-Age MetaCenter, [1965]. *Note:* Not seen.

311. ———— . *Broadcasting Light, for Operation Landing Light.* 2 vols. Miami: Mark-Age MetaCenter, [1968]. 73p.

312. ———— . *Christ Awareness.* Miami: Mark-Age MetaCenter, [1964]. *Note:* Not seen.

313. ———— . *Christ Consciousness.* Miami: Mark-Age MetaCenter, [1963]. *Note:* Not seen.

314. ———— . *The Church and the New Age.* Miami: Mark-Age MetaCenter, n.d. 16p. *Note:* Not seen.

315. ———— . *Cosmic Lessons: Gloria Lee Channels for Mark-Age.* 5 vols. Miami: Mark-Age MetaCenter, [1969-1972].

316. ———— . *Earth Man on the Moon.* Miami: Mark-Age MetaCenter, [1971]. 12p.

317. ———— . *Evolution of Man.* Miami: Mark-Age MetaCenter, 1971. 160p.

318. ———— . *Externalization of the Hierarchical Board.* 4 vols. Miami: Mark-Age MetaCenter, [1969-1970]. 163p.

319. ———— . *Gloria Lee Lives! My Experiences Since Leaving Earth.* Miami: Mark-Age MetaCenter, 1963. 40p.

320. ———— . *Golden Era Children.* Miami: Mark-Age MetaCenter, [1963]. *Note:* Not seen.

321. ———— . *Group Guidelines for New Age Light Centers.* Miami: Mark-Age MetaCenter, 1971. 39p.

322. ———— . *Growing in God.* By Jeanene Moore. 2 vols. Miami: Mark-Age MetaCenter, [1969]. 72p.

323. ———— . *Hierarchical Board Decrees and Announcements.* Miami: Mark-Age MetaCenter, [1966]. 21p.

324. ———— . *Hierarchical Board Tour.* Miami: Mark-Age MetaCenter, [1967]. *Note:* Not seen.

325. ———— . *The Hierarchical Plan for Our Planet and Solar System*. 5 vols. Miami: Mark-Age MetaCenter, [1962-1963].

326. ———— . *How to Achieve Christ Consciousness on Earth, by Jesus The Christ*. Miami: Mark-Age MetaCenter, [1966]. 36p.

327. ———— . *How to Do All Things: Your Divine Use of Power*. Miami: Mark-Age MetaCenter, [1965, 1970]. 144p.

328. ———— . *I Am Guidance*. 2 vols. Miami: Mark-Age MetaCenter, 1973-1974. *Note:* Not seen.

329. ———— . *Impending Events*. Miami: Mark-Age MetaCenter, [1960-1961]. *Note:* Not seen.

330. ———— . *Into the Fourth Dimension*. 7 vols. Miami: Mark-Age MetaCenter, [1964-1966]. 300p.

331. ———— . *John Kennedy Lives*. Miami: Mark-Age MetaCenter, 1964. 34p.

332. ———— . *Let It Begin*. Miami: Mark-Age MetaCenter, [1967]. 28p.

333. ———— . *Life in Our Solar System*. Miami: Mark-Age MetaCenter, 1963. 49p.

334. ———— . *Linking of Lights*. 6 vols. Miami: Mark-Age MetaCenter, [1970-1971].

335. ———— . *Manifestation*. Miami: Mark-Age MetaCenter, [1965]. 37p.

336. ———— . *Mark-Age Broadcasts: Questions and Answers*. 4 vols. Miami: Mark-Age MetaCenter, [1968].

337. ———— . *Mark-Age Functions*. Miami: Mark-Age MetaCenter, 1973. *Note:* Not seen.

338. ———— . *Mark-Age Period and Program*. 2 vols. Miami: Mark-Age MetaCenter, [1965-1966]. Vol. 1 (1958-1961); vol. 2 (1962-1965). 76p.

339. ———— . *Mark-Age Period and Program*. Miami: Mark-Age MetaCenter, 1970. 350p. Revised as *MAPP* to Aquarius*. Ft. Lauderdale: Mark-Age MetaCenter, 1985. 351p.

340. ———— . *Mark-Age Roles and Missions*. 3 vols. Miami: Mark-Age MetaCenter, [1970]. 148p.

341. ———— . *The Master Plan for the Spiritual Earth, 1972-1983*. Miami: Mark-Age MetaCenter, [1973]. 42p.

342. ———— . *Mortal Versus Immortal: Your Battle of Armageddon*. Miami: Mark-Age MetaCenter, 1972. 50p.

343. ———— . *A New Heaven and a New Earth*. Miami: Mark-Age Meta-Center, [1966]. 58p.

344. ———— . *New Jerusalem*. 2 vols. Miami: Mark-Age MetaCenter, 1967.

345. ———— . *1000 Keys to the Truth: Spiritual Guidelines for Latter Days and Second Coming*. Miami: School of Education/University of Life/Mark-Age, 1976. 155p.

346. ———— . *Operation Show Man*. Miami: Mark-Age MetaCenter, [1964?]. *Note:* Not seen.

347. ———— . *Physician, Heal Thyself*. Miami: Mark-Age MetaCenter, 1962, 1981. 10p.

348. ———— . *Plan a Nation: Spiritual Self-Analysis for I am Nation Citizenship*. Miami: Mark-Age MetaCenter, 1975. 200p.

349. ———— . *Program Jesus*. 2 vols. Miami: Mark-Age MetaCenter, [1963]. *Note:* Not seen.

350. ———— . *Questions and Answers*. 6 vols. Miami: Mark-Age MetaCenter, [1961-1963].

351. ———— . *Rending the Seventh Veil*. 3 vols. Miami: Mark-Age Meta-Center, [1967-1968].

352. ———— . *Second Book of Acts*. Miami: Mark-Age MetaCenter, [1964]. 68p.

353. ———— . *The Second Coming of Jesus the Christ*. Miami: Mark-Age MetaCenter, [1966]. 37p.

354. ———— . *See and Be the Light*. Miami: Mark-Age MetaCenter, [1965]. *Note:* Not seen.

355. ———— . *Serene Meditations*. Miami: Mark-Age MetaCenter, [1965]. *Note:* Not seen.

356. ———— . *Servers of Light*. 4 vols. Miami: Mark-Age MetaCenter, [1971-1972]. *Note:* Not seen.

357. ———— . *Seven Rays of Life*. Miami: Mark-Age MetaCenter, [1963]. *Note:* Not seen.

358. ———— . *Soul Records*. 3 vols. Miami: Mark-Age MetaCenter, [1966-1968]. 134p.

359. ———— . *Spiritual Awakening*. Miami: Mark-Age MetaCenter, [1964]. *Note:* Not seen.

360. ———— . *Stories for Children of Earth*. Miami: Mark-Age MetaCenter, [1969]. *Note:* Not seen.

361. ———. *Transmutation*. 3 vols. Miami: Mark-Age MetaCenter, [1969]. 135p.

362. ———. *Unified Space Program*. Miami: Mark-Age MetaCenter, [1960]. *Note:* Not seen.

363. ———. *University of Life*. Miami: Mark-Age MetaCenter, 1972. 38p.

364. ———. *Visitors from Other Planets: Operation Show Man*. 3 vols. Miami: Mark-Age MetaCenter, [1966-1967]. *Note:* Also three supplements, February-April 1967.

365. ———. *Visitors from Other Planets: Operations Show Man and Landing Light*. Miami: Mark-Age MetaCenter, 1974. 334p.

366. ———. *Ye Are the Sons of God*. Miami: Mark-Age MetaCenter, [1965]. *Note:* Not seen.

367. ———. *Youth in Action: Master Discourses for Youth Meditation Meetings*. 3 vols. Miami: Mark-Age MetaCenter, [1970]. 124p.

UNARIUS-SCIENCE OF LIFE (RUTH NORMAN)

368. Adirije, Nwabueze. *Man of Earth and His Endless Journeying through the Stars: The New Age Science Evolutionary Principles of Life*. Oweril, Nigeria: Unarius Educational Foundation-Africa, 1987. 79p.

369. Antares. *Satan Is No More! He Has Been Overcome . . . and He Too, a Lightbearer Has Now Become!* El Cajon, Calif.: Unarius Academy of Science, [1985?]. 10p.

370. Ellerman, Dorothy. "A Spacewoman Speaks from Planet Earth." *Search* 133 (Winter 1977): 51-52.

371. ———. "Unarius: Science of Life." *Beyond Reality* 5 (August 1973): 21-22, 24-25, 28.

372. *New Hope!!!* El Cajon, Calif.: Unarius, 1984. 48p.

373. Norman, Ernest L. *The Anthenium*. El Cajon, Calif.: Unarius Educational Foundation, 1956. 142p.

374. ———. *Cosmic Continuum*. Santa Barbara, Calif.: Unarius-Science of Life, 1960. 263p.

375. ———. *The Elysium: Parables of Light*. Vol. 1, illus. Don Burson. [Pasadena, Calif.: Ruth E. Norman], 1956. 117p. Separate ed., vol. 1 [sic], illus. Don Burson. Pasadena, Calif.: Ruth E. Norman, 1956. 53p. 3d ed., Glendale, Calif.: Ruth E. Norman, n.d. 71p.

376. ———— . *The Infinite Concept of Cosmic Creation: An Introduction to the Interdimensional Cosmos.* Glendale, Calif.: Unarius-Science of Life, 1970. 596p. *Note:* A compilation of courses separately published earlier. "Number one course: 1-13 lessons given in 1956 [pp. 3-434]. Advanced course: 1-7 lessons written in 1960 [pp. 435-548]."

377. ———— . *The Infinite Contact.* Santa Barbara, Calif.: Unarius-Science of Life, 1960. 48p. 3d ed., 189p.

378. ———— . *Infinite Perspectus.* Glendale, Calif.: Unarius-Science of Life, 1962. 440p.

379. ———— . *The Story of the Little Red Box.* Glendale, Calif.: Unarius-Science of Life, 1968. 138p. 2d ed., El Cajon, Calif.: Unarius-Science of Life, n.d. 138p.

380. ———— . *Tempus Interludium.* El Cajon, Calif.: Unarius Educational Foundation, 1978. Part 1, 290p. *Note:* Part 2 not seen.

381. ———— . *Tempus Invictus.* El Cajon, Calif.: Unarius Educational Foundation, 1965. 496p.

382. ———— . *Tempus Procedium.* Glendale, Calif.: Unarius-Science of Life, 1965. 480p. Revised ed., 1968. 480p.

383. ———— . *The True Life of Jesus of Nazareth: The Confessions of St. Paul.* Glendale, Calif.: Unarius-Science of Life, [1969?]. 500p. *Note:* Not seen; ad in *Fate,* May 1970.

384. ———— . *The Truth about Mars.* Los Angeles: New Age, 1956. 61p. 3d ed., El Cajon, Calif.: Unarius-Science of Life, 1967. 56p.

385. ———— . *The Voice of Eros.* Los Angeles: Unarius, 1958. [264p.] 2d ed., El Cajon, Calif.: Unarius-Science of Life, n.d. 261p. *Note:* Pulse of Creation Series, vol. 2.

386. ———— . *The Voice of Hermes.* Los Angeles: Unarius-Science of Life, 1959. Pp. 465-718 [253p.]. *Note:* Pulse of Creation Series, vol. 3.

387. ———— . *The Voice of Muse-Unarius Elysium.* Montrose, Calif.: Unarius-Science of Life, 1964. Pp. 949-1210 [261p.]. *Note:* Pulse of Creation Series, vol. 5-7.

388. ———— . *The Voice of Orion.* Santa Barbara, Calif.: Unarius-Science of Life, 1961. Pp. 719-948 [229p.]. *Note:* Pulse of Creation Series, vol. 4.

389. ———— . *The Voice of Venus.* Los Angeles: New Age, 1956. 198p. 2d ed., Pasadena, Calif.: Unarius Spiritual Dynamics, [1957]. 198p. 3d ed., Santa Barbara, Calif.: Unarius-Science of Life, n.d. 198p. 4th ed., Glendale, Calif.: Unarius-Science of Life, n.d. 198 + [5]p. 5th ed., El Cajon, Calif.: Unarius-Science of Life, [1972?]. 177p. *Note:* Pulse of Creation Series, vol. 1.

390. Norman, Ernest L., and Ruth E. Norman. *Unarius.* 6 vols. [Los Angeles: New Age], 1956. Vol. 1, 28p.; vol. 2, 26p.; vol. 3, 39p.; vol. 4, 25p.; vol. 5, 26p.; vol. 6, 25p.

391. Norman, Ruth E. *Biographical History, Unarius Educational Foundation.* 4 vols. El Cajon, Calif.: Unarius Educational Foundation, 1982. Vol. 1, 348p.; vol. 2, 360p. *Note:* other Volumes not seen.

392a. ——— . *Bridge to Heaven: The Revelations of Ruth Norman.* Glendale, Calif.: Unarius-Science of Life, 1969. 506p.

392b. ——— . *A Brief Outline of the Basic Unarius Principles.* El Cajon, Calif.: Unarius Publications, 1986. 33p.

392c. ——— . *By Their Fruits (Shall They Be Known).* By Ruth Norman and Unarius students. 2 vols. El Cajon, Calif.: Unarius Educational Foundation, 1978. 408 + 372p.

392d. ——— . *The Decline and Destruction of the Orion Empire.* 4 vols. El Cajon, Calif.: Unarius Educational Foundation, 1979. 372 + 360 + 375 + 381p.

392e. ——— . *Early Biography of Ruth Norman.* El Cajon, Calif.: Unarius Educational Foundation, n.d. *Note:* Not seen.

392f. ——— . *Easter Message from Jesus of Nazareth (Now Archangel Raphael).* El Cajon, Calif.: Unarius Educational Foundation, 1984. 10p.

392g. ——— . *Effort to Destroy the Unarius Mission Thwarted.* El Cajon, Calif.: Unarius Educational Foundation, 1984. 407p.

392h. ——— . *Facts about UFOs.* By the Ambassador of the Interplanetary Confederation. El Cajon, Calif.: Unarius Educational Foundation, 1982. 19p.

393. ——— . *Have You Lived on Other Worlds Before? An Emissary for Thirty-Two Worlds Speaks to Earth.* 2 vols. El Cajon, Calif.: Unarius Educational Foundation, 1980. 352 + 268p.

394. ——— . *Historical Biography of the Unarius Educational Foundation.* El Cajon, Calif.: Unarius Educational Foundation, 1980. 402p.

395. ——— . *History of the Universe.* 3 vols. El Cajon, Calif.: Unarius Educational Foundation, 1981. 429 + 443 + 450p.

396. ——— . *Lemuria Rising.* 4 vols. El Cajon, Calif.: Unarius Educational Foundation, 1976-1977. 199 + 372 + 370 + 376p.

397. ——— . *Light from the Window.* El Cajon, Calif.: Unarius Educational Foundation, n.d.

398. ——— . *Man's Proof of Survival.* El Cajon, Calif.: Academy of Parapsychology, Healing and Psychic Sciences, [1972?]. [16p.]

399. ———— . *My 21 Days "Out-of-the-Body" Experience.* El Cajon, Calif.: The author, n.d. 13p.

400. ———— . *My 2000 Year Psychic Memory as Mary of Bethany—13th Disciple to Jesus of Nazareth.* El Cajon, Calif.: Unarius Academy of Science, 1987. 75p.

401. ———— . *Osiris-Isis Return!* El Cajon, Calif.: The author, n.d. 5p.

402. ———— . *A Pictorial Tour of Unarius.* El Cajon, Calif.: Unarius Educational Foundation, 1982. 162p.

403. ———— . *Preview for the Spacefleet Landing on Earth in 2001 A.D.* El Cajon, Calif.: Unarius Academy of Science, 1987. 128p.

404. ———— . *Proof Cases.* El Cajon, Calif.: Academy of Parapsychology, Healing and Psychic Sciences, 1972. [8p.]

405. ———— . *The Psychology of Consciousness.* El Cajon, Calif.: Unarius Educational Foundation, 1985. 725p.

406. ———— . *A Resume of Unarius in a Nutshell.* [El Cajon, Calif.: Unarius], n.d. 10p.

407. ———— . *Return to Atlantis.* 3 vols. El Cajon, Calif.: Unarius Educational Foundation, 1982. 350 + 275 + 375p.

408. ———— . *A Space Woman Speaks from Planet Earth.* El Cajon, Calif.: Unarius-Science of Life, n.d. 23p. Also a paper, 6p.

409. ———— . *Spaceman Delivers Science of the Future to the Earth World.* El Cajon, Calif.: Academy of Parapsychology, Healing and Psychic Sciences, [1972?]. 6p.

410. ———— . *Television Interviews of Ruth Norman.* El Cajon, Calif.: Academy of Parapsychology, Healing and Psychic Sciences, 1973. [14p.]

411. ———— . *Tesla Speaks.* 13 vols. El Cajon, Calif.: Unarius-Science of Life, 1973-1978.

Vol. 1, *Scientists*, 1973. 334p.
Vol. 2, *Scientists and Philosophers*, 1973. 451p.
Vol. 3, *Scientists and Presidents*, 1974. 499p.
Vol. 4, *32 Earth Worlds of the Intergalactic Confederation Speak!! (to Planet Earth).* Transmitted by Ruth E. Norman, Vaughn Spaegel, and Thomas Miller, 1974. Pt. 1, 621p.; pt. 2, 362p.; pt. 3, 411p.
Vol. 5, *24 Earth Worlds Speak to Planet Earth*, 1975. 298p.
Vol. 6, *The Celebration of the Millennium: Crystal Mountains, Cities, and Temples*, 1974. 93p.
Vol. 7, *Countdown!!! To Space Fleet Landing, or George Adamski Speaks Again from Planet Venus*, 1974. 186p.

Vol. 8, *The Masters Speak*, part 1, 319p.; part 2, 385p.
Vol. 9, *Uriel and the Masters Speak*, part 1, 1978. 400p.
Vol. 10, *Whispers of Love on Wings of Light*, 1975. 228p.
Vol. 11, *Keys to the Universe and the Mind*, 1977. 367p.
Vol. 12, *Martian Underground Cities Discovered!*, 1977. 341p.
Vol. 13, *The Epic*, 1977. 278p.

412.. —————. *Testimonials and Relatings of Unarius Students*. El Cajon, Calif.: Unarius Educational Foundation, [1978]. 43p.

413. —————. *That Incredible Hierarchy (of the Universe)*. El Cajon, Calif.: Unarius Educational Foundation, 1973. 10p.

414. —————. *Unarius in a Nutshell*. [El Cajon, Calif.: Unarius], n.d. 9p.

415. —————. *The Unarius Library*. El Cajon, Calif.: Unarius Educational Foundation, [1983]. 30p.

416. —————. *The Visitations: A Saga of God and Men*. El Cajon, Calif.: Unarius Academy of Science, 1987. 564p.

417. —————. *Welcome to Unarius: Love in Action, the New World Teaching*. [El Cajon, Calif.: Unarius], n.d. 15p.

418. —————. *Your Encounter with Life, Death and Immortality*. El Cajon, Calif.: Unarius Educational Foundation, 1978. 83p. Also a pamphlet, 1978. 19p.

419. Norman, Ruth E., and Thomas Miller. *The Epic*. El Cajon, Calif.: Unarius Educational Foundation, 1977. 278p. *Note:* Tesla Speaks Series, vol. 13.

420. —————. *Martian Underground Cities Discovered!* By Cosmic Visionary. El Cajon, Calif.: Unarius Educational Foundation, 1977. 341p. *Note:* Tesla Speaks Series, vol. 12.

421. Norman, Ruth E., and Vaughn Spaegel [Charles von Spaegel]. *The Conclave of Light Beings: or, The Affair of the Millennium*. El Cajon, Calif.: Unarius-Science of Life, 1973. 22 + 583p.

422. —————. *History of the Universe: And You a Star Traveler*. 3 vols. El Cajon, Calif.: Unarius Educational Foundation, 1981-1983. Vol. 1, 429p.; vol. 2, 443p.; vol. 3, not seen.

423. —————. *Preview for the Spacefleet Landing on Earth in 2001 A.D.* El Cajon, Calif.: Unarius Academy of Science, 1987. 141p.

424. —————. *Principles and Practice of Past Life Therapy*. El Cajon, Calif.: Unarius Educational Foundation, 1984. 397p.

425. —————. *Testimonials by Unarius Students*. El Cajon, Calif.: Unarius, 1985. 141p.

426. ———— . *Who Is the Mona Lisa? Through Astral Flight (Psychic Attunement) or E.S.P. Is Discovered the Long Sought Answer to this Question*. El Cajon, Calif.: Unarius-Science of Life, 1973. 88p.

427. *A Resume of Unarius*. El Cajon, Calif.: Unarius Academy of Science, [1985?]. 19p.

428. Speigel, Charles. *The Virgin Mary vs. Mary of Bethany: A Misconception in Identity*. El Cajon, Calif.: Unarius Educational Foundation, n.d. 10p.

429. Stevens, Lianne. "Questions and Answers: Cosmic Leader Uriel." *California UFO* 2, 1 (January-February 1987): 2-23.

430. Swanson, Jeff. *The Restoration: Rejoining the 33 Confederation Planets*. 2 vols. El Cajon, Calif.: Unarius Educational Foundation, 1981. 228 + 200p.

431. Unarius Students. *Glowing Moments*. El Cajon, Calif.: Unarius Educational Foundation, 1982. 170pp.

432. *Universal Hierarchy: A Pictorial Tour of Unarius*. El Cajon, Calif.: Unarius Educational Foundation, 1982. 166p.

UNDERSTANDING (DANIEL FRY)

433. Fry, Daniel W. *Alan's Message: To Men of Earth*. Los Angeles: New Age, 1954. 43p.

434. ———— . *The Area of Mutual Agreement: A Practical Approach to Mankind's Most Critical Problem*. Alamogordo, N.M.: Understanding, Inc., [1962?]. [9p.] Revised ed., Tonopah, Ariz.: Understanding, Inc., n.d. 16p.

435. ———— . *Atoms, Galaxies and Understanding*. El Monte, Calif.: Understanding, 1960. 109p.

436. ———— . *The Curve of Development*. N.p.: The author; Lakemont, Ga.: CSA, 1965. 75p.

437. ———— . "Human Consciousness." *The Searcher* 3 (January 1962): 95-97.

438. ———— . *Steps to the Stars*. Lakemont, Ga.: CSA Press; El Monte, Calif.: Understanding, 1956. 83p.

439. ———— . *To Men of Earth, Including the White Sands Incident*. Merlin, Oreg.: Merlin Publishing, 1973. 118p. *Note:* Combined edition of *Alan's Message* and *The White Sands Incident*.

440. ———— . *U.F.O. Logic*. [Merlin, Oreg.: Understanding], n.d. 8p.

441. ———— . *The White Sands Incident*. Los Angeles: New Age, 1954. 66p. Revised ed., Louisville, Ky.: Best Books, 1966. 120p. *Note:* Includes *Alan's Message*.

442. ———— . *The White Sands Incident, and To Men of Earth*. Merlin, Oreg.: Understanding, 1964. 66 + 41p.

443. ———— . "The Work of the Saucer Groups." *Flying Saucer Review* 5, 5 (September/October 1959): 12-13, 16.

444. Gast, Ann. *Understanding, Inc.* Los Angeles: The author, n.d.

445. Girvan, Calvin C. *The Night Has a Thousand Saucers*. El Monte, Calif.: Understanding, 1958. 168p.

446. Norman, Marke A. *Many Shall Be Called*. El Monte, Calif.: Understanding, 1959. 103p.

447. Rowe, Kelvin. *A Call at Dawn: A Message from Our Brothers of the Planets Pluto and Jupiter*. El Monte, Calif.: Understanding, 1958. 198p.

448. Telano, Rolf [Ralph M. Holland]. *A Spacewoman Speaks*. El Monte, Calif.: Understanding, 1960. 93p. *Note:* See other titles by Telano.

449. Tumlin, John S. *A Genderal Description of the Public Lecture by Daniel W. Fry for Unit Number 50 of Understanding, Incorporated*. Milwaukee, Wisc.: The author, [1962?]. [15p.]

450. *Understanding Incorporated: History, Present Status, Future Objectives*. Merlin, Oreg.: Understanding, Inc., n.d.

451. Whitworth, Eugene E., and Ruth E. Whitworth. *Diary into the Unknown*. El Monte, Calif.: Understanding Publishing Co., 1961. 171p.

UNIVERSARIUM FOUNDATION

452. *Cosmic College (Educational Series)*. Portland, Oreg.: Sadhana-Western Publishers, 1961.

453. *How the Forces of Love Can Overcome the Forces of Hate*. Portland, Oreg.: Universarium, n.d. [9p.]

454. McNames, Lucille E. [Sari, pseud.]. *Startling Revelations*. Portland, Oreg.: Universarium Foundation, 1980. 319p.

455. ———— . *United Friends of Earth*. By Phrado, through the channelship of Lucille McNames. Portland, Oreg.: Universarium Foundation, [1978?]. 48p.

456. Master A-N. *Navigating the Seas of the Emotions*. Tucson, Ariz.: Universarium Foundation, 1983. 78p.

457. *Oh! Urantia: (Earth-Share-Shan) Whither Goest Thou*. Portland, Oreg.: Universarium Foundation, [1958?]. 40 [=42]p.

458. Prins, Ethera. *Miracle of Love and Life*. Portland, Oreg.: Universarium Foundation, 1974. 220p.

459. Roberts, Leroy, Zelrun Wallace Karsleigh, and Jeannette Cleavenger. *The Voice of Universarius*. Portland, Oreg.: Sadhana-Western Press, 1959. 112p.

460. Rodehever, Gladys Kemp, comp. *The Book of Ra/Lord Ra*. El Paso, Tex.: The Fourth Dimension, 1983. 86p.

461. Saint Germain. *Violet Fire—The Torch of Freedom's Holy Light*. Tucson, Ariz.: Universarium Foundation, 1983. 56p. 2d ed., 1985. 78p.

462. *Space Messages of 1960*. Vol. 3. Portland, Oreg.: Sadhana-Western, May 1961. 116p. *Note:* Other volumes not seen.

GEORGE VAN TASSEL AND THE ASHTAR COMMAND

463. Ashtar. *In Days to Come*. Received through automatic writing by E. P. H. [Ethyl P. Hill]. Los Angeles: New Age, 1955; Clarksburg, W.Va.: Saucerian Books, [1975]. 91p. Other eds., not seen: Auckland, N.Z.: Heralds of the New Age, [195-]. 3 vols., Los Angeles: New Age, [195-]. 7 + 7 + 15p. *Note:* Translation of *In Kommenden Tagen*. Wiesbaden, Ger.: Ventla-Verlag, 1954.

464. Cooney, Denise R. *Beyond a Master*. Saddlebrook, N.J.: The author, 1986. 86p.

465. Gallup, Betty. *Star Song*. Deming, N. Mex.: Guardian Action, 1982. 196p.

466. Ireland, Bonnie. *Inner Views of the Galactic Command*. N.p., n.d. *Note:* Not seen; mentioned by Tuella.

467. Krastman, Hank. *George W. Van Tassel and the Space Aliens*. Encino, Calif.: The author, 1991. 18p.

468. Rodriguez, Carol Ann, ed. *The New World Order: Channeled Prophecies from Space*. New York: Global Communications, 1982. 68p.

469. Tarvis [Richard T. Woodmaster], comp. *The Master Symbol of the Solar Cross*. Compiled by Tarvis with channeling by Tuella [Thelma B. Terrell]. Durango, Colo.: Guardian Action, 1984. 239p.

470. Tuella [Thelma B. Terrell], ed. *Ashtar: A Tribute*. Durango, Colo.: Guardian Action, 1985. 178p.

471. ———. *The Dynamics of Cosmic Telepathy*. Aztec, N. Mex.: Guardian Action, 1983. 214p.

472. ———. *On Earth Assignment*. Salt Lake City: Guardian Action International, 1988. 179p.

473. ———. *Project: World Evacuation, by the Ashtar Command*. Deming, N. Mex.: Guardian Action, 1982. 180p.

474. ———— . *The Universal Concerto*. Durango, Colo.: Guardian Action, 1984. *Note:* Not seen; listed by Tarvis.

475. ———— . *World Messages for the Coming Decade: A Cosmic Symposium*. Columbus, N. Mex.: Guardian Action, 1980, 1981. 80p. 4th ed., Deming, N. Mex.: Guardian Action, 1981. 134p.

476. Tuieta. *The Council of Light*. Ft. Wayne, Ind.: Portals of Light, 1984. 55p.

477. ———— . *Gathering in the Light*. Ft. Wayne, Ind.: Portals of Light, 1983. 35p.

478. ———— . *Gifts from the Prophet*. Ft. Wayne, Ind.: Portals of Light, 1985. 55p.

479. ———— . *The Law as Given by the Father-Mother GOd*. Ft. Wayne, Ind.: Portals of Light, 1985.51p.

480. ———— . *Letters from Home*. 3 vols. [Ft. Wayne, Ind.]: Portals of Light, 1985.

481. ———— . *The Mighty Council*. Ft. Wayne, Ind.: Portals of Light, 1986. 61p.

482. ———— . *Project Alert*. Fort Wayne, Ind.: Portals of Light, 1986. 73p.

483. ———— . *Thru the Windows of Light: Aquarian Preparation*. Ft. Wayne, Ind.: Portals of Light, 1985. 182p.

484. [Van Tassel], Dorris. *Suzie's Sudden Saucer*. Santa Ana, Calif.: Total Graphics, 1976. 37 + [3]p.

485. Van Tassel, George W. *The Council of Seven Lights*. Los Angeles: DeVorss and Co., 1958. 156p. Reprinted as *Religion and Science Merged*. Yucca Valley, Calif.: Ministry of Universal Wisdom, 1968. 156p.

486. ———— . *I Rode a Flying Saucer! The Mystery of the Flying Saucers Revealed through George W. Van Tassel*. Los Angeles: New Age, 1952. 44p. Revised ed., Los Angeles: New Age, [1954?]. 51p.

487. ———— . *Into This World and Out Again: A Modern Proof of the Origin of Humanity and Its Retrogression from the Original Creation of Man*. Yucca Valley, Calif.: The author, 1956. 94p. 2d ed., Los Angeles: DeVorss and Co., 1957. 94p.

488. ———— . *Messages from the Golden Density*. Landers, Calif.: Omniversal Ministry, 1978. 97pp.

489. ———— . *Proceedings of the College of Universal Wisdom*. Yucca Valley, Calif.: The author, [1957]. [464p.] *Note:* Bound ed. of vols. 1-4 (October 15, 1953-October 1956) of his journal.

490. ———— . *When Stars Look Down*. Los Angeles: Kruckenberg Press, 1976. 198p.

491. *White Star Yearbook 1970-71*. Joshua Tree, Calif.: White Star, 1971. 62p. *Note:* Bound volume of White Star publications (Ashtar Command bulletins).

Additional Contactee Literature of the 1950s

492. Alford, Milton H. *We Who Live*. Phoenix, Ariz.: The author, [1958?]. *Note:* Not seen; ad in *Fate*, November 1958.

493. Anchor [Ann Grevler]. *Transvaal Episode: A UFO Lands in Africa*. Corpus Christi, Tex.: Essene Press, 1958. 48p.

494. Anderson, Carl A. *Two Nights to Remember!* Los Angeles: New Age, 1956. 55 + 5p.

495. Bailie, Alfred J. *Spiritualism Exposed: or, The Inner Circle*. New York: Vantage, 1957. 91p. *Note:* Not seen; ad in *Flying Saucer*, December 1958.

496. Barnhouse, Perl T. *My Journeys with Astargo: A Tale of Past, Present and Future*. Denver: Bell, 1952. 212p. *Note:* Some copies have *My Flight to the Moon* as cover title.

497. Bodin, Edward Longstreet. *Upper Purgatory*. Daytona Beach, Fla.: College Publishing, 1955. 159p.

498. "A Bonny Quarter." *Doubt* 48 (1955): 334.

499. Brown, Dulcie. "Search Visits a Flying Saucer Lecture." *Searth* 31 (April 1959): 78-83.

500. Carr, Otis, T. *Dimensions of Mystery*. Baltimore, Md.: Millennium, [195-]. *Note:* Not seen; mentioned by Margaet Storm.

501. Constable, Trevor James [Trevor James, pseud.]. *Spacemen: Friends and Foes*. 2 vols. Los Angeles: New Age, 1956. 18 + 18p.

502. Crandall, Lee. *The Venusians*. Los Angeles: New Age, 1955. 76p.

503. ———— . Untitled mimeograph. Alhambra, Calif.: C&M Publishing House, 1956. 40p.

504. Drake, Eugene H. *Life of the Planets: A Visit to Venus*. Los Angeles: Fellowship of Golden Illumination, 1950. 38p.

505. ———— . *Visitor from Space*. Los Angeles: Fellowship of Golden Illumination, [1951]. 34p.

506. Gibbons, Gavin. *They Rode in Space Ships.* London: Neville Spearman; New York: Citadel, 1957. 217p. Reprinted as *On Board the Flying Saucers.* New York: Paperback Library, 1967. 192p.

507. Girvin, Calvin C. *The Great Accident.* Los Angeles: The author, 1957. *Note:* Not seen.

508. ———. *The Night Has a Thousand Saucers.* El Monte, Calif.: Understanding, 1958. 168p. Paperback ed., 168p.

509. ———. *A Vital Message to All People from Space People Themselves.* Los Angeles: The author, 1958. *Note:* Not seen; ad in *Search,* August 1958.

510. Heralds of the New Age. *Further Telepathic Communications from Venus and the Satellites of Jupiter.* Auckland, N.Z.: Heralds of the New Age, [195-]. 21p.

511. Hoffman, Beatrice W., and John C. Hoffman. *The Flying Saucers Are Here.* N.p.: The authors, 1958. 51p.

512. Holloway, Gilbert N. *Coming of the Space People.* Los Angeles: Holloway School of Philosophy and Religion, January 1954. 13p.

513a. ———. *Communion Between Worlds.* Los Angeles: Holloway School of Philosophy and Religion, [1953?]. 7p. *Note:* Not seen; ad in *Flying Saucer News,* March 1955.

513b. ———. *Conquest of Space and the New Saucer Phenomena.* Los Angeles: Holloway School of Philosophy and Religion, 1953. 7p.

514.. ———. *Flying Saucers: The Mystery Deepens!* Los Angeles: Holloway School of Philosophy and Religion, 1953. 6p.

515. ———. *Flying Saucers: Vanguard of the New Age.* Miami, Fla.: New Age Church and School of Truth, 1958. 16p.

516. ———. *Let the Heart Speak.* Los Angeles: DeVorss and Co., 1951. pp. 120-30.

517. ———. *Messages from the Space People.* Los Angeles: Holloway School of Philosophy, Health and Religion, 1955. 15p.

518. ———. *Seven Years 1958-1965 that Changed the World.* Miami, Fla.: New Age Church and School of Truth, [1958?]. *Note:* Not seen; listed in his *Miami Saucerlore,* Spring 1958.

519. ———. *This Way Up: A Psychic Autobiography and Guide to Spiritual Development.* Chicago: Henry Regnery, 1975. 278p.

520. Kelly, William Franklin. *"Flying Saucers."* N.p.: The author, 1953. 28p. Reprinted as *"Flying Saucers" Metaphysical.* Los Angeles: DeVorss and Co., 1953; New York: Flying Saucer News, 1963, 1967. 28p.

521. LaVigne, Ruth. *There Shall Be Signs*. Bristol, Conn.: The author, 1957. *Note:* Not seen; ad in *Flying Saucer News*, August 1957.

522. Light, Gerald. *The Book of Light*. [Los Angeles]: Lodge of Light, n.d. *Note:* Not seen. Gerald Light was a Los Angeles occult teacher who produced numerous small pamphlets with an extraterrestrial theme.

523. ———— . *The Human Personality*. [Los Angeles]: Lodge of Light, n.d. 26p.

524. ———— . *Peru: Temple of Jupiter*. [Los Angeles]: Lodge of Light, [1955?]. 7p.

525. ———— . *Signs in the Skies*. Los Angeles: R. G. McFarland, 1954. 28p.

526. ———— . *Spirit Speaks*. Los Angeles: R. G. McFarland, 1954. 29p.

527. ———— . *Tibet: Temple of Mars*. [Los Angeles]: The Lodge of Light, [1955?]. 6p.

528. Maccarini, Nilo. *The March Towards the Sun*. Translated by J. Rush. Tucuman, Arg.: The author, September 1953. 203p. *Note:* Translation of *La Marcha Hacia El Sol*. Typescript.

529. McCoy, John O., Jr. *Flying Saucers*. Corpus Christi, Tex.: The author, 1957. 16p. *Note:* Reprint of article in *Life*, April 7, 1952.

530. ———— . *Soarings of the Eagle*. Corpus Christi, Tex.: Essene, 1958. 81p.

531. ———— . *They Shall Be Gathered Together*. Corpus Christi, Tex.: The author, 1957. 74 + 8p. Hardcover edition, 66p.

532. McCoy, John O., Jr., Ray Stanford, and Rex Stanford. *Ave Sheoi: From Out of this World*. Corpus Christi, Tex.: Essene, 1957. 66p.

533. Martin, Dan. *Prince Michael and the Prince of Persia*. Detroit: The author, [1959?]. *Note:* Not seen.

534. ———— . *Seal of Daniel, Broken*. Detroit: The author, [1959?]. *Note:* Not seen.

535. ———— . *Seven Hours Aboard a Space Ship*. Detroit: The author, [1959]. 29p. Reprinted as *The Watcher: Seven Hours Aboard a Space Ship*. Clarksburg, W.Va.: Saucerian Books, n.d. 17p. 3d ed., 1969. 32p.

536. *Messages from Space Ships Received at Florence, Oregon*. Florence, Oreg.: Interplanetary Study Group, [1957?]. 11p.

537. Michael, Cecil. *Round Trip to Hell in a Flying Saucer*. New York: Vantage, 1955. 61p. Revised ed., Auckland, N.Z.: Roofhopper Enterprises, 1971. 65p.

538. ———. *Signs and Wonders*. Reseda, Calif.: Mojave Books, 1977. 218p.

539. Miller, Will, and Evelyn Miller. *We of the New Dimension: Communications with Other Worlds*. Los Angeles: The authors, 1959. 115p.

540. Mitchell, Helen, and Betty Mitchell. *We Met the Space People: The Story of the Mitchell Sisters*. Clarksburg, W.Va.: Saucerian Books, [1967]; Kitchener, Ont.: Galaxy, 1973. 15p. 2d ed., Jane Lew, W.Va.: New Age, 1981. *Note:* These addresses were delivered at the Buck Nelson Convention, June 28, 1959.

541. Morley, George. *Etherian Ships*. N.p.: Kosmon Press, 1955. 12p. *Note:* Not seen; ad in *Flying Saucer News*, August 1964.

542. Nicholson, John. "The Contact Cases." *Fantastic Universe* 8 (August 1957): 41-46.

543. Norkin, [John] Israel. *Saucer Diary*. New York: Pageant, 1957. 137p.

544. Probert, Mark. *Flying Discs and Current Topics*. 3 vols. San Diego, Calif.: Inner Circle Kethra E'da Foundation, [1950?].

545. Reeve, Bryant. *The Advent of the Cosmic Viewpoint*. Amherst, Wisc.: Amherst Press, 1965. 311p.

546. Reeve, Bryant, and Helen Reeve. *Flying Saucer Pilgrimage*. Amherst, Wisc.: Amherst Press, 1957. 304p. Reprinted as Issue D-4 (Fall 1965) of *Inspired Novels*. Mundelein, Ill.: Palmer Publications, 1965. 304p. British ed., London: Neville Spearman, n.d.

547. Rember, Winthrop Allen. *Eighteen Visits to Mars*. New York: Vantage Press, 1956. 439p.

548. Schafer, J. Bernard. *Flying Saucers*. N.p.: The author, [195-]. 22p. 2d ed., New York: Flying Saucer News, [1966]. 22p.

549. Schmidt, Reinhold O. *The Kearney Incident*. N.p.: The author, 1958. 15p. Revised ed., *The Kearney Incident and to the Arctic Circle in a Spacecraft*, edited by Anna E. Keppy. Hollywood, Calif.: The author, 1958. 39p. Revised ed., *The Reinhold Schmidt Story*. Los Angeles: Amalgamated Flying Saucer Clubs of America, 1960. 18p. Reprinted as *The Edge of Tomorrow: The Reinhold O. Schmidt Story*. Hollywood, Calif.: The author, 1963. 64p.

550. ———. *The Kearney Incident: Up to Now*. Phoenix, Ariz.: Spacecraft Research Association, 1958. 16p.

551a. The Scientist of Venus [pseud.]. *The Race to the Moon*. London: Regency, 1958. 71p.

551b. ———. *Venus Speaks: Direct Revelation Regarding Flying Saucers and Life on Venus*. London: Regency, [1955, 1958]. 63p. *Note:* Messages received through the medium Cyril George Richardson; authorship also attributed to William Thorner. Introduction written by Myrtle Tyson.

552. Spiva, Frank. *America Know They Destiny*. N.p., 1959? *Note:* Not seen; mentioned in *AFSCA World Report*, November/December 1959.

553. Stanford, Ray, and Rex Stanford. *Look Up*. [Corpus Christi, Tex.]: The authors, 1958. 66p.

554. Storm, Margaret. *Return of the Dove*. Baltimore, Md.: The author, 1959. 294p. 2d ed., Mokelumne Hill, Calif.: Health Research, 1972. 294p.

555. ————. *A Vital Message to All People Everywhere from the Space People Themselves*. [Baltimore, Md.]: The author, 1957. 10p.

556. Sumner, F. W. *The Beginning of the New Age*. Los Angeles: New Age, [1958]. 8p.

557. ————. *The Coming Golden Age: The Great Cosmic Changes Now in Progress and What the Future Holds for Us*. Los Angeles: New Age, 1957. 206p.

558. Telano, Rolf [Ralph M. Holland]. *The Flying Saucers*. San Diego, Calif.: Borderland Sciences Research Associates, 1952. 11p. 2d ed., Clarksburg, W.Va.: Saucerian Books, 1963. 45p.

559. ————. *A Spacewoman Speaks*. El Monte, Calif.: Understanding, 1960. 93p.

560. Thomas, Dorothy. *The Coming of the Great White Chief!* Los Angeles: New Age, 1955. 30p.

561. ————. *Concerning Flying Saucers and Communication with Spacemen*. Los Angeles: New Age, [1955]. [5p.]

562. ————. *Life on Mars According to the Great Mystics*. No. 7. Los Angeles: New Age, 1955. [9p.]

563. ————. *Life on Venus According to the Great Mystics*. No. 8. Los Angeles: New Age, 1955. [10p.]

564. ————. *Who Are the Chosen Ones*. N.p., 1958? *Note:* Not seen; ad in *Search*, August 1958.

565. Thomas, Franklin. *"We Come In Peace!" A Martian Lands in Austria*. Los Angeles: New Age, 1955. 53p.

566. Trepanier, Clyde L., and Helen Trepanier. *Man, Consciousness and Understanding: Communications from Extraterrestrial Beings*. Redmond, Wash.: The authors, 1956-. Vol. 1, 1956-1959. 70p. *Note:* This is a multi-volume set. A volume II (or is it 11?) was published in 1974, [91p.]. According to Don Elkins and Carla Rueckert, a volume 4 was published in Detroit by Understanding of Detroit in 1962 and volumes have appeared annually since 1959.

567. X, Dr. "Visitor from 50,000 A.D." *Fate* 7 (August 1954): 61-66.

CONTACT SINCE 1960

The contactees of the 1950s set the image of the contact phenomenon for many people, however, the experience of contact has continued at a steady pace during the thirty years since Gloria Lee's death. A few of the 1950's contactees, such as George King and Ruth Norman, are still alive and communicating new messages from space on a regular basis. Two new contactees did much to keep the phenomena before the public as well as discourage serious research. Both Uri Geller and Eduard "Billy" Meier became well-known for their claims of contact, and both suffered from heavy criticism as hoaxers. While attaining a high degree of fame, both Geller and Meier are atypical of contactees. Also, during the 1980s, popular writer Brad Steiger, who holds the distinction of having written more UFO-related books than any other person, moved from discriptive reporting to become an advocate of the "star people" variation on the contactee theme.

The Prominent Contactees

MICHAEL X. BARTON (AKA MICHAEL X, AKA M. VINCENT BARTON)

1. Barton, Michael X. [Michael X, pseud.], ed. *Amazing Visions of the Endtime.* Los Angeles: Futura, 1967; Clarksburg, W.Va.: Saucerian Books, 1970. 37p.

2. ———. *Danger on the Moon.* Clarksburg, W.Va.: Saucerian Books, 1970. 29p. Revised ed., New York: Global Communications, [1982]. 32p.

3. ———. *The D-Day Seers Speak.* Los Angeles: Futura, 1959; Clarksburg, W.Va.: Saucerian Books, 1969. 35p.

4. ———. *Discs, Destiny and You.* Santa Barbara, Calif.: Futura, 1956. 10p. Reprinted in *Flying Saucer Revelations*, pp. 50-61.

5. ———. "Does He Talk to Flying Saucers?" *Real* (December 1966): 16-17, 61, 79.

6. ———. *Dynamic Mind-Power.* Los Angeles: Psychology Publishing Company, 1951. 52p.

7. ———. *Flying Saucer Revelations.* Los Angeles: Futura, 1957. [61p.] Later ed., Clarksburg, W.Va.: Saucerian Books, 1969. 61p.

8. ———. *Flying Saucers at Giant Rock.* Santa Barbara, Calif.: Futura, [1956?]. 11p. Reprinted in *Flying Saucer Revelations*, pp. 15-26.

9. ———. *The German "Saucer" Story.* Los Angeles: Futura, [1968]. 88p.

10. ———. "Ghost Out of the Past." *New Age World* 4 (October 1966): 8-9; (November-December 1966): 8-9, 29.

11. ———. *Icarus '68.* Los Angeles: Golden Dawn, 1967. 35p.

12. ———. *The Incredible Search for Dr. Halsey.* Los Angeles: Futura, 1965. 29p.

13. ———. *It Will Happen in February!* Los Angeles: Futura, 1961. 34p.

14. ———. *It's All in Your Super-Mind.* Los Angeles: Futura Press, 1963. 41p.

15. ———. *The Magic of the Ether Ships.* Santa Barbara, Calif.: Futura, [1957?]. 11p. Reprinted in *Flying Saucer Revelations,* pp. 38-49.

16. ———. *Nikola Tesla: Man or Spaceman?* Clarksburg, W.Va.: Saucerian Books, 1970. 38p.

17. ———. *Rainbow City and the Inner Earth People.* Los Angeles: Futura Press, 1960. Reprinted, Clarksburg, W.Va.: Saucerian Books, 1969. 31p.

18. ———. *Release Your Cosmic Power.* Los Angeles: Futura, 1961. 33p. Reprinted, Clarksburg, W.Va.: Saucerian Books, 1969. 31p.

19. ———. *The Saucer People on Earth.* Santa Barbara, Calif.: Futura, 1957. 12p. Reprinted in *Flying Saucer Revelations,* pp. 1-14.

20. ———. *Secrets of Higher Contact.* Los Angeles: Futura, 1959; Clarksburg, W.Va.: Saucerian Books, 1969. 30 + [3]p.

21. ———. *Secrets of the Saucer People.* Santa Barbara, Calif.: Futura, 1957. 10p. Reprinted in *Flying Saucer Revelations,* pp. 27-37.

22. ———. *The Seven Golden Prophecies.* Los Angeles: Futura, 1961. 34p. Reprinted, Clarksburg, W.Va.: Saucerian Books, 1984. 34p.

23. ———. *The Spacemasters Speak.* Los Angeles: Futura, 1960; Clarksburg, W.Va.: Saucerian Books, 1970. 34p.

24. ———. *Time No More.* Los Angeles: Futura, 1965. 37p.

25. ———. *Venusian Health Magic.* Los Angeles: Futura, 1959. 61 + [8]p. 2d ed., Clarksburg, W.Va.: Saucerian Books, 1972. 62p.

26. ———. *Venusian Secret-Science.* Los Angeles: Futura, 1958; Clarksburg, W.Va.: Saucerian Books, 1970. 71 + [6]p.

27. ———. *We Want You.* Los Angeles: Futura, 1960. 39p. Reprinted as *We Want You: Is Hitler Alive?* Clarksburg, W.Va.: Saucerian Books, 1969. 39p.

28. ———. *The Weeping Angel Prediction.* Los Angeles: Futura, 1964. 33p.

29. ———. *Your D-Day Destiny*. Los Angeles: Futura, 1958. 38p.

30. ———. *Your Part in the Great Plan*. Los Angeles: Futura, 1960; Clarksburg, W.Va.: Saucerian Books, 1972. 30p.

31. Brooke, Anthony, and Michael X. Barton. *Prophecy 67*. London: Futura, 1966. 46p.

32. *Harmony Grove Lectures: Book 3*. [Michael X. Barton, ed.?] Los Angeles: Golden Dawn, 1963. 30p. *Note:* Contains: "Subud: What It Is and Isn't," Victor Royal; "Return of the Gnostic Wisdom," Michael X. Barton; and "Will You Escape This Life Alive?" Orfeo Angelucci. On Angelucci, see 155.

URI GELLER

33. Bailey, Herbert. "Uri Geller: The Man Who Makes Weird Things Happen." *Argosy* (May 1974): 64-70.

34. Beckley, Timothy Green, and Harold Salkin. "Psychic Uri Geller." *Saga* (July 1974): 28-30, 54-58.

35. Bockman, Dwight. "Uri Geller Discusses Fame, Fortune and His Personal Mission for the Future." *Psychic World and the Occult* 8 (March 1977): 42-48.

36. Ebon, Martin, ed. *The Amazing Uri Geller*. New York: New American Library, 1975. 168p.

37. ———. "Is Andrija Puharich a Press Agent for Outer Space?" *Occult* 6 (July 1975): 32-35, 91-93.

38. Fuller, Curtis. "Geller, Puharich and the Sky Intelligences." *Fate* 27 (October 1974): 68-71. *Note:* (Letters), David A. Krouse, 28 (March 1975): 128; Henry E. Jessup, (September 1975): 112-13.

39. "Geller and UFO." *The News* 3 (March 1974): 7.

40. Geller, Uri. "Interview: Uri Geller." *Psychic* 4 (May-June 1973): 6-11, 30-31.

41. ———. *My Story*. [Ghostwritten by John G. Fuller.] New York: Praeger, 1975. Pp. 211-82. Paperback ed., New York: Warner, 1976. Pp. 213-77. British ed., London: Robson, 1975. British paperback ed., London: Corgi, 1977.

42. ———. *Pampini: A Novel*. New York: World Authors, 1980. 228p.

43. Puharich, Andrija. "Interview: Andrija Puharich, M.D." *Psychic* 5 (September-October 1973): 6-11, 26-28.

44. ———. *Uri: A Journal of the Mystery of Uri Geller*. Garden City, N.Y.: Anchor, 1974. 285p. Paperback ed., New York: Bantam, 1975. British ed., *Uri: The*

Original and Authorized Biography of Uri Geller, The Man Who Baffles the Scientists. London: W.H. Allen, 1974. 285p. British paperback ed., London: Futura, 1974. 285p.

45. Randi, James. *The Magic of Uri Geller.* New York: Ballantine, 1975. Pp. 112-28. Revised ed., *The Truth About Uri Geller.* Buffalo, N.Y.: Prometheus, 1982. Pp. 87-89.

46. Vaughan, Alan. "The Phenomena of Uri Geller." *Psychic* 4 (May-June 1973): 12-18.

47. White, John. "Uri: A Critique." *Psychic* 6 (May-June 1975): 40-43.

48. ———— . "Uri Geller: The Outer Space Connection?" *Gnostica* 6 (January-February 1979): 28-33, 70.

49. Zeibell, Ila. "Through the Looking Glass with Uri Geller." *Psychic* 6 (January-February 1976): 16-19.

EDUARD "BILLY" MEIER

50. Berlet, Artur. *UFO Contact from Planet Acart.* Tucson, Ariz.: UFO Photo Archives, 1988. 214p.

51. Deardorff, James W. *Celestial Teachings: The Emergence of the True Testament of Immanuel (Jesus).* Tigard, Oreg.: Wild Flower Press, 1990. 323p.

52. Denaede, Stefan. *Operation Survival Earth.* Pocket Books 1977. 159p. Revised ed., Stefan Denaede and Wendelle C. Stevens. *UFO Contact from Planet Iarga.* Tuscon, Ariz.: UFO Photo Archives, 1982. 364p.

53. Dibitanto, Gioggio, and Sherwood. *UFO Contact from Angels in Starships.* Tucson, Ariz.: UFO Photo Archives, 1990. 160p.

54. Elders, Lee J., and Brit Nilsson-Elders. *UFO . . . Contact from the Pleiades: Volume II.* Phoenix, Ariz.: Genesis III, 1983. 72p.

55. Elders, Lee J., Brit Nilsson-Elders, and Thomas K. Welch. *UFO . . . Contact from the Pleiades: Volume I.* Supervised by Wendelle C. Stevens. Phoenix, Ariz.: Genesis III, 1979. [70p.] Revised ed., 1980. [70p].

56. Kinder, Gary. *Light Years: An Investigation into Extraterrestrial Experiences of Eduard Meier.* New York: Atlantic Monthly Press, 1987. *Note:* A sympathetic defense of Meier's claims.

57. Korff, Kal K. "Billy Meier Hoax." *Frontiers of Science* (March-April 1981): 31-33.

58. ———— . "The Meier Incident: The Most Famous Hoax in Ufology." *MUFON UFO Journal* 154 (December 1980).

59. ———— . *The Meier Incident: The Most Infamous Hoax in Ufology.* With the editorial assistance of William L. Moore. [Prescott, Ariz.: Town Scribe Press], 1981. 124p. *Note:* The most comprehensive presentation of the evidence that Meier's claims amount to a hoax.

60. Korff, Kal K., and William L. Moore. *"Contacts from the Pleiades" in Fact and Fiction: A Categorical Response to Wendelle Stevens and Genesis III.* [Prescott, Ariz.]: William L. Moore, 1982. 15p.

61. Meier, Eduard "Billy." *Decalogue, or the Ten Bids.* Alamogordo, N.M.: Semjase Silver Star Center, 1975. 151p.

62. ———— . *The Meditation.* Alamogordo, N.M.: Semjase Silver Star Center, 1975. 102p.

63. ———— . *Message from the Pleiades.* N.p.: privately published, 1984. 401p.

64. ———— . *The Psyche.* Alamogordo, N.M.: Semjase Silver Star Center, 1975. 80p.

65. Moya Cerpa, Antonio. "The Ummo Affair: A Summary." *Search* 140 (Fall 1979): 48-49.

66. Ribera, Antonio. *UFO Contact from Planet Ummo.* Tucson, Ariz.: UFO Photo Archives, 1985. 354p.

67. Sanchez-Ocejo, Virgilio, and Wendelle C. Stevens. *UFO Contact from Undersea.* Tucson, Ariz.: Wendelle C. Stevens, 1982. 190p.

68. Steinman, William S. *UFO Crash at Aztec: A Well-kept Secret.* Tuscon, Ariz.: UFO Photo Archives, 1986. 623p.

69. Stevens, Wendelle C. *UFO Contact from the Pleiades: A Preliminary Investigation Report.* Edited by Janet Davidson. Tucson, Ariz.: UFO Photo Archives, 1982. 542p.

70. Stevens, Wendelle C., and William James Herrmann. *UFO Contact from Reticulum: A Report of the Investigation.* Edited by Sharleen M. Spivak. Tucson, Ariz.: Wendelle C. Stevens, 1981. 398p.

71. *Talmud Jmmanuel.* Hinterschmidriti, Switz.: Freie Interessengemeinschaft, 1984. 124pp.

72. Van Vlierden, Carl, and Wendelle C. Stevens. *UFO Contact from Planet Koldas.* Edited by Amy S. Davidson. Tucson, Ariz.: UFO Photo Archives, 1984. 320p.

73. Ziegler, Julie H., and B. L. Greene, trans. *The Talmud of Jmmanuel: The Clear Translation in English and German.* Tigard, Oreg.: Wild Flower Press, 1990. 295p.

BRAD STEIGER

74. Steiger, Brad [Eugene Olson], ed. *The Aquarian Revelations*. New York: Dell, 1971. 158p.

75. ———. *The Fellowship: Spiritual Contact Between Humans and Outer Space Beings*. Garden City, N.Y.: Doubleday, 1988.

76. ———. *Gods of Aquarius: UFOs and the Transformation of Man*. New York: Harcourt Brace Jovanovich, 1976; London: W.H. Allen, 1977. 264p. British paperback eds., London: Sphere, 1977; London: Panther, 1980. 304p. American paperback ed., New York: Berkley, 1981. 274p.

77. ———. *Revelation: The Divine Fire*. Englewood Cliffs, N.J.: Prentice-Hall, 1973. 316p. Book club ed., 287p. Paperback ed., New York: Berkley, 1981. 291p.

78. ———. *The Seed*. New York: Berkley, 1983. 202p.

79. ———. "UFOs and the Transformation of Man." *Beyond Reality* 23 (November-December 1976): 34-39, 49.

80. ———. *You, Too, May Be from Krypton*. [Scottsdale, Ariz.]: The author, n.d. 9p.

81. Steiger, Brad, and Francie Steiger. *Discover Your Past-Lives Your True Roots on the Starbirth Odyssey*. [Scottsdale, Ariz.]: The authors, n.d. 6p.

82. ———. *The Star People*. New York: Berkley, 1981. 201p.

83. Steiger, Francie. *Reflections from an Angel's Eye*. Cottonwood, Ariz.: Esoteric, 1977. 105p. 2d ed., New York: Berkley, 1982. 202p.

84. Steiger, Francie, and Brad Steiger. "Discover Your True Roots: Starbirth Odyssey." *Beyond Reality* 40 (November-December 1979): 36-37, 48.

FRANK STRANGES

85. Stranges, Frank E. *Danger from the Stars: A Warning from Frank E. Stranges*. Venice, Calif.: International Evangelism Crusades, [1960]. 14p.

86. ———. *Flying Saucerama*. New York: Vantage, 1959. 115p. 2d ed., *New Flying Saucerama*. Glendale, N.Y., and Venice, Calif.: International Evangelism Crusades, 1962. 117p. 3d ed., *Flying Saucerama*. Glendale, N.Y., and Venice, Calif.: International Evangelism Crusades, 1963. 117p. 4th ed., Glendale, N.Y., and Venice, Calif.: International Evangelism Crusades, 1966. 117p. 5th ed., Van Nuys, Calif.: International Evangelism Crusades, 1974. 128p.

87.. ———. *German Saucer Mystery*. Van Nuys, Calif.: International Evangelism Crusades, 1982. 32p.

88. ———— . *The Great East Coast Blackout.* Venice, Calif.: International Evangelism Crusades, [1967]. *Note:* Not seen; mentioned in *Probe*, Spring 1967.

89. ———— . *Like Father—Like Son.* Palo Alto, Calif.: International Evangelism Crusades, 1961. 30 + [10]p.

90. ———— . *My Friend from Beyond Earth.* [Palo Alto, Calif.]: International Evangelism Crusades, 1960. 17p. 2d ed., New York: Flying Saucer News, [1967?]. 17p. 3d ed., Kitchener, Ont.: Galaxy, 1972. [24p.] Revised ed., Van Nuys, Calif.: International Evangelism Crusades, 1974, [1981]. 59p.

91. ———— . *Nazi UFO Secrets and Bases Exposed.* Van Nuys, Calif.: International Evangelism Crusades, [1982?]. *Note:* Not seen; ad in *Flying Saucer Review* 28, 4.

92. ———— . *The Parade of the Planets.* Van Nuys, Calif.: International Evangelism Crusades, 1975. 15p. Revised ed., 1981. 15p.

93. ———— . *The Stranger at the Pentagon.* Van Nuys, Calif.: International Evangelism Crusades, 1967, 1972. 201p.

94. ———— . *The UFO Conspiracy.* Van Nuys, Calif.: International Evangelism Crusades, 1983. 105p. 2d ed., 1985. 168p.

95. ———— . "What Caliber People?" *New Age World* 4 (October 1966): 10.

96. Stranges, Frank E., and Robert L. Park. *Strange Sightings from Outer Space.* Venice, Calif.: Truth Publications, 1964. 50p.

Additional Contactee Literature Since 1960

For information on the different contactee groups of the last generaion, see the entries in the *Encyclopedia of American Religions* (4th ed., Detroit: Gale Research, 1992).

97. Abramson, Charles. (Letter}, "Mountain Mission." *Fate* 16 (January 1963): 112-13.

98. Adkins, Diana. *Introduction Confrontation.* 2 vols. Wassenaar, Neth.: Servire, 1970. Part 1, 162p. Part 2, not seen.

99. Aho, Wayne Sulo. *Mojave Desert Experience.* Eatonville, Wash.: New Age Foundation, 1972. 10p.

100. ———— . *Prophet's Return.* Eatonville, Wash.: New Age Foundation, 1973. [14p.]

101. ———— . *The Prophet's Return II.* Eatonville, Wash.: New Age Foundation, 1975. 8p.

102. ———— . *Saucer Intelligence.* Eatonville, Wash.: New Age Foundation, [1966]. [12p.]

103. ——— . *What the Lord Said: The Ancient of Days.* Eatonville, Wash.: New Age Foundation, n.d. 4p.

104. Alamar. *Teaching of Alamar.* N.p., n.d. *Note:* Not seen.

105. Ald, Roy. *The Man Who Took Trips: A True Experience in Another Dimensions.* New York: Delacorte, 1971. 245p.

106. *Alien Encounter: Evolutionary Intelligence Manual.* Friday Harbor, Wash.: Guild, [1984?]. *Note:* Not seen; ad in *Fate,* May 1984.

107. Amelpha. *Planet Earth at Crisis.* [Phoenix, Ariz.: Franky G. Miller], [1961]. 11p.

108. Anka, Darryl. *Bashar: Blueprint for Change; A Message for the Future.* Simi Valley, Calif.: New Solutions Publishing, 1990. 302p.

109. ——— . *New Metaphysics.* Beverley Hills, Calif.: Light and Sound Communications, 1987. 99p.

110. Antaree, Joseph, and Allen Michael. *Journey to the Great Central Sun: The Movie.* Stockton, Calif.: Starmast Productions, 1986. 204p.

111. Aquarma. *Children of the Sun.* London: Regency, 1961. 132p.

112. Armstrong, Virgil (Posty). *The Armstrong Report: ETs and UFOs— They Need Us, We Don't Need Them.* Village of Oak Creek, Ariz.: Entheos Publishing, 1988. 145p.

113. ——— . *The Lesser Gods and Their Religion.* Village of Oak Creek, Ariz.: Heirgive Foundation, 1988. 9p.

114. ——— . *Nature Spirits and Elementals.* Village of Oak Creek, Ariz.: Heirgive Foundation, 1988. 11p.

115. ——— . *The Twelve Women Apostles.* Village of Oak Creek, Ariz.: Armstrong Publishing, 1988. 241p.

116. ——— . *What NASA Did Not Tell Us about the Moon.* Village of Oak Creek, Ariz.: Heirgive Foundation, 1988. 9p.

117. [Bachman, Fritz]. *Brothers from Partially Materialized Spheres of the Universe Serve in the Redemption Work of the Son of God.* [Pelham, N.H.]: Homebringing Mission of Jesus Christ, [1982]. 38p.

118. ——— . *Five Messages to Mankind from Outer Space.* New York: Homebringing Mission of Jesus Christ, [1983?].

119. Baines, John. *The Secret Science for the Physical and Spiritual Transformation of Man: Hermetic Philosophy, Book One.* Translated by Evelyne Brown. Edited by Judith Hipskind. St. Paul, Minn.: Llewellyn, 1980. 196p. *Note:* Translation of *Los Brujos Hablan.*

120. Baker, Douglas M. *The Occult Significance of UFOs*. Wellingborough: Thorsons, 1977. 68p. 2d ed., Little Elephant, [S. Africa?]: The author, 1979. 108p. *Note:* Several editions exist; one includes Mark Stenhoff, "Twelve Cases of Unidentified Flying Objects: A Special Report," and Geoffrey Hodson, "Other Hierarchies of Life Using Our Planet."

121. Ballister, Barry. "Who Killed the Toronto Peace Festival?" *Rolling Stone* (December 24, 1970: 37-43.

122. Bartsch, Leo. *Supernatural Deceptions and Supernatural Revelations: The Greatest Deception on Earth Exposed by the UFO*. Coos Bay, Oreg.: The author, [1976?]. [21p.]

123. ———— . *UFO Electric Living Creatures*. Coos Bay, Oreg.: The author, n.d. 2p.

124. ———— . *UFO Living Chariots*. Coos Bay, Oreg.: The author, [1969?]. [14p.]

125. ———— . *UFO Living Creatures Not of This World: Are You Ready?* Coos Bay, Oreg.: The author, n.d. [2p.]

126. ———— . *The UFO that Changed My Life: Testimony*. Revised 2d ed., Coos Bay, Oreg.: The author, 1964. [4p.] Revised 3d ed., 1965. [4p.] *Note:* This author has issued many 1 to 2 page press releases with titles similar to those listed here.

127. Bateman, Jo Nel. "Prediction Proven on TV Show." *New Age World* 4 (September 1966): 8-9.

128. Batis, Olga. "Electra, Who Came from Another Planet, Speaks to 'Woman.'" *Pursuit* 14 (1981): 11-12. *Note:* From *Gynaika*, April 23, 1980.

129. Beckley, Timothy Green. *The Contactees*. N.p., [1981?]. *Note:* Not seen; offered as free with any order in his December 1981 catalog.

130. ———— . *A Guideline on How to Contact the Space People*. N.p., [1981?]. *Note:* Not seen; offered as free with any order in his June 1981 catalog.

131. ———— . *The Mysterious Flying Saucers; The Men in Black; The Contactee Enigma; Flying Saucer Hostility*. New Brunswick, N.J.: ESP Library, 1971. 30p.

132. ———— . *Prophecy: Key to the Future*. New Brunswick, N.J.: The author, 1970. 224p. *Note:* Not seen; ad in *Saucer News*, no. 75.

133. ———— . *Psychic and UFO Revelations in the Last Days*. New York: GLobal COmmunications, 1980. 67p.

134. ———— . *Strange Encounters: Bizarre and Eerie Contact with Flying Saucer Occupants*. New York: Global Communications, 1980. 68p.

135. ———— . *Timothy Green Beckley's Book of Space Brothers*. Clarksburg, W.Va.: Saucerian Books, 1969. 114p.

136. ———— . *Timothy Green Beckley's Book of Space Contacts*. New York: Global Communications, 1981. 68p.

137. Beere, D. Chessman. *Fail-Sure-Win-Safe!* Del Mar, Calif.: USP Press, 1980. 55p.

138. ———— . *USP—Physics for Flying Saucers: An Interpretation from Memory of a Communication from ATOS Xetrov, Visitor*. Del Mar, Calif.: USP Press, 1973. 54p.

139. Behlor, Reigh H. *All Is One: A Year with Mentor*. Grass Valley, Calif.: Golden Sierra Printing, [1977]. 243p.

140. Bender, Hildegard E. *Knights of the Solar Cross: Messages from Outer Space*. London: Regency, 1968, 1970. 97p.

141. Bennett, Jo Ann. (Letter), "Star Person Speaks Up." *Fate* 37 (December 1984): 128-29.

142. Bent, Dave W. *New Age Primer*. For Lauderdale, Fla.: The author, n.d. 9p.

143. Bergstrand, Amy Dorinda Carter. *Spaceships of the Gods*. Hinckley, Ill.: Godimats Jehovah Isms, 1982. 31p.

144. Bey, Hamid. *The Meaning of Flying Saucers in Reference to the New Age*. Los Angeles: Coptic Fellowship of America, n.d. 10p.

145. Binder, Otto O. "Flying Saucer Prophet of Doom." *Saga* (April 1971): 22-25, 70-75.

146. ———— . "The Incredible Truth Behind the UFOs Mission to Earth." *Saga* (September 1970: 22-25, 52-56.

147. ———— . "Psychic Pearl Harbor." *Saga* (October 1971): 22-25, 58-62.

148. ———— . "'Spokesman' for the UFOs?" *Saga* (August 1970): 22-25, 90-94.

149. ———— . "Ted Owens: Flying Saucer Missionary." *Saga* (March 1971): 22-25, 78-84.

150. ———— . *Ted Owens, Flying Saucer Spokesman: The Incredible Truth Behind the UFOs Mission to Earth*. Clarksburg, W.Va.: Gray Barker, [1971?]. [15p.]

151. ———— . "UFO's + Ted Owens' PK Jinx = The Freakiest Season in Pro Football." *Saga* (January 1972): 26-29, 80-86.

152. Blazs, Ben. *Interplanetary Carriers and Venusian Scouts.* Detroit: UFO International, 1967. 17p.

153. ——— . *UFOs and Flying Clouds.* Detroit: UFO International, 1975. 17p.

154. Bockman, Dwight. "UFOs: Updated." *Omega Magazine and Directory* (June 1975): 11.

155. Bodin, Edward Longstreet. *First Century Healing.* Lakemont, Ga.: Marcap Council, 1962. 80p.

156. Bowman, Frank. *New Horizons Beyond the World.* Los Angeles: DeVorss and Co., 1969. 368p.

157. Brady, Enid Joan. *Atlantis Rediscovered.* [Holly Hill, Fla.]: The author, n.d. 7p.

158. ——— . "Where Are the Space People?" *Orion* 8 (APril 1963): 13-14.

159. Brom, Elgar. *Sagasha: Mysterious Dust from Space.* New York: Global Communications, 1980. 68p.

160. Brooke, Anthony. *Towards Human Unity.* London: Mitre, 1976. 133p.

161. ——— . *The Universal Line Revelation.* London: Universal FOundation, 1967. 35p.

162. Brooks, Fred R. *Borup's Spiritual School: Second Coming, Part Three.* Borup, Denm.: Universal Link, [1979]. 9p.

163. [Brown, Adelaide J.]. *Advice to a Man from a Higher Sphere.* Los Angeles: DeVorss and Co., [1957?], 1967. 32p. Reprinted in *The Book of Space Ships* (DeVorss edition).

164. ——— . *The Book of Space Ships in Their Relationship with the Earth.* By the God of a Planet near Earth and Others. Los Angeles: DeVorss and Co., 1965. 44p. 2d ed., Clarksburg, W.Va.: Saucerian Books, [1966]. Introduction by Gray Barker. 70 + [9]p. Reprinted as *The Space Gods Speak.* New York: UFO Review, 1983. 65p. *Note:* Originally published as a series of eleven booklets; Saucerian Books edition only printed eight.

165. ——— . *From Jupiter, Planet of Joy.* Los Angeles: DeVorss and Co., [1957?], 1967. 15p. *Note:* Reprinted in *The Book of Space Ships* (Saucerian Books edition, pp. 49-52).

166. ——— . *From Pluto, Planet of Brotherly Love.* Los Angeles: DeVorss and Co., [1957?], 1967. 32p. *Note:* Reprinted in *The Book of Space Ships* (Saucerian Books edition, pp. 22-30).

167. ———— . *God of the Planet Earth Speaks to His Children.* Los Angeles: DeVorss and Co., [1957?], 1967. 16p. *Note:* Reprinted in *The Book of Space Ships* (DeVorss edition).

168. ———— . *Invitation from Planet Venus.* Los Angeles: DeVorss and Co., [1957?], 1967. 20p. *Note:* Reprinted in *The Book of Space Ships* (Saucerian Books edition).

169. ———— . *More Advice from a Higher Sphere.* Los Angeles: DeVorss and Co., 1967. 16p. *Note:* Reprinted in *The Book of Space Ships* (DeVorss edition).

170. ———— . *Neptune from Experience Gives Advice.* Los Angeles: DeVorss and Co., [1957?], 1967. 16p. *Note:* Reprinted in *The Book of Space Ships* (Saucerian Books edition).

171. ———— . *Planet Mercury Sends Greetings.* Los Angeles: DeVorss & Co., [1957?], 1967. 32p. *Note:* Reprinted in *The Book of Space Ships* (Saucerian Books edition).

172. ———— . *The Prophet Isaiah Speaks Again.* Los Angeles: DeVorss and Co., n.d. 60p. *Note:* Not seen; listed by Rasmussen.

173. ———— . *Saturn Planet of Peace Sends Warning.* Los Angeles: DeVorss and Co., [1957?], 1967. 31p. *Note:* Reprinted in *The Book of Space Ships* (Saucerian Books edition).

174. ———— . *Three Undiscovered Planets.* Los Angeles: DeVorss and Co., [1957?], 1967. 15p. *Note:* Reprinted in *The Book of Space Ships* (Saucerian Books edition).

175. ———— . *Uranus, Lover of Man.* Los Angeles: DeVorss and Co., [1957?], 1967. 29p. *Note:* Reprinted in *The Book of Space Ships* (Saucerian Books edition).

176. Brownell, Winfield S., comp. *UFOs: Key to Earth's Destiny!* Lytle Creek, Calif.: Legion of Light, 1980. 214p.

177. Bunze, Juanita V. *Voluntary Encounters with UFOs and Extra-Terrestrials.* Anaheim, Calif.: The author, 1980. 6p.

178. Burns, Donald A. "Maui Loa Talks to Flying Saucers." *Search* 103 (March 1973): 74-79.

179. Caddy, Eileen. *The Spirit of Findhorn.* New York: Harper and Row, 1976; Romford, London: L.N. Fowler, 1977. 127p.

180. Campione, Michael J. "Space Visitors Are Here." *Search* 134 (Spring 1978): 20-21.

181. ———— . *UFO Contactee.* Cinnaminson, N.J.: Delval UFO, n.d. 6p. *Note:* Not seen; ad in *Ohio Skywatcher* 2, 4.

182. Cannon, Frances. *Miracle of Life*. Dallas, Tex.: Cannon Productions, 1984-1985. Vol. 1, 1984, 15p.; vol. 2, 1985, 11p.; vol. 3, 1985, 24p.

183. Carlson, Naomi J. (Letter), "Astral Trip to Mars." *Fate* 13 (August 1960): 112-14.

184a. Carroll, St. Thomas Marion. *Aliens*. Reseda, Calif.: Mojave, 1974. 52p.

184b. Carter, Joan Frances. *Fourteen Footsteps from Outer Space*. Dallas, Tex.: Royal, 1966. 168p.

185. Chalker, Bill. "Cigar-UFO Occupants." *Paranormal and Psychic Australian* 2 (October 1977): 6-9, 27-28.

186. ———— . "UFOs: The Psychic Connection." *Psychic Australian* 1 (December 1976); 12-15, 25-27; 2 (January 1977): 20-23, 25-26.

187. Chaney, Earlyne. *Beyond Tomorrow*. Upland, Calif.: Astara, 1985. 171p.

188. Chovanec, Frank. *About Your S.I. Photograph*. [Taylor, Tex.]: The author, 1970. 4p.

189. Church of Christology. *Kidnapped by UFO*. San Diego, Calif.: Church of Christology, [1978]. [6p.]

190. Clark, Jerome. "Indian Prophecy and the Prescott UFOs." *Fate* 24 (April 1971): 54-61. *Note*: (Letter), Red Cloud Mason (September 1971): 142-44.

191. Clarke, Miriam Teel. "Extra-terrestrial Visitor?" *Mystic* 7 (December 1954): 20-23.

192. Clendenon, William D. *Mercury: UFO Messenger of the Gods*. Owl Press, 1990. 123pp.

193. Coe, H. Albert. *The Shocking Truth*. Beverly, N.J.: The Book Fund, 1969. 112p.

194. Colson, Lucy B. [Lucien, pseud.]. *1982: Cosmic Countdown*. Deming, N.Mex.: Guardian Action, 1981. 44p.

195. ———— . *1985: An Update*. Ojai, Calif.: The author, 1984. 36p.

196. ———— . *Tell My People*. By Joshua. Ojai, Calif.: The author, 1983. 83p.

197. Comella, Thomas M., Jr. [Peter Kor, pseud.]. "Behind the Contact Claims." *Search* 135 (Summer 1978): 22-26.

198. Conna [Barbara G. Finney]. *Starnet: Introductory Information*. [Addison, Pa.: Starnet, 1984]. 3p.

199. *Conscious Channeling: An Extraterrestrial Approach*. Sedona, Ariz.: Earth Mission Publishing, 1989. 83p.

200. Contreras, Marco A. *My Friend from Outer Space*. [San Francisco, Calif.]: The author, 1981. 149p.

201. Cortez, Ramona. "The Stranger." *Beyond Reality UFO Special Report* 2 (1979): 40-41, 58.

202. ———— . "The Unearthly Voices in My Ears." *Beyond Reality UFO Special Report* 2 (1979): 45, 64.

203. *Cosmic Awareness Messages*. Seattle, Wash.: Servants of Awareness Publication, n.d. [1970].

204. Coundakis, Anthony L. *Mannerism on Space Communication: Some Methods and Some Reflections*. Smithtown, N.Y.: Exposition, 1981. 174p.

205. Cox, Norma. *Secrets*. Marshall, Ark.: The author, [197-]. 48p.

206. Crenshaw, James. "The Great Venusian Mystery." *Fate* 19 (June 1966): 32-39. *Note*: (Letter), Gene Dorsey (September 1966): 121-24.

207. Criswell, Beverly [Lavandar, pseud.]. *Quartz Crystals: A Celestial Point of View*. Reserve, N.Mex.: Lavandar Lines, 1983. 31p.

208. Croft, Lenora. *Contact Point*. Eatonville, Wash.: [New Age Foundation, 1966?]. [9p.]

209. Cummings, Martin M. "Do People from Other Planets Really Live Among Us?" *Beyond* 2 (November 1969): 22-27.

210. "Cups or Saucers?" *Time* (September 9, 1957): 67.

211. Dardanelli, Albert. *Mind Powers, Transmutation, and U.F.O.s*. N.p.: Dial, [1988]. 128p.

212. Darling, Thomas J. [Sundar, pseud.]. *Rainbow Bridge Space Channeling Guide*. Santa Cruz, Calif.: Rainbow Bridge Construction Company, 1976. [48p.]

213. Davies, Owen. "UFO Update." *Omni* 7 (December 1984): 144; (September 1985): 83.

214. Davis, Isabel. "Meet the Extraterrestrial." *Fantastic Universe* 8 (November 1957): 31-59.

215. ———— . *Meet the Extraterrestrial*. N.p.: Would-You-Believe, 1984. 42p. *Note*: Reprinted from *Fantastic Universe* articles.

216. "Deadly Wait for a UFO." *Pursuit* 15 (1982): 181.

217. Dean, John W. *Flying Saucers and the Scriptures*. New York: Vantage, 1964. 173 + [63p].

218. ———— . *Flying Saucers Close Up*. Clarksburg, W.Va.: Gray Barker, 1970. 224p.

219. Decard, Bob. *The California Connection*. Manhattan Beach, Calif.: Constellation Press, 1986. 73p.

220. Denaerde, Stefan. *Operation Survival Earth*. Translated by Jim Lodge. New York: Pocket Books, 1977. 159p. *Note:* Translation of *Buitenaardse Beschaving De Planet Iarga*. Deventer, Neth.: N. Kluwer, 1969.

221. Denaerde, Stefan, and Wendelle C. Stevens. *UFO . . . Contact from Planet Iarga: A Report of the Investigation*. Tucson, Ariz.: UFO Photo Archives, 1982. 364p.

222. Dewey, Mark. *A Man from Space Speaks*. Houston, Tex.: The author, 1966. 38p. *Note:* "Dictated by Amano."

223. Deyo, Stan. *The Cosmic Conspiracy*. Morley, West Austral.: West Australian Texas Trading, 1978. 200p.

224. Dickhoff, Robert Ernst. *Behold . . . The Venus Garuda*. New York: The author, 1968. 71p.

225. ———. *The Eternal Fountain: A Kaleidoscope of Divine Inspired Thought Sparks*. Boston: Bruce Humphries, 1947; Mokelumne Hill, Calif.: Health Research, 1954, 1965. 128p.

226. ———. *Homecoming of the Martians: An Encyclopedic Work on Flying Saucers*. Ghaziabad, India: Bharti Association, 1958; Mokelumne Hill, Calif.: Health Research, 1964. 175p.

227. ———. *The Martian Alphabet and Language: The Mother Culture*. N.p., 1957. 8p.

228. Dickson, Richard. "UFO Encounters in Japan." *Beyond Reality* 21 (July-August 1976): 24.

229. Dilts, Russell LeRoy. *Ignorant About UFOs: Facts You Should Know*. [South Bend, Ind.]: The author, 1978. 8p.

230. Dongo, Tom. *The Alien Tide!* Sedona, Ariz.: Hummingbird Publishing Co., 1990. 128p.

231. Doreal, Maurice. *Flying Saucers: An Occult Viewpoint*. Sedalia, Colo.: Brotherhood of the White Temple, [1964?]. 48p.

232. Doulos, Chris. *Outer Space Creatures Are on Earth Now*. Memphis, Tenn.: The author, 1977. 122p.

233. Dutta, Rex. *Flying Saucer Message*. London: Pelham, 1972. 117p.

234. ———. *Flying Saucer Viewpoint*. London: Pelham, 1970. 115p.

235. ———. *Reality of Occult/Yoga/Meditation/Flying Saucers*. London: Pelham, 1974. 199p.

236. Duverus, Delamer. *The Golden Reed*. Seligman, Mo.: The author, 1973. 214p.

237. El Morya, and Miriam. *The Beloved Chohans Speak Their Peace*. Grass Valley, Calif.: Golden Sierra Printing, n.d. 25p.

238. *An Embassy for Extraterrestrials*. Geneva, Switz.: International Raelian Movement, 1972. 27p.

239. Environ. *Flying Saucer Occupants: What They Look Like, Ways to Contact Them*. [Hebron, Ill.]: Unidentified Flying Ojbects Supporters of North America, 1973. 7p.

240. Eolia, St. Germain. *The New Guide for Students in God's Golden Age*. Grass Valley, Calif.: Golden Sierra, 1978. 142p.

241. Esthesia, Goddess, Ruler of Planet Uranus. *Spiritual Questions and Answers*. Cottonwood, Ariz.: Cosmic Light Center, 1985. 119p.

242. Evans, Hilary, and Michel Piccin. "Who Took Who for a Ride?" *Fate* 35 (October 1982): 51-58.

243. The Evergreens [group of entities speaking through Michael Blake Read; sessions directed by Philippa M. Lee]. *The Evergreens Speaking for Ourselves*. Edited by Beth Kendall. Toronto: Michael Read and Philippa Lee, 1977. 28p.

244. ———. *Monsters and Mysteries*. Toronto: Michael Read and Philippa Lee, 1976. [37p.]

245. ———. *Mysteries of History*. Toronto: Michael Read and Philippa Lee, 1977. [20p.]

246. ———. *UFOs: Why?* Toronto: Michael Read and Philippa Lee, [197-]. [20p.]

247. ———. *Visitors of Time and Space*. Toronto: Emanation Press, 1978. 36p.

248. [Finch, Bill], ed. *I Am Ishcomar: The Voice from Beyond Our Stars!* No. 1. Cottonwood, Ariz.: Esoteric Publications, 1978. 38p.

249. ———. *An Introduction to Ishcomar: The Voice from Beyond Our Stars!* Sedona, Ariz.: Esoteric Publications, n.d. 14p.

250. Findhorn Foundation. *The Findhorn Garden*. New York: Harper and Row, 1975; London: Turnstone, 1976. 180p.

251. Finney, Barbara G. (Letter). *Fate* 35 (September 1982): 129.

252. Fletcher, David. (Letter), "A Covert Operation?" *Fate* 38 (August 1985): 114-17. *Note:* (Letters), Ava E. Scott, Donald E. Evett (December 1985): 115-16.

253. "Flying Saucer in South Africa." *Search* 20 (May 1957): 6-12.

254. Foreman, Laurence W. *Passport to Eternity*. Los Angeles: The author, 1970. 112p.

255. Francis, Marianne [Aleuti Francesca]. *The Call of the Phoenix*. Central Point, Oreg.: Solar Light Center, n.d. 15p.

256. ———. *Egyptian Light*. London: Regency Press, n.d. 159p.

257. ———. *Frequency Change and the Second Coming*. Central Point, Oreg.: Solar Light Retreat, n.d. 12p.

258. ———. *God—Man or Animal—Man*. Central Point, Oreg.: Solar Light Retreat, n.d. 12p.

259. ———. *Manifestation*. Central Point, Oreg.: SOlar Light Retreat, n.d. 17p.

260. ———. *The New Dimensions and the New Age*. Central Point, Oreg.: Solar Light Center, n.d. 10p.

261. ———. *Starcraft Contact*. Central Point, Oreg.: Solar Light Center, n.d. 12p.

262. Freitas Guimares, Joao de. "I Flew Aboard a Flying Saucer." *True or False* (April 1958): 39, 60-61.

263. Fuller, Curtis. "The Men Who Ride in Saucers." *Fate* 7 (May 1954): 44-47.

264. Gaines, J. R. "New UFO Cult." *Newsweek* (October 20, 1975): 32.

265. Gaylord, Lyman. "Men Who Ride in Flying Saucers." *Challenge* (November 1955): 16-18, 56-58.

266. Gilbert, Phyllis. "I Was a Member of the UFO Cult." *Pageant* 31 (March 1976): 45-50.

267. Gilbert, Violet. *Love Is All: A Discourse by the Ancient One*. Grant's Pass, Oreg.: Cosmic Star Temple, 1969. 24p.

268. ———. *My Trip to Venus*. Grant's Pass, Oreg.: Cosmic Star Temple, 1968. 55p.

269. Goetz, A. William. *My Trip to Mars: A Personal Psychic Experience*. Houston, Tex.: Jewell, 1960. 22p.

270. Goetz, Warren H. *The Intelligence of the Universe Speaks*. De Tour Village, Mich.: The author, 1974. 205p.

271. Gordon, Ian. *The Andronicus Tapes*. Melbourne, Vict.: Andronicus Foundation, 1983. 256p.

272. Grant, Kenneth. *Outside the Circles of Time*. London: Frederick Muller, 1980. 316p.

273. Greenberg, Marian. *An Extraterrestrial Conspiracy: A Case Study*. Los Angeles: Falcon Press, 1988. 256p.

274. Gualda, Jose Maldonado. *A True Story, Showed as Fiction or a Fiction Showing a Story? Concerning Extra-Terrestrial Phenomena, Human Reality and Flying Saucers*. Paris: Centre Ummo d'Investigation, n.d. [5p.].

275. Guery, Appel. *Timeless Voyage: Earth Sky Convention*. Fevrier, France: Macedo Appel-Guery, 1987. 103p.

276. [Guthrie, Wayne]. *Visitors from Other Planets*. 2d revised ed. Los Angeles: Fellowship of Universal Guidance, November 1968. 32p.

277. Gutsche, Clara. "Life Beyond Earth: In Advance of the Landing, Folk Concepts of Outer Space." *Photo Communique* 6 (Summer 1984): 30-34. *Note:* (Commentary), Doug Curran, 35-43.

278. Haigh, John S. *Serving Planet Earth*. Bellingen, N.S.W., Austr. Sontar Communications, 1981. 101p.

279. Halsall, Patricia. *The Science of Distance*. Leeds, Yorke: Arts, 1981. 32p. *Note:* Not seen; mentioned in *Earthlink*, no. 15.

280. Halsey, Wallace C. *Cosmic End-Time Secrets*. Los Angeles: Golden Dawn, 1965. 102p.

281. Hamilton, William F., III. *Geometry of the Grid*. Glendale, Calif.: Nexus and Nexus News, 1983. 71p.

282. ———. *The Secret Code of the UFOs*. N.p., n.d. *Note:* Not seen; according to *Gray Barker's Newsletter*, no. 13, writing was in progress.

283. Hannaford, Kathryn. *Cosmic Cookery*. Berkeley, Calif.: One World Family, 1974. 254p.

284. Harrison, Sam. *The Krone Chronicles: A True Story*. Virginia Beach, Va.: Donning, 1981. 186p.

285. Hastings, Philip. "Scientific Wonders Predicted from Another World." *The Searcher* 3, 1 (January 1962): 72-76.

286. Hawken, Paul. *The Magic of Findhorn*. Boston: East-West Journal, 1974. 60p. Revised ed., New York: Harper and Row; London: Souvenir, 1975. 216p. Paperback ed., New York: Bantam, 1976. 343p.

287. Henley, Cerra de Puy. *A Man from Mars*. N.p., n.d. 67p. *Note:* Not seen; mentioned in *Bufora Journal* 10, 2.

288. Hind, Cynthia. "South African Woman Reports: A Ride in a UFO." *Fate* 22 (August 1969): 42-46. *Note:* (Letter), Ira B. Cross (November 1969): 145-46.

289. Hoag, Helen I., ed. *Dawn of Creation*. By Mara Menara from the Planet Yama in the Sixth Universe. North Miami, Fla.: Metaphysical Research Group, 1968. [39p.] Some editions paginated, [1982?]. 41p.

290. ———— . *The Glowing Wall*. Hollywood, Fla.: Awareness Research Foundation, 1982. 20p.

291. ———— . *My Lives on Atlantis*. North Miami, Fla.: Metaphysical Research Group, 1969. 43p.

292. ———— . *My Visits to Other Planets: The Sun, Moon and the Star, Capella*. North Miami, Fla.: Awareness Research Foundation, 1970. 119p.

293. ———— . *The 3 Missing Planets*. North Miami, Fla.: Awareness Research Foundation, 1974. 32p.

294. ———— . *What Happens Between Lives*. North Miami, Fla.: Awareness Research Foundation, 1969. 39p.

295. ———— . *Your Future on this Planet*. North Miami, Fla.: Awareness Research Foundation, 1972. 48p.

296. Hogben, Crystal. *Quella, E.T.* Leeds, Yorks: Arts, [1982?]. *Note:* Not seen; mentioned in *Earthlink* 15, 8.

297. Holland, William Larry. *Not of this Earth: The Planto Connection*. Sheffield, Ala.: The author, 1977. 36p.

298. Holroyd, Stuart. *Prelude to the Landing on Planet Earth*. London: W.H. Allen, 1977. 337p. Reprinted as *Briefing for the Landing on Planet Earth*. London: Corgi, 1979. 351p.

299. Howard, Frank. *An ExtraTerrestrial Message to the Nations*. Auckland, N.Z.: Stellar, 1983. 187p.

300. ———— . *Journey in Space with Alizantil*. Brisbane, Queensland: The author, [1979?]. 83p.

301. ———— . *A Planetary Saga and Return of Alizantil*. Brisbane, Queensland: The author, [1979?]. 83p.

302. ———— . *A Planetary Saga and Return of Alizantil and Journey in Space with Alizantil: Combined Edition*. Mt. Shasta, Calif.: Association Sananda and Sunat Kumara, 4th ed., 1981. 132p.

303. Howard, Joan. *Genesis to Eternity*. N.p., n.d. *Note:* Not seen; mentioned in *Saucers, Space and Science*, no. 64, p. 10.

304. ——— . *The Space or Something Connection.* Toronto: The author, [1982]. 85p.

305. Hubbard, Harold W., and Woodrow W. Derenberger. *Visitors from Lanulos.* New York: Vantage, 1971. 111p.

306. Ibrahim, Yosip. *I Visited Ganymede: The Wonderful World of the UFOs.* Lima, Peru: The author, 1974. 201p. *Note:* Not certain whether there are more than a few copies of this manuscript. Translation of *Yo Visite Ganimedes: El Mundo Maravillosos De Los Ovnis.* Lima: The author, 1972.

307. Iner, Stella, "UFO Update." *Omni* 4 (October 1981): 169.

308. Innocente, Geraldine. *God's Divine Plan for Our Solar System.* St. James, N.Y.: Bridge to Freedom, [1957?]. 36p.

309. Ireland, Bonnie. *First Lessons in Mastership by the Ascended Masters.* Garland, Tex.: The Institute of L.L.U. *Note:* Not seen.

310. ——— . *Meditate with the Masters: 33 Nights of Inner Wisdom.* Garland, Tex.: The Institute of L.L.U. *Note:* Not seen.

311. ——— . *The Meditations of Soft-Foot.* Garland, Tex.: The Institute of L.L.U. *Note:* Not seen.

312. ——— . *Shekinah Speaks: Messages from a Lady Master with Inner Views from the Intergalactic Command.* Garland, Tex.: The Institute of L.L.U., 1984.

313. Irwin, Enid M. *Message from Atlantis.* Jane Lew, W.Va.: New Age, 1983. 86 + [20]p.

314. Jarnagin, Roy C. *UFOs: The Extrauniversal Connection.* Hicksville, N.Y.: Exposition, 1977. 133p.

315. Jensen, Aage. *Borup's Spiritual School.* Naestved, Denm.: Universal Link, 1968. 23p.

316. ——— . *Summa Summarun!* Translated by Gunvor Jensen. Naestved, Denm.: Universal Link, 1969. [14p.]

317. ——— . *Universal Link: Denmark.* Naestved, Denm.: Universal Link, February 1969. [10p.]

318. Jenson, Lillie May. (Letter), "Lecture on UFOs." *Fate* 10 (December 1957): 126-27.

319. Jig, Hermann. *Thinking in Cosmic Terms.* Lubeck, W. Ger.: M. Drager, 1982. 26p. *Note:* Translation of *In Kosmischen Bahnen Denken.* Lubeck: Buchdienst M. Drager, [1979?].

320. Johnson, David H. *Salos: Another World.* Moore Haven, Fla.: Rainbow, 1983. 199p.

321. Johnson, Frank. *The Janos People: A Close Encounter of the Fourth Kind.* Sudbury, Suffolk: Neville Spearman, 1980. 198p.

322. Jones, Mary C. (Letter), "UFOs and Automatic Writing." *Fate* 9 (October 1956): 113-16.

323. Joshua [Richard Shapiro], ed. *Journeys of an Aquarian Age Networker.* Palo Alto, Calif.: New Life, June 1982. 333p. Revised ed., October 1982. [489p.]

324. Keel, John A. "America's Unrecognized UFO Experts." *Saga* (April 1973): 34-37, 68-71.

325. ———. "Ancient Astronauts, Modern Mysteries." *Saga* (February 1975): 14, 44, 50-52.

326. ———. "Strange Messages from Flying Saucers." *Saga* (January 1968): 22-25, 69-74. *Note:* (Letter), Joan Siohan, April 1968, p. 4.

327. King, Beti. *Diary from Outer Space: As Dictated by Bernie to Beti King.* Mojave, Calif.: Desert Specialties, 1976. 73p.

328. ———. *A Psychic's True Story of Life, Death, and Flying Saucers.* Part One by the deceased (d. 1974) Bernie King. Mojave, Calif.: Desert Specialties, 1976. 34p. Later ed., [1980?]. 47p.

329. ———. *Reincarnation and UFO.* Mojave, Calif.: Desert SPecialties, 1976. 8p.

330. ———. *Spiritualism and UFO.* Mojave, Calif.: Desert Specialties, 1976. 5p.

331. ———. *UFO and Life After Death.* Mojave, Calif.: Desert Specialties, 1976. 8p.

332. ———. *Vibrations Are Real.* Mojave, Calif.: Desert Specialities, 1976. 5p.

333. ———. *You Will Never Die!* Mojave, Calif.: Desert Specialties, 1975. 6p. 2d ed., 1976. 11p.

334. ———. *You, Your Psychic Development, and How It Can Improve Your Life!* Mojave, Calif.: Desert Specialties, 1978. 21p.

335. Klarer, Elizabeth. *Beyond the Light Barrier.* Translated by Manfred Landeck. Sparta, N.J. and Capetown, S. Africa: Howard Timmins, 1980. 191p. *Note:* Translation of *Erlebnisse Jenseits Der Lichtmauer.* Wiesbaden, W. Ger.: Ventla-Verlag, 1977.

336. Knight, Oscar F. *Wolverton Trail Event: A Visitor from Venus.* Strathmore, Calif.: The author, 1963. 11p.

337. Kolson, Ann. "A Seeker of Truth." *Fate* 36 (December 1983): 44-48.

338. Kooistra, Walter A. (Letter), "Right around the Moon." *Fate* 23 (September 1970): 134, 145.

339. Koslouski, Paul. *Are We Children of the Universe? My Contact with Space People*. Mississauga, Ont.: UFO Media Publications Group, 1979. 52p.

340. Krebs, Columba. *The Moon Is Inhabited*. Williams, Ariz.: The author, 1962. 129p. *Note:* Not seen; mentioned in Glemser's *UFO Report*, vol. 1, no. 2.

341. ———. *Visiting Spacemen?* [Williams, Ariz.]: Symbolart, 1961. 28p. *Note:* Not seen; ad in *Flying Saucers*, March 1962.

342. Kron, Fritz, and B. Ann Slate. "The Great UFO 'Ride.'" *Fate* 24 (May 1971): 38-50. *Note:* (Letter), Cyndia Valree Hanna (November 1971): 139-40.

343. Krouse, David A. (Letter), "Curious 'Coincidence.'" *Fate* 29 (November 1976): 124.

344. Kullgren, William, comp. *Messages from Higher Planes*. Atascadero, Calif.: The author, [1960]. 117p.

345. Lael, Ralph I. *The Brown Mountain Lights*. Morganton, N.C.: Outer Space Rock Shop Museum, 1965. 28p.

346. Lane, David Christopher. "The Himalayan Connection: UFOs and the Chandian Effect." *Journal of Humanistic Psychology* 24 (1984): 75-89.

347. Laub, Edith Yarowsky. *God-Or: A Psychic Communication with Outer Space*. Ardmore, Penn.: Dorrance and Co., 1976. 156p.

348. Lavery, Frank. "UFO Contactee Interviewed." *Cosmos: The Living Paper* 4 (November 1976): 4-5.

349. ———. "UFO Super-Gods Training Victorians!" *Psychic Australian* 2 (July 1977): 6-9, 29-30.

350. Leary, Timothy, and Lynn Wayne Benner. *Terra II*. San Francisco: Imprinting Press, 1973. Ch. 19.

351. Le Fountain, Doris. *Are Space Visitors Really Here?* Hawthorne, N.J.: The author, [1961]. 26p.

352. Lewis, David H. *Beyond Our Galaxy, Book 1*. St. Petersburg, Fla.: Science Research, 1978, 1980. 159p.

353. ———. *The Days Before Tomorrow*. St. Petersburg, Fla.: Science Research, 1978. 260p.

354. ———. *The Deon Chronicles*. St. Petersburg, Fla.: Science Research, 1983? *Note:* Not seen; may not have been published.

355. ———. *Survival of the Remnant*. St. Petersburg, Fla.: Science Research, 1980. 175p.

356. ———. *The Universal Oneness: Beyond Our Galaxy, Book 2.* St. Petersburg, Fla.: Science Research, 1979. 175p.

357. Lloyd, David. *The "I AM" Discourses.* Schaumburg, Ill.: Saint Germain, 1980. 417p.

358. Lobsang Rampa, Tuesday [Cyril Henry Hoskins]. *The Hermit.* London: Corgi, 1971. 159p.

359. ———. *My Visit to Venus.* Clarksburg, W.Va.: Saucerian Books, [1966]. 31p. 2d ed., Kitchener, Ont.: Galaxy, [1973?]. [28p.].

360. Long, Mary. *I, Osiris.* London: Regency, 1970. *Note:* Not seen; reviewed in *Gemini,* vol. 1, no. 3.

361. ———. *Our Son Moves Among You.* London: Bachman and Turner, 1974. *Note:* Not seen; mentioned in *Cosmic Frontiers,* November 1976. Another ed., published by Grant Helm, 1974?, according to *BUFORA Journal* 4, 4.

362. Looney, Bill. *Radix.* Fort Worth, Tex.: Branch-Worth, Inc., 1970. 208p.

363. LoPear, Bertha, and G. Ross. *World in Translation, with References for Further Study.* Glendale, Calif.: SFTAUFOS, 1987. 352p.

364. Lucchesi, Dominic C. *Flying Saucers from Khabara Khoom.* Jane Lew, W.Va.: New Age, 1984. 105p.

365. MacDonald, Howard Brenton. *Flying Saucers and Space Ships: And the Unknown Planets from Whence They Come.* New York: The author, 1955; New York: Flying Saucer News, [1967]. 6p. Revised ed., St. Catherines, Ont.: Provoker, 1970. 32p.

366. ———. *Spirit Revelations Concerning Flying Saucers and Spaceships Received Thru the Pendulum Mediumship of Dr. Howard Brenton MacDonald.* New York: The author, [195-]. 7p.

367. Macer-Story, Eugenia. *Congratulations! The UFO Reality.* Los Angeles: Crescent, 1978. 118p.

368, MacLaine, Shirley. *Out on a Limb.* New York: Bantam, 1983. Pp. 212, 227, 240-55, 262, 295-96, 302-39, 341-43, 347-51, 357, 372.

369. Magocsi, Oscar. *Beyond My Space Odyssey in UFOs.* Toronto: Quest Group, 1983. 52p.

370. ———. *My Space Odyssey in UFOs.* Missassauga, Ont.: UFO Media Publications Group, 1979. 8 ½ × 11" format. 146p. Regular format, Toronto: Quest Group, 1980. 209p. *Note:* Originally published in 1975, according to Rasmussen.

371. Mallan, Lloyd, "The Man Who Saw Venus." *Mechanix Illustrated* 64 (May 1968): 58-60, 110-12.

372. Mann, Rod. "The Commune." *Cosmos* (August 1969): 4-5.

373. Marcus [Richard Watson]. *Celestial Raise: 'Tiers of Light' Pouring Forth from the Son.* Mt. Shasta, Calif.: A.S.S.K., 1986. 228p.

374. Martin, Dan. (Letter). *Fate* 13 (December 1960): 120.

375. Martin, Dorothy [Sister Thedra, pseud.]. *Excerpts of the Prophecies from Other Planets Concerning Our Earth.* [Mt. Shasta, Calif.]: The author, 1962. 17p. *Note:* Sister Thedra heads the association of Sananda and Sanat Kumara.

376. Marystone, Cyril. *The Origin of Comets in Planet Magnetotails.* [Bronx, N.Y.]: The author, March 1983. 120p.

377. Mason, Peggy. "Psychic Signs in the Sky." *Two Worlds* (April 1970): 108-11.

378. ———. "The Space People Have a Purpose." *Two Worlds* (February 1976): 35-38.

379. Mathes, Joseph H., and Lenora Huett. *The Amnesia Factor: Extraterrestrial Communications Breakthrough.* Millbrae, Calif.: Celestial Arts, 1975. 169p.

380. Matthews, Arthur Henry. *The Wall of Light: Nikola Tesla and the Venusian Space Ship the X-12.* Mokelumne Hill, Calif.: Health Research, 1973. 117 + [41]p.

381. May, Antoinette. "The Findhorn Experience." *Psychic* 6 (July-August 1978): 39-43.

382. Mengel, Elmer O. (Letter), "Up the UFOs!" *Fate* 25 (September 1972): 142.

383. (Letter), "Message from Aldebaran." *East-West Journal* 9 (February 1979): 6.

384. Messiah's World Crusade. *"Seeking the New Age? Help to Create It!"* Berkeley, Calif.: The Crusade, n.d. 8p.

385. Mezra. *Morning Star: Chronicles of a Star Traveler.* Triad Communications, 1989. 137p.

386. Miller, George. "Sylvia." *Search* 87 (September 1969): 64-69.

387. Miller, Max B. "The Men Who Ride in Saucers." *Fate* 13 (February 1960): 32-38. *Note:* (Letters), Zan Overall (June 1960): 116-20; Carl L. Barton, Keith Robertson (July 1960): 113-16.

388. Miller, Richard T., ed. *Star Wards: Welcome Home Earthman.* Campbell, Calif.: Solar Cross Foundation, 1979. 365p.

389. Mishara, Eric. "Airport for Extraterrestrials." *Omni* 6 (February 1984): 90.

390. ———. "Aliens Among Us." *Omni* 6 (May 1984): 96.

391a. ———. "Space Pets." *Omni* 7 (February 1985): 94.

391b. Mishlove, Jeffrey. "The Wrath of the 'UFO Prophet.'" *Fate* 32 (February 1979): 62-70. *Note:* (Letters), Judith Gee (June 1979): 114; Jeffrey Mishlove, Judith Gee (June 1979): 113-14; Ted Owens (December 1979): 115-17; Stan Farnsworth, 33 (June 1980): 119; Judith Gee (July 1980): 116-17.

392. Moeller, Elouise. *The Science of Living.* N.p., n.d. *Note:* Not seen; mentioned by Tuella.

393. Montgomery, Ruth. *Aliens Among Us.* New York: G. P. Putnam's Sons, 1985. 240p.

394. ———. *Ruth Montgomery: Herald of the New Age.* Garden City, N.Y.: Doubleday and Company, 1986. 277p.

395. ———. *Strangers Among Us: Enlightened Beings from a World to Come.* New York: Coward, McCann and Geoghegan, 1976. 254p.

396. ———. *Threshold to Tomorrow.* New York: Putnam's, 1983. 269p.

397. ———. *The World Before.* New York: Coward, McCann and Geoghegan, 1976.

398a. Moody, Marjorie B. *Master Krishan Venta.* Grass Valley, Calif.: Golden Sierra Printing, n.d. [1976]. 51p.

398b. Moon, Margaret, and Maurine Moon. *The Jupiter Experiment: A Love Story of this World and the Next.* St. Paul, Minn.: Llewellyn, 1976. 213p.

399. Morris, Maria. (Letter), "Terrifying Beings." *Fate* 36 (December 1983): 118.

400. El Morya and Miriam. *The Beloved Chohans Speak Their Peace.* Grass Valley, Calif.: Golden Sierra Printing, n.d. 25p.

401. Moyer, Ernest P. *God, Man and the UFOs.* New York: Carlton, 1970. 422p. Reprinted as *The Day of Celestial Visitation.* Hicksville, N.Y.: Exposition, 1975. 304p.

402. Mullens, Henry. "Nepal Monks Announce Forthcoming Visit of Inhabitants of Dying Star: Reveal Elaborate Reception Plans." *Beyond* 1 (November 1968): 81-88.

403. Mulvin, Colleen. "Venus: Who Needs a Starship to Get There." *ECK MATA Journal* 2 (1977-78): 20-21.

404. Mustapa, Margit. *Book of Brothers*. New York: Vantage, 1963. 196p.

405. ———— . *Spaceship to the Unknown*. New York: Vantage, 1960. 243p.

406. Nelson, Bernard. "The Pluto/UFO Connection." *The Illustrated Cosmic Machine* 1, 4 (Vernal Equinox 1979): 7.

407. *The New Age Testament of Light*. Auckland, N.Z.: New Age Light, 1979? *Note:* Not seen; mentioned in *Earthlink*, Autumn 1979.

408. Newton, Silas. *Some Implications of the Spaceships and the Space Command*. London: Universal Foundation, 1969. 16p.

409. Nigl, Marian E. *Messages from Space*. N.p.: The author, n.d. 12p.

410. Noel, Mel [Noel Brice Cornwall]. *The Mel Noel Story: The Inside Story of the U.S. Air Force Secrecy on UFOs*. Inglewood, Calif.: The author, 1966. 26p. 2d ed., Clarksburg, W.Va.: Saucerian Books, n.d. 26p.

411. [Noonan], Allen Michael. *ETI Space Beings Intercept Earthlings*. [Stockton, Calif.]: Starmast, 1977. 158p.

412. ———— . *The Everlasting Gospel: God, Ultimate Unlimited Mind, Speaks*. Stockton, Calif.: Starmast, 1982. 457p.

413. ———— . *The Everlasting Gospel: To the Thought of the World*. Berkeley, Calif.: Starmast and Universal Industrial Church of the New World Comforter, 1973. 350p.

414. ———— . *UFO-ETI World Master Plan*. [Stockton, Calif.]: Starmast, 1977. 160p.

415. Northdurft, Milton H. *Between Two Worlds*. Prescott Valley, Ariz.: Mountain Valley Press, 1985. 152p.

416. O'Brien, Glenn. "The Saucer Men of Tennessee and the Unspeakable Things They Did to Stanley Ingram's Daughter." *OUI* (August 1977): 90-98, 106-108.

417. O'Connor, Mary Jane. "I Lived on Another Planet!" *True or False* (April 1958): 30-33, 55-57.

418. Omoleye, Mike. *Mystery World Under the Sea: A Vivid Account of a Woman Who Found Herself in a Beautiful City Under the Sea After a Ship Disaster*. Ibadan, Nigeria: Omoleye, 1979. 51p.

419. Oribello, William Alexander. *The Final Solution*. New Brunswick, N.J.: Inner Light Publications, 1985. 51p.

420. Oswanta, Yashah. *Divine Guidance from the Space Brothers*. Salmon Arm, Br. Col.: Alahoy Publications, 1987. 94p.

421. *The Outsider*. Ardmore, Pa.: Dorrance, [1982?]. *Note:* Not seen; mentioned in *Fate*, June 1982.

422. Owens, Ted. (Letter), "Batting Average." *Fate* 19 (December 1966): 146-47.

423. —————. *Flying Saucer Intelligences Speak: A Message to the American People from the Flying Saucer Intelligences*. New Brunswick, N.J.: Interplanetary News Service, [1966]. 8p. 2d ed., Cape Charles, Va.: The author; Kitchener, Ont.: Galaxy, 1972. [32p.] 3d ed., Clarksburg, W.Va.: Saucerian Books, 1979. 12p.

424. —————. (Letter), "Help from Another Quarter." *Fate* 37 (March 1984): 129.

425. —————. *How to Contact Space People*. Clarksburg, W.Va.: Saucerian Books, 1969. 96p. *Note:* A tabloid reprint also exists.

426. —————. "How You Can Communicate with UFO Space Intelligences." *Saga* (February 1972): 34-37, 66-74. *Note:* (Letter), Ted Owens (March 1972): 8.

427. —————. (Letter), "The SI's." *Fate* 20 (June 1967): 128-29.

428. —————. (Letter), "The SI's Want to Help." *Fate* 20 (December 1967): 131-32.

429. Paige, Frank L. "Museum Curator Claims to Have Visited the Planet Venus." *Beyond* 4 (February 1971): 70-75.

430. Pallmann, Ludwig F. *Cancer Planet Mission*. London: Foster Press, 1970. 216p.

431. Pamale. *Signal from Space*. New York: Vantage Press, 1987. 228p.

432. Partridge, Samuel Goerge. *Golden Moments with the Ascended Masters*. Grass Valley, Calif.: Golden Sierra, 1976. 380p.

433. Pease, Beth. "Flying Saucer Circus in Tonopah." *Psychic Observer* 32 (July 1971): 46.

434. Pestalozzi, Rudolph H. *Letters to You from Baloran: A Space Being's Observation of Earth*. Auburn, Calif.: Solar Cross Fellowship; San Francisco: K Publishing, 1965. 154p.

435. Pettinella, Dora M. "Messages from Other Worlds." *Fate* 30 (November 1977): 73.

436. Pflock, Karl T. "Anatomy of a UFO Hoax." *Fate* 33 (November 1980): 40-48. *Note:* (Letters), Karl T. Pflock, George Kuchar, 34 (February 1981): 120-21.

437. *The Planets Visit Mother Earth*. Naples, Fla.: Vander Nell, 1981? *Note:* Not seen; ad in *Fate*, September 1981.

438. *Plans for World Improvement.* N.p.: D'Angelo, 1972. Reprinted as *Predictions to the Year 2000.* Monterey, Calif.: Angel Press, 1974. 31p.

439. Prabhupada, A. C. Bhaktivedanta Swami. *Easy Journey to Other Planets.* Los Angeles: ISKCON Books, 1969. 49p. Reprinted, Los Angeles: Bhaktivedanta Book Trust, 1970, 1975. 96p. Later ed., New York: Macmillan, 1972. 96p. *Note:* Other editions and translations also exist.

440. Price, John Randolph. *The Planetary Commission.* Austin, Tex.: Quartus Foundation for Spiritual Research, 1984. 176p.

441. Pritchett, E. Blanche. *Excalibur.* Lakemont, Ga.: CSA, 1964. 272p.

442. ———— . *Explosions in Galaxy M-82.* N.p., n.d. *Note:* Not seen; ad in *Search*, March 1973.

443. ———— . "The History of Marcap Council." *Orion* 7 (April 1962): 21-22.

444. ———— . *Japhalein, Mother Ship of this Galaxy.* Arlington, Wash.: Marcap Council, 1961. 174p. 2d ed., 1968. 169p.

445. ———— . *Transcripts Of "44."* 3 vols. Arlington, Wash.: Marcap Council, 1965-1967. 36 + 32 + 21p.

446. ———— . *View 11: The Architectonics.* N.p., n.d. *Note:* Not seen; ad in *Search*, March 1973.

447. Prophet, Elizabeth Clare. *Planet Earth: The Future Is to the Gods.* Malibu, Calif.: Summit University, 1981. *Note:* Not seen; mentioned in *Fate*, February 1982.

448. Prophet, Mark L. *The Soulless One: Cloning a Counterfeit Creation.* Malibu, Calif.: Summit University, 1965, 1980. 214p.

449. Prophet, Mark L., and Elizabeth Clare Prophet. *Pearls of Wisdom, 1965: Volume Eight.* Malibu, Calif.: Summit University, 297p.

450. Puccetti, Roland. *Persons: A Study of Possible Moral Agents in the Universe.* London: Macmillan, 1968. 145p.

451. Puttcamp, Leland, and Rita Puttcamp. "Some Have Entertained Angels." *Fantastic Universe* 11 (December 1959): 92-99.

452. Randall, John B. *Cars from the Stars.* 14 vols. [San Clemente, Calif.?]: The author, [1978-].

Vol. 1, *Introduction to UFOs.* 10p.
Vol. 2, *Six Types of Aliens to Our Planet.*
Vol. 3, *Do the Space Aliens Self-Impose Restrictions?*
Vol. 4, *Who Are the Unfriendly Aliens?*
Vol. 5, *The Stunning Effect of the UFO.*

Vol. 6, *The Type of Ships Used by the UFOs.*
Vol. 7, *The Reticulum: Home Base for 6 UFO Groups.*
Vol. 8, *UFO Descriptions of Lights and Malfunctioning Auto and Aircraft Engines and Why.*
Vol. 9, *UFOs Ahead Technically 200 Years.*
Vol. 10, *Defenses against UFO Weapons.*
Vol. 11, *Type of Engine Used by UFOs.* 14p.
Vol. 12, *Who Are the Friendly UFOs and from What Star Do They Call Home Base?*
Vol. 13, *Looking Ahead: UFO Comparison.*
Vol. 14, *Closing the Gap between Civilizations.*

453. Randis, Alexander. *Aboard a UFO.* Sherman Oaks, Calif.: The author, [1982]. *Note:* Not seen; ad in *Fate,* October 1982.

454. ———— . *My UFO Journey to Venus.* Los Angeles: The author, [1980]. *Note:* Not seen; ad in *Fate,* October 1981.

455. ———— . *The UFOs Are Coming!* Los Angeles: The author, 1976. 5p.

456. Randles, Jenny. (Letter), "The Janos Case." *Fortean Times* 36 (Winter 1982): 3, 58.

457. Raphael [Ken Carey]. *The Starseed Transmissions: An Extraterrestrial Report.* Kansas City, Mo.: Uni-Sun, 1982. 95p.

458. Reiss, Andy. "UFO Contact." *PSI Review* 1 (November 1983): 28-29.

459. Reyna, Ruth. *Sukra: The Story of Truth.* New Delhi, India: Sagar, 1969. 87p.

460. Richardson, Petrillio C., ed. *Special Report,* Volume 1, No. 1. Aurora, Colo.: Denver Extraterrestrial Research Group, 1979, 1982. 72p.

461. Richman, William. "They Came from Inner Space: UFOs, Is Seeing Believing?" *Mother Jones* 3 (December 1978): 33-39.

462. Riley, Terri. "Starseed Claims You Don't Have to Die." *Fate* 29 (April 1976): 49-57.

463. Robinson, Charles M. *Spirit: A Message to Planet Earth as Received Through the Trance Mediumship.* La Jolla, Calif.: Planet Earth, 1977. 149p.

464. Rogers, Ann. *Soul Partners.* San Jose, Calif.: Abiblical Society, 1979? *Note:* Not seen; ad in Beckley's *UFO Review,* no. 5

465. Rondinone, Peter. "Extraterrestrials Only." *Omni* 6 (March 1984): 93.

466a. ———— . "UFO Update." *Omni* 5 (April 1983): 115; 6 (November 1983): 151.

466b. Roy, Lillian Ray. *The Prince of Atlantis*. Grass Valley, Calif.: Golden Sierra Printing, n.d. [1970?]. 178p.

467. Sachs, Margaret. "UFO Ports." *Omni* 4 (December 1981): 133.

468. St. Germain, Jules B. "The Strange Affair at Highbridge." *Argosy* (November 1957): 39-41, 100-104.

469. Sande, Frances F. *A Life and Work with Men from Outer Space*. N.p., n.d.

470. ———— . *The Truth About Men from Outer Space*. N.p., n.d. *Note:* Both titles not seen.

471. Saunders, Alex. "Are Saucer Sighters Hypnotized?" *Search* 101 (January 1972): 19-24.

472. Savizar and Silarra, comp. *Conscious Channeling: An Extraterrestrial Approach*. Sedona, Ariz.: Earth Mission Publishing, 1989. 82p.

473. ———— . *Extraterrestrial Earth Mission. Book One: The Awakening*. Sedona, Ariz.: Earth Mission Publishing, 1989. 155p.

474. ———— . *The Superconscious Technique*. Sedona, Ariz.: Earth Mission Publishing, 1988. 43p.

475. Schaufler, Larry E. [Solar Edan, pseud.]. *This Is All There Is*. 3 vols. Santee, Calif.: The author, 1979. pt. 1, 73p.; pt. 2, 72p.; pt. 3, 78p.

476. Schiller, Robert. "A Being from the Fifth Dimension Answered My Prayer." *Search* 86 (July 1969): 31-33.

477. Schmidt, Reinhold O., and Wambly Bald. "I Spoke to Space Men." *Challenge* (January 1959): 9-11. 49-51.

478. Schrader, Del, Catherine Callaway, Kathy Hurley, and Cheryl Ann Carpenter, eds. [Earth-Cosmic Task Force]. *You and the Cosmic, or Heaven Unveiled*. Arcadia, Calif.: Santa Anita, 1980. 129p.

479. "Scooped by a UFO." *New Scientist* 78 (1978): 241.

480. Scott, Eugene C. "First Contact with Outer Space!" *Real* (October 1967): 32-33, 60-65.

481. Seargent, David A. J. "UFOnauts from Inner Space." *Psychic Australian* 1 (November 1976): 22-25, 28-30.

482. "Seeds from a 'Contactee.'" *Pursuit* 4 (April 1971): 30. *Note:* (Update), (October 1971): 96-97.

483. Seifer, Marc. "A Graphological Analysis of the Handwriting of Individuals Claiming Contact with Extraterrestrials." *Journal of Occult Studies* 1, 1 (May 1977): 50-75. *Note:* (Correction), 1, 3 (Winter-Spring 1978): 206.

484. Shapiro, Bob, and Edouard Mabe. *Allies*. Edited by Allyn B. Brodsky. N.p.: The authors, 1983. 80p.

485. Shapiro, Joshua. *UFOs, Space Brothers and the Aquarian Age*. Los Gatos, Calif.: J & S Aquarian Networking, 1985. 118p.

486. Shaver, Richard S. "Comment on Reinhold Schmidt." *Search* 41 (June 1961): 50-55.

487. Shelton, Vaughan. *The View from Eternity*. Pocatello, Id.: Forbes Nichols, 1983? *Note:* Not seen; mentioned in *Fate*, November 1983.

488. Shockley, Paul. *Awareness in the Age of Aquarius*. Portland, Oreg.: Akasha Publications, n.d.

489. ———. *Cosmic Awareness Speaks*. 3 vols. Olympia, Wash.: Servants of Awareness, [1967]. 28p. Vol. 2, Olympia, Wash.: Cosmic Awareness Communications, 1977. 76p. Vol. 3, Olympia, Wash.: Cosmic Awareness Communications, 1983. 94p. *Note:* Shockley was trance medium in volume 2 and 3; vol. 1's "interpreter" died in 1967 and remains anonymous.

490. ———. *Government of the Aquarian Age*. Portland, Oreg.: Akasha Publications, [1974?].

491. ———. *Predictions for the Aquarian Age*. Olympia, Wash.: Cosmic Awareness Communications, 1973, [1977]. 36p.

492. Short, Robert. *Beyond These Portals: "A Solar Tour."* [Joshua Tree, Calif.]: The author, 1981. 45p.

493. ———. *California Fault Activity*. Joshua Tree, Calif.: Blue Rose Ministry, 1981. 15p.

494. ———. *Record in Stone: "The Pyramids."* Joshua Tree, Calif.: Blue Rose Ministry, 1977. 35p.

495. ———. *Revelation: "The Number of the Beast."* Joshua Tree, Calif.: Blue Rose Ministry, n.d. 8p.

496. Shubow, Robert. *The Voyagers*. Frankfurt, Ger.: Spiritual University Press, 1981. 33p.

497. Silva, Charles A. *Date with the Gods*. [Melville, N.Y.]: Coleman Graphics, 1977. 411p.

498. Smith, Beatrice S. "Super-Bees and Contactees: A Collection of UFO Nonsense." *Odyssey* 2 (May 1980): 12-14, 18-19.

499. Smith, Dan. *Roots of the Earthman*. El Cajon, Calif.: Unarius Educational Foundation, 1981. 44p.

500. Smith, Enid Severy. *Adventures with Modern Space Visitors*. Tonopah, Ariz.: The author, January 6, 1978. 8p.

501. ———. *Experiences with the Space People*. Tonopah, Ariz.: The author, n.d. 6p.

502. ———. *General Information: Universal Faith and Wisdom Association*. Tonopah, Ariz.: Universal Faith and Wisdom Association, [1971?]. [12p.]

503. ———. *News from Space People*, December, 1964. Tonopah, Ariz.: The author, n.d. 4p.

504. ———. "Our Guardian Angels: Spacemen." *Psychic Observer* 31 (December 1970): 30-33.

505. ———. "Our Space Friends." *Psychic Observer* 34 (February-March 1973): 136-43.

506. ———. "Outer-Space Communications." *Psychic Observer* (July 1970). *Note:* Not seen.

507. ———. "Outer Space Research." *Psychic Observer* 31 (September 1970): 9-11.

508. ———. *Sky Ships from Venus*. Tonopah, Ariz.: The author, July 10, 1967. 8p.

509. ———. "Space Friends." *Psychic Observer* 33 (June 1972): 48-51, 65-68.

510. ———. "The Space People: Guardians and Reaping Angels." *Psychic Observer* 31 (November 1970): 22-25, 44.

511. ———. "Space Visitors: Are They from Outer or Inner Space?" *Psychic Observer* 31 (October 1970): 34-39.

512. ———. "The Truth about Apollo 13." *Psychic Observer* 31 (July 1970): 29-31.

513. Smith, Susy. "Hands Across Space." *Beyond Reality* 10 (July-August 1974): 21-23, 59.

514. Smith, Warren. "Sensational Contact with a UFO Crew!" *Saga* (May 1973): 34-36, 66-70. *Note:* (Letter), G. W. Purois (July 1973): 2.

515. ———. "UFO Contact Inside the Bermuda Triangle." *Saga* (June 1976): 26-27, 60-68.

516. Smith, Wilbert Brockhouse. *The Boys from Topside*. Edited by Timothy Green Beckley. Clarksburg, W.Va.: Saucerian Books, 1969. 96p.

517. ———. *The New Science*. Ottawa, Ont.: Fenn-Graphic, 1964. 72p. 2d ed., Keith Press, 1978. 72p.

518. "Sound Off." (Letter). *Saga* (June 1968): 6.

519. Spangler, David. *Links with Space*. Forres, Moray, Scotland: Findhorn Trust and Universal Foundation, [1971?]. 24p. 2d ed., 1976. 41p. American ed., Marina del Rey, Calif.: DeVorss and Co., 1978. 41p.

520. Specter, Ann. *United Friends of Earth UFOs*. Ivyland, Pa.: Delval UFO, 1983. 11p. *Note:* A 19p. edition also exists.

521. Spielmann, Peter. "Watch the Skies! UFOS . . . A Fact of Life." *Bugle American* (Milwaukee, Wisc.) 8, 40 (December 10, 1976): 10-13.

522. [Staples, Crawford E., and Jean Offut Staples]. *Argent, Another World: Transmissions Transcribed by Oster: Classified and Typed by Dazit and Cham*. 4 vols. Pittsburgh: The authors, [1976?]. Unpaginated.

523. Staples, Jean Offut. *He Was My Brother, or "How, God?"* Hicksville, N.Y.: Exposition, 1975. 63p.

524. [Staschek, George]. *Ultimo: The Book of Divine Revelations of Echen, the Eldest and Higher-Than Divine Son of God the Father, to the Remnant of the Gentilite Peoples on Earth*. Reno, Nev.: The Echenian Church, 1977. Revised ed., 1978. 84p.

525. Steinberg, Gene. "Law Socks It to Stranges." *Caveat Emptor* 9 (September-October 1973): 33.

526. Stellar, Ann. *Correct Perspective of God and Spaceman*. Redlands, Calif.: Citograph Printing Company, 1978. 61p.

527. Stevens, Eric. "Haunted by Ancient Astronauts." *Beyond Reality UFO Special Report* 2 (1979): 14-15, 50.

528. Stevenson, Bryan. "Russians Seize Czech Orphan Who Claims to Have Come from Another World." *Beyond* 2 (February 1969): 59-65.

529. Stevic, Milenko S. *Exploration of the Cosmic Space: Part I and II*. N.p.: The author, 1961-1962. 19 + 23p. Revised ed., 1964-1965. *Note:* A part 3 [1969?] may also exist.

530. Stuart, John. *UFO Warning*. Clarksburg, W.Va.: Saucerian Books, 1963. 82p.

531. Sundar. *Rainbow Bridge Space Channeling Guide*. Santa Cruz, Calif.: Golden Bridge Construction Company, 1976. 48p.

532. Syll-Davis. *Aum*. New York: Brotherhood AUM, 1984. 112 + [4]p.

533. Talmist, Gist. *Spiritual Ecology and Psychic Powers: Bible of Creative Religion, Psychistic Science Transmortality*. New York: Psychistic System, [1982?]. 322p.

534. Tarree, Kathy O. *Earthseeds: Reflections and a Prophecy*. N.p.: The author, 1975. 44p.

535. Taylor, Josephine. *Eternity*. Grass Valley, Calif.: Golden Sierra, n.d. 73p.

536. ———. *Monal's Esoteric School for Students Seeking Guidance in God's Golden Age*. Grass Valley, Calif.: Golden Sierra Printing, n.d. 122p.

537. Taylor, Lee Roger, Jr. "Wyoming UFO-Contactee Runs for Governor." *Skeptical Inquirer* 7 (Winter 1982-83): 13-15.

538. Taylor, Wayne H. *Pillars of Lights*. Melbourne, Fla.: Pillars of Light, 1965. 116p.

539. Teich, Mark. "UFO Update." *Omni* 5 (August 1983): 91.

540. Teresi, Dick. "Anti-matter." *Omni* 3 (October 1980): 155.

541. Tessman, Diane. *The Transformation*. New York: UFO Review, 1983. 64p.

542. [Tessman], Diane, and Tifus. *We Are Among You*. [Poway, Calif.]: Starlight Center, [1985]. 22p.

543. Thompson, Bretta Lynn. "Other Planet People." *Search* 50 (December 1962): 42-49.

544. Thring, Brynhild Wooldridge. *Flying Saucer: Gurdjieff Visits Earth*. Daglingworth, Gloucestershire, UK: Coombe Springs Press, 1979. 205p.

545. Topper, Michael. *UFOs: An Initiated Account*. Beverly Hills, Calif.: Order NUMA'ION, 1984. 111p.

546. Trask [Greg Smith]. *They Shall Call Me Trask (The Truth You Never Heard)*. Glendale, Calif.: Great Western Publishing, 1979. 143p.

547. Triton. *The Magic of Space*. Introduction by John Hay. Larchmont, N.Y.: Triade, 1962. 314p.

548. Troxell, Hope. *Bases of Faith*. Portland, Oreg.: Universarium, n.d.

549. ———. *Christ of the Cosmos*. Portland, Oreg.: Universarium, n.d.

550. ———. *Cosmic Attainment*. N.d., n.p. *Note:* Not seen; mentioned in *Flying Saucers* (March 1966): 70.

551. ———. *From Matter to Light*. June Lake, Calif.: School of Thought, 1968. 93p.

552. ———. *The Mohada Teachings: From the Galaxies, Book 1*. Independence, Calif.: School of Thought, [1965], 1969. 43p.

553. ———— . *The Mystery of the Spirit of Truth.* Bishop, Calif.: Chalfant Press, 1974.

554. ———— . *Seven Outstanding Lectures.* [June Lake, Calif.: School of Thought], n.d.

555. ———— . *Through the Open Key: Poetry from the Spheres.* El Monte, Calif.: Understanding, [1957?]. 12p.

556. ———— . *The Twelve Great Future Temples of the World.* Independence, Calif.: School of Thought, 1963. 12p.

557. ———— . *The Winged Life of Cosmos: Testimony of Sister Hope.* Bishop, Calif.: Chalfant Press, 1974. 240p.

558. ———— . *The Wisdom of the Universe.* El Monte, Calif.: Understanding, 1957. 206p. 2d ed., Pasadena, Calif.: Jensen Printing, 1963.

559. Twiggs, Denise, and Bert Twiggs. *Secret Vows: Our Lives with Extraterrestrials.* Tigard, Oreg.: Wildflower Press, 1993. 206p.

560. Twitchell, Cleve. *The UFO Saga.* Lakemont, Ga.: CSA Press, 1966. 94p.

561. UFO Contact Center International. *On the Wings of Eagles: A Collection of Poems Composed by Contactees.* Seattle, Wash.: UFO Contact Center International, 1984. 20p.

562. *The URANTIA Book.* Chicago: URANTIA Foundation, 1955. 2097p. *Note:* Concordex by Clyde Bedell published in Santa Barbara, Calif., 1971. 315p.

563. Valerian, Valdemar. *Matrix.* I-III. Yelm, Wash.: Leading Edge Research Group, 1991-1992.

564. Valiant Thor (Frater VIII, pseud. of Harry J. Gardener]. *Fire, Water, Earth and Air.* Los Angeles: Golden Dawn, 1962. 32p. *Note:* Gardener wrote numerous titles on various occult topics which were published by the Golden Dawn Press.

565. ———— . *Magic of Flying Saucers.* Los Angeles: Golden Dawn Press, 1954. 24p.

566. ———— . *Outwitting Tomorrow.* Los Angeles: Golden Dawn Press, 1939, 1941, 1948. [Printed in 1952]. 64p. Another Ed., credited to Valiant Thor, Van Nuys, Calif.: International Evangelism Crusades, 1978. 64p. Other eds. in 1956, 1960.

567. ———— . *Watch Jerusalem.* Los Angeles: Golden Dawn, 1948. 26p.

568. Vallee, Jacques. *Dimensions: A Case Book of Alien Contact.* Chicago: Contemporary Books, 1988. 304p. Reprinted, New York: Ballantine Books, 1989. 294p.

569. ——— . *Messengers of Deception: UFO Contacts and Cults.* Berkeley, Calif.: And/Or Press, 1979. 243p. Paperback ed., New York: Bantam, 1980. 272p.

570. ——— . "Space Age Cults: Masks of Deception." *East-West Journal* (March 1979): 48-56. *Note:* From his book, *Messengers of Deception.*

571. ——— . "UFO Update." *Omni* 5 (May 1983): 115. *Note:* (Letter), Cyril Permutt, 6 (October 1983): 12.

572. Van Vlierden, Carl. *The Twelve Planets Speak.* Q. Publications, 1990. 263p.

573. Vegan, Partana. *Telah Speaks!* N.p.: Telah Press, 1961; Mokelumne Hill, Calif.: Health Research, n.d. 47p.

574. Verner, Yul. *The Book of Yul: The Secret Life of a Space Incarnate.* New York: Vantage, 1977. 137 + [16]p.

575. Vest, Paul M. "Venusians Walk Our Streets." *Mystic,* no. 5 (August 1954): 8-20.

576. VIVenus. *Starchild.* New York: Global Communications, 1982. 68p. Attributed to Diane Tessman.

577. *The Voice from Heaven: Important Message to Mankind.* N.p., 1979? *Note:* Not seen; review in *Earthlink,* Fall 1979.

578. Von Krueger, Frederick, and William J. Eisenman. *The Transparent People.* New York: Vantage, 1972. 33p.

579. Vorilhon, Claude [Rael, pseud.]. *Let's Welcome Our Father from Space.* Vadnz, Liechtenstein: Raelian Foundation, 1986. 213p.

580. ——— . *Sensual Meditation.* Tokyo, Jap.: AOM Corporation, 1986. 152pp.

581. ——— . *Space Aliens Took Me to Their Planet.* Montreal, Quebec: Canadian Raelian Movement, 1978. 349p. *Note:* Translation and combined edition of *Le Livre Qui Dit La Verite: J'ai Rencontre un Extra Terrestre* (Clermont-Ferrand, Fr.: Editions du Message, 1974. 157p.) and *Les Extra-Terrestres M'Ont Emmene Sur Leur Planete: Le 2e Message Qu'ils Mont Donne* (Brantome, Fr.: Editions du Message, 1975. 159p.).

582. Wade, Carlson. "Are Flying Saucers Supernormal?" *Astrology Guide* (February 1967). *Note:* Not seen.

583. Wallace, Baird. *Commentaries on Further Unfoldment of the Space Story and the Inner Light.* Grosse Ile, Mich.: The author, September 1973. [18p.]

584a. ——— . *The Space Story and the Inner Light.* Grosse Ile, Mich.: The author, 1972. [59p.]

584b. Walosin, Frank C. "Derenberger a Fraud?" *Bachelor News* 2 (May 11, 1968): 7, 31.

585. Walter, Hallie, and Julius Walter. *"To Bear Witness Unto Truth": (Starcraft and Special Lessons).* Portland, Oreg.: The authors, 1972. 86p.

586. Watkins, Edward L. *The Teachings of Sazar, Book One/The Liberation, Book Two.* 2 vols. in one. Mt. Shasta, Calif.: Association Sananda and Sanat Kumara, 1977. 68 + 68p.

587. Watson, Carol J. "Transcript." *Search* 142 (Spring 1980): 53-54.

588. Watson, Nigel. "Enigma Variations." *Fortean Times* 30 (Autumn 1979): 43-45; 42 (Autumn 1984): 56-57.

589a. Watts, John Langdon. *Hello Venus! An ESP Epic.* New York: Vantage, 1973. 167p.

589b. ———. *Here Is Where It Is! "A Mystery Solved."* [South Daytona, Fla.]: The author, 1984. 16p.

590. ———. *In My Own Way.* N.p., n.d. *Note:* Not seen.

591. ———. *The Reason for Life; and Now, Visit Venus.* Port Orange, Fla.: Dixie Venus Books, 1975. 28 + [151]p.

592. ———. *Religious Philosophies of the Planets.* Port Orange, Fla.: Dixie Venus Books, 1971. 43p.

593. Webb, Dorothy Duckworth. *Great Cosmic Council.* Grants Pass, Oreg.: The author, 1977. 28p.

594. Webb, Ripley. *The Eternal Pilgrim: His Past, Present, and Future.* London: Fowler and Co., n.d. 136p.

595. Wedd, Tony [J. A. Dunkin Wedd]. *To Our Friends on Earth.* N.p., 1970? *Note:* Not seen; may not be contactee.

596. White, Nancy. *Once Upon Venus: A Musical Fantasy.* Grass Valley, Calif.: Golden Sierra, n.d. 68p.

597. White Dove [pseudonym of Ida Partridge] and Samuel George Partridge. *Golden Moments with the Ascended Masters.* Grass Valley, Calif.: Golden Sierra Printing, 1976. 381p.

598. ———. *Jesus Still Teaches.* Grass Valley, Calif.: Golden Sierra Printing. 1980. 223p.

599. Whiteside, I. W. *Sharon's UFO Code for Outer Space.* Glenview, Ill.: The author, 1982. 54p. 2d ed., Smithtown, N.Y.: Exposition, 1983. 43p.

600. Whitfield, Joseph [pseud.]. *The Treasure of El Dorado: Featuring "The Dawn Breakers."* Washington, D.C.: Occidental Press, 1978, 1981. 213p. Indian ed., Bombay: K.S. Renade, 1978.

601. Wilcox, Hal. *Contact with the Master.* Los Angeles: Galaxy Press, 1963. Revised ed., 1984.

602. ———. *Gateway to Superconsciousness.* Los Angeles: Galaxy, n.d. [1965?].

603. ———. *Going Up! Practical Methods of Astral Projection.* Hollywood, Calif.: The author, 1964. 41p.

604. ———. *UFO Flight: Visit to Planet Selo.* Azusa, Calif.: Galaxy, 1968. 94p.

605. ———. *Zemkla: Interplanetary Avatar.* Los Angeles: Galaxy, 1966. 57p.

606. Wilkerson, Clark. *Celestial Wisdom.* N.p.: The author, 1965; Reprinted, Gardena, Calif.: Institute of Cosmic Wisdom, 1965. 57p.

607. ———. *Wisdom from Venus.* Playa del Rey, Calif.: Institute of Cosmic Wisdom, 1968. 184p.

608. Williams, Margaret, and Lee Gladden. *Hands, the True Account: A Hypnotic Subject Reports on Outer Space.* Warner Springs, Calif.: Galaxy, 1976. 272p.

609. Willow, Ji. *Why Me?* East Syracuse, N.Y.: Deerfield Enterprises, 1978. 96p.

610. Wilson, Robert Anton. "Timothy Leary Is Loose Again, Headed for the Stars." *Psychic* 7 (September-October 1976): 8-14.

611. Womack, John H., and Hugh Helms. *I Was Picked up by a U.F.O.* Cullman, Ala.: Helms Publications, 1975. [18p.]

612. "Woman Dies Waiting for UFO." *Fate* 36 (May 1983): 44.

613. Wonder, Robert A. "Outer-Space Armada." *Psychic Observer* (July 1970).

614. Woodrew, Greta. *Memories of Tomorrow.* New York: Doubleday, 1988.

615. ———. *On a Slide of Light: A Glimpse of Tomorrow.* New York: Macmillan; London: Collier Macmillan, 1981. 176p. Revised ed., Black Mountain, N.C.: New Age, [1985]. 180p.

616. Wyllie, Timothy. *The Delta Factor: Dolphins, Extra-Terrestrials, Angels: Adventures among Spiritual Intelligences.* Farmingdale, N.Y.: Coleman Publishing, 1984. 215p.

617. Young, June [Bright Star, pseud.]. [*Elvis Presley Series*]. Milwaukee, Wisc.: Arising Sun Interplanetary Newsletter of the Elohim, 1976-1977. Nos. 1-6.

618. Zarkon [Kenneth Raynor Johnson]. *The Zarkon Principle*. London: Everest, 1975. 225p. American ed., New York: New American Library, 1976. 241p.

619. Zoonch of the Planet Zyanthia. *The Not So Secret Secret of Life*. Edited by Harvey Cohen. Beverly Hills, Calif.: Psycho-Dynamics Press, 1986. 98p.

INDEX

Lightning Source UK Ltd.
Milton Keynes UK
UKOW03f1846280417
300155UK00001B/116/P

9 780791 423301